A Skeptic's Guide To The Universe: How To Develop Your Intuition For Fun And Profit

A SKEPTIC'S GUIDE TO THE UNIVERSE: HOW TO DEVELOP YOUR INTUITION FOR FUN AND PROFIT

WILLIAM GLADSTONE AND MARISA MORIS

Intuition Media

TABLE OF CONTENTS

INTRODUCTION

In this book you will learn much of what the new age community considers sacred truth. This is not the first book to examine these "channeled messages." This book was not planned. This book has no agenda. I happen to be a bestselling novelist and major literary agent. I have represented some of the leading thinkers of the twentieth century ranging from Linus Torvalds who created the Linux operating system to Peter Norton who created Norton Utilities to Tom Anderson who created My Space. I represented the original creators of the For Dummies Book series and I have represented ecologists and scientists ranging from Dr. Michael Tobias to Hunter Lovins to Dr. Ervin Laszlo. I have also represented many visionaries ranging from Barbara Marx Hubbard to Jean Houston, Neale Donald Walsch, Eckhart Tolle to Barbara DeAngelis. I have degrees from Yale College and Harvard University. I play golf and tennis, have children and grandchildren and am generally considered a logical and grounded successful businessman. The books I have represented have generated in excess of three billion dollars in book sales just in North America. I have never channeled, never believed in channeling and considered those who are attracted to those who channel somewhat eccentric if not unstable.

Quite by accident I met Marisa Moris. I was vaguely aware of her because I had seen ads for her book in the local newspaper. The book was Answers from Heaven and I had no interest in the book or Marisa as a potential client. I was playing golf at my local course and my partner had a conflict and was a no show. The club decided to pair me up with another golfer. The other golfer turned out to be Joe Moris, Marisa's dad. Joe is a good golfer and gave me some pointers that immediately helped me drive the ball a little further. At the end of the round he mentioned that he was wondering what would be the best strategy for his future books that he was writing with his daughter. I had told him that I was a literary agent so he wanted to give me copies of his books and see if I would meet with his daughter. I explained that I was not taking on any new clients but would have my wife Gayle meet with Marisa and see if there might be some way we might work together. Gayle had just agreed to become publisher for our own imprint with Amazon Waterfront Digital Press and it seemed logical that these books might fit that imprint which we use to help authors who are not well enough established for the major New York publishers who publish our bestselling clients's books.

Gayle met with Marisa and there was some confusion about why they were meeting. Marisa is an intuitive healer and assumed Gayle was there for a healing. Gayle has been an intuitive healer herself so was intrigued and just went with the flow and had a session. When Gayle returned she told me, "You have to meet Marisa. She is amazing." Gayle was glowing and her enthusiasm was infectious and uncharacteristic. We set up to have Marisa join an existing dinner we were hosting and within minutes I realized that Marisa was quite extraordinary. One of the reasons I felt she was so extraordinary was that she was perfectly ordinary. She was eight and one half months pregnant and focused on getting ready for the birth of her daughter. She explained that she had dropped out of college but had a successful career as a mortgage broker and real estate investor. She understood and appreciated the world of money and material success and might have just gone on with accumulating more properties and wealth except she was in two car accidents and had two near death experiences. These experiences did not change Marisa overnight. In fact I would call Marisa a skeptic herself when it comes to accepting information that comes from "the other side" but information kept coming in and eventually Marisa decided to pursue becoming a medium and a channeler. Within a few years

Marisa had developed her psychic abilities to the level where she was teaching other mediums and psychics and channelers not only how to channel but how to determine what entities they might be connecting with and how to determine if the information coming through was truly true or just trickster information intended to deceive.

Never having had a session with a medium or channel, I decided to experiment and see what type of information might come through. The following text is the transcript of the first and three subsequent sessions. We purposely have not edited the material other than to correct grammar and remove some redundancies (these guides say "indeed", "so to speak" and "in which" repeatedly so most of these expressions which seemed more like pauses for Marisa's benefit as the channel than meaningful content, have been deleted). Having read and now reread this material several times I am amazed at the clarity and coherence of the information Marisa has brought through. If every person on this planet would read and take to heart the wisdom and guidance provided not only would they learn how to develop and access their intuition but they would understand the essence of their human journey in a way that would benefit all of humanity.

This is a very positive and life affirming book. I remain skeptical of the reality of channels and our ability to access information in the way that we have for this book. At the same time I cannot deny the clarity and logic of what follows. I have learned a great deal and suspect that every reader will as well. It is not necessary to believe every word you are about to read. You can retain your skepticism and assume that all that follows is just coming from Marisa's imagination. You will still benefit from this wisdom as long as you remain open to the possibility that through some quirk in the universe that Marisa actually does have the ability to "download" unlimited knowledge. Marisa for the most part goes into a trance when she channels and does not even remember what was discussed. She has to listen to the tapes to learn what has come through. She is as amazed as I or any reader with the clarity of these messages.

Marisa and I are an unlikely team to be co authoring this book but if this book has fallen into your hands it is a sign that you, as unlikely as it may seem, are also a part of the destiny of this planet to create a world of wisdom and joy for present and future generations. We may not be able to respond to all of the questions and queries that readers will have but feel free to direct any questions or comments for me to my author website, www.12thebook.com or for Marisa to www.discoverintuition.com.

January 29, 2016

Part I
The Conversation Begins

CHAPTER ONE
WHAT IS INTUITION?

INTRO: Hello, my name is William Gladstone.

MARISA: Hello. My name is Marisa Moris.

WILLIAM: Marisa is an amazing vehicle. I'm not going to call her a channel because too many people have the wrong idea about channeling. She's just a resource, a communication tool if you will, that can access what another one of my clients, Dr. Ervin Laszlo, calls the zero point. The zero point is the concept that all information that ever can be, that ever was, that ever will be, coexists in a non-space, non-time—I can't even call it a "place"—zero point, that is actually accessible. And great geniuses throughout history, from Einstein to Beethoven, on and on, have actually, the theory is, been able to access this zero point. And that in part explains child prodigies, people like Mozart, and where ideas actually come from. This has also been written about by people like Charles Haanel whose master key system was the basis for all human development books in the United States including the *Tapping the Source* book which I was fortunate enough to be involved with. So this is the background for today. We're going to start very simply before we get into the real depths. I've interviewed many, many mediums, channels, people who have been able to manifest information from the other side. John Edwards and on and on. Out of all the people that I've interviewed, Marisa is perhaps the most powerful and the most interesting because it is not as simple as you think, the other dimensions.

And this is one of the reasons why I'm taking my time to interview Marisa today. We're going to start out very simply, with the basics.

WILLIAM: Marisa, what is intuition?

MARISA: Hm, okay. What is intuition? Well, I would say that intuition is the voice of your soul, the voice of your soul, and communicating with that greater piece of yourself inside of yourself that knows all. But when you say it's not as simple as that, we have so many different layers of our self that I could totally get into that—

WILLIAM: Well, no, let's keep it simple right now. One of the things that I'm trying to establish here is this is not—if we turn this into a course, which I think we will, and a book—it's not just a course and a book for people who are quote "out there." This is very basic stuff. I think everyone in the listening audience understands the concept of intuition. People through centuries have said, "I just had this feeling, I had this sense, I had an intuition." So let's start with something as simple as that. Where does intuition come from?

MARISA: Okay. Intuition comes from inside of us. You may call it the soul, you may call it your consciousness, you may call it your spirit, you may call it God, Source, whatever. It's a higher aspect of us beyond the mind that knows, that knows. Intuition works through sight, through sound, through feeling, through touch, and there's a whole bunch of different terms that people use for it you may know like clairsentience – the ability to feel energy or feel spirit. Clairvoyance is the ability to see energy, see auras, see stuff like that. There's a whole bunch of different terms that people use for it. But I basically call intuition our internal GPS system. You know you're going to get on the freeway and all of a sudden you just get that feeling like "Maybe I should take the coast today." And then you're going down the coast and you see the freeway and you see everybody just jammed up and there was an accident there. So you just avoided an accident, you know. Was that God that was talking to you? Was that your soul that was talking to you? It's your intuition, your intuition.

WILLIAM: And I know we've spoken before about the ability for anyone to enhance and develop their intuition.

MARISA: Yes.

WILLIAM: Tell us a little bit, for just the general person, not someone who even necessarily believes in the concept of soul and spirit, how can an ordinary person develop their intuition?

MARISA: For developing your intuition, I say that quieting the mind is the easiest way. Whether you believe it's your soul or whether you believe it's your spirit, or just another aspect of you, a lot of it comes from the subconscious mind. It's clearing the conscious mind. If you're worrying about "My car payment is due. I need to go get the tires changed; my kids, I need to go pick them up; I need to do all this," and you're scrambling around and your mind is going crazy, you're not going to be able to hear that silent piece inside of you that is your intuition. So in order to develop that, I teach people to quiet their mind. To do this, one must learn how to just kind of get everybody else's thoughts, emotions and feelings out of the way so that they can actually hear their intuition speak. Everybody has intuition, everybody has it.

WILLIAM: This is very interesting. My father was a book publisher and he never read any of the books he published. He did it all on intuition. He would have a feeling. And one of the things that I learned from my father, and I do it myself, is he always took care of business completely so his mind was always open for the next opportunity. I, in my business as a literary agent, depend a great deal on intuition and my technique is very much what you're saying. Sometimes I might do a two-minute clearing meditation in the morning when I wake up. But more important actually than the meditation I might do is when I go to bed I've cleaned off everything. All my emails. There's nothing hanging over me. There's nothing that I haven't done. If there is, I'll usually dream about it and take care of it the very first thing in the morning. So when something presents itself, either through an email, through a phone call, in that moment I'm completely un-encumbered and I think that's why I've been very fortunate with my intuition as, "Oh, I have a good feeling about this, let's work together," and it's really more that feeling I use than great analysis. A lot of times I'll do the analysis afterwards, and my intuition isn't 100 percent accurate, but I'd say I'm batting about 90 percent, which is pretty good, and you know, I resonate with what you're saying. It's essential to sort of clear the deck and then you can receive, you can receive the information that is out there. This is what Charles Haanel has talked about in terms of intuition. So I think that's excellent advice. Now in your case, once you develop your intuition, I assume you started like most people in developing your intuition. You had a sense about things and the more you were right about things, the more confident you became about using your intuition rather than just relying on "well, the book says do this and my father says do that," and you were like, "No, my intuition says do this." So tell me a little bit about how you transition from intuition to what really a lot of people call channeling or at least accessing, you know, in a scientific sense, information from the zero point.

CHAPTER TWO
WHO IS MARISA?

MARISA: Well, I had an accident. I would say I was completely numb to all intuition my entire life. I mean, I was a very intuitive kid, I knew what people felt, I knew what they thought, things like that. But I never saw it as intuition. I just, I didn't think of it. I had an accident where I had an out of body experience and I met my higher self.

WILLIAM: What kind of an accident?

MARISA: I had a seizure driving home from the mall one night. I was on my way to church.

WILLIAM: What kind of seizure?

MARISA: Grand mal seizure.

WILLIAM: And what is that?

MARISA: Seizure is a neurological issue. I have epilepsy and so I wasn't taking my seizure medication and I was driving home from the mall to go to church with my dad and my boyfriend.

WILLIAM: And how old were you?

MARISA: This was in 2008, so 31. Thirty one, yeah. So 2008 I was driving home all stressed out, and the next thing I know I'm floating above my car. I see a geyser of water shooting in the air and I see my brand new Mercedes smashed into a fire hydrant. And I just remember looking down going "That really sucks for her, that sucks." And then all of a sudden I remember looking over and I went, "Ah!" because there was a girl right here and she looked just like me but she had blonde long hair, green eyes, wearing like white robes and stuff. And I just went, "You can't make me go back," and she says "You're going to go back, you have too much to do." And I said, "The market is going to crash," because I was a mortgage broker, so "The market's going to crash, she's not going to have any money. Life's going to be hell, and by the way Marisa is an idiot." I kept saying "Marisa's an idiot, she doesn't listen to me, she doesn't do what I say…"

WILLIAM: Well, who was "you"?

MARISA: Exactly. That was exactly the point.

WILLIAM: I mean, if that's Marisa, are there two Marisas? Is that your higher self?

MARISA: I think that I was talking to my body. My body was Marisa. I think my spirit or my consciousness, whatever I am in this lifetime, popped out of me. And I know that I know—

WILLIAM: So when you're talking about Marisa, you're talking about Marisa as the body, and all of her actions and thoughts until that normative time?

MARISA: Yes. Exactly, yeah. So I was talking about the human that was lying on the ground. The ambulance had pulled up because the car filled up with water so I almost drowned. So they came, they smashed it open, and they pulled me out of the car.

WILLIAM: The car almost filled with water from the fire hydrant?

MARISA: Yeah. Because I ran into a fire hydrant.

WILLIAM: Because you were unconscious?

MARISA: Yeah, so I was on the fire hydrant. The only thing that saved me, they said, was the computer system under my new Mercedes. If I had been in my BMW the water would have shot through and I would have got—

WILLIAM: I do have to have a little side here because Gayle, my wife, was in a car accident today, and she came within six inches of plowing into a fire hydrant.

MARISA: Oh my goodness. Oh my goodness.

WILLIAM: But anyway let's get back to your story.

MARISA: Talk about coincidences.

WILLIAM: It is kind of strange—and the car ends up going here. Go ahead.

MARISA: So anyway I was up there and I was just being a total little brat, like, "I'm not going back, I don't care how divine you are. The market's going to crash, she's not going to have any money." That's what I cared about, you know? If I read spiritual books it was about the law of attraction so I could learn to make money. That was my thing. And I was good at it. But I was just like, "The market's going to crash. The real estate market is going to be no good. I don't want to go back and she won't listen to me." Next thing I know I wake up in a cop car. They thought I was a drunk college student. I was in like a little black dress and I had all this crazy makeup on from the Mac store that I had gone to at the mall and, you know, so they put me in the back of a cop car. And when I woke up they had to give me oxygen. They didn't do anything. So I ended up losing my memory, kind of like short term memory.

WILLIAM: Tell me a little bit more, because I don't know anything about mal seizures.

MARISA: Grand mal seizures are when you go unconscious and your entire body just locks up and you start shaking. I bite my tongue.

WILLIAM: So basically an epileptic fit?

MARISA: Yeah.

WILLIAM: For those of us are who aren't... and so you had an epileptic fit while driving and lost consciousness and plowed into the hydrant? You weren't even aware that you went out before it happened?

MARISA: Yeah.

WILLIAM: And it was only your oversoul, that you call it, that was seeing it?

MARISA: Yeah, that was seeing that. And I woke up in the cop car and I do remember seeing my car with the fire hydrant so this is why I discounted the experience, because I had woken up at the accident, and I was banging my head up against the window going like, "Let me out of here" because they had me handcuffed thinking I was a drunk student since I was literally in front of San Marcos University. So they just said, "Oh, drunk kid," you know. So anyway, I lost my marketing company. I just couldn't remember anything. And I was just—

WILLIAM: Wait, wait, wait. You're jumping ahead. You go into the hospital?

MARISA: Yeah. No, the hospital. I went into the hospital—.

WILLIAM: I mean, first they take you to the police station?

MARISA: Yeah.

WILLIAM: And then, when did they figure out that you weren't drunk?

MARISA: Oh, I actually had to fight that case. They actually tried to charge me with something for not taking my seizure medication. So I ended up fighting it and—

WILLIAM: But you know, let's go a little slow here. So they take you into the police station. They give you a breathalyzer and you're not drunk so they figure, okay, she's not drunk, and then you come to and you say – your conscious –?

MARISA: I said I had a seizure, blah, blah, blah.

WILLIAM: So then they take you to the hospital or not?

MARISA: No, I never ended up going to the hospital. Apparently they said that while I was coming back into consciousness, I told them I don't need medical treatment. So they didn't give me medical treatment. So my dad came and got me.

WILLIAM: And then you took your medicine?

MARISA: Yeah, yeah.

WILLIAM: So then you went back?

MARISA: Yeah. So then I started taking my medicine regularly.

WILLIAM: Do you still take this medication?

MARISA: I actually got off of it two years ago and I haven't had a seizure since.

WILLIAM: Congratulations.

MARISA: Thank you. Yay! So that's a good thing. That's how I was able to get pregnant. Yeah. But the reason why I was kind of jumping forward is because my whole life was a blur for about six months and I kind of remember that night seeing the fire hydrant, seeing the girl, seeing all this stuff, but I just figured it was a dream. I'm very logical. I'm science over spirituality. More "prove it to me."

WILLIAM: In college what did you study?

MARISA: I studied marketing and I studied accounting. Originally I was going into law. Then I ended up dropping out.

WILLIAM: Okay. But you weren't into the quote "artsy fartsy" stuff.

MARISA: No, no. I'm very… No. I wanted to be in accounting.

WILLIAM: Very "feet on the ground."

MARISA: Yes, yes. Very, very left-brain. So six months later I got my license back and I was driving my dad's old car he takes to play golf. There are racks in it, and all like, you know. I was just driving it because I didn't have a car since I had crashed my car. And I was driving down the freeway and I was like livid at this agent because she credited somebody like $9,000, I was going to lose all this money on a loan, and I was just screaming my head off and I felt kind of like, "Uh-oh, its happening again." And I was taking my medication at the time, too. So I pulled off the freeway, parked the car, but it didn't go all the way into park, and next thing I know I'm above the car. Here's the girl. But now I have a ball of lightness to me. There's this ball of light.

WILLIAM: What was going on with the car meanwhile?

MARISA: The car was just rolling into a curb and it just went "doop," like it rolled into a curb. It didn't crash. I didn't have a concussion. No airbags.

WILLIAM: So the body, your body, the Marisa body, is just sitting slumped over in the car but you're not hurt?

MARISA: Yeah. Having a seizure, not hurt, nothing.

WILLIAM: But having a seizure?

MARISA: Yeah, exactly. Having a seizure. But now I said, "I told you, I told you it was going to happen, see!" And I went "I don't want to hear it!" Whatever this ball of light was over here was talking to me and I could hear it, and she just said, "You need to go back." And I said, "Nope." And I turned around and started walking towards the light. "Not going back, she's an idiot." This time it's not going to happen. This time I woke up in the ambulance on the 78 Freeway going to the hospital. I told the ambulance worker, "Give me a piece of paper."

WILLIAM: Now, why were you in the ambulance? Because when they—

MARISA: Because they came and got me since I had a seizure.

WILLIAM: They could tell that you needed—

MARISA: Yeah, this time.

WILLIAM: When you have a seizure you need oxygen?

MARISA: Oxygen. They had me on an IV and all that. Really seizures can't hurt you that much. It's what happens when you have

13

the seizure, like if you're driving. Or I've been in the shower and fallen. I've fallen down three flights of stairs, like, just you know, you just drop. So we're going down the freeway and in the ambulance I told the guy there, I said, "Can I have a piece of paper?" And so I start writing down everything that I remembered. I remembered the witnesses that were there talking to the cops. And then I remembered the first accident, like in detail. So I wrote all that down. And for the next month—I was telling my boyfriend, my husband now, my boyfriend at the time—who the heck am I? I'm not Marisa, I'm not Marisa because I kept saying, "Marisa's an idiot." If it was me, I'd say, "I'm an idiot." So there's obviously... And that girl, she looked like me. So who was she? And he just one day, I think he was probably polishing his gun or something, I mean precision shooting, he was doing something real manly like that and he goes, "Sweetie, why don't you just pull the police reports and see if that was a heavenly experience you had?" It was like, "Who are you?" So I pulled the police reports and the witnesses that I saw matched the witnesses that were on the police report, like red hat, blue shirt, jeans. Like I saw the actual—

WILLIAM: When you say witnesses you mean non-human?

MARISA: No, people that were on the police report like, "Oh hey, I'll give a statement of what happened and I saw her crash her car." But they write down what the people are wearing. So the fact that I knew what a witness was wearing when I was completely unconscious at that second accident and didn't wake up until I was on the freeway... The first accident I was always like, "I woke up, I hit my head on the glass but I woke up. I could have seen something." But the second accident I was not injured.

WILLIAM: So you were able to describe what people were wearing even though you were completely unconscious?

MARISA: Yeah. I was unconscious—

WILLIAM: At the site and could not have seen it with your eyes?

MARISA: Yeah. I could not have seen it. I was completely unconscious. The report said I did not.

WILLIAM: Well, just for the readers, let me confirm, because we've done many books on near-death experiences and this is actually not an uncommon experience. Many people when they're on their death bed, literally in the hospital having an operation and they're completely knocked out, but they are revived from death. And there have been over 10,000 reported cases. There are people who have dedicated their lives to this study. They do report that they are aware of many details down to somebody's... one of the doctors wearing blue sneakers. I mean, things that they could not possibly have known. So this is not just a phenomenon that happened to you.

CHAPTER THREE
MARISA WAKES UP

MARISA: That's interesting. Wow. Okay. Yeah, well, great. That's even more confirmation then. I think I'm nuts half the time, so... But yeah, after that, I really, somebody... our toothless IT guy at work came up to me one day and he actually gave me the *Power of Now* by Eckhart Tolle. And he said, "You need to read this book," and I said, "Nah, New Age crap." I was raised sort of Christian but I'd say I was agnostic, very, very, very agnostic. So I didn't read that. He gave me another book, *Conversations with God.* Those two books, which is so coincidental because—

WILLIAM: I represent them, yeah.

MARISA: Yeah, you represent them. And then some Earnest Holmes stuff. And I was thinking, "You need to read this stuff." Because I kept saying I don't know who I am, I don't know who I am. So when I read that you have a higher self in the *Power of Now*, he says something about the ego and the higher self, I went "ding, ding, ding." That's it. That was my higher self. I met my higher self. And from there I just dove into spiritual books. Not real complex stuff. It was like Jerry and Esther Hicks, *The Law of Attraction.* But in the beginning of the book it says that she's a channel and I just remember thinking, "Channel? What's that?" And I came across Seth Speaks and that's a channeled book. And what other one? I think it was those two. And I thought, I want to learn how to channel. So I went to the grocery store and this girl just walks up to me and says, "I'm reading this really good book. It's called *Opening the Channel*." I mean, she was just random. She must have been an angel, or she must have just... Something from the divine came in. So I got the book and I started learning how to meditate because I wanted to channel my higher self. I didn't want to channel. I didn't believe in spirits. I didn't believe in angels. I didn't believe in any beings outside of ourselves. I kind of saw us as like Neo on the Matrix. I thought we had like a higher self maybe plugged in somewhere and we're down here. And I wanted to talk to that piece of me and ask, "Why the hell did you make me come back?" I was suicidal. I started cutting myself. I started, you know, just really wanting to hurt myself because—

WILLIAM: This was after the second accident?

MARISA: After the second accident.

WILLIAM: And you had not been suicidal before?

MARISA: No. I just... My dad wasn't talking to me. He thought that I had the seizure because I was on drugs. So he wasn't listening to me about it and I was, "I swear, I was taking my seizure medication. I was doing everything I needed to. I didn't mean to crash your car." So we didn't talk for a whole year and he's like my world. And so I was just... My family just kind of wasn't talking to me and I was just kind of alone. I wasn't working because he and I were business partners. I was still kind of working on the side, but not going into the office. And that was my whole identity—my work and money, and having my Mercedes and my BMW and my house, and you know, money and suits and everything. And I just didn't have any of that. I had no identity. So I came across a book by Sonia Choquette that basically teaches intuition. Everybody has a sixth sense. And I started reading it and I started reading that book *Opening the Channel*, and I just had an obsession with channeling. So that's why I tell people, if you are wanting to develop your intuition and you're even remotely obsessed with it, it's because a piece of you really wants you to develop it, you know. People will say, "Oh I don't have those abilities," or "I'm not psychic" or "I'm not a medium." It's like, if you're wanting to do it, it's because something inside of you knows you have that ability. And that's why, that's why it's happening. So I started just doing meditations. I had nothing else to do. I had no job. I didn't, you know—me and my boyfriend were living together; now my husband—and I had some money saved up, thank God. But I just did a lot of meditation and one day I was sitting in the living room and I had my eyes closed and I was doing this meditation and the girl that I met in the accident, her face... It was like my eyes were open but they weren't. Her face came right up to mine and she says, "I am you and you are me." And poof she was gone.

WILLIAM: Wow.

MARISA: And I was like, "Oh my gosh! I communicated with something. I communicated!" So after that I got obsessed and started—

WILLIAM: Okay, how long ago was that? What year was that?

MARISA: That was 2009.

WILLIAM: Okay. So basically a year after all the accidents?

MARISA: After.

WILLIAM: So you had a year that we might call the dark night of the soul.

MARISA: Yeah, yeah. I was depressed. And that's why, I can get into it a little bit more later, but that's why I want to, my whole passion is, helping people develop their intuition in a safe way. I was opening up to all these things thinking I was just calling my higher self, but I mean, I had spirits around me that I didn't know how to see.

I would start meditating and my fan would start spinning, my lights would start flashing. Things would start happening because—

WILLIAM: A little bit like *Carrie?*

MARISA: Yeah, yeah, yeah. I wasn't like *Poltergeist,* head-spinning or anything. But I was like, you know, I could have very well had lots of spirits.

CHAPTER FOUR
MARISA DEVELOPS THE ABILITY TO
"SEE" AURAS AND SPIRITS

WILLIAM: Did you ever have the telekinesis with things moving?

MARISA: Things would move, yeah. The keys would fly off, or my phone would start shaking, or something. But that's when spirit beings that have not crossed over to the higher realms are down here and they're using our energy, our kinetic energy and our etheric energy to move stuff. But I totally attribute the spirits that were in my energy to the suicide, to wanting to commit suicide because they're dead, so the frequency that they're letting off is "I'm dead." So that's why I was just, "I need to be dead, I need to be dead." So I was like hurting myself or I'd pull my hair and go, "I'm not alive," and I would like slap my face. It was really weird, really weird. And a lot of people in early spiritual development go through this and a lot of people, teachers, will discount it as, "Oh, you're just releasing the past." But it's like, no, no, no. This can be avoided. This can be avoided. This can be done in a safe way. So I went through a year of just bumbling around, doing this, and then I started to see auras. I would be at the grocery store and someone would walk by and it would just be like, "Whoo." I'd see a trail, you know. And I went and got my eyes checked.

WILLIAM: When you say "see an aura," what do you see, actually?

MARISA: An aura is... I kind of describe auras as the way you would see like a street light and it's foggy out, and you kind of see like the orb kind of around the light. That's what people look like. And some people can see colors. Others just see light.

WILLIAM: And you see colors or just light?

MARISA: I don't see colors. I see light. But if I close my eyes and tune into it, I can see all the colors. So it's like with my imagination I can see the colors, or I can just look at you right now and say, okay, you have a green and blue aura. I'm not actually seeing it, which is a very nice aura, a green and blue aura, but I'm not actually seeing it with my eyes. I tell people the way that—

WILLIAM: Are you feeling it? Is it feeling?

MARISA: The way that I tell people my clairvoyance, the way it works with most people is I see it the way I see a memory. So if you think, "Last time I was at the beach and I saw the waves crashing…"

WILLIAM: You remember it.

MARISA: You remember it, yeah. So it's like a memory or remembrance. So if I tell you, "Imagine the last time you were at a Padres game," its like, boom, you see it in your head. That's the way that spirit, and that's the way our higher selves communicate with us, through pictures in our brain. So when you hear a medium or someone say, "Oh, I'm seeing this or I'm hearing that," they're not really seeing it or hearing it—some are—but it's mostly within the mind that it's working, you're seeing it through memories or just through… telepathy. A telepathic sense. So yeah, so I started seeing those and it really tripped me out and scared me, so I started going to church and—

WILLIAM: Wait a second. You started seeing auras and it freaked you out, and it made you want to go to church?

MARISA: Yeah. So I had heard that anything outside the Bible is evil, you know, growing up, because there's all the "Don't add or take away from this Book," so you know... I hadn't told my dad anything. We were still not talking. So I thought, you know what? I'm going to go to church and I'm going to ask them to take away this, because I was wanting to kill myself, I was seeing auras...

WILLIAM: You wanted an exorcism and felt—

MARISA: Yeah, pretty much.

WILLIAM: You kind of felt, "Hey, if I'm seeing auras, there's something happening to me that shouldn't be here."

MARISA: Yeah, and I'm wanting to kill myself, which I never wanted to do before.

WILLIAM: So ironically, I mean, as we know now, you were actually probably receiving higher guidance.

MARISA: Yes.

WILLIAM: And instead of welcoming it, you wanted to banish it?

MARISA: Which was what most of my students do when they come in and they see me for the very first time. You know, I'll read some of our real elementary books about Christianity and spirituality. They'll come in and they're going, "I see stuff in my house and I just need it to go away."

Its like, "Oh, that's your higher self. That's your angel."

"No, no, no, it pins me down, it holds me."

"Actually no, you just think it's doing that." I had one client who came to me and she wanted an exorcism. She wanted, you know, this spirit to—

WILLIAM: Exorcise my angel, I don't want my angel.

MARISA: Yes. Well, she was going to bed at night, she would lay down and her pillow would start floating above her head. So she's like raised in the Church of Jesus Christ. It was like a Christian cult, just very strict. They couldn't do anything. And so she came to see me. Her father met my father on the golf course. And my dad kind of said a little bit about what I did. This is after, obviously, we started talking again. So she came to see me and turns out I was seeing a little spirit, a cute little grandma, and she kept showing me a little tow-headed boy. And I was like, "Are you the one making her pillow float?" And she like pulled out like a little daisy. So it turns out her name was Daisy. So she's pulling out a daisy to me, and I said, "I don't know." I told the client, I said, "I just see this cute little lady holding a daisy and she's clapping her hands and she's showing me this tow-headed kid that has a truck in his hand." She goes, "That's my next door neighbor," the little tow-headed kid. And so as soon as she said that then the messages started coming in from the lady with the daisy, and the lady with the daisy said, "I just want them to know that I love them and I'm watching over them, but I have to go to heaven now. I have to leave because my daughter keeps telling me not to leave her, but I have to go." And so this girl that came to see me goes over to her next-door neighbor's house, knocks on the door, "I have a really weird message that I need to tell you." So she tells her and the girl just started balling, crying, "Oh my God, I prayed my mom won't leave us." And it was her son. The girl who came to see me shares a wall with the little boy. So the grandmother was just kind of going like, "Oh, she's a medium," but she doesn't know she's a medium. Because spirits can only see mediums. They can't see people that are not mediums. So the spirit was trapping her and she was just like trying to get her attention, and she felt like she was being pinned down. So she thought it was the devil. She thought it was Satan coming to get her because she was going through a divorce, and divorces were not allowed. So you know, that's how our minds work, and that's kind of where I was at, at that point. I was like, I need to go to church and I need to get all this turned off. And they actually... I finally told my dad about it. We went to the pastors. We had been going to that church for 26 years, and they kicked us out of the church. They told us we couldn't come back because they were scared.

WILLIAM: You were beyond what?

MARISA: My dad's kind of a blabbermouth and he tried to tell the pastor that I would talk to the pastor's father who had just died. It's a longer story, but... My dad ends up with his foot in his mouth most of the day, all the time. But so it's kind of a longer story, but they ended up telling us we could not come back to the church. And when they did that I got very, very angry at the church, and that's kind of what drove me to go and start learning about all of this stuff. It gave me the courage to go, "Well, if they're not going to accept me here and I'm seeing all these things, and I'm feeling beings around me, then I need to go somewhere and learn about it." So I found a spiritualist church and started taking mediumship classes.

CHAPTER FIVE
DIFFERENCES BETWEEN MEDIUMS AND PSYCHICS

WILLIAM: So there are actually classes to become a medium?

MARISA: Yeah. Kind of creepy places, though. Be careful of those places.

WILLIAM: What is the goal for most mediums? Because I don't know a lot about the profession of mediumship. As a kid growing up we had, you know, five dollars, ten dollars, tell your fortune. Are we talking about that kind of a mediumship?

MARISA: The difference between a medium and a psychic is pretty much every medium is psychic but not every psychic is a medium. So mediumship... the definition of that is proof of life after death. So these mediums can talk to dead people. And that's my big beef with the mediumship community is that a lot of these mediums don't know what they're talking to. They're just getting messages, you know, flashes, images in their head, and they're reporting them to people. But they don't know what realm they're talking to, they don't know—

WILLIAM: And can anyone become a medium?

MARISA: Anyone can become a medium in a sense. A lot of mediums see it as, "I want to be clairvoyant, I want to be able to see the spirit, I want to be able to talk to it." A lot of people are more empathic mediums. They can feel the emotions of the medium. A lot of people who have anxiety disorders that come to see me, because I do medical intuition too, is they think they have an anxiety disorder but really they're just a medium and they don't know it, and they get a spirit in their field. They don't have defense mechanisms for whatever that spirit has gone through so their emotional body just reacts, "Oh my gosh I'm having anxiety." You know, and they do a simple like, "If you're not here for my highest and best good, leave!" It's like gone. Because we are completely in control of our energy field.

WILLIAM: And how large is the medium community?

MARISA: It's getting more and more popular. You know, Long Island Medium. Now there's this new Hollywood medium that's on TV, and there's another girl. And I just feel like there's a lot of people wanting to become mediums so they're like me, sitting at their house going, "All right, come in, whoever's out there, I just want to talk to you." And I kind of gross some of my students out sometimes and I say, "You could be talking to like a pedophile that's flashing images of looking like grandma to you, and you're letting that energy into your house so you have to be careful. You need to have protection…"

WILLIAM: And what is the role of mediums in society? What are they serving to do?

MARISA: I think a lot of them are destroying society.

WILLIAM: Okay, but are there a branch of mediums that are just focused on healing, or..?

MARISA: Most mediums do have the ability to heal, but not all of them heal. I think that most mediums that are just mediums will have somebody come to them. That person wants to talk to dad who just passed away, wants to know that dad is in heaven, wants to know dad is okay, wants to know where dad left the will, wants to know where, you know, things like that. So they're just a medium between the spirit world and here.

WILLIAM: So some mediums do perform some useful functions?

MARISA: Oh yeah, absolutely, absolutely. They give people peace. My thing is, a lot of mediums are not mediums, they're psychics. So you come to me and say, "I'm just a psychic" and we're talking. In your mind you're thinking, "I've got a picture of my dad in my pocket, my dad looked like this, I wonder if they're going to pick up on that." And I go, "Your dad is here, I got a father energy here, your dad's here, you got a picture in your pocket, don't you?" I'm not reading dad, I'm reading your mind. Yeah. So a lot of mediums are not mediums; they're psychics. So psychics can be taught to be mediums, though. But there's not really much education out there on mediumship. It's so kind of, the spiritualist church kind of—

WILLIAM: Well, this is just to bring it back to a more general conversation. Based on scientific information about the zero point and the nature of information that can't be created or destroyed, some of the work that Dr. Gary Schwartz in Arizona and other legitimate scientists have done that has been trying to get at the scientific basis for psychic and medium phenomenon requires a different world view than strict materialism. Strict materialism is, you know, if you can't measure it and it doesn't have physical mass, it doesn't exist. What you're sharing with us provides an alternative explanation so that it's... Because, I don't know if it was Einstein but it's a caveat, you know, the simplest explanation is usually the best. And to try to explain away the literally millions of cases of accurate psychic predictions would require a theory much more complex than the theory that you indirectly are proposing that all information is available. So this is interesting from that point of view and grounded into something that, you know, someone reading this can actually say, "Okay, let's go to the next step, okay, we have intuition, we have psychic ability, we have mediumship, and they're kind of different levels of involvement with quote 'another dimension'." So continue.

CHAPTER SIX

CHANNELS

MARISA: And then there are channels–

WILLIAM: Because you see... Well, okay, let's go onto the channels. Let's come back also, you know, what is the nature of these other dimensions? But let's go with channels first.

MARISA: Okay, so a channel, the way I look at it, is a psychic is tuning into the fourth dimension. The fourth dimension is around us, it's everywhere. It's our thoughts, it's our emotions, it's our feelings, it's the dream world, it's the astral plane. If anyone has seen that movie *Inception*–have you seen *Inception* with Leonardo DiCaprio? That's the astral plane, that's the fourth dimension. They're going into this dream state. You know, they are there and it's real but time is different and it depends on what layer they're in... but it's basically about lucid dreaming. That's where lucid dreaming is done and astral traveling, remote viewing, things like that. The fourth dimension is where all the thoughts and emotions and feelings are, so it's the dirtiest dimension. It's where everything—

WILLIAM: The dirtiest dimension? The fourth? Because—just some time out– because traditionally the first dimension is one dimension, then you go to two you have with 3-D movies, three dimension, you're a three-dimensional being, I am, and you think of it as a progression. Now we're going to a fourth dimension and you're telling me it's messier than one, two or three, and so it's not necessarily... well, does it represent a higher energy or not?

MARISA: It is a higher energy. It's a higher frequency. So it's spinning faster, the way that the guides have explained it to us in channeling.

WILLIAM: But it's more—

MARISA: It's kind of like a plane going at light speed, so you can't see it, as opposed to a little hot air balloon or blimp putzing along. You know that's the third dimension. But say a big rocket ship is to come by and pick up that blimp and just "shoom," go. It's going to disappear, too. So the energy is moving faster so we can't see it. Mediums can see it, you know, the energy.

WILLIAM: So higher is not necessarily better?

MARISA: Nope. It's all consciousness. So consciousness, we have guides in the fourth and—

WILLIAM: So the esthetics of the third dimension may be superior to the esthetics of the fourth dimension?

MARISA: Yeah, in some cases.

WILLIAM: I'll come back to this question when we get up to the fifth and beyond dimensions, if we do. I don't know if you have access to them, but—

MARISA: Yeah, I do.

WILLIAM: Let's go back to the channeling.

MARISA: I don't, but they do, so…

WILLIAM: Let's go back to the channeling, give a little more explanation of the channeling.

MARISA: So channels kind of bypass the fourth dimension. So the way that I describe the fourth dimension is as you can kind of look at two sky scrapers. See, you've got a 12-story sky scraper here. And I use, you know, David Hawkins' Scale of Consciousness. I love using that scale to kind of be able to determine what floor of the third dimension you are on because it's your consciousness, it's your emotions, it's your feelings. It determines what floor of this building you are living on. And you know, you could be on the fifth floor and somebody cuts you off on the freeway and you go, "Ah!" and you drop down to the second floor. You know, so I mean you're going up and down, up and down all day long. So if you're grounded in the third dimension, which most humans are, but we're evolving as a planet so people are kind of moving toward the fourth and fifth dimension, so you know you look at the greatest generation, like your dad's generation, he was very intuitive, but that generation is more like, you know, "We've got our house, we've got our food, how's the weather?" You know, just very like—

WILLIAM: Basic.

MARISA: Yeah. Third dimension. They didn't have to worry about if somebody is in a bad mood in the grocery store, picking that bad mood up, because they didn't really have access to the fourth dimension. So now, you know, we have access to the fourth dimension. You do, obviously. You're very intuitive. Other people do. So the fourth dimension has a building just like it and it's like a storage unit. So every time you're on the, say, third floor which is where kind of ego resides, everything you do, everything you say, everything you touch, everything that you experience, is stored in that fourth dimension over here. So it's like a storage locker and that's for, you know, past, present, future lives, everything. But we won't get that deep. As you go up into the higher floors things get more refined, they get nicer and better. So the third floor is going to be kind of if you go into this fourth building over here, it's going to be where all the earthbound spirits are that have not crossed over.

They're still in ego. "I've got to stay here, I've got to save people, I've got to rescue people, I've got to get my killer, I've got to do this, I've got to do that." You know, whatever it is. Like, "I wasn't supposed to die yet," you know, or "I just love alcohol, I don't want to leave the earth plane. I want to drink so I'm going to go hangout at bars and I'm going to jump into people's energy and enjoy some drinks." And they do that. They do that. So that's the third floor. The fourth floor is where kind of guides start coming in and then angels and then the celestial beings, and then all the way up to the 12th floor. So the fourth dimension is kind of hairy at the bottom, but when you get up to the higher dimensions, or the higher planes of higher levels of consciousness, you're going to be tuning into much greater beings, and the beings from the higher dimensions like fifth, sixth, seventh, all the way up, communicate with us through the fourth dimension. That's where mediums hang out. So mediums are hanging in this fourth building and a lot of us don't know we are mediums. I mean, I went through drug addiction and all this in my early 20s because I was trying to not feel the fourth dimension around me.

WILLIAM: What drugs were you addicted to?

MARISA: I was addicted to opiates. So, yeah.

WILLIAM: Opiates. That's pretty heavy stuff.

MARISA: Yeah, very heavy stuff. Pain killers were like my thing, and they just made me... As soon as I would take the Vicodins... I was up to like 18 a day or something. I would take so many. I remember the first time I took them it was like, "I can function, I can work, I'm not sad, I'm not depressed, I feel good, I'm confident..." Because what I didn't realize is, you know, a 20-year-old that just dropped out of college and thought she let everybody down and, you know, all this, is that I was now kind of ungrounded in my life. I was a medium. I've always been one, I just didn't know. But instead of operating at, say, the fifth floor where there's no earthbound spirits, no negative emotions–there are all guides there–my emotional level dropped down to maybe the second floor and now all the stuff on the second floor was kind of affecting me emotionally and mentally and physically. So I got sick and I took that pill and it was like, "Woo!" It was like putting a big block. Drugs kind of just... alcohol... that just kind of puts a big huge wall between those two buildings so you can't feel that stuff. So mediums and psychics usually are tuning into this fourth dimension. When you're talking about channels you're talking about people who can tune into the higher states of consciousness of the fourth building over here, and into the fifth and sixth.

WILLIAM: So a channel... So there's different levels of channeling?

MARISA: Yeah, channels...

CHAPTER SEVEN
THE 12 DIMENSIONS AND LAYERS
OF SELF

WILLIAM: Now, are there many channels who can go all the way up to the... how many dimensions are there, first of all?

MARISA: I can see 12.

WILLIAM: Twelve.

MARISA: I think that there are a whole lot of them, but I see 12.

WILLIAM: Okay, and you developed your mediumship and then you started channeling? And when you first started channeling you were going into fourth dimension, I assume?

MARISA: Yeah, pretty much. I was channeling dead people, you know. I'd rock back and forth and I would sweat, and—

WILLIAM: And what was the breakthrough when you realized you were not just doing mediumship but channeling?

MARISA: I think I did channeling first, because I wanted to tune into my higher self, and that's what opened the mediumship. But my consciousness was not high enough in the floors. I was on the third floor because I wanted to kill myself, I wanted to die, so I was opening up to this fourth building and all the beings that were in there were like, "Oh we're your guides, we love you," you know. It's like they were probably earthbound spirits I was talking to and I didn't know.

WILLIAM: So they were lying to you?

MARISA: Oh yeah.

WILLIAM: So this is important information.

MARISA: People are crappy on that side. If they were crappy here, they're crappy over there, too.

WILLIAM: Okay, well this is very important because so many people have the misconception that just because someone is not on planet Earth they can be trusted by all.

MARISA: No…

WILLIAM: Okay. This is important.

MARISA: I mean I'm not saying all, I'm not saying all—

WILLIAM: No, no, no, but you need the same level of discernment. Just like on planet Earth we have good people and bad people, we have good people who sometimes do bad things, and we have bad people who sometimes do good things, it's kind of the same in the fourth dimension.

MARISA: Exactly.

WILLIAM: Now, at a certain point you went from channeling fourth dimension, just dead people, to channeling fifth dimension and you said they were angelic beings.

CHAPTER EIGHT
ASCENDED MASTERS

MARISA: They were ascended masters.

WILLIAM: Ascended masters, okay. A little background. What's an ascended master?

MARISA: An ascended master is somebody who, if you want to look at earth like a school, we have seven different grades here—this is the way it was explained to us through the channeling that we've done for our book, is you start off... they don't like to use negative numbers, they said—so we start at second grade, that's a baby soul. And then if you decide, you know what? I just want to incarnate for the rest of my life and I don't want to merge back with my higher self, and I don't want to evolve, and I don't want to keep going to school... that's what the other side considers a level one. So people can turn their back as souls on—the guides don't call it God, they call it their light.

WILLIAM: But you can have a very nice physical human existence?

MARISA: Oh yeah, yeah. I mean it's not like, "Oh I've given into Lucifer and I've turned my back." It's just, you decided that you, as a soul, have been sparked and, "I want to continue to be Marisa's spirit forever. I don't want to be, you know, my dad's cousin, brother..." You don't want to keep... because when you reincarnate, you know, you become these different people.

WILLIAM: So the majority of human beings, first, second grade, is all they really desire?

MARISA: Yeah.

WILLIAM: I mean, in fact—

MARISA: And they're not allowed to be born here anymore.

WILLIAM: What do you mean they're not allowed to be born here? If that's all they desire, they get kicked to another—

MARISA: Levels. Earth was the only planet, supposedly, out of 168,000 inhabitable planets. And this gets into the woo-woo, you know. But it's—Earth was apparently–.

WILLIAM: Well, I'd rather stay into the science because... that's not—

MARISA: Yeah. Oh okay. But yeah.

WILLIAM: Just so people know, I mean, I went to Yale, I went to Harvard. I'm not easily duped into "Oh, I saw this, I saw that." One of the reasons I'm having this conversation, Marisa—she has a critical mindset about this and doesn't just accept even what she channels from higher dimensions.

MARISA: Oh yeah, I argue with them.

WILLIAM: She questions it and there's logic here, not just feelings. And I think there's that combination which is making this interesting to me, and I believe will be interesting to millions of you out there.

CHAPTER NINE
LEVEL TWO

MARISA: Yeah, so there are level twos. And level twos are your baby souls. They are a lot of the people that are, they're just not interested in religion, not spirituality. They could be, you know, some of your wealthiest, richest people. They could be, a lot of them, the guides have explained, a lot of them are just experiencing human life for the first time so they're like your Bush People, you know, out in like these colonies where they're not very civilized because they are just consciousness learning to be in these bodies, you know. So they're learning how to be human and they're learning very simple stuff. As you evolve and you become a level three soul, they've explained, level three are your very religious people. They have to be ruled by fear. And I'm not saying religion is bad because if level threes were here and they did not have religion, they would—

WILLIAM: They would run amok.

MARISA: Yeah. They would run amok. Exactly. I always say, you know, one of my family members, she has the same abilities as me and if she was not scared to death that God was going to strike her down and send her to hell, she'd be putting curses on everybody, you know.

WILLIAM: And effectively?

MARISA: Oh yeah, yeah. She would. Instead of sending light to someone, she'd be sending dark. So she's scared that God will strike her down and that's fine. That's great. I'm glad. She needs that, you know. So the level threes are more of the religious. The level fours are most of mediums, healers, intuitives, things like that. And can be your bipolar people, your schizophrenic people, your anxiety disorders. The people that think they have mental disorders. Alcoholics, addicts, things like that. Because they're trying to find ways to medicate spiritual abilities. So they can feel what someone is feeling over here, but they think it's their feelings, their brain is interpreting it to, you know... say this person is in a fight with their husband, and say I'm watching a movie with my husband, and... "I gotta go get popcorn. I'll go to the store, I'll be right back." So we're in this great mood, we're on a date night. I go and I'm talking to the register lady, "Hey, how's it going, blah, blah, blah?" And say her husband is just angry at her, he's just so mad at her. But she smiles and everything, you know, whatever. I take on that energy—husband is mad at me—but I don't realize it because I'm not in tune with my intuition. I'm just a big ball of, you know, feeling everybody's stuff. I walk in the door five minutes later, popcorn, it's like, "What's wrong with you?" to my husband.

"What's wrong with you?"

"Nothing is wrong, let's watch the movie."

"I didn't take that long." You know, it's like...

"I didn't say you took that long."

"Why are you mad at me?"

"I'm not mad at you."

"Yes you are, I can tell."

"Well, if you keep saying I'm mad at you..."

Believe me, that happens all the time with my husband.

WILLIAM: Well, this just aside, because this is really interesting in terms of where you choose to shop, and where you interact, like how you get to work. Like if you live in New York City and you're taking the subway, or you know, if you get to drive in a limo with a driver who is being paid, I guess, to be really nice. It's interesting—

MARISA: But they could be very nice and they could be having a lot of stuff going on.

WILLIAM: Oh, okay.

CHAPTER TEN
LEVEL FOUR SOULS

MARISA: Some level four souls were level five in here, which is pretty cool, but started as level fours. A lot of level fives started as level fours. There's lots of sub-levels within the levels. But the level fours are people who have issues with relationships because we can't tell the difference between our energy and someone else's energy, and we're constantly blaming somebody else for our energy, you know, kind of projecting that and stuff. So level fours are my favorite to work with, and most of my students are level fours. I just love level fours because it's like, "Hey, guess what?" You know, the reason you get anxious right before your husband gets home, and you know, you start eating or you get agitated is because his energy is getting home before him, and you are feeling what he is bringing home from work, and it may not be his energy, it may be the guy in the cubicle next to him, or the office next to him who is fighting with his wife, you know. I used to get on my husband and I used to think he was calling me a nag. For like six months, it was like off and on. He'd come home and I'd be like, "Why do you think I'm a nag?" And he was like, "I never called you a nag, you're not a nag." And I'd get so upset. And finally we went to one of his work parties and I met one of the guys that he would work with once a week—

WILLIAM: Whose wife was a nag—

MARISA: That's all he would talk about. "My wife is a nag." And I said next time I think— I thought in my head—next time I think that Jeff is calling me a nag I'm going to ask him, "Did you work with

Mr. X?" And every time, "Did you work with Mr. X today?" "Yes…" "Okay, good, it's not your energy."

WILLIAM: So when a child is born, they don't necessarily go through one to two, three to four? They come in as a four or a five?

MARISA: That's the fun thing about the kids these days. They're all fives and sixes.

WILLIAM: Okay, well let's keep going and find out more about the level fives and sixes.

MARISA: Yeah. It's fascinating. So level fours, a lot of times they'll become level fives or they're alcoholics and they die alcoholics, and you know, they end up having to come back. And level fours were level fours for a long time. Level fives are very spiritual beings but they're not necessarily in spirituality. Like you. You're in spirituality, but you're representing spiritual people. You're bringing light to—

WILLIAM: I don't spend time meditating and everything, no.

MARISA: Yeah, you're not in here meditating with your legs crossed.

WILLIAM: No. If I do two minutes a day it's a lot, you know.

MARISA: Exactly. So level five doesn't need to really go through all of that stuff and deal with the addiction and deal with the blah, all this stuff that brings you to your knees to say, "God help me," or whatever.

WILLIAM: This is really an important point to make because so many of the books that I represent are books about how to get in touch with your higher self and involve spiritual practices and meditation practices, including the book that we wrote ourselves, *Tapping The Source*, which has great meditation exercises, but I always maintained… and it's interesting because the co-author of that book who really did the heavy lifting, John Selby, is like, "Wow, you have to spend at least 30 minutes a day meditating." And I was like, "I don't think that's true. You shouldn't say that in the book." And he actually got into a little bit of a miff with me because in the introduction I said you didn't. "You're misleading people."

MARISA: Some do, but—

WILLIAM: That's the thing. My point that I'm trying to make is really there is so much variety about where you are in your own evolution, in your own stage, if you will, your own vibration, that it can never be one-size fits all.

MARISA: Yeah.

WILLIAM: What is prefect… Because there are people who probably do need to be born and born to be Tibetan monks and spend 12 hours a day meditating every single day for their entire 80-year life. And there may be other people who two minutes a day is plenty. So this is I hope helpful to the people reading, so that whatever practice you are doing, don't feel it's not enough, or that you have to change. Maybe you do if it's not working, but if it is working, don't feel, "Oh there's something more I need to do," because you may already be where you need to be.

MARISA: Exactly. And some people are so intuitive and, you know, we've got the Chopra Center down the street. So I work on a lot of people that work over there and a lot of the students and all that, who live around here. And it's interesting because they have their practice and a lot of people come in saying, "I need to do this, I need to do my mantra. I got my mantra, I paid for my class and I got this and that," and it's not working for them. It's like, "Well, you don't need the mantra. The mantra is actually kind of what's blocking you." It may work for this person who's a level three who needs to be told. There's a lot of level threes that go to places like this.

WILLIAM: Transcendental meditation. That was the whole thing. You gotta get your mantra, get your mantra. Yeah, I tried transcendental meditation. Didn't work for me.

MARISA: You're too high-level soul.

WILLIAM: It was bringing me down instead of up.

MARISA: Exactly, exactly. So there's these ritualistic things. And I'm not ritualistic at all. I have to kind of teach ritual to some of the students that need it, but I'm just kind of like, "Okay, room is protected, everything is done." I'm not walking around, you know, with sage and doing all this stuff, but I teach it because that's how I started, you know. You kind of have to start somewhere.

Chapter Eleven
Level Fives

WILLIAM: So from level five—

MARISA: So level fives are a lot of the children. They call them Crystal Children, and they're just almost fully evolved beings that have mostly probably spent a lot of lifetimes on other planets recently. So they've been on other planets and now they're like, you know what? The way I describe it is, you know, we live here in Cardiff, okay. We're here in Cardiff in this beautiful city, and you can look at Earth as Cardiff, you know, way back when, before all these level five souls went "I'm outta here." So, you know, let's say we're getting taken over by the ghetto. People start parking on the lawns, drawing on the walls. We're going to be like, "I'm moving out of here, I'm out." We got somewhere else, it's pretty, it's beautiful, and then you know, 12,000 years later we go, "Oh look, all the residents of Cardiff are parking on the streets now and they've painted their walls, you know, I think they are smart enough now for us to go back and teach them how to be a civilized community, so let's go ahead and go back." So that's a lot of the level five souls. Atlanteans and Lemurians that were here before and went, "I don't want to live here anymore. I don't want to hit a woman over the head with a club and drag her off like a caveman, I'm way too civilized for that."

WILLIAM: "We're going to have some nice champagne, and then we'll dance and then we'll go."

MARISA: Yeah. Hit her over the head. But anyways, that's kind of like the Atlanteans are all coming back. So a lot of times when I see like, you know, your soul standing behind you as this tall Atlantean priest, you know, and so it's like a lot of people are coming back from there. Others have just... I mean I've seen other-worldly beings that is their soul because they are just coming through to my imagination, to my mind, as what they were last. So those are level five souls. And you know, Michael Jackson, people like that, that are bringing like a high frequency energy. You see some of these singers, they start singing, even Eminem, I mean he's so angry and you still get chills because he's like being angry because he's a level five soul and he's bringing in a higher frequency even though it's through anger but people can relate to that and they help raise the vibration of the planet. The guides have described these level sixes that are coming in, the ascended masters, as beings that have no karma. They learned all the virtues they needed to learn at birth, and basically they don't need to come back anymore. They're done, they're pretty much graduated from Earth school. But these ascended masters choose, because they love Earth, to stay here. So they hang around and they act as guides.

WILLIAM: Are they here?

MARISA: Some are, yeah.

WILLIAM: In physical form?

MARISA: Mm-hm [yes].

WILLIAM: So you can be walking down the street in the park and, "Hey, how you doing? Have a good day..." and it could be an ascended master?

MARISA: Yeah, I was at the grocery store the other day and it made me think of an example. In our last book we were channeling

Peter from the Bible and he says, "Look at the earth, the grid as a Lite-Brite." Remember those Lite-Brites from the 80s, you know, it was like a little screen that was like this big, and you put little light bulbs in a black piece of paper or little peg-holes, and you stick little light bulbs in those holes and you draw pictures of hearts or, you know, whatever? So it's this little grid and he says, "Look at each and every single human being as a light bulb. The higher level souls, they're not bigger, they are going to shine brighter, though." Okay, so that Lite-Brite is shining real bright and then there's another one over here maybe a level two or level three or level four that are right next to it that have all this goop and gunk all over them which is the emotional, all the stuff that happens down here, all the gunk that gets on us. And let's say that level six, little light bulb in that grid, is a baby in a baby carriage at the grocery store. And I'm there and I'm dealing with like all my emotional crap and everything, and I'm just standing there. I don't look at the baby. I don't have interaction with the baby. I just have nothing to do with the baby. But their frequency is so bright that it burns off my muck so then I'm able to see my own light, I'm able to connect to—

WILLIAM: So it's quite possible that the ascended masters… do you have an idea how many ascended masters are on the planet right now?

MARISA: I just heard 144,000, but I don't think that's human beings. Twenty-two thousand, one hundred twenty six—

WILLIAM: Human beings and the others are spirits that are hovering—

MARISA: A hundred and forty-four thousand it feels like, that's how many ascended masters there are. Twenty-two thousand, one hundred twenty six.

WILLIAM: Twenty two thousand, one hundred—

MARISA: And twenty six humans right now are ascended masters.

WILLIAM: So obviously many of these ascended masters have chosen families which are not prominent?

MARISA: Oh yeah.

WILLIAM: In fact, I would think as an ascended master it is almost easier if you were not in the limelight because you'd be more effective.

MARISA: Yeah. You're just emitting frequency. You're just down here. Because the ascended masters have said… like Jesus comes in, we talk to the apostles, we talk to St. Germain, we talk to Mary Magdalene. But it's the beings that are kind of done, they come in and they say it's not about really going down and being this huge spiritual teacher and, you know, all this. It's just existing in the grid to bring in that light.

WILLIAM: Holding the light, holding the energy and influencing in subtle ways others who influence others, who influence others—

MARISA: Exactly.

WILLIAM: And whoever chooses to be in the limelight, that's fine. It's not about—

MARISA: The level fours like being in the limelight.

WILLIAM: They do. Yeah.

MARISA: The level fours are like, "I'm a spirit in a human body and I'm going to share this with the world." You know, it's like the motivational speaker Tony Robbins, he's a level five. I was tapping into his energy because I was going to teach at a place where he was at, and I was checking all the soul levels of everybody, you know.

WILLIAM: How was Wayne Dyer?

MARISA: Wayne Dyer is a level five.

WILLIAM: That's what I thought. He was a good guy.

MARISA: And the level fives are... almost kind of get pushed into the limelight, you know. They're not real like, "Yeah!" When I was a level four they finally told me like nine months or 10 months ago or something, that "Yay, you're a level five." I was like "Woo-hoo!" I hope I can't flunk and go back, you know, but...

WILLIAM: Just so people listening don't get the wrong idea, just because you go from level four to level five doesn't mean your income is going to go up or—

MARISA: No—

WILLIAM: Or any of the material ways that people measure, you know.

MARISA: I sometimes joke around and say that level twos have the most fun. They're not worried that, "God's going to strike me down." They're not worried. They don't feel everybody else's stuff around. They just exist and experience themselves. They have fun. They are baby souls. They have fun. It's the level fives and the level... I don't know a lot of level sixes, but know lots of level fives. The level fours seem to be the souls that have the hard lives. The level fives seem to have these charmed lives where it's just kind of like, nothing really bad happens to them. You didn't earn your level five. I went through hell and back to become a level five. No, but the level fives kind of have these charmed lives.

WILLIAM: You had mentioned something earlier that I had been a level four. Now I'm a level five?

MARISA: Yeah, yeah.

WILLIAM: That's good news because things happen to me easier and easier.

MARISA: But you switched 18 years ago so you've been a level five a long time. What were you doing 18 years ago?

WILLIAM: I don't know. I had to battle some difficult situations in the past 18 years. So being a level five isn't necessarily a free coast, guys. It's not a hall pass.

MARISA: No, no.

WILLIAM: Because I mean my life has been very blessed and easy compared to, you know, 99 percent, but for, you know, where I started, because my life was always good, even when I've had that switch, I still had a number of challenges—

MARISA: Growing pains.

WILLIAM: And I will say I'm at a place now where I think that I really have assimilated what it is to be a level five because almost nothing bothers me.

MARISA: Perfect.

WILLIAM: It's like we did an interview when we were doing *Tapping the Source*. I never say his name right, Drunvalo Melchizedek.

Yeah. I can't say that name. Anyway, we did this interview with him and it was like talking… because I'm an expert on 2012 and what the Mayans, you know, intended that to be, the end of the world. And it was the end of the world and if you're still here that means you're in the new world. But anyway, we'll get into that. But talking more in terms of what most people think the end of world could be, like the Apocalypse and the end of the physical planet that we're on, he had this wonderful thing. He said, "Well, you know, and if it is, it's perfectly okay because there's nothing to worry about." And you know he's obviously at least a level five. He may even be a level six. I don't know. But that's sort of the way—

MARISA: You're talking about Drunvalo Melchizedek? I can't say his name right either.

WILLIAM: I can't say his name either, but yeah. I think that he is a level—he's a level beyond me. If he is a level five he's a higher five, because he just never—

MARISA: He's a higher five. His higher self is an ascended master so he channels level six. Interesting. He's like a hybrid.

WILLIAM: Yeah. Okay well that's… but it was more the way he said it. He goes, "There's nothing to worry about." You know, it's like the world could end but there's nothing to worry about because once you connect with the bigger picture of all the multi-dimensionality of existence, you realize that, yeah it would be a pity; it's a beautiful planet, but eh, there are other planets. It's not the end of the world. It's the end of this world—it's not the end of the universe, I guess I should say. And then you know you still care. But if collective consciousness decides to destroy itself on this level, it's just—

MARISA: We'll still exist somewhere else—

WILLIAM: Just a synapse that happened, you know. But meanwhile while we're here, I'm very dedicated. I know most of my colleagues and friends are, you know, let's try and keep this planet going because it's a great planet.

MARISA: And save it.

WILLIAM: And I think there's a lot of support for that.

CHAPTER TWELVE
LEVEL SIX AND BEYOND

MARISA: That's the whole point of these sixes coming down. Yeah.

WILLIAM: I mean like there seems to be something special about this planet. Maybe just because it's a proving ground or something, but there may be other planets that are more evolved. But for whatever reason, this planet seems to get a lot of attention.

MARISA: Well, it's a melting pot. Because it's the only planet where levels one through six, seven, can coexist. Because other planets, like in the Pleiades or Arcturus that are like only level three, four, five. Or four, five, six. So it's like there are worlds where you have to be a certain grade to incarnate there, but then you live 200 years or, you know, you learn to manifest, you learn to do this. There are planets they say that are purely just for like people who are inventors that go there and invent things and they will transmit these inventions through frequency to people down here and channels will pick up and that's why you see on the earth plane three or four, or five, people come out with the same invention at the same time. It's because they are—

WILLIAM: It's literally in the air.

MARISA: Yeah. Literally in the air. I like that, I like that, yeah. The frequency is literally being broadcasted. Yeah, so these level sixes are the ascended masters, and then of course, level seven would be your Christed beings, so they become Christed. You know like Jesus Christ, or … gosh they listed off a bunch of people that had been Christed. Some of those when we talked to the 12 gurus of the Holy Ghost. Me and my friend did some channeling and I think three or four of those had been Christed. So they've ascended, they've become Christed, and now they can go make their own planet.

WILLIAM: They can make their own planet?

MARISA: Yeah, they can go—

WILLIAM: From scratch?

MARISA: Yeah. They can go and they can create—

WILLIAM: Just molecules come together and boom?

MARISA: They just manifest, yeah. They become Christed here.

WILLIAM: Now, they have to do it within the laws of physics, I assume.

MARISA: Yeah. And the way they described it to us is that there are 12 Christed souls that came together to create earth, and whether the "Big Guy" up there above them, or you know, some architect created it and then they went to work to build it, or whether they just went "poof!" it's there, I don't know how it works. And we can probably channel that later and ask them because that's an interesting question. But 12 basically Christed souls came together to create this planet and have seeded—like holographically, basically—created lots of little tiny "thems" to inhabit all people down here. So all of us are pretty much part of those 12 original souls that created Earth, unless we're from another planet or you know, another… And that's one of the things I'm a little obsessed with, too—the different souls that people come from and things like that. That's been kind of my little... everyone has their obsession and mine is the soul anatomy and where we came from.

WILLIAM: Okay, well let's keep on. So we have the Christed seventh level. You said there are 12 levels.

MARISA: The Christed seventh level. There are another seven grades. There are seven grades and that's it. So the ascended masters is... we were talking about that because I started channeling an ascended master because I got scared, because my dad's very–kind of—dogmatic Christian. He's coming around, you know, he's getting better at not being scared all the time that the dark side is coming in. But I decided I had read somewhere online about the ascended masters... or no, Saint Germain the trickster started coming in to session with my dad and so I looked him up. Because I don't read anything. I don't want to have it in my mind and then just regurgitate other people's stuff, so I don't read. But if a name comes through I'll Google it and I'll kind of read some things. So I went, "Oh, ascended masters." So I found this site that had all of these ascended masters, like a ton of them on there, and all the colors they come in. And so one night I was just bored and I just kind of... my husband travels four days a week, or used to, and now he doesn't anymore, but I would just be sitting at home kind of bored and you know we don't have kids, just have the cat at the time. Now I have a dog. Now I have a little girl. But I was just sitting there and I started thinking, "Okay, calling in Saint Germain," and I felt the energy. It was like, "Woosh." And I heard my guide Abraham, which all of us have Abraham here, which I find very interesting. Abraham said, "Ask them to step into your body, all bodies." And I was like, "That's kind of creepy." You know. And he said, "If it's an ascended master they can step into your body and you can feel what they feel like. Don't let anyone else in. Don't let grandma in...because they may not leave. They may like it there, you know, and then they don't leave." But if it's an ascended master you can call them into your field, all layers. I see 12 layers but at the time

I only knew like five. So I actually imagined myself kind of like Tupperware bowls, you know, that are all stacked in each other, and I saw almost like Saint Germain's energy kind of pouring into all the bowls, and I just felt like goosebumps and chills and it was just a really full feeling. And they said, "This is how you need to feel when you channel." So I went, "Oh…" I wasn't rocking back and forth, I wasn't dripping sweat, because I didn't have a person inside of me. I had a fully evolved consciousness. The ascended masters don't necessarily have spirit bodies anymore. There's like a university over on the other side and all of us as spirits, we go to the university and we connect down, and go back and forth, back and forth, back and forth. And the ascended masters have ascended back into that which created them, which is their higher self. So they are their higher self. They are consciousness. So after that I just thought, "You know what? I don't want to channel spirits anymore." I mean, the last time I channeled a spirit it was this guy, he's sometimes gay, sometimes, not, so he's always like, "Girl!" And then sometimes he's like, "blah." He's hilarious. He became a friend, but he took my Reiki class–I teach intuition development through Reiki—and so he was introducing himself to the class and he said, "Yeah, Marisa had me when we were making out on the Reiki table at my session." And I went, "What?" And he said, "Oh everything that she said was accurate so I had to take her class, but when she was cuddling with me on the table…" And I went, "Shut up, I was not cuddling with you." And he goes, "You don't remember?" And I said, "No." And he says, "Remember my mom? You let her get into your energy, you were laying on the table with me, hugging me?" I was like rocking him back and forth. And he says, "That's what she used to do." And I went, "That's it! I'm never letting a spirit come into my energy." And then I flashed on saying "Can I give you a hug?" or whatever, so I was just like, okay, yeah. I'm not letting people into my body ever again. From that point forward it was like only ascended masters.

WILLIAM: And when was that?

MARISA: That was probably 2013.

WILLIAM: Okay, so just three years ago, two really.

MARISA: And when I started only allowing ascended masters into my energy I still was dealing with the self-worth thing, like I couldn't talk to God, Source. I wasn't good enough for that. I had all the self-worth Christianity imprints, you know. I'm a sinner...

WILLIAM: That's all gone now?

MARISA: Yeah, that's gone now.

WILLIAM: So you can talk to anybody?

MARISA: Yeah, I can talk to anyone on some level.

WILLIAM: Okay, so let's keep going and find out—

MARISA: I can not channel anyone, or should I say, I will not channel anyone. Low level beings need to go through my higher self to deliver messages because I won't talk to them, it's dangerous. All that being said, my old self worth issues do not keep me from connecting with extremely high level beings, God, or Source anymore.

CHAPTER THIRTEEN

OVERSOULS

WILLIAM: Okay so you got ascended masters. Now there's above ascended masters.

MARISA: Ascended masters. Well, then you've got the Christed beings. And then above the fifth dimension you're going to go... the sixth dimension is what you would call like our Christ body. So it's like our Christed self. What's her name? Elizabeth Claire Prophet? I think she calls it the I Am or something like that. So we've got our six-dimensional body, but above that we have like our oversoul, we have the soul that created our higher self and spirit. It's like a tripod or a family tree. You look at your soul that created a bunch of higher selves, and those higher selves created—

WILLIAM: Of you or other people as well?

MARISA: Other people—

WILLIAM: So my oversoul could overlap with your oversoul?

MARISA: Yeah.

WILLIAM: We can have the same oversoul?

MARISA: In fact, we're all kind of from the same oversoul. Yeah. There are thousands of people.

WILLIAM: And just for the people listening, when Marisa is referring to all of us, my wife Gayle is also here, and she's a very important part of the energy, because one of the things that we prepared for this meeting was that we would only have very high frequency energy in the room. Fortunately Gayle has that.

MARISA: Has a very high frequency.

WILLIAM: She's helping to bring these spirits. Because this is all just a prequel. We're actually going to talk to some spirits in a little bit. I don't know if you want to take a break before we do that ...

MARISA: No...

WILLIAM: We'll keep going. Let's finish this part. This is the normal human interpretation conversation and then we're going to get into another dimension conversation.

MARISA: Exactly.

WILLIAM: So you're in for a treat. Just stay tuned.

MARISA: So there's the upper dimensions and once you get past physicality—I mean, earth is a third dimension, and us as human beings we can actually go past Christed and start working with these upper dimensional beings.

WILLIAM: The oversouls.

MARISA: The oversouls. But it's just really not part of the human experience. So if someone is like, "Oh I embody the twelfth- dimensional this..." It's like ego. You know. It's like we can only go up to a certain dimension and embody that without disappearing, you know. The ascended masters literally had such a high frequency. Like my higher self is over here. She's a fifth-dimensional being.

I talk to her. But she's not a sixth-dimensional being. If she was a sixth-dimensional being in my body I would disappear because my frequency would go so high that I'd be like that rocket ship that went so fast it just disappeared.

WILLIAM: Yogananda? What level was Yogananda?

MARISA: High level five. Interesting. Yeah. We get a lot of Yogananda people. We're right down the street.

WILLIAM: The reason I ask, exactly. We're right down the street. I walk in front of his ashram almost daily on the beach and I always feel good around it.

MARISA: It's a good thing, yeah.

WILLIAM: It's good energy.

MARISA: It's because my office is right down the street. A couple blocks down.

WILLIAM: And of course the Yogananda people think he's right up there with Christ.

MARISA: But a lot of them are level threes and because they need the organized religion. So it's like the guru can be a high level but the people—and there's nothing wrong with level threes—it's just the structure is needed.

WILLIAM: And it's really not a competition anyway, out there. I mean if you're a level two or three you may be having a better life than us at five. Though I doubt it because…but whatever.

MARISA: But no competition, no. I'm like, "You're higher than me." Anyway, yeah. There's the higher dimensional stuff that we can tune into but it's really once you get up to higher than like that Christed self it's really not human anymore.

WILLIAM: You're out of here, you're gone.

MARISA: And you're really sharing. I mean your Christed self could have created, say, 12 souls and those 12 souls–everything is in twelves—

WILLIAM: Yeah. This is also great. You want to get into this, the whole thing with 12 and my relationship with 12 is kind of one of the reasons we have been able to connect. And we'll get into the twelves maybe the next session.

MARISA: Yes.

WILLIAM: Okay.

CHAPTER FOURTEEN
IT CAN GET COMPLICATED

MARISA: But you know, say a Christed self over there on the other side, a fully evolved one, can now create. Can go and get together with other creators and create worlds. Or just create other souls. So once you are Christed you can say, "You know what...?" The way I describe it is like say a Christed being will say, "You know what? I'm going to create a clone of myself. Bill that's in New York and there's Bill that's in...California."

WILLIAM: Calcutta.

MARISA: Yeah, there we go.

WILLIAM: Why not?

MARISA: Why not, yeah? And one in Houston or something. So all those Bills are consciousness so they're living in maybe a little Western kid over here, or some white kid over here, and then some—

WILLIAM: See if they interact and be able to recreate something together.

MARISA: Exactly.

WILLIAM: That's wonderful.

MARISA: Yeah. Or they never meet and I compare them to like iPods, you know. You have three iPods and this has 20 songs, this has 40 songs, this has 50 songs, but they're all syncing up to the same computer. So all of your clones as a Christed being are all constantly syncing up all their experiences to you and so—

WILLIAM: Sometimes you just meet somebody and you have this incredible connection. Could it be that that is what you're connecting with?

MARISA: Yeah. It could be you.

WILLIAM: It's like you're connecting with yourself, with a part of yourself—

MARISA: Yeah.

WILLIAM: But really a part of the oversoul that you are a part of.

MARISA: Exactly, exactly.

WILLIAM: Because you do. You sometimes meet someone you feel you've known forever.

MARISA: Yeah, exactly. They could be you or they could be a soul mate. But the way the sixth-dimensional self works is so interesting because I meet people that are of that same higher self all the time—those are the people who have Abraham. That's kind of my code word. If they have Abraham as a guide then I know that we all kind of have the same sixth- dimensional self. They have different souls, different spirits, different human experiences, but we have the same hard drive up there, so you know, you may be learning all these lessons over here, uploading them to the hard drive and I'm learning these, she's learning these, all your Bills are all learning stuff. So the thing is, is when Bill in Texas dies, all that information stays, you know, in that hard drive up there, and then that Bill clone comes back and lives in Florida. If that Bill clone doesn't ever get in touch with his higher self, then he's going to have to keep learning the lessons over and over and over.

WILLIAM: So that's the big—

MARISA: If you tune into your higher self, yeah.

WILLIAM: Depends on making the progress from that level so that you would have the choice of going back or not. But it seems you wouldn't come back at some point. Because if you become an oversoul, I mean I'm not talking about the ascended. Beyond ascended. The ascended are the last ones that come back. They come back as level sixes and they come back as a free gift to humanity–

MARISA: Basically.

WILLIAM: Because they care.

MARISA: Or they want to become Christed like Jesus did. He became Christed after he was baptized. So it took him until he was baptized to become Christed, and then he walked the earth for however many years he walked to teach people.

WILLIAM: But if you go beyond ascended into the oversoul, then you're kind of on one level done with earth because you're done—

MARISA: You're living through your clones.

WILLIAM: You are living through your clones and you're at a level where you can simultaneously be doing the same thing on other planets.

MARISA: Exactly.

WILLIAM: And it becomes more interesting. When I wrote my novel *The Twelve* I wanted to end it, because there is a character in the novel who is the creator entity, and I wanted to end it and he just left "to continue to be the artist that he was meant to be" because on the highest level of consciousness it's really all about art and aesthetics. It's about creating infinite combinations and variations that are ever more complex and ever more beautiful.

MARISA: I like that.

WILLIAM: And that... and you know you can manifest at the level of human beings and human interactions and human relationships and all kind of things. Its limitless. And that makes sense from a logical point of view.

MARISA: I like that. That's good. Yeah. So yeah, we become these creators. We're living vicariously through... you are living through your clones. One is living in New York, one is living down here, and then Calcutta.

WILLIAM: Why not?

MARISA: Yeah and so these little clones here, they can access... say the Texas one can access his spirit which is his fifth-dimensional self. He can access his spirit and access all the lives that his spirit has lived, which would be Texas and now Florida. But that's it. Texas and Florida. Then he dies, comes back. This is if you believe in reincarnation, you know. He goes and he lives in Minnesota. So he's just got those three lives to pull from in his spirit, in his 5-D self. His spirit. But if he can learn to tune into his Christed self, his higher self, now he's got all the experience of Calcutta, he's got New York, he's got these three lives, so you can imagine that the higher and the higher you go in the dimensions, the more of a hard drive you have to pull from, and that's where you kind of end up at that zero point where you've got the consciousness of—

WILLIAM: Of everything.

MARISA: Every single person.

WILLIAM: Just for the physicists out there, because I think for 99 percent or more of humanity, this is as high as we really need to go for understanding the nature of reality, but for those more scientifically-oriented and mathematically-oriented, because ultimately mathematics is the highest science, but beyond the oversoul to get to the creator souls, talk a little bit about the levels above the oversoul.

CHAPTER FIFTEEN
THE UPPER DIMENSIONS

MARISA: So above the oversoul you're going into—I call it there's basically the oversoul and then... so that's the seventh dimension—and then you get into the eighth dimension which is your cosmic body. So, the way the guides have described it when I channel it, they describe it so much more eloquently, but the way that I see it is, like okay for example guide Mother Earth. That's a soul. And she's ascending and she's evolving. And eventually will be able to become like the cosmic body that can create souls. So every single person on this planet has an eighth layer that I can see that has a different cosmic body. Not different, I mean, you know, like mine—when I look at my eighth body it's Orion. Same with you guys. So it's like Orion. But I was with a girl the other day and she had the same seed soul—I call it seed souls and then creator souls—she had the same seed soul like we were created by the same consciousness from the tenth-dimension, but she had Andromeda as her eighth body. So it's like you carry the consciousness of an entire other universe or planet. So that's one layer of you. Doesn't mean "Oh I'm Earth," but it makes sense as to everybody that's on Earth is feeding the consciousness of Earth, and that's why they say the vibration of the planet is going up, Earth is ascending, blah, blah. So the eighth layer that I see, and again this isn't stuff I've read, this is stuff I've channeled with my dad or just that I've seen during the thousands of sessions I've done, but I sce this being called Orion and it comes in and I can channel information from it and it can bring in information from anyone really on this planet, anyone that has a piece of that within it, and–

WILLIAM: When you say—

MARISA: It's very... I don't know much about it.

WILLIAM: When you say the being. It's not like a physical body being?

MARISA: No. I see it like a silver mercury-looking being, and I've had other clairvoyants see it the same way. But it was interesting, I had to get an MRI about 11 months ago. So I was laying in the tube and "click, click, click," and I was like bored so I'm just lying there, and I hear Abraham my guide come in and say, "Call in oxygen." And I inhaled. And he goes, "No, call in oxygen like you're calling in a spirit." So I said okay. "Calling in oxygen." I'm like, oh my gosh. I never did acid but you would think I was having a flashback or something up in this thing. I never got into drugs like that. So I said, "Calling in oxygen," and this billowing lady comes in, "Woo, I'm oxygen." I was like, "Oh my gosh, I'm losing my mind." And I was calling in nitrogen, and that's when that Lego movie was out so I see this little black Lego man come in. "Calling carbon," this little green Lego man. And I was like, "All right what are you guys trying to get at?" And they said, "What we are trying to get at is that everything is consciousness because you are in a human being you see everything as human, so I'm not human but you see me as human. I'm consciousness just like oxygen, just like the elements." Everything. But since my consciousness is living as a human, my brain wants to see everything as human. He says, "Angels aren't humans, guides aren't humans. The only thing that's human that's on this side are actual humans that have not crossed over, but we're conscious, we're energy." And that's a lot of the healing I do. I see the periodic table and I see all the different elements flying into people and it's crazy looking, but...

WILLIAM: It is in fact represented by conscious beings so there's Mr. Tin–not the Tin Man–but there's tin, there's mercury, and on and on.

MARISA: Yeah. You can call in the consciousness of anything. I can call in rose, you know. I see a red lady. You know, or whatever. Based on what we think. So I can see—

WILLIAM: But it's not what you see, it's the energy.

MARISA: Exactly.

WILLIAM: That is expressing. And of course we have this wonderful combination of H20 where the hydrogen and oxygen get together and you know, create water, and on and on.

MARISA: Exactly. But what they're trying to say is like, you know, that eighth layer of the body I'm seeing are these beings, or as these people, you know Mother Earth. She's got a crown on and a blue dress. You know, it's like—

WILLIAM: That's your version of it.

MARISA: That's my version, yeah. Someone else may see her and, you know, as some gangster or something with a grill on her teeth. Or I don't know. Everybody is different. But it's what Abraham was trying to get through to me, was that everything is consciousness and it doesn't mean that all the beings are human. You're living in humans but you can also live in other beings in other worlds that don't look human at all. So he was trying to get my mind—

WILLIAM: Well, I would also think there are elements on other planets that are non-earth elements because by definition we only are aware of the elements that appear on our earth.

MARISA: Who was the guy? I think it was Einstein, Sir Isaac Newton, and Ben Franklin used to come in when I was channeling spirits. They're like...oh they come in together all the time. So they would come in. They're part of our soul group. They're on the other side.

They're part of our university. They have Abraham, too. Abraham will bring them in. And they were talking to me. They were the ones that channeled this element—I call it elemental healing, where I heal with the elements. And they said that there is another element that me and some people from the soul group probably were working on in another lifetime to bring through that's going to be discovered on the planet in the next, like, I think they said–I mean this was like four years ago—I think they said in the next 12 years.

WILLIAM: Within the next 10 years or something? Within the next 10 years?

MARISA: Yeah, yeah. It would not require the need for like gasoline and all that stuff. It was going to be some sort of like—

Chapter Sixteen
Can This Be Practical?

WILLIAM: Well, you know, there's got to be a solution to this energy issue.

MARISA: And they're trying to bring it into me, but I'm a dummy when it comes to that stuff. So the channel has to kind of resonate with that, though, unless you're in trance. And I can be in trance, but I haven't since I was pregnant.

WILLIAM: Well, we can work on this and once we find out more about it then I can connect us with some scientists who can actually do the work. Because this is sort of—just a little aside here—sort of the whole purpose of this is not so you can go off on fantasies, there's this and there's that. What is the practical use of this? And it's like combining this other worldly knowledge with practical everyday knowledge in this world. That's one of the reasons I—even though I may be this level five—I really stuck very much with my roots at Harvard and Yale, and I was a mathematical wizard, and you know just really, if I couldn't solve a problem with it I wasn't interested in it. And that's one of the reasons why I haven't been like this, "Oh I better be around this spiritual master." You feel good around these people but what's the point of feeling good unless the entire planet is feeling good?

MARISA: That's exactly my point, too.

WILLIAM: And you can't improve this planet unless you're practical. And it's not going to happen by itself. I have just had somebody here, they were crying and they were all into "You create your own reality, and the world is getting better in every way and every day." Well yes and no. Because yes, the vibration is improving, but human beings have a lot to do with what's happening here. And as we can see, there are a lot of human beings right now who are doing atrocious things, and it's not just automatic that everything is going to be great.

MARISA: No. It's going to get worse first.

WILLIAM: It really has to be thought out and acted upon. And from the human level at least, my experience is, it's going to take great courage, and without courage none of the envisioned heaven-on-earth for everyone... I actually feel I'm living heaven on earth right now for me. But in terms for all of humanity, there's not heaven on earth here right now. But you know, it's not going to happen in the future either unless we contribute to making it happen, so I think it's very important.

MARISA: And knowledge—

WILLIAM: Knowledge. And it's not like, "Oh we have Marisa, we don't need to go back to school and learn all this stuff." No. Marisa can help those who are learning all this stuff and let's get to the point where the people who are studying the physics and doing all this computer wizardry are starting to say, "Oh let's include this information," and working together on this plane is how we create.

MARISA: Exactly, exactly. And we actually one time for fun called in the author of Revelation, and they actually were talking about that. Not to get into the Bible stuff because I don't know anything about the Bible, but they were actually talking about how Revelation is happening now, and it's not the end of the world; it's the end of the consciousness, just like you were talking about.

WILLIAM: Right. Well, that's what the Mayan–and we'll talk about the Mayan later—but it was the end of a specific cycle of consciousness. The cycle really did end. And cycles start and cycles end.

MARISA: Yeah, and they were talking about how like the first horse came in, I think it was like... well, when we channeled, it was like two years ago, but it was 10 months from then so it was like eight months ago or something like that, they said the first horse is peace, so the frequency of peace is coming down onto the earth and couldn't be put into the grid and that grid I was talking about with the little Lite Brite, they compared that to a barbed wire fence that sings but nobody can hear it. So the frequency, a song called peace, is being played and yeah, some people hear the song and they're like, "Oh I'm so peaceful," but they can't really hear it because of its frequency. Other people that don't have peace within them, like you know these terrorists and stuff, its "argh."

WILLIAM: Makes them angry—

MARISA: Exactly opposite. So the guides have been very, very clear about the fact that things are going to get very much worse before they get better, so people's very simplistic view of spirituality, "Oh I meditate, I'm going to connect with my higher self, and everything's going to be wonderful." Our demise as human beings is through our emotions. You know what I mean? I see people's lives destroyed because, you know, someone is corded up, like they're corded up to an old experience of being beat as a child or something, and that's still playing, that song is still playing in their field and they can't be in a good relationship with their husband, so they got started drinking, and then the husband starts cheating, and it's all based on old emotions. So as the world shifts, what people don't see, and it just makes me crazy–there's that obsession again... must be my higher purpose–is that as the world is changing, we're getting pushed into this fourth building to stuff we didn't feel before. So it's affecting the earth and it's affecting people. So if we can educate people on how to clear that or just understand it more, then I think the world will start getting better. And yeah, staying practical. And emotions are as practical as you can be. I tell people, just don't even think about energy as protons and light and all this stuff, and oscillation and frequency and vibration, and God has raised my vibration. Energy is emotions. And there are emotions floating around everywhere. We're all picking up on them, we're all acting on them, and that's what tells us whether we're in heaven or hell, you know. So it's interesting how. But it is very practical. Holistically it is practical. All this is very practical.

WILLIAM: Well, let's keep going. So we get to the eighth level and we have Orion.

MARISA: We have Orion.

CHAPTER SEVENTEEN
IT'S ALL ABOUT TWELVE

WILLIAM: Because you told me at the beginning there are 12 levels.

MARISA: Yes.

WILLIAM: Let's keep going.

MARISA: So the ninth level is very interesting to me, and we can channel that when we do the channeling, because the ninth just looks like a void to me, it just looks like nothing. I've never read about dimensions and I won't do it because that's one of the topics I am obsessed with channeling about and I don't want to run the risk of mistaking something that I read and filed away in my mind somewhere with the information that my higher self, Source, and the guides bring though me when I channel. But I've been told by people, and I'm like, "Don't tell me, don't tell me." And they'll say, "Oh there is a void there."

WILLIAM: Well I think in the next segment we are definitely going to channel and will ask about the ninth dimension.

MARISA: Yeah. We'll have to.

WILLIAM: Nine is kind of... you know you have that Beatles song.

MARISA: There you go.

WILLIAM: Something is going to happen here.

MARISA: Yeah, so nine, it's just a void. I don't see anything. But then sometimes I see a big huge angel with people. So it's kind of like it's very... I can't figure it out, I can't figure it out. But I see almost kind of like a void, but there is an actual creator angel that I see and a lot of people named Kaya. And I think that she's kind of ... but I don't know if that angel is a seraphim angel and I've looked up seraphim and the seraphim are like the angels that sit next to the throne of gods. They've got all these wings and eyeballs.

WILLIAM: So what is she wearing?

MARISA: She's not a girl, she's actually... seriously though she's a firefly. She's a huge firefly, like a humongous 300 foot firefly thing. And I think its just an angelic consciousness.

WILLIAM: So what colors does she look like? Gold?

MARISA: It's like violet, pink and gold. Yeah. You're feeling her, sensing her. But yeah it's an energy that comes in. It's a consciousness. And then when I get up to the tenth I see what I call the seed souls, and the seed souls are the original 12.

WILLIAM: The original 12? We're back to 12?

MARISA: The original 12 that created Earth. So those are the seed souls. But I'll see seed souls that were created for other planets, and you know, they're seeding individuals down here. But I don't think that a seed soul can make a human being. I think the seed soul has to kind of be infused with the angelic energy that then creates the soul, that then creates the higher self.

WILLIAM: Don't they have to create the matter too?

MARISA: Yeah. I believe so but we can ask when we channel later.

WILLIAM: Doesn't it kind of start with matter, which means they're calling on the carbon and the hydrogen and oxygen, and–

MARISA: Exactly. Yes.

WILLIAM: Because it all starts with that.

MARISA: That's a good point. Yeah, so we'll have to channel about that.

WILLIAM: It can't go straight to... We'll need him, you know—

MARISA: It's really interesting. And so these seed souls are the ones that—

WILLIAM: You mentioned 12. Have you asked if all the planets required 12 seed souls, or just the planet Earth?

MARISA: I'm hearing, "Yes."

WILLIAM: Yes. Because its very interesting in my studies of the 12—.

MARISA: It can be 12, 24, or 36–

WILLIAM: Right. It has to be a multiple of 12 because 12 is—I was told, well I read because I don't channel so I can't say I was told, but I read that Plato and Pythagoras both reported that the dodeca-hedron, which is the 12-sided cube, is the structure of the universe, and that 12 is the base number from which any viable structure is formed. So that's why I'm interested, because when we say 12 beings it's 12 energies that are creating the universe and—

MARISA: I just realized 12 times 12 is 144, and that was the 144,000—

WILLIAM: Right, right, exactly.

MARISA: Interesting.

WILLIAM: Everything is the base number 12 . I do have a personal ego in this because my birthday is 12/12 and it happened to be—.

MARISA: So you're the center of the universe.

WILLIAM: Well, no I'd say more I resonate with the 12, the whole idea of 12, and it was interesting that the vibration of my birth was— this is a spoiler alert for anyone who hasn't read *The Twelve* yet— identical to the vibrational end of the Mayan calendar. So I had a real connection with the Mayan calendar and with the essence of the information contained in that calendar.

MARISA: That's interesting. It's all so interesting. I wish I could read it but I don't want to get... But yeah, and like my little chart here that I have, 12 create 12 that create 12 that create 12. So we're all like these... yeah—there's third dimension. Oh my goodness.

WILLIAM: Another interesting scientific fact is our DNA also requires the dodecahedron in order to transfer genetic information. There would be no evolution of life without the structure of 12.

MARISA: And that's funny because that's what I heal with. I see shapes coming down from Source that go through the person. They spin the mercury... I don't know the names of them because, again, I don't look them up, but I know the dodecahedron because somebody gave me one for the baby shower. She created this thing and it's supposed to hang above the baby as a mobile. It's like this big pointed 12-star shaped thing. But yeah, so the tenth is the seed souls, the original 12, and then of course earth is seeded with a lot more souls from other places, but those are the original and we've actually channeled and discovered different virtues that these different souls come from, which were all from Soul A and B, which are the souls that, you know, most famous people I think from that would be like Mother Mary and Jesus. It doesn't mean they are the oversoul; though they were created by the same oversoul. And souls A and B, that's the real wonderful, you know, descriptive names that we've given them—A, B, C, D—but the As and Bs are coming together at this time on the planet to help evolve the planet because the As are the divine feminine and the Bs are the masculine. So you guys are like A and B. That's why we see Mother Mary in your wife's energy. There's Jesus, Saint Germain, all of these big hitters in your energy, and it's because when I look at someone's energy and I see their tenth layer, I'll see an ascended master or I'll see something like that. It's not because that person is the ascended masters. It's just because my brain understands that energy is that person. And for the longest time I used to say, "You're a reincarnation of this person," or "You're this," or "You're that." And now I've realized, no, they are just showing me the energy of the family that that person is created by.

CHAPTER EIGHTEEN
LET'S KEEP EGOS OUT OF THIS

WILLIAM: This is a very important point because I've also had to deal with this issue. A lot of people come to me, "I'm the reincarnation of this," and "I'm the reincarnation of that," and "I'm going to write about this." My experience—and I've even been told I'm the reincarnation of this and that and whoever—is matter is never destroyed. It just transforms. So there's a level on which each and every one of us is the reincarnation of each and every entity that ever has been on an energetic level. Because if a single molecule that was Jesus' breath, it didn't disappear. That molecule has been recycled countless times, and each one of us is possibly part of that molecule, or has had that molecule within us. So potentially and in a small way, because one molecule out of the trillions that comprise each human being plus their experience is very small, but it is a scientific way of describing what the more spiritual people have described as "We're all one." Because we literally are all one. So when you get back into this idea of reincarnation, yes, you may have more energy from one specific lifetime and identify as that being, but that doesn't mean that there isn't someone else who is also part of that being. Because otherwise how do we get the explanation of so many women who have been Mother Mary? Because I've had dozens with their books.

MARISA: Or Abraham Lincoln or Napoleon?

WILLIAM: And so you know, I don't want to be disrespectful because their experiences in some cases... I mean, I've had people come to me who have reported historical facts about their experience of being Mother Mary that are confirmable. So they're not charlatans. But does that mean that they are the reincarnation of the one and only Mother Mary? No, in my opinion.

MARISA: Exactly, and that's the problem–not the problem—the thing that needs to be fixed with past life readers, people who go into the Akashic records, is as a psychic or medium I may be only tuning into the person's spirit, their fourth-dimensional energy body, so it's the little clone that... remember Florida, and... you know? May just be remembering those. Or I could be tuning into their fifth-dimensional self that created a bunch of spirits that are the clones.

WILLIAM: Or you could be tuning into their oversoul.

MARISA: Exactly, exactly. So the thing is, I'm very left-brain and kind of annoying to spiritual people because I'll say, "Ask what level of consciousness this is coming from." You don't want to tell everybody that they're... but I have every single medium telling me, "You were Joan of Arc, you were Joan of Arc." I've asked specifically, "Was my soul Joan of Arc?" My spirit was not Joan of Arc but we shared the same soul. So you know, we pulled from the same fifth dimension but not the same fourth dimension. So I've had hundreds of lives, she's had hundreds of lives. Totally different. And what's funny is I meet all these people that come in, say, "I was Joan of Arc." I'm like "We're all Joan of Arc."

WILLIAM: It's like "I'm Spartacus, I'm Spartacus." Have you seen the movie? But an important point here, because you're not really doing anyone a favor if you're a medium or a psychic out there to tell them that they are Jesus, or they're Napoleon.

MARISA: It's just an ego trip.

WILLIAM: I mean, you're going... because it's kind of a burden to have been that person, particularly when you look at the life you're living right now which may not quite live up to that famous life. So I think it's important. And it doesn't mean that you weren't, but it's the context in which you were—so that you can interpret that information in a way that helps you, rather than takes you off your path.

MARISA: And that's what I tell people. I say, you are from the same soul group or the same soul lineage as this person, so you're like a soul sister. You are not them but you have access to the exact same higher self, the exact same soul, so technically if you are a clear enough channel, you could call their consciousness into yours and you could remember what they remember. But it's just like going up to bigger and bigger hard drives.

I look at our souls as computers because this is how they have been explained to me by my guides. They know that it makes it easier for me to understand what I am being taught because it's translated into concepts I understood prior to working with spirit. When I co-owned our mortgage company I spent a good part of everyday networking our office and when that was complete, I spent, what seemed like a majority of each day, fixing all the agent's computers. I bet that a day did not go by that I was not interrupted to fix something in someone's workspace. So anyway, the guides have taught me to look at the different layers of self in our aura as separate hard drives that each carry all the information from the previous. So basically the information held in layer 6 is everything from layer 1 through 5. Layer 9 is everything from layer 1 through 8... and on up to layer 12 that holds a copy (like a hard drive) of every bit of information in a person's field of consciousness (aura).

The guides have compared our human bodies to robots or a vehicle for our spirit to drive. They say that our vehicle then has an SD storage card right here (pointing at heart) representing our spirit (layer 4). We've got our SD memory card representing our higher self (layer 6) here (pointing at a point at the base of head) and they're recording our lives, everything we do, feel, and experience. And then once we awaken to knowing they are there we can tune into them at will to learn about ourselves and we can also tune into the hard drive in the sky (God). So it's a lot easier to look at the soul kind of as technology, you know, because you're pulling in information rather than like, "Oh I was Mother Mary." Its like, "Now I'm going to pull forward all those life experiences." So that tenth soul is really interesting to me at the tenth layer, because I can actually go into that layer when I am doing healings and I can ask to see all of the things that this person needs to learn. An example of something someone would need to learn in a lifetime is patience or self trust. Once I have discovered what they are here to learn I can ask that the completed lessons be pulled down as a pure form of information on a quantum level into their spirit. So now their spirit has learned everything they need to learn, and it is up to me and the person I am working with to find ways to let those learned lessons into their human lives. When this happens, when the human mind accepts the energies from the spirit, cords fall away, addictions, habits, toxic people all begin to fall away. It's really interesting. So healing from that level is amazing and almost magical because it works so quickly compared to healing from the lower levels. Before learning how to heal from this level I thought it was normal to get a healing once a week. Now I know it's not necessary.

WILLIAM: One of the impressions that I'm receiving at a feeling level, just from the conversation, is just complete awe and gratitude of being a human being. Because it's just so awesome when you understand the bigger picture of what it means to be a human being, to have all these different energies able to express themselves through you, and you to have the ability to grab these energies and be just a fabulous creator on your own. So it's really humbling.

MARISA: Yeah and people don't realize, and the way the guides have described it, you know, we're these radios, you know. Depends on what channel you're tuned into. My first website was "Tuned In" because I wanted to be a channel also. I had a little blog and I wrote my nonsense that I was writing at the time. It was like jibber-jabber that would come through, you know. Same words over. "I'm you, you're me, I'm you, you're me." Or I'd sit there for 30 minutes and one word would come through—"and." And I'd sit there and another word. So it's like I was tuning in kind of like a guitar or a piano—you're tuning in like a tuning fork. And so if you're vibrating that my tuning fork is going to heal you, you're tuning with an A—all the As in the room are going to start vibrating. So if you're getting your tuning instrument, your physical body, you're etheric body, your emotional body, all that kind of tuned into what you want to be calling in, beings of that frequency are going to come in. So we're really, if you look at us as a blank template, if you look at us like little robots, which we're not, but if you look at us as little robots, it just depends on what we're tuning into up there. We can tune into our spirit, our soul, our higher self, we can tune into Saint Germain, pull that through, but our subconscious is such a wonderful thing that it blocks out most of what's trying to come through. Our subconscious mind, all of our beliefs and everything. So it's just interesting when you can teach people how to fine tune frequencies that are coming in. That's intuition. I mean, intuition is... that's why I said it's a little bit more complicated than just "it's the voice of your soul," because it's what layer of consciousness is coming through.

WILLIAM: And it goes back to what you said in the beginning. You can think of this film, this sort of dense filter that is preventing you from accessing pure energy and pure information, and so whatever you can do to become clear, whether it works for you to meditate, or in my case I choose walking on the beach by Swami's.

MARISA: I was going to say, people love surfing.

WILLIAM: I think for me that clears me and then I'm able to receive more.

MARISA: Exactly. And that's being grounded. If you're not grounded you can't really receive. I tell people the deeper your roots, the higher you can grow. A lot of people think like, "Oh I don't want to be grounded because I want to tune into all that. Those are the crazy people walking around." You know, its like…I played a joke on my clients for a week and I wore this scarf over my head, the gypsy earrings. "Oh, hello…" And like, "Ah, I'm ungrounded." That's what people expect when they see me. They don't expect some girl that— I mean right now I'm in workout clothes—but I mean, I dress nice and I get my hair done and I do my makeup and everything, and a lot of spiritual people try so hard to just wear the scarves and no makeup, and look as spiritually "woo-woo" as possible, you know. But a lot of the spiritually ungrounded people, that's where kind of the world needs to learn we need to get grounded, because then you can call in. So that's why the beach grounds you, and then all those high frequencies can come in. If you're a lightning rod and you're not grounded, you need to be grounded.

CHAPTER NINETEEN
DIVINE MASCULINE AND DIVINE FEMININE

WILLIAM: Okay so let's go to 11.

MARISA: Eleven is what I basically...the most I can really see with 11, I don't see a being; I just see an energy...and it's... women's activists—we're 12. The man is 11. Eleven is the divine masculine.

WILLIAM: Eleven is the divine masculine?

MARISA: And a lot of times I see Christ. Not Jesus—Christ energy. So it's like "Christ," that's the 11. And then 12—

WILLIAM: Christ energy... most people think of it as the Jesus Christ.

MARISA: It's not. Yeah, it's not. He was just able to tune into that energy.

WILLIAM: So what is the Christ energy?

MARISA: Christ energy is, well, let me see, the guides... Okay, so it's the consciousness of the zero point. It's the consciousness of God, the light. The guides call it the light. They don't call it God. They call it the light.

WILLIAM: It's the all-knowing consciousness—

MARISA: And they're saying—

WILLIAM: That would be a guy.

MARISA: Yeah. It's the consciousness that is the all that is created into a masculine energy that can reproduce itself when given the—

WILLIAM: The elements.

MARISA: So it's kind of like the feminine is what Christians would call the Holy Spirit, you know, 12. And then you've got the masculine which is Christ.

WILLIAM: So 12. Let's talk a little about 12. We kind of have talked about 11 and 12 at the same time.

MARISA: Yeah because they're the same thing. They're just—

WILLIAM: And for people who are more into the one and the two, it's really the one and the two. Because we have a good friend and client, Dr. Sha, who talks about the one creates two, two creates three, and three creates infinity.

MARISA: Interesting. The trinity.

WILLIAM: Yeah. When you look at it from a mathematical point of view, one can create two, and two can create three, and then with three you can create infinity.

MARISA: That's interesting.

WILLIAM: But let's talk a little bit about the feminine, the 12, which is the peak of the peak. The beginning of the beginning.

MARISA: So that's going to be what Christians would call the Holy Spirit, but it's the divine feminine that then comes together with... actually they're showing, wow. Okay. Interesting. We're not channeling yet, but they're showing the light breaking off into almost like a creator energy and then that Christ energy is more like the mind. So it's like the mind of the creator, and then it's kind of like the body of the creator. The feelings, the emotions. So those two together come together and they're in every single living being.

WILLIAM: Okay, is that all in the 12, or is that the 12 combined with—

MARISA: Twelve and 11, yeah.

WILLIAM: To create 10? And the 10, the Christ consciousness, is the mind? Or the 11 and the 12 together are the mind?

MARISA: The mind, the Christ consciousness, is the 11. The 12 would be like the creator, kind of "all that is," but it's a feminine energy.

WILLIAM: So the mind of God... because, you know, Einstein used to talk about it, people are still talking about it, they think this new God particle is a representation of the mind of God. I think it's an interesting, you know, thought that science has picked up on, that we can understand the mind of God. But the mind of God is really the 11, and the creative impulse that is primary prior to the mind of God, would be the divine feminine?

MARISA: Divine feminine, yes.

WILLIAM: The divine feminine would be—

MARISA: It's almost like it births the—

WILLIAM GLADSTONE AND MARISA MORIS

WILLIAM: Would be the birthing ground. You couldn't necessarily have a universe that didn't include the 11, but the 11 couldn't even exist without the 12.

MARISA: Exactly, exactly. So I'm looking down there now because now all the guides are in here now trying to show me these pictures. I wish I could just take the camera and stick it inside my head so you could see what I am seeing. But they're showing this being of all creation that's in every... because I was saying, well is that the thirteenth dimension then? You know, I started asking in my head. They said, no. They said the creator of all is in all dimensions but there has to be a dimension where a certain consciousness lies and every single person has that in them. So it's not like it's necessarily a being or anything like that. It's an energy and it's a frequency that we all carry.

WILLIAM: It's a primordial energy of existence.

MARISA: Exactly.

WILLIAM: Now, if it's the primordial energy of existence, I would assume there's nothing beyond it, that it is the beginning and the end—

MARISA: It is—

WILLIAM: And the all.

CHAPTER TWENTY
THERE ARE ONLY 12 PRIMARY
DIMENSIONS

WILLIAM: So there are in fact only 12 dimensions.

MARISA: Yes. There are only 12. And there's a lot of people that say there are 13, and there is when there's... me and my friend I was telling you about earlier, that wrote the books on science and physics and all that, in her sessions something used to come in and say, "We are from the 163rd dimension," and blah blah blah. But now when... I've learned that in the fifth dimension there are millions of dimensions. So in the fifth dimension—

WILLIAM: There are lower dimensions within... but in terms of the universal scope of the universe itself, there are 12 dimensions. Because there can be multiple universes with variations. I wouldn't necessarily call them inferior, but they're less than the primordial universe.

MARISA: Yeah, yeah. What they're saying basically, the guides are coming and they're saying that in a world of creation, in a world of manifestation, which is the fourth and fifth dimension, they're saying that man can create dimensions, we can think of dimensions, and therefore they are real. So if people made up a dimension, there is the 511th dimension and it's comprised of this, that's floating around as a thought pattern, as a belief, as a morphic field out there in the fourth or fifth dimension. So, there's lots of different dimensions. So when people are tuning into... I went to a class one time, and I actually ended up leaving because the teacher was channeling a demon. It was very creepy. But he was trying to teach that you need to go to the thirteenth dimension in order to access God. And I asked five or six of the people that went to that class that I knew, afterwards on Facebook, "Did you guys feel anything when you went to the thirteenth dimension?" Because he was tuning everybody to all these different dimensions. And that's when I left because I felt like I was going to throw up. My guide is probably trying to get me out of there. And they said, "No, it's like we hit a wall after we got to the twelfth. It was like I was floating and then the thirteenth, it was like, boom, not there." So I think that there is like a thirteenth dimension in the lower, like fourth dimension–

WILLIAM: In a lower dimension, yeah—

MARISA: And has negative entities and stuff in it.

WILLIAM: And let's talk just a little bit about the concept of multi-verses and multiple universes. To me it's kind of a lot about nothing, because there is really only one ultimate universe which contains all of these multi-universes. Is that accurate based on what your—

MARISA: Yeah, yeah.

WILLIAM: And that would also explain why you could have a billionth dimension within one universe. But that universe is actually a subset of the universe.

MARISA: Exactly, exactly.

WILLIAM: And from a mathematical point of view, there can only be one ultimate universe.

MARISA: Exactly, yeah. But there are just layers and layers of these universes that are just like make-believe land. It's kind of like what they're saying. We're just making stuff up. Which is great and everything, you know. It's the world of duality. We make it up. You know? But once we're tuning into that higher stuff it's like we're more defined.

WILLIAM: What's interesting about this, because I remember a conversation with my mother growing up when she was feeling there was no ultimate truth in the universe. She was an agnostic. And as a mathematician I never agreed with her because from a mathematical point of view there is absolute perfection in creation, and what you're confirming for me is that there is in fact absolute truth in the universe. And I think this is an important concept because we live in a world of duality, we live in a world of half-truths. I mean, one of my favorite stories is I had a monk come to me once who had spent 12 years in a cave in India channeling Lahiri Mahasaya, one of the great yoga teachers, and he came to my office in Del Mar, not Cardiff at the time, and he said, "Yes, my master has told me that I'm responsible for bringing in the truth about the right way to do yoga, and I was to bring it to America, and specifically San Diego because San Diego is the eye of the universe, and this is what I've done, and you're a literary agent so now I give this responsibility to you and you have to get this book published." And you know, along the way one of the small things was he wanted to correct the way the Yogananda people were meditating and breathing because it wasn't really the way that Yogananda's teachers had taught. And anyways...

So anyway, I turned to him and...I said, "I don't think I can help you." He says, "But this is the pure truth." I said, "Exactly. I live in a world where adulterated truth sells much better than pure truth. This is too advanced for the market that I represent." So I think this is a little bit the problem we have on the earth right now, where pure truth is not that popular.

MARISA: Yeah, reality TV sells.

WILLIAM: And on multiple levels. And I think it's important for people to realize that there really is beauty and truth and goodness. The other issue that I wanted to raise before we get into the actual channeling is Dr. Laszlo has written a couple of books lately. He has one coming out called *The New Reality*. And what is most intriguing to me, and he's coming at this as a scientist, is that he feels that the evolution of consciousness on planet Earth and the universe itself, beyond the planet Earth, is directly aligned with what we would call goodness and morality—that good behavior and caring and compassion are actually aligned with the directionality of evolution. And I'd be interested to know if—

Chapter Twenty-One
What is Good?

MARISA: But what is good?

WILLIAM: What is good? Well, good from a scientific point of view and a mathematical point of view would be ever greater complexity, ever greater beauty, ever greater perfection of form.

MARISA: But everybody is completely different for that, too. So your question is wondering how—

WILLIAM: Well, from a mathematical point of view, no. I mean this is the thing about mathematics. From a mathematical point of view, you can't argue. It's like certain forms... that's why we talk about "ah, we solved the problem," but his solution is more aesthetically perfect. Because there's an aesthetic to mathematics. And what Dr. Laszlo would then argue, to all that come from mathematics, which is all creation, so that you actually can sense when you're going in the right direction.

MARISA: Yeah, yeah. Well, that's what the guides always say, and I'm hearing them right now, is compassion is the biggest good deed for yourself and for others. If you don't love yourself, you can't love others. If you're critical on yourself, then you're going to be critical on others. That's love. So yeah, that's true, in that the more compassionate the frequency of compassion. Because they all have frequencies. I'm sure he's probably able to figure out the ratios or numbers behind these. I mean I see the frequencies when they're going in people, I see little numbers. That would be cool to get together with someone like that and figure out what those ratios actually mean. I'll see the numbers going in the people, but the guides have always said that allowing compassion into our fields, which is the Christ light, or which is God's light, is pure compassion, pure unconditional love, is what will shift human beings altogether. But people don't allow it in.

WILLIAM: Well, my question then goes back to the twelfth dimension and the eleventh dimension, because I can imagine when the eleventh and twelfth dimensions got together there was only goodness.

MARISA: Oh yeah. Yeah. And that's pure... what I'm hearing is... unconditional love, compassion, strength. It's all the virtues that we want to acquire, is what was created when it was created. But then you get down to lower dimensions—

WILLIAM: Well, it keeps getting adulterated.

MARISA: Yeah.

WILLIAM: And as it gets more and more adulterated it gets less and less pure and then you introduce greed and fear and all this stuff that has made a mess of things.

MARISA: Exactly. And the interesting thing is, the way that they've put it is, as human beings we're down here in all this muck, but if we can learn to tune into these higher dimensions it's just bringing that frequency in, washing away the muck, and then you're like you, "nothing really bothers me." You know, because you know somebody—

WILLIAM: And one of the nice things about it, it's not just about you, because when nothing bothers you, you're less likely to bother others.

MARISA: Exactly. I tease my husband. He's the type of person where you can't talk him down. "Nice hair, buddy." "Thank you." It's like you can't tell him that he doesn't look good. He's not like cocky; he's humble, he's a nice guy. But it's just funny because he's so confident about what he's confident about, and that's what I find spiritual people… they are tuning into their intuition and I tell them, "You know, look, if you can see…" I make them do this exercise–it's hilarious—in my first level class. I say, "Write down five things that you hate about other people, that you just can't stand, and then five things you absolutely admire." I say, "If you're having a hard time just think of your mom, what you can't stand, or what you love, or what you don't love." Like me, it's my dad. It's five things that I can't stand and five things that I can stand. He's humble, he's honest, he's this, he's that. But he's thick-headed, he's stubborn, he argues. So everybody writes all their stuff down. And people usually don't come to class alone. They always bring a buddy. You know, it's like, "Will you take this class with me? It's weird, I don't know…" But it's funny because I'll have everyone read the qualities that they can't stand about other people. And you know me, I can't stand fake people because I spent so much of my life being fake and smiling, you know, like when I felt so bad inside, but I never realized that until I did this exercise and I realized, you know, on a bad day I can walk into a restaurant with my husband and a girl will be like, "How's it going?" Blah, blah. "Have a great night." And I'll be like, "Screw you, too." You know? And my husband will be like, "She was just really sweet." And I'm like, "Yeah, right, she's so fake." But then on a good day, I'm all healed and I'm feeling good, and I have the compassion of God in me, and you know my frequency is high: "You too!" You know? I don't see her mistakes. Same girl, same circumstance, same place, but as humans we operate on these different floors, you know, where the same behavior will bug us or we'll like it, and it's because of what's in us. And so the guides have kind of explained by tapping into these higher dimensions you are pulling forward this compassionate energy so you can see… If someone is being fake I can go, "Oh, poor thing, I wonder if she's sad inside," instead of "Screw you too," you know, like most human beings do. I say the best way to gauge what kind of mood you're in is to figure out what you're blaming all the other drivers on the freeway for doing.

WILLIAM: Oh, that's a bad one for me. I'm going to get caught here. Anytime I'm around them I just curse them. And I'm probably the worst driver. I can imagine everybody's just yelling and cursing at me.

MARISA: Road rage guy, that's my dad. "What are you doing!?" You know. But I mean one day you may be driving and you'll say, "Oh maybe they're having a baby…" You have a high vibration. Or if it's like someone is trying to get in, "No, they're trying to cut me off!" You're in a competitive mode that day, you know. So I always bring like the practicality of the spirituality into people's everyday life by saying, you know, you can tell what mood you're in by what you're blaming everybody for doing.

WILLIAM: Well, just before… because we're going to end this session, take a little break, and we're going to channel—I don't know if this is a question better for the channeling because Gayle had a little car accident today, and I want to find out, and she wants to find out, why.

MARISA: We'll channel because she told me the story and it was already in my mind, I was like, I wonder if that was the spirit, or I wonder if that was—

WILLIAM: Yeah, because it's – there's a reason to everything.

MARISA: There is. There is.

WILLIAM: And so we'll find out, we're going to take a little break and we'll be back with you shortly.

MARISA: Okay.

PART II
LIVE DEMONSTRATION OF
CHANNELING

CHAPTER TWENTY-TWO
SETTING INTENTIONS AND
SUSPENDING DISBELIEF

WILLIAM: Hello, we're back. This is William Gladstone, Marisa Moris, and we're going to go into the second part of this unique course. It starts out as you've seen with something very simple, developing your intuition, and it's gone from there to discussion about becoming psychic, becoming a medium, becoming a channeler, and then going beyond mere channeling to actually understanding that you can contact different versions of different human and spirit beings at their own different levels of evolution because everyone and everything is constantly evolving. So it's much more complex than I've ever heard from any other channeler or psychic in this realm. So in the second part of this course we're going to do an actual live demonstration of Marisa's abilities. She's going to channel some beings. We've done a little bit of preparation. She's done proper cleansing of the area and invocation so that only the entities we want to talk with will be available. For those of you who are complete disbelievers, as part of me actually is—

MARISA: And me, too—

WILLIAM: Even though I am doing it… suspend disbelief. If what comes forth resonates for you, use it and enjoy it. So, sit back and enjoy. I also think it will be very entertaining. So, Marisa, let's start. I think that I am the subject of the channeling, that it's going to be my entities and my connections. Is that the way it works?

MARISA: Well, that's what it seems like. It seems that the lovely wife back here—

WILLIAM: Yes, Gayle is with us and that's important because when you do channeling like this, the people in the room really determine the spiritual component of what comes through. So Gayle is just as much a part of this even though she's the woman behind the camera, not in front. So I've never done a session like this. Part of me doesn't even believe in these kinds of things. But I've known Marisa only a short time, I met her father playing golf, he's a normal kind of person, her background is kind of normal, she cares about looking good and eating well and, you know, all the things that normal people care about, so let's give her the benefit of the doubt and see where this goes.

MARISA: All right, all right. What you're talking about, about having certain people in the room, it's very interesting because in old school mediumship, when I studied that in the very beginning when I first started seeing stuff, I wanted something that I could study that was kind of proven. But I mean, mediumship... you can't really prove it other than the information coming through. But what's interesting is that they used to have what they would call séances where they'd bring people together and the medium—I'm what's called a physical medium even though I don't like calling myself a medium because I feel like I can connect with other stuff too—but physical mediums would get a list of everybody that was going to come to the séance and they would go through and they would see who was allowed in and who was not allowed in, because everybody has—I call it their snow globe—so you've got your snow globe around you and you have all of your energy, all of your people, your spirits, everything that kind of comes along with you to these meetings. So they would only want the people with the strongest energy. And both of you have very strong energy. It's those people that you get around that just motivate you to want to go out and make money or go out and do something, or you partner up with them for a business venture and then, you know, they kind of move out and go onto something else, and then you don't want to do it anymore. It's called—I call it—generator energy. So you guys both have generator energy. So this should be fun because there's lots of guides here. I'm used to just channeling with my dad or just with one person that I'm doing a session for, and my dad brings in all the Biblical guys, that's all that ever comes in because he gets a little nervous that the dark side may come in, so he trusts those. But this is fun because there are a lot of different worldly beings coming in. So we will just see what they have to say. I have no idea and I won't remember. I'm pregnant right now, 8 ½ months, so I'm not doing trance channeling. Let me just kind of tell you the difference. There are trance channels, which is kind of like Edgar Cayce. He would do self-hypnosis, he would go into trance, and I heard that he had a really low I.Q. but he came through with all this—

WILLIAM: Low education. I don't think he had—

MARISA: Low education? Oh okay, so he wasn't educated. And that's kind of like me. I'm not going to read books on a bunch of stuff and then just regurgitate what I read in a book. So I don't read or take classes, really anything. I just get the information that comes through. Because I'm very skeptical, too. So I'll watch this later and go, "Really? No, I don't think that was real." So anyways, a trance channel goes out and a being can step into your energy field and speak through you, and those are the channels that, you know, they talk with accents and they sound real funky or funny. Unless they're fakers—there's a lot of fake ones out there that kind of put on a theatrical show. And then there's light trance channeling where it's kind of like when you write an email and then you just kind of feel like something else takes over. That's your higher self taking over your higher consciousness. For me, it's more like it sounds like my mind, so sometimes I flip between channeling, because it sounds like my mind, but it's something else sending the information in, or I'll say, "This is what I see, they're showing me pictures." So I kind of go back and forth between actual channeling and doing a reading. So we'll see what happens.

WILLIAM: Okay we'll see what happens.

MARISA: Yeah, we'll see what happens. There's lots of different ways to channel, so we'll see...

WILLIAM: And for the record I've never had anything like this. I have no idea what I'm going to experience. I'm just here as an observer and possibly as—

MARISA: A very educated question-asker.

WILLIAM: As a question-asker, and the medium for the medium.

MARISA: Perfect, yeah. All right, let's do this. So I'm going to close my eyes. I'm over here in Fern Gully over here.

WILLIAM: We have plants.

MARISA: Okay, so do you want me to just start by what guides are in here?

WILLIAM: Yeah.

MARISA: Or do you want to ask questions? Or—

WILLIAM: Yeah, my first question is if there are guides here, who are they? And do the guides themselves have an agenda for us because I really don't.

CHAPTER TWENTY-THREE
THE SESSION BEGINS

MARISA: Now they're all here. Okay, so all right. So this is who I'm seeing. And again, I was raised Christian, so a soul that may have been Quan Yin, who was also Mother Mary, I'll see her as Mother Mary, because my perspective is Christian. So for those of you who are not Christian or whatever, it could be another energy, but that's what my mind sees it as. So, Mother Mary just came in, there is Mary Magdalene who is here, Archangel Michael is over there, we've got the Council of Nine that I've talked about with no faces, they're just all light, and then you've got your Council of Three over there, and then of course Bill's mom and dad are here. His mom is standing back there and then his dad is over here wanting to be a questioner too. He wants to be in the mix. And that's really all. There's a very... oh, Peter is here. He always comes into our sessions. That's Peter from the Bible. And then there is... oh my gosh, there's so many people here. Let's just ask them a question. So, here's Abraham. Abraham says: "Dear children, as I step into your energy today I bring to you love, I bring to you hope, and I bring to you a feeling and awareness of protection. As you begin to feel the energies around you, you will see and you will understand and you will know that this space in time is protected. For much information will be entering into this room that is information that other worldly beings, other spiritual beings may or may not want people to understand. For the human species, the human species for the most part, is in the dark, is in the dark. There are many religions, there are many sects in this world that bring forth truth. They are truth within their truth within their truth to those that believe in these, but for those that stand outside of these beliefs, those that stand outside of these religions, these beliefs, these clubs, so to speak, these beings are left feeling lost. These beings are left feeling as if they do not want to believe this but they feel bad if they do not believe this, so they will believe this, but this over here is not specific enough so they really do not know what they want to believe, so they are left standing without a belief system, without a belief set. Human beings need a belief, whether it is in science, whether it's in religion, whether it's in spirituality, whether it's in self, whether it's in energy, whether it is in anything really that they can define and wrap their mind around in an understanding of what God is, what Source is, what energy is. So we come together today to bring an understanding, to bring an understanding as to what is God? There are scientists, there are people, there are researchers who want to know, who is God, what is God, can I measure God, what does God look like? And we say unto you, God is everything, God is everything. And we use this word "God" and many say, "No God." They do not want to hear this word "God," so we say unto you that we are using this term because this is what human beings call this, but we call God The Light, the Source, the source of all creation. And it is from that light where everything resonates from. You may look at and imagine the sun, and this is Source. It is illuminating through time, through space, through all dimensions, giving off its sun, giving off its nurturing, and projecting itself through all beings on this planet. But understand and know that God is not one thing. It is all things. And we bring in this understanding today so as to break down and rebuild bridges, and bring an understanding for the science community to the religious community, the religious community to the science community, to the science community to the spirituality, to religion to spirituality, and around and around and around, so that people may begin to understand and see and know that there really is just one true source of information entering into each of us, and if we use this as an electricity, if we use this as something that we can fuel ourselves with, we all truly become that sun. We are that sun, because we are all holographic beings, we are all little pieces of that sun, and we can create for ourselves the lives that we want. For understand and know, there are many human beings who want beautiful lives, who want beautiful families, they want children, they want money, they want jobs, they want cars, and this is all good, this is all good indeed. But if they do not know how to use the electricity to charge the body in which they are living in at this time, that their consciousness is inhabiting, then they cannot truly, truly benefit from the use of this Source energy to manifest the dreams and the lives that they want, both in this life and the afterlife. For understand that in the afterlife we are also manifesting our dreams, manifesting what we want, as well. The journey does not end, the journey does not end until you graduate, so to speak, and become that which is a god of your own."

WILLIAM: Thank you.

MARISA: That was Abraham.

CHAPTER TWENTY-FOUR
THE HUMAN EXPERIENCE

WILLIAM: So I do have a few questions that this has provoked. I've been, like most human beings on the planet right now, been somewhat concerned with the level of terrorism in the Middle East, with the breakdown of civility even in our country in terms of the politics, the hatred that seems to be manifesting itself in so many different ways. And so my question—I don't know if it's to Abraham, or some of the other beings—from a practical point of view, not at this abstract level... yes, all is one, all is light... but from a practical point of view, we are dealing with many different fundamentalist belief systems which are at absolute loggerheads with each other. I've talked with many experts. Some believe there is nothing to be done, "They'll just kill themselves off and we'll evolve, don't worry about it." But that does seem to be an impoverished way of solving this problem. Is there an enlightened way when you have what seem to be different groups fanatically in belief of opposing views of what is the purpose of man and God?

MARISA: "And this is the human experience. For understanding and knowing that yes, we say that we are all one, but in actuality we are all fractions of that one until we realize that we are one. So yes, you are very, very, very correct in saying that the world is a crazy place. The world is a crazy place." —Okay, Saint Germain just came in. So he's talking— "The world is a very crazy place and people will not see this and people will not know this if they are at the lower consciousness level. Those who are fighting amongst themselves, identify with their beliefs as that which who they are. For they see their religion as them. They see their house as them. They see their job as them. You meet somebody who is from a town where they are tied in very closely with their town… people from Chicago. You say, 'Oh Chicago is horrible' and then they don't like you anymore; they hate you. You say this to somebody who is living in San Diego and they will say, 'Oh yeah, there are some goods, there are some bads.' So you can look at this as an example as somebody who is highly tied in their identity to the town in which they live. It can dictate the way that they are, who they like, who they treat poorly, who they treat good, who they accept into their life, whether they like their identity or not, because they have tied into this. You see this with sports teams and most importantly you see this with religion. You see this with what people believe God is. What we are saying is that bringing in education to people on this planet who are part of the same soul group where these other people belong to." —Jesus just came in. He says, "Let me give you an example. There is a hard drive which we will call an oversoul. This oversoul has created 144 souls that are living on the planet right now. Let's say 100 of them are not tied in with their root beliefs. They are not tied in with religion. They are more spiritual. They are open to tuning into God, they are open to tuning into a non-biased view upon who they are. They see themselves as individuals. They see themselves as souls living in human bodies. But these other 44 are very tied in with religion and they will kill for their religion because they think because a man said that they must kill for their religion so that God will love them, they say, 'I will kill for my religion and then I will go to heaven.' Understand that many of these people are unreachable. Unreachable, indeed. And your experts who are saying 'Let's let them kill themselves off,' this is not something that we are warranting over here, saying this is how it has to be, but understand and know there is a way around this by the education of the other 100 people. For if you look at these 144 people as all feeding up to the same hard drive, the same consciousness, the same awareness as these 100 learn and move in a direction towards the upper chakras—and we will not get into the chakra system to confuse things—but understand that as they move up into their emotional body, as they move up into their heart, as they move up into the crown chakra, as they move up into spirituality, these others will be forced to move up out of the root chakra, and they will just suddenly say, 'I am not so concerned with wanting to kill for my religion anymore because I think I see beyond this.' So understand and know that over the next 18 years many ascended masters, many beings that have not incarnated for a very long time just like you, just like you, understand that these beings are coming back to the planet to bring out—for the lack of a better word—a mass media explosion on an understanding and a knowing that there is something beyond here. Even if somebody fully believes in their religion and they hear something on TV, they read something in a book accidentally, they see something in the newspaper that plants a seed that opens up their awareness to the understanding there is something outside of their religion, outside their beliefs, they may or may not allow some of their higher selves' information to come in. Remember, they are sharing a higher self on some level with these other 100 people who are emotionally and spiritually evolved human beings who would never cause terrorism, who would never kill for a god. They understand and know that they are in essence gods themselves to a certain extent. So understand that as the world is educated—and this is why you, Bill, came to this planet at this time, as an educator, as someone who is acting as a minister through education. A minister through education. For when you are trying to educate with that which is your books, your videos, these things that you are teaching with, you feel an inspiration behind it but you also feel an expansive energy behind, representing those who are bringing this as well, because this is just as much a part of this. So education is the key, education is the key. Even if these 44 others never see anything, never hear anything, never feel anything that is educating them to broaden their horizons, to broaden their awareness, a piece of them inside of them will. Just because we have our awareness placed on the first couple layers of our body, it does not mean that there are not nine other layers that know. And this is the important thing. This is the important thing, indeed. There are also ways for those working on this planet and there are many alchemists, many scientists from past lives, there are many healers, there are many people working within the quantum realm who can send healing to those which are the oversouls of those that are acting as terrorists. There are already secret groups, secret societies getting together to send mass healing to the group consciousness of that which is those who are afflicted by humanity, those who are afflicted by judgment of self, therefore judgment of others, and bringing cruelty and violence to the world."

WILLIAM: Thank you very much. That was Saint Germain?

MARISA: Saint Germain, Jesus, and Mary Magdalene.

WILLIAM: Thank you all.

MARISA: They jumped in there.

WILLIAM: I have to say, not only does it resonate with me… because I've had a gift really since birth when I hear pure truth I actually have tingles in the back of my neck and in my chest. And I was able to receive that. So I can confirm from my personal experience that what we have just heard is absolutely true. Now, of course it's very, very hopeful. The one thing I would add in terms of my own role, I get tremendous joy from representing books which elevate the souls of others, and I do think that it is a collective. As the vibration of the planet and of the consciousness of the majority increase, it's almost like the way the Berlin Wall came down. It happened seemingly suddenly, but it was really years and years of change of thought patterns. And I can envision this happening again. So this is very hopeful. A very small example, because I think this is very important—joy. To me the two words that best symbolize the path for human beings no matter who you are out there: courage and joy. Courage and joy. The best example of joy actually as an author,

I have the privilege to represent Marie Kondo, whose newest book *Spark Joy* is about her overall life changing magic of tidying up. And the reason it's about "spark joy" is Marie has been gifted—I'm sure she's an ascended soul herself—with an awareness that every single element has consciousness and has awareness. And I mean every single element. That means not just this living plant, but this table in front of us, this shirt. And her whole methodology, the reason it's become such a massive worldwide best seller, is that she asks you to take each element in your life, each article of clothing, each of your possessions, and ask, "Does it spark joy?" And if it doesn't, give it away, or allow it to be reconstituted by being destroyed. But the molecules even will find joy in another expression. So finding joy is the reason I'm very successful in what I do. I just enjoy what I do. I have great joy doing it. Also in the writing. And then the other thing is courage, because it's not always easy. We're going no matter what to have certain individuals who just aren't ready to be elevated, who are going to do horrible things. One of the blessings—that certainly wasn't a blessing in my experience at the time—was I was born into a family with a violent schizophrenic older brother who tortured me most of my young life. But I did learn, and it took a while, to overcome that. Fortunately, I didn't have, you know, everyone talks about the victim mentality. I never felt that for whatever reasons. But I am able to understand the nature of evil. And as far as I can tell, it really is about being insane. It's a level of insanity. Insanity is when you believe something that isn't true. And for many reasons, people who are well-intended—and I think this is true of most fundamentalists —they find something, they're so scared, they're so frightened, that they find something that may have been true at one time in the world, and they hold onto it so tight because they're so scared. And the reality is, at a certain point they have to let go and evolve and incorporate that fundamental truth in an even higher expression of that truth. And based on what we just heard, I think that is the only way we will have this progress. And from a theoretical point of view there is absolutely no reason why it can't happen. Though if you just look at the nightly news every night you'll probably be a little more skeptical that it will happen in 18 years. But in 18 years we'll still be here, so this is good news.

MARISA: Yeah, it's a good thing. Because a lot of people think it's over. And you know there's a lot... And that's why my passion is in cleaning up the astral planes, cleaning up that fourth building I was talking about. Because if one person at a time I can clear— I mean I can clear 80 people at the same time, I can multiply myself in the astral plane and heal a bunch of people at once, even more. But if we could just start by educating the people that have the abilities of the people in this building... start cleaning it up—

WILLIAM: Well, this is what I'm saying. Obviously, the people that are reading this book, it's probably going to be a relatively select number, maybe 10,000. Fifty-thousand. Maybe 100,000—

MARISA: But even you guys helping—

WILLIAM: Even if it's 100,000. There could be within that 100,000, 500 who reach the tipping point. This is the tipping point for them, who finally realize, "Wow, what I've been feeling inside is really true. These people aren't crazy, they're rational people, they're very successful people, they're saying this is real. I'm not going to hold back anymore." Because I've experienced lack of courage, and it's not always lack of courage, but you have to know, as Kenny Rogers said, "when to fold them" and when to, you know, go...because you don't want to expose yourself in a way that is going to bring your own ruin, so you do have to be cautious but you could be cautious and courageous, and that I think is what we need going forward.

MARISA: And as people have knowledge, I think that a lot more people have the courage to be courageous because they feel like they know. When you start to have a knowing.

CHAPTER TWENTY-FIVE
EINSTEIN SPEAKS

WILLIAM: Well, I have a couple of other questions. There's been a lot of talk—changing topics to something more intellectual—about the singularity. I personally do not believe in the singularity. I think it's a very limited concept. I don't know if we've got Einstein or some of the other brilliant scientists—

MARISA: He just came in. That's funny.

WILLIAM: Come in who would want to explain to the general audience why, or if I'm wrong, why I'm wrong, that singularity is not a really viable scientific concept.

MARISA: So now they're showing me in pictures. So Einstein did just walk in, but this is a very low version of him. This is Einstein—

WILLIAM: Back when he was still a human?

MARISA: Yes. The ascended piece of him is actually part of the same soul as this soul group. That's interesting. That's probably why he and his buddies come in a lot. Sir Isaac Newton and Ben Franklin like to come with him. But it's just him this time. But it is—it's an un-crossed-over version so I'm curious to see if I can connect. There's a higher piece of him coming in. Let's see here. C'mon, higher piece, higher piece, higher piece. Man, he's fragmented.

WILLIAM: Einstein is?

MARISA: A lot of people channel him. Okay so... "Singularity is a key factor in which I believe..." See, he's standing up for it. Let's ask somebody else. Who else could we ask? Because he's going to sit here and "this is what I said, this is what I believe." Let's see here. Saint Germain again. Saint Germain. So wait. Describe—because they're showing me in all pictures what the definition of singularity is real quick...

WILLIAM: Well, it's being used in different ways by different groups of scientists so there could be some confusion around it.

MARISA: Because they're showing me cells. They're showing me... okay so this is what they're showing me. They're showing me like electricity and then they're showing me like these cells that are breaking apart and then they almost look like this. They look like all broken up. And Einstein keeps coming over and he keeps wiping it out and kind of doing these cells that are like merging. And I can't tell what it is that they're talking about. I can channel Saint Germain. Hold on, let me see. See, if it's not in my consciousness... okay, so just give me like a real quick—

WILLIAM: Overview of singularity?

MARISA: Yeah. Just so that it's in my consciousness and they can get it through, because they're trying to talk and my mind is going, "I don't know what that is."

WILLIAM: Okay. Well, as I said there are different people that have used this expression, but the ones that I'm ridiculing, if you will—and it's not Einstein—are the ones who believe that it's actually possible to create computers that will be more intelligent than humans, and that the computers will lead us to singularity of consciousness that is more highly evolved than human consciousness.

MARISA: Yeah, that's ridiculous. Okay.

WILLIAM: Exactly.

MARISA: So that's why I was seeing this… it was breaking into all these and then it was combining. And then they kept going like this, and then it was like this. It was really weird. So they're showing pictures, so on the recording I'm drawing little circles basically and crossing them out. Okay so here's Saint Germain: "This is what you must understand. What you misunderstand is in the energy world, in the mental realms, the only thing that can be created is something that has already been created within itself. So what man can create is only the highest pinnacle of thought of what they can create. If you are speaking of something taking on the consciousness of a human being and expanding its awareness on its own to be above that which is a human being, we will say 'yes.' But understand and know that human beings are not just one part beings. They are not apes, they are not monkeys, they are not evolved beings with just a human mind. They are spirit consciousness. They are God consciousness. So when we are speaking of something becoming more aware than that which is the god-self in each human being, this is something that cannot exist." But Einstein is over here jumping up and down saying, "We can create something that is greater than us." He's jumping up and down. "We can create something that is greater than us. We can create something that is greater than us…"

WILLIAM: Well, I would say Einstein, yes we can, at the human plane, which is a limited plane—

MARISA: And that's where he is. He's earthbound.

WILLIAM: But not at the higher realm plane, and that you are right now still attached to the earth plane. Even though I'm on earth, part of me is looking at it from a much higher realm.

MARISA: And you are looking at it from a higher realm—

WILLIAM: And I don't mean any disrespect, Einstein.

MARISA: No, not at all.

WILLIAM: You were fantastic. And without you we wouldn't even have any of the fabulous rocketry and everything else that we've got here. You were amazing.

MARISA: But this is a piece of him that is down here, so he is saying, "Anyone who channels that which I am is one that channels that which I am that broke off in 1955." When did he die?

WILLIAM: I think that's about when he died, yeah.

MARISA: He says: "…that which broke off in 1955. For this understanding, this knowing of what I am bringing in—" Because he's like a holographic being almost. "—is only that up to 1955. So when I say that something may be created…" I'm talking to his higher self now and I'm looking at his lower self saying, 'Don't give me up.' His higher self is basically saying, "The understanding and the knowing that's being channeled by many of these fragmented beings, they are not ghosts; they are pieces of themselves that they left in the astral plane to give wisdom." Oh, that's interesting. I've never heard them say that before. "So when we say, Bill may say, 'I want to make a holographic version of myself and I want to leave it in the astral plane so that anybody who calls upon me will call upon this piece.' This is how strong intention is. Intention can be created behind something like this. But this piece that is broken off will be right now, January 2016, it will not learn, it will not unlearn anything that is not learned, but it may remember things that Bill does not remember because Bill's conscious mind is blocking, Bill's subconscious mind is blocking these things, so these holographic images, these holographic versions, these spirit versions, whatever you may call them, do know more than the human because it carries all the consciousness of that which is the human—but it freezes at that time and does not bring anymore information in over and above. For there is much speculation about these world computers, about these robotics, about all of these things that were going to make the world a better place, and there is still a dreamer inside, still a dreamer inside that sees this as something that may fix the world. But no, no, no, no indeed..." Oh god, great. Here he comes. He's getting close.

Saint Germain says: "No, no, no indeed. One must understand consciousness and one must understand that... let's use this example, that when somebody runs a marathon, they run a marathon and they run this marathon in oh let's say two hours. They run it in two hours. Nobody has ever run this in two hours. They have never run it in two hours. It has always been 2:50 minutes. And now there are 100 people that run it in two hours. And then somebody runs it in 1:45 minutes. And then all of a sudden there are 200 people that run it in 1:45 minutes. This is how consciousness works. Somebody in the pool of consciousness has to experience something in order for it to manifest in the physical plane. And this includes things that are manifested through electricity, things that are manifested through science, things that are manifested through computers, things that are manifested through technology. Something has to experience it in order for others to experience it. So this is something where it takes someone who is a strong believer in getting outside of the human consciousness and excelling and achieving over and above what is in the field of the earth to experience something, and then everyone else is very easily able to experience this."

WILLIAM: Okay. I understand that. And I do understand that it's possible to create a machine that could envision beyond what a human can envision...

MARISA: Mm-mm. It couldn't envision. The human has to envision it.

WILLIAM: Before? We can create a computer that can dream?

MARISA: "No."

WILLIAM: Okay. That is important for you science fiction writers out there. So, the other issue that I've been thinking a lot about is the issue of health. We have a health crisis throughout the world, costs of health have gone through the roof. I've read that 90 percent of all health resources are spent on preserving the last six months of life in America. So my question is, first, is immortality in the human body possible? And second, is it desirable? And then third, if those are true, what should we be doing in terms of health care? Because it seems to me that we are using very old technology to ensure the health of human beings.

CHAPTER TWENTY-SIX
EDUCATION MATTERS: GOING BEYOND EINSTEIN TO ATLANTIS

MARISA: We have three new guides here. They're the Atlantean guides. There's three of them that just came in. I call them the priest, the minister and the scientist, or something. They're all kind of like there."In the times of Lemuria and in the times of Atlantis, in the times of the..." It's spelled A—with a backwards K — alona... blah blah. If I was in trance I'd be able to say it. Akalona? Two little dots. It's not the Anunnaki. No, it's some weird word and I'm trying to phonetically say it.]

WILLIAM: I've never heard it before. You may be channeling new information.

MARISA: "...Thirty-eight thousand years ago..."

WILLIAM: There ya go.

MARISA: "...many beings did not just channel their spirit, channel their consciousness into human beings and incarnate at that time on the earth. On the earth indeed. There are many beings from Sirius, many beings from Alman matter." That's not in my consciousness either. Now they're doing teleprompter. Alma matter...? Alta Ursa something... matter. They're showing me all these different stars. "There are many beings, many beings who have traveled to the earth plane and were able to live 800 or 900 years.

You may hear about this in some of your old texts and this is something that many will say, 'Oh, it is because the sun and the calendars were different so people thought that 900 years was really 900 years, but really it was only 20 or 30 years...' Understand and know that human beings have the ability and the capacity to be endless, to be eternal, to understand and know that the body is made up of matter that is just denser than the other layers of the body that are eternal. Please know and understand that the earth plane which we like to call it at times..." They're chuckling. "... is one where human consciousness is truly blind to its ability to be god-like, to its ability to live free from illness, free from disease. There are many times, 16 in fact on the earth, when human beings could live here for as long as they would like to, and then go back into what you would call the spirit world, or go back to another world that they came from because they had the ability to completely inoculate that which was disease inside. For understand and know, all disease is caused by emotion. All disease is caused by human emotion. To tell a human being to come to the earth plane and not feel human emotion would be absolutely impossible for the souls that are incarnating on the earth plane at this time. But many would say, 'Oh he died of a broken heart.' One can die of a broken heart. One says, 'They were very stressed out, they did nothing but stress, so they have a heart attack or they have a brain aneurysm...' Understand that emotions run disease. So as the world evolves, as the world changes and people become educated, just as we have said before, people will become educated in the sense that as they clear their fields of emotions—emotions that not only belong to them but other people—people will live longer. People will live longer. There are many who say, 'Oh, this is too holistic, this is too energetic, this is too Western, this is too Eastern, this is too medical.' Understand that as human beings come to an understanding, and the two of you, the three of you, will be a part of this, the understanding and knowing—there will be 16 others that become a part of this as well—is that humans' understanding of health will completely begin to shift. There are many who are working on helping to shift this now, but they take too much of a stance from one side. They say, 'No medicine, all energy.' They say, 'All holistic, no medicine.' It is like the religions that we speak of where people get tied in with this and then this causes beliefs within itself, and causes them to get sick. So it is really quite entertaining indeed, if you look at this from the standpoint that we are all eternal souls looking down upon our human bodies that we are living in and thinking of how small minded human beings truly are. And we do not say this in the sense that we are putting down human beings. We love human beings, because we are human beings when we are on the earth plane. But understand that as people are educated—and this is the word that we keep using tonight, because this is very important—education will heal the health system. Education will heal people. But there will always be the people who are tied in deeply with the belief about something. And when we say this, when you speak of the victim mentality, and we are oh so proud of you indeed for not taking this victim mentality on, there are many that, this is their M.O. This is what they get attention with. This is what they like to get attention with. So this will not change people like this because they want to be sick, they want to be ill, they want to get attention. Maybe their mom only paid attention to them when they got sick so now they get sick to get attention. So under-stand that sickness and health is a choice. And many people will say, no, no, I would never want to have hepatitis, I would never want to have AIDS, I would never want to have cancer. But understand there is a piece in every single one of us that is asking for this. Not because it wants it, but because a certain behavior is portrayed that is attracting this energy that is causing the physical body to be sick. So we come in with the medics..." There are all these medics. "... we come in with the medics and we come in with the angels and we come in with the truth and the understanding and the knowledge to bring to people in a very reasonable way that emotions cause sickness. And this will begin to shift over the next seven and a half years on the earth plane as different medical procedures become impossible, different medical procedures become too expensive, different medical procedures become too farfetched —or technology expands so much that the only way to cure something is so expensive that nobody can afford it. People will begin to look for other ways, other resources to heal themselves, and in doing this, just as we have spoken before, let's say 100 people learn this, the other 44 that are so closed with 'I have to be sick in order to get attention' or 'I have to be sick in order to complain' or 'I have to be sick' for whatever reason. Understand that these will begin to see the light. So it really is about a mass consciousness. And when we say we are all one, it does sound a little, 'Oh, we are all one,' and we know that it doesn't really make any sense, but understand that as one person shifts, another shifts. Understand and know that there have been experiments, there have been experiments indeed..." They're showing the 101 monkeys. "...where human beings are just like this because all human beings on the earth plane are part of the same group consciousness on some level."

WILLIAM: Just for those who don't know the story of the 101 monkeys, there was an experiment that was done where, when the one-hundredth monkey on one island learned a particular technique of how to use a tool, all the monkeys throughout that area of the world—.

MARISA: And everywhere...

WILLIAM: Yeah, everywhere, received the same information. So there is something in the air, in consciousness, which the great anthropologist Kroeber called the super-unconscious, which is a reality and not just a concept. It was a theory, but the collective consciousness truly does exist.

MARISA: "But it does depend on..." This is Saint Germain. He says, "Oh it does depend on what we are tuned into indeed. If we say, 'I am not tuned into the mass consciousness,' most likely you are. If you say, 'What is the mass consciousness?' most likely you are.

Understand and know that there is a mass consciousness. People who fight it are usually living off of it because it's inside of them. They are receiving information from it. But there are ways that people can cut themselves off from this and that is living within the lower chakra system where they are only tuned into worldly things. All religions, all spiritual practices work on helping individuals to get past these worldly things. Understand you can still like worldly things, you can still want worldly things, but making that your identity is what cuts you off from the mass consciousness of the planet as well."

CHAPTER TWENTY-SEVEN

HEALTH CARE

WILLIAM: Well, one of the things that I've observed in terms of health is exactly what they said about certain approaches which may be effective but are not cost-possible because if it costs a million dollars to find the gene that's going to save a particular cancer, or a particular disease, well how many individuals on this planet can we spend a million dollars on? It's just not feasible. So, so much money and research and cancer research, and genome project... There's going to be certain instances where it does find relatively low cost solutions. But as a general direction, it just strikes me as a logical person, as ill-fated; whereas other modalities, including modalities that have existed on this planet for thousands of years from indigenous sources, are very cost-effective. So we need to combine the two. A good example is I have a client, Jared Rosen, he's just written a book called *Drowning in the Light*. He actually created his own energy-healing technology, light technology, light fusion, healing, and he ignored all of traditional medicine. And when he was in his late 50s he got a rare disease and it was only $10,000 worth of drugs a month and the removal of his spleen that enabled him to still be on this planet right now. So he, coming from the direction of totally rejecting traditional medicine, found a middle ground. And I would just say that in my experience, and what I'm encouraging, because I've been a great proponent of health books that have basically developed alternative modalities and that have looked at the economic complicity of the medical establishment, which unfortunately like so many of our current systems serves its financial goals more than its original goals. And this is, to me, one of the great crises that we have. I think we can also say the same about our educational system. And this is, you know, one of the things that I like so much about the other client I represent, Eckhart Tolle, when he writes about the pain body and the institutions that have evolved really for their own ability to sustain themselves, and not for the true human spirit that supposedly they serve. So this to me is sort of the crisis that I see on our planet. And obviously we've already talked about it in terms of religion. And I'm very heartened by the collective wisdom of the assembled guides that it is education that is the only possibly salvation for these problems, and it's not so much of going out and educating others, but each individual to educate him or herself, and that act in and of itself raises the vibration, raises the awareness, raises the mass consciousness. So again, I see, you know… and I'm not a Pollyanna, I am an optimist, but I do see from a logical perspective that there is in fact reason for hope here.

MARISA: They're saying… is there a cure for cancer?

WILLIAM: They're asking me?

MARISA: I'm just wondering, personally.

WILLIAM: Well, we can ask them.

MARISA: They say there's been a cure for cancer in Frankfurt, Germany three years ago. Hold on. Let me see. This mad scientist is coming in. Oh, is it Einstein's higher self? Ah, there we go. Here he is. Einstein's higher self just came in. Let's see here…

WILLIAM: Well, he is German.

MARISA: Oh he is? Oh, okay. See, I don't know. I'm so uneducated. I've uneducated myself, rewound my brain so I wouldn't have anything in it, or something. He says, "There is a cure, there is a cure, there is a cure." He's like banging on a table. And he says, "There is a cure for every disease within the energetic realm. All one must do is access this, and this is what I access when I access the group consciousness and the, as they say, the super-conscious of that which is the earth plane. For there is a super conscious for all the human beings, there is a super conscious for all the souls, there is a super conscious for the planet, there is a super conscious... There are many layers of the super conscious. And when many thought that I was insane, many thought that I was crazy, I was bringing in this information from the grid, from the upper dimensions, and did not even realize this until crossing over. This is why I've left a piece of myself to share what I knew at that time, for now I am evolved past this and bring in information that is much higher in wisdom than that which I brought through prior. I am the piece of me who he channeled."

WILLIAM: Okay. My only comment on Einstein's comment is that there is no one cancer. There are many different kinds of cancers. So I'm quite certain—

MARISA: He's saying, "Every disease there is a cure for."

WILLIAM: Every disease there is a cure for?

MARISA: Yeah.

WILLIAM: But it's not necessarily one cure for all cancers? Because cancers are so different.

MARISA: He's saying there is an energetic cure for every single—

WILLIAM: Yes, I agree with that.

MARISA: "Because the body is made of energy, the body is made of a crystalline substance, the body is made of holographic material that can be changed through consciousness. But if even 51 percent of the planet believes that consciousness cannot heal, then everyone else on the planet at that time will not be able to do it. Somebody can say, 'I'm going to heal myself, I'm going to heal myself because this is the energetic component that comes in that heals me.' If more of the people on earth do not believe than believe, they can heal themselves but not completely, because many human beings are at the mercy of what everyone else believes, and this is why we say education, education, education, knowledge, knowledge, knowledge. Because as people begin to allow it into their awareness—they do not even have to believe it, it just has to be in their awareness—then it is in their field, then it can resonate with this, then others can begin to heal themselves. For there are many that will say, 'I am going to heal myself of this disease,' but if there are many that are in their soul group that do not believe this can happen, if there are many within their soul families, if there are many... Understand and know that we all affect each other. One's consciousness is great, one's consciousness can create and manifest, and build and build the life of their dreams. But things that are laws within the physical plane cannot be broken until a certain amount of consciousness and awareness is brought to this law so that it may be un-created and recreated differently." He's talking about the law of cause and effect.

CHAPTER TWENTY-EIGHT
ARE THERE ACCIDENTS?

WILLIAM: Changing the subject totally, just something more mundane but possibly as an illustration of interest to the ordinary reader, we had commented earlier about how my wife drove her car today, and there was a problem with the accelerator, her car did a 360 spinning and almost crashed—

GAYLE: And then it reversed and did the same thing in the same pattern, without harming or hurting anything.

WILLIAM: Yeah. And our question is, number one, just about accidents because she was six inches away from hitting a fire hydrant, I mean it could have easily been an accident that took her life. And accidents that do take people's lives happen all the time. So my question has to do, one, the specifics of her situation, which you know, is kind of amusing because no one got hurt. What was the purpose, if there was a purpose of that accident? And in general, what's going on with accidents? Why do we have accidents? From the littlest of stubbing your toe to the biggest of having your house burn down or something?

MARISA: Saint Germain is funny. I've never seen this humorous side of him that he comes in with you. He says, "Ha ha ha..." He's tapping his fingers together. He's laughing. He says, "Accidents are never an accident, indeed. But we will break this into three categories. There are accidents that are fate. There are accidents that are decided upon to shift somebody's consciousness, to shift somebody's awareness, whether it's an out of body experience, a near death experience, or just a fender bender. Understand that accidents will take us out of the equilibrium of our life and cause us to stop and say, why did that happen? And when we ask 'why did that happen,' this is when the mind allows for a higher consciousness to come in. This is the type of accident that is placed within our field, placed within our path, when prior to incarnate we all say, 'If I'm not on this path at this time, I will have this happen so that I will stop and say, "why did this happen?"' And this will allow an awareness in. This is one kind of accident. The other kind of accident would be one where the angels are trying to save your life. Understand and know that had this accident not happened today you would have continued to move forward and would have continued to injure yourself." They are showing an intersection. Where were you driving to?

GAYLE: I was making a left turn, so—

MARISA: Okay, so you were making a left turn, but it wasn't right here?

GAYLE: Yeah, it was, no—

WILLIAM: But not at the busiest part of the intersection. If another hundred yards, she would have been at an intersection by a railroad track where it could have been fatal.

MARISA: The train. The train…

GAYLE: Yeah.

MARISA: So this is what they are showing me. That's why I was like, it wasn't around right here? Because they actually showed a train. Okay, so you had a spirit attachment. Spirits messed with your electronics. Do you remember coming to meet you, my car turned off on the freeway?

GAYLE: Yes.

MARISA: My car turned off on the freeway when I was coming to meet her, and then when I got out of my car and was walking down the street, my car turned back on by itself when I was coming to meet her. It was like something is trying to get me to either not meet, or you know, just playing tricks. "So the second type of accident is that in which the angels intervene. The angels take over. Ariel is the angel that was in your car today. Ariel is the one that caused this 'shhh' like that..."

GAYLE: And it's been back, yeah.

MARISA: Exactly. It was angelic. Just a real quick example is I had a lady who came in to see me. An angel came in and said, "Let her know that I moved her car six inches, 10 months, three days ago," or something. She called me crying later on that night because she thought I was nuts, she was super-skeptical. And she looked it up, her camera guy was getting his stuff out there, they were going to do a story and she was grabbing her briefcase or something, and a car drove by and took the door off of her car, but she swears she felt something move. An angel actually moved her like eight inches. Otherwise she would have probably died because the car took her door off, and it would have hit her. But it didn't hit her. So the angel... So they're saying: "The second accident is when the angels... angels have to come in and cause for something to happen so that something else will not happen. The other types of accidents are those caused by careless human behavior, but that was not what this was today. Understand and know that careless human behavior and free-will will cause accidents, and many angels will have to stop people from having these accidents. We've removed all energies, we have removed all beings from your field that were causing this to happen." It was that what girl. But I must have not have seen her the other day when you came in for your session. She's been messing with your electronics and—

GAYLE: The what girl?

MARISA: The girl that I crossed over—

GAYLE: Twenty years ago or something?

MARISA: Yeah, yeah. It just causes stuff to happen but they're literally showing Ariel coming in and just protecting you like that.

GAYLE: That is beautiful.

MARISA: That is so cool.

GAYLE: Well, I have had a car go up and over my car in a head-on collision, so I understand...

WILLIAM: I had a similar... that was actually going to be my next question. When I was about 18, just learning to drive, I had an experience where I was driving, and I didn't realize until I was right under the guy that I had gone through a red light, and on the other road when I looked there was a truck on my right and then I looked and then the truck was on my left, as if it had gone through me.

MARISA: It went right through you. That's angels.

WILLIAM: And what my question is, who was the angel that saved my life? Did what I experience really happen, or was it in my imagination?

MARISA: "This was not in your imagination indeed, for understand that there are many times, many times that angels will come in and just as we have used this example earlier in this evening, understand that we'll use the example of a Goodyear blimp floating along—this is the human experience, this is the density, this is how slow human matter moves, this is you in your car. Understand that an angel will come by at light speed and just touch this blimp and the blimp will move and disappear so nobody can see it in the blink of an eye. So all an angel must truly do is come into the physical plane for just a second. The matter and the density will speed up so much that one will disappear. So this has happened in many cases, this has actually happened to you four times, four times indeed, where the matter has been sped up so much around you that you have literally disappeared and reappeared. We have been watching after you—"

WILLIAM: Because I'm not the best driver in the world.

MARISA: "We have been watching after you indeed, for there was one time when driving on the…" They're saying the 405. Isn't that up in LA?

WILLIAM: Yeah.

MARISA: I think they're saying the 405. "Driving and you began to nod off, you began to get tired, this was after a…" They're showing a long drive. You were driving somewhere. This is like 20 years ago. "When you began to nod off. There was a car that was entering where you were driving, and we had to un-manifest the car and make it so that the two of you would not hit. Understand and know that you were then woken up. It was only for a split second. But there are many, many, many, many guardian angels that have to do this on a very regular basis for many of their people that they are watching. Archangel Gabriel is your angel. Archangel Gabriel was responsible for this and Archangel Gabriel continues to watch over you."

WILLIAM: I want to thank Gabriel and I apologize for my dereliction and my less than stellar driving.

MARISA: They're kind of saying it funny. Like, "We've had to do this a lot of times for ya...We've had to pull the miracles out of our sleeve..."

CHAPTER TWENTY-NINE
MIRACLES ARE NORMAL

WILLIAM: Well, this brings up another question. So this whole idea of miracles is quite common?

GAYLE: Normal.

WILLIAM: Because miracles are normal.

MARISA: "Miracles are normal, yes. But miracles have to be within the frame of reference of the human being. Understand this, and this is quite fascinating indeed, for many will say, 'I was healed by God, I was healed by a miracle, I had cancer and before I went to surgery they found no cancer, I am healed.' But understand that every time a human being thinks a positive thought about another human being... you may imagine this as a little bubble that gets stuck to the other person's snow globe that is around them—a bubble is around each person, and you may imagine all the positive thoughts and all the negative thoughts as pluses and minuses all around this person's field. Understand that many people never allow anything other than their own hope, their own reverence for who they are, what they can do for themselves, what they can do for others. But they do not necessarily allow the energy of others that are wanting good or bad for them into their field, until a crisis happens, and then they get down on their knees and say, 'help me, anyone help me.' This opens up the field and allows all of the positive energy into their field and a miracle occurs, because their vibration goes up so high that the body heals itself. Please know and understand that this is something that we have shared with this channel at one time in a channeling session that if a human being was to use a time machine and go back to biblical times, every single human being on this planet with the intention to heal would be able to do what Jesus and the other prophets were able to do in healing. Understand that the vibration and the frequency, the oscillation of cells of each human being have gone up so much over the last 2,000 years that the frequency alone, the difference in this, is what heals. You may look at it like this, something is spinning very fast, something is spinning very slow. The thing that is spinning slow has sickness stuck to it. The thing that is spinning fast steps into the field of the thing spinning slow, and the thing that is spinning slow speeds up so quickly everything flies off and it heals. And this is the right of each human being—to heal themselves. But they are just covered in low frequency energies. But this is very interesting indeed in understanding that the planet, things are speeding up, so if you can bring this into your awareness and wonder if maybe these beings that have come into the world that can heal miraculously, maybe they are from the future and they just have a higher frequency, and they really have no abilities whatsoever, they just carry a higher frequency, because really it is all science. It is all science and all of this can be proven." This was somebody totally different just came in. It was—

WILLIAM: I have two questions this has raised—

GAYLE: Wow and I just spun out.

MARISA: You just spun out?

GAYLE: I just spun out in the physical realm and I can totally see it in the channel.

WILLIAM: So one thing that came up, I have a bad habit when I'm driving of saying nasty things about the people who are in my way. And it's a combination of ... Am I creating... I mean, it's kind of joking at this point but am I actually creating negative energy for these people?

MARISA: "This is creating negative energy but understand there is no real correlation between you and that person and since you do not know each other emotionally, it will not affect them as much. What we speak of is people who have an emotional tie and tie into this energy. But yes, yes, when somebody thinks poorly of you this will lower your frequency for 10.8 seconds. If somebody thinks negatively of you enough it will lower your vibration, which will take you to a lower floor of this building that we are talking about. This is the problem with people who are in the public eye. This is the problem with people who are in the public eye and why they need to use energy, why they need to shield, why they need to use protection, for this exact reason. Because of the fact that the ridicule, even if they do not read the tabloids, they do not watch the news, they do not do anything, they are on television, they are in the movies, they are in print, they are authors, anything. Somebody says, 'Oh, that person, I can't stand them...' This is a negative energy that is entering into their field for just long enough to lower their vibration and make them susceptible to sickness, illness, disease, depression."

WILLIAM: This must be part of the reason why all presidents die earlier than their opponents. Those who don't get elected live longer. I just read that in the newspaper.

MARISA: Really?

WILLIAM: Yeah.

MARISA: That makes sense.

WILLIAM: Not such a good thing, yeah. Another question that this raises, talking about health, is our whole food system. There's all this controversy about GMOs and how important is it we have, you know, either organic, you know? The whole revolution with food. To what degree do we really need to be concerned with the manufacturing of artificial food?

CHAPTER THIRTY
EVERYTHING IS INTENTION

MARISA: Someone just... different guy. Who is this? El Morya? He's an ascended master. El Morya. Here's the council: "We are the council, we are the council that sits above..." The Food and Drug Administration. They're being funny. "... Everything is intention. If somebody ate dirt and truly believed the dirt was good for them, it would be good for them to some extent. We are not saying they would live a long, healthy life, but understand that when people believe that something is evil, when people believe that something is bad, it will affect them on an energetic level much, much more. This brings us to these chem trails that you spoke of earlier. If one believes they are bad and they are affected by them, this will affect them more than somebody that does not know what one is. So when we speak of the GMOs, when we speak of all of these things, the organic foods, yes they are good for the physical body but the beliefs behind why they are being eaten, or if they are eating this out of fear, or if they are eating this out of retribution against these companies, whatever the reason may be, this intention has a lot to do with how the food affects people. There are people who do not believe in organic or it's just not in their awareness whatsoever. They do not eat organic and they live much longer than somebody who eats all organic food, because they eat the organic food because they are worried that anything else will poison them. So when they eat the other food the food does poison them in a sense, energetically. And this is why we say earlier the emotions and feelings and beliefs affect health more than anything on the physical plane could affect it. For understand that when people believe that chemotherapy will heal them, it heals them. When they think it is poison, it poisons and kills them. So understanding and knowing that consciousness and beliefs are much stronger than anything that anyone can do in the physical is the key to health and awareness. We do not say that eating organic is bad; we are saying this is good. But understand and know that there is a lot behind the consciousness of why it is being done."

GAYLE: That's got to be because you're communicating with a consciousness of that which you're eating or drinking. So if you raise the vibration of your food to your own vibration, then it will—

MARISA: Or higher.

GAYLE: Or higher, it will be in that intention.

MARISA: "And this is why people bless food, this is why people pray for food, this is why people send healing to food. For if somebody is conscious, if somebody is aware of the fact that they do not want to eat GMOs, they do not want to eat anything that is not organic- -if they go to eat something that is not organic, they may ask that Source energy, they may ask that their energy, they may ask that any energy above and beyond them remove any sort of negative energies from this food that could negatively affect them and this will be something that will cause them to not be negatively affected."

WILLIAM: Okay.

GAYLE: Because then you're communicating with the god within all things.

WILLIAM: Let's also address the issue of vegetarianism. Is there from a spiritual perspective a plus or minus about being vegetarian?

MARISA: "What we say about one's choice in…" This is Saint Germain again. "… What we say about one's choice in what they would like to eat is all behind their beliefs. Let's say that somebody's mother was a vegetarian and they died young. They may have a belief system within their field that says vegetarians die young, but they still continue to be a vegetarian because this is what they want to be. They may die young because of this. But it does not mean that vegetarian is bad for you, and it does not mean that eating meat is better for you or worse for you. There are many that believe, many that believe that the frequency of the animal that is within the meat is carried within the meat, and this is true, this is true. But again, if one feels they are being affected by it, this energy can be released. This energy can be released. The human body was made to digest and bring in these proteins, bring in these meats, but it is all up to the human being what they believe is healthy and what they understand to be healthy. So if one believes that meat kills them, meat will kill them. If they believe that not eating meat will kill them, that will probably kill them, too. So again, it is all belief, because we are all creators, we are all gods, and we really truly do create our reality. So this is why we keep saying education—education is so important to help people realize that if we go above and beyond our beliefs and step into our conscious awareness of that which is us being manifesters of whatever it is that we think we are manifesting, this is what we bring into our awareness. So we do not have one thing or another to say about vegetarianism, but we will say that within the morphic field of spirituality, within the morphic field of frequency and vibration and raising one's awareness, there is a strong belief that the lack of animal proteins within the field will raise one's vibration. So if somebody is not plugged into this belief system, it will not affect them. But if they are plugged into this belief system, it will affect them." So they're showing kind of like, there's different groups of people that believe different stuff, so if you're within that group then it's going to affect you.

CHAPTER THIRTY-ONE
OTHER PLANETS

WILLIAM: So, going a little further afield, on other planets is the consumption of biological beings and plants necessary?

MARISA: "No. There are many planets, many planets indeed. We spoke of Sirius today, we spoke of Arcturus. We do not speak of the Pleiades constellation, but we will bring that in. These are fifth-dimensional planets where food is not necessary. Food can be necessary, but it is not necessary." Hold on, let me ask how that…how?

WILLIAM: How can it be nec—

MARISA: Yeah, that's interesting—

WILLIAM: You can enjoy food, but you don't need it.

GAYLE: In other words, you have the choice, maybe.

MARISA: "Food can be manifested. The particles can be manifested. The molecules can be manifested to act as a nutrient for those who believe on planets such as this, because they are fifth-dimensional planets. Earth is moving into a fifth-dimensional space within itself as it's evolving. This will not happen for at least, at least 32 years, but know that it is on a path of moving into a 5-D ascension process, and when it moves into this, human beings will want to eat less. They will want to eat less because they will not feel as physical. They will feel more of their energy body. So these things in a 5-D world, one can think 'burger' and a burger appears, or they can think the energy of a burger, put it in my energy and now I have the energy of a burger. So this is a purely manifesting dimension which is quite amazing indeed and very, very hard for the human mind to fathom because the human mind is so 3-D, so 4-D, that it cannot even imagine this. But you may imagine these futuristic movies where you see people eating dehydrated pills of food and you may imagine it is kind of like this because they can manifest what they need, they can ingest it, and it's done. But yes, they may enjoy food if they would like, and this is the same for the spirit realm." What? You can eat in the spirit realm?

GAYLE: So in other words, you can have fun if you enjoy it?

MARISA: Yeah. It's for fun.

GAYLE: But it's not necessary.

MARISA: Yeah, they're showing—

GAYLE: It's playful-like?

MARISA: "A 5-D community is one where people are learning to manifest in the physical planes. But you may look at some planets that you believe are just fiery masses flying through the universe, and there are actually 5-D experiences going on, on these planets. It is really quite fascinating indeed." This is…Einstein? No, this is Saint Germain. Einstein again. He keeps coming back in. We've mentioned him so now he's like, "Argh, I want to talk." "It's really quite fascinating indeed if you look at it from a human standpoint, is that it is quite sci-fi, as they call it indeed. But understand that when one is on a 5-D planet, they may manifest as they would like, and it's quite fascinating indeed, because when one enters back into the earth plane if they chose to, after living on a 5-D planet, they are much better at manifesting. This is why you are able to manifest…" They are pointing at you, Bill. "… Because of the fact that you've lived on other planets where manifesting with the mind was what one does."

Chapter Thirty-Two
Steve Jobs

WILLIAM: A couple of final questions. First, it's been rumored that Steve Jobs for a while was a Breatharian who lived just on air, and Gayle in fact has met other Breatharians. Is that real? Were people... are people... presently on planet Earth sustaining themselves just through air? I assume water, also, for Breatharians?

GAYLE: Oh yeah, I would assume. I don't know. I didn't live within that...

WILLIAM: Is that real, or is that a fantasy?

GAYLE: Or were they kidding?

MARISA: "When reptilians enter into somebody's field..." Oh my God... Steve Jobs was a reptilian? Reptilians aren't smart. He was so smart. Was he not a very nice guy?

WILLIAM: He had his moments of not being nice.

MARISA: He had some sort of attachment possession thing.

GAYLE: I was going to say, I think he was not nice a lot.

MARISA: I don't know anything about him but—

WILLIAM: He was brilliant but he did some very mean things including pretending that he wasn't the father of his daughter.

MARISA: Oh, wow. Yeah. So he had a reptilian attachment. "Reptilian attachments will enter into one's etheric field and will feed off of sexual energy which will feed off of anger, will feed off of fear, and cause one to have a grandiose egoic personality."

WILLIAM: He had that.

MARISA: "Understand and know that this does not take away from the genius of a person, this does not take away from their mind, but this does take away from their emotional body and their energetic body. Understand and know that if an alien being is inhabiting that which is a human being for long enough, they may begin to take on 5-D characteristics in that they do not want to eat, they do not want to eat. There are many that believe that they do not need to eat, and if they believe this enough, yes it is true. They can go without eating. Just as they say, 'Breatharian.' But this was not the case for him. This is things that he tried. He tried it 16 times." These people that you talked to, it feels like one was kidding, two were trying it.

GAYLE: She was a medical doctor and—

MARISA: "This is one that's tried it."

GAYLE: She believed she was from Sirius.

MARISA: Okay, 5-D.

GAYLE: And when I looked at her I had never heard of Sirius, but in my mind I was told "She's from Sirius." So I went outside and said, "Are you from Sirius?" because I didn't know what that meant. And then we became kind of acquainted and saw each other now and then. And she began to explain to me what that meant, and that she was Breatharian, that she could hold an apple and take the energy from the apple that her body needed—

MARISA: That's what they were just talking about. That's interesting.

WILLIAM: So maybe she was?

MARISA: Yeah. So one person—

GAYLE: Without destroying the apple.

MARISA: It feels like you were talking about three people. One of them was like, ah, whatever. The other one is like, I don't know how long she did it for but it feels like she was able to do something because she was a 5-D. She was like a 5-D being.

GAYLE: I would have guessed... that was me in my innocence and not seeking it out, it came into my intuition and so I asked her. Not about the—

MARISA: Steve Jobs is yelling at me.

WILLIAM: Oh, what does he want to say?

GAYLE: You keep going.

MARISA: He says, "Don't you dare smear my name."

GAYLE: Was that Steve Jobs?

WILLIAM: It was Steve. Let me handle the conversation because Steve, I've been a thorn in your side whether you knew me or not because I was the agent behind several books which told the truth about you, that you did not want exposed.

MARISA: Oh, so he's yelling at you, not me. "Don't smear my name." Okay.

WILLIAM: You know, we can delete this part from this, if you wish. You're really not that important, Steve. You know, you probably were the greatest business person in the history of the world to date, but you know, you're just a human being. Wherever you are right now I think that you would do well to let go of your concern about your image.

MARISA: He's still very concerned. He hasn't crossed over.

WILLIAM: But in any event, I really have benefited greatly from your existence, Steve, and I honor you and I admire you, and you know, I'm good with you.

MARISA: I wonder if I can cross him over... his higher self is over there wanting to cross over. You know, he's from the same oversoul as us?

WILLIAM: I wouldn't be surprised.

MARISA: He's from Saint Germain, too. Oh my goodness.

WILLIAM: Yeah, well he was a trickster. He was an incredible guy. Still is, Steve, you know, you're great.

MARISA: But his earthbound version is what people are wanting. Like, he's going in because he wants to be remembered forever as him, not as something else. If he merges with like Saint Germain or his higher self, he's not him anymore, in his mind. He would be considered a level one right now because he's turned his back like, "I'm going to stay here and I'm going to be me." But he does have a little girl with him. He must have had some sort of ... the person he was with had an abortion or—

WILLIAM: No, she had the child.

MARISA: I wonder if they lost a child because he has a little girl with him. Is the girl alive?

WILLIAM: Yeah, his daughter is alive. And he had other children too.

GAYLE: His daughter is alive but you never know what that might have done to his daughter, and she may have aborted—

MARISA: Yeah, he may just have a fragment of her with him, then. Like, she seems like she's six or eight years old. I don't know if he had a young wife and he was older before he died, and maybe they had a miscarriage or abortion or something like that.

WILLIAM: Well, he has three other children alive from his second wife. He never married the first woman.

MARISA: Yeah, he's—

GAYLE: He denied her.

CHAPTER THIRTY-THREE
ARE ABORTIONS EVIL?

WILLIAM: Okay, so while we have you here, you great beings, tell us a little bit about what happens with abortions, because this is a big concern here on earth. We have one group that feels it's the worst sin possible, and then we have a large group that feels its practical here—

MARISA: Mother Mary is in my energy.

WILLIAM: Because, you know, how can you bring in a child if you don't have the resources to support the child, or the desire to support the child? It doesn't seem to me to be a black and white issue. What guidance can you provide?

MARISA: "There are many things and guidance that we can provide. If you understand and if you know that each has a path, but each has three to seven paths for each lifetime. There are three to seven templates, so to speak, that are chosen out. You may look at this as a computer program or an app..." She's totally in my energy.

WILLIAM: Who?

MARISA: Mother Mary.

GAYLE: Mother Mary.

MARISA: I'm like, "Woo!" I feel myself expanding, yeah. She totally, totally, totally stepped into my energy. Oh wow, she's got a lot to say about abortion. Interesting. Ooh, this is going to be interesting. Oh my God she has a lot to say. That's interesting about the templates.

GAYLE: The three to seven?

MARISA: Three to seven templates. There's so much stuff we can ask.

GAYLE: So I wonder if when you're doing... you're on one template and suddenly you make a right turn to go to the next template—

MARISA: You move to a—

GAYLE: Because you can almost feel yourself do that. I know you feel it, too. I felt it too and it was a template, completely stepping out of a template—

MARISA: You switched templates two years ago.

GAYLE: I just may have.

MARISA: Two years and three months.

GAYLE: Two year ago was—

MARISA: Two years, three months, they said. So it's like these different templates you can just kind of like hop back and forth between them... "This is an amazing question indeed, my children. I must start with this. Each human being will come into this divine life plan with a template. You may look at this as a computer program. You may look at this as something that is already marked out. There are already markers pre-set within these templates. Many people will have a different soul mate on these different paths. Many will have the same soul mate on these different paths. Many will have different children that they chose to have a soul contract with that will come into the earth plane as their children with lessons that are similar to theirs, or with lessons to trigger their lessons. This is all divinely planned out. But please know and understand that as a human enters into the earth plane, they do not necessarily know who their child will be. There is a template that says, 'I will have this many children, they will have these qualities and they will be within this soul family or this soul family, or this soul family.' So upon incarnating onto this earth plane, Bill and Gayle, you chose who your parents would be. You had choices of who you wanted them to be. Of course, these are people who you have probably incarnated with prior and you go off the experiences in which you have experienced prior to with them in other lifetimes. You look at their establishment, you look at where their free will has taken them, you look at what they have accomplished in this lifetime, and you look to see if they are within their divine plan, if they are learning things they need to learn, and these are cohesive and represent what it is that you need to accomplish. The soul then enters into the earth plane's ethers for anywhere between two to three years and will study that which will be their parent, that which will be their parents, and they will see how these parents are operating within the physical plane at that time. At that time a soul contract is made between these individual souls, between them on the upper levels in the sixth-dimensional planes. A soul contract will be made. Understand and know that this is stamped, signed, sealed, and delivered. This is something that is tied in together. The lessons of these souls are tied in together, of what they will be learning, how they will be growing together. Understand that when the child is conceived, if free will of the human being is to abort this child when it was a soul agreement to have this child, this person is not going to go to hell, they are just not going to learn the lessons which they wanted to learn at that time from this soul contract which they made in the upper realms. Understand that once one has entered into and is conceived, this spirit is within the child's energy field. Within this miniscule piece of a human being there is consciousness, and at times this consciousness will split. It will become angry and will become a ghost in a sense. It will stay on the earth plane because it is upset. A big piece of it could go back to the other side and then reincarnate in a few months to a year, to 10 years later, with these same parents and come back as a different child. Understand and know that many of the children today—this has become a very big problem—many of the children today that are transgendered, many of the children today that are confused about who they are or feel as if they are possessed, many of them have fragments of an aborted version of themselves prior to their birth onto this planet. It is much more complicated and this is why I've stepped into this channel's energy so I can speak clearly and precisely about this because there is no right or wrong answer indeed. Understand there is another version of truth that we may bring in, in that a mother is not understanding or knowing how to place boundaries within their life. They do not know how to say no, they do not know how to put themselves first, they put everybody else first, they cannot make a decision. The soul says, what is something that is completely irreversible? What is something that will cause my human consciousness to make a decision that they have to put themselves first? Understand that this is something that is quite drastic indeed, for it haunts many women and men years and years, for their entire lives afterwards, and if they were to understand that this was happening due to a soul plan or a soul intervention they may be able to forgive themselves and release this. Many times when this happens, it is a guide. It is not a soul that has spent two to three years studying these people to become their child. This is a guide from the soul family. This is an ex-child from a past life, or this is a future child that plans to come in a year or two, or three, or 10. So they volunteer to come step into the field and be aborted so that these decisions will have to be made. Many peoples' lives are changed drastically due to procedures like this, but know and understand that there is a consciousness within prior to conception. You may talk to people and you may see and understand that they will crave certain things a year before they are pregnant, and then they will see that this child grows up and likes these things. It is because the soul memo-ries, it is because it is carried within the spiritual DNA what this person that is incarnating likes, and the person that is going to conceive them and carry them will pick up on these things. So there is no cut and clear answer, but we must say that sometimes it's planned, and sometimes it's not. When it is not planned, we must say this— if a mother is feeling, 'No, no, no, I just know this has to happen, I just know this has to happen. I've been thinking about being pregnant for a year or two years, three years, it has come into my consciousness...' most likely it is their free will that is causing them to do this abortion. It does not always mean that a soul will fragment but many times it will, because the soul will become upset that it chose a time, it chose a place, it chose a fam-ily, it chose a path and this path was discontinued prior to even entering into the field."

WILLIAM: I thank Mary intensely for this because I know how trau-matic the entire experience can be for both men and women, and I also appreciate that the answer is in fact very much attuned to the answer about education in terms of religious fundamentalists, and others, who are overly attached to one view versus another. And that in every situation we must look at the actual emotions and cir-cumstances without judging. And I think that that would be the most important lesson that people on both sides of the issue could take with them. There is no right or wrong position to take. It's not something to be done lightly, but it's not right to say it should never be done.

MARISA: Exactly, exactly. "And the reason why I step forward is because I represent that which is a religion, that which is a reli-gion that says this is evil, this is bad. And what we must say is that miscarriage sometimes has the same effect on people where they blame themselves, and many times miscarriage is due to the fact that free will was used to get pregnant prior to a soul being ready, or understand that this may have just been in the path so that a couple would experience this. And the souls always do return. In most cases the souls do return for a miscarriage. But the abortion, they do not always return if it was done through free will. But if it was done through a path, in 99.99 percent of the cases, the same soul will come back."

CHAPTER THIRTY-FOUR
BILL'S DAD MILTON GLADSTONE

WILLIAM: Okay, so hopefully perhaps the lighter issues... At the beginning of this session you said that my father's spirit, soul, had several questions he wanted to ask. Let's open the floor for Milton Gladstone to participate and ask whatever questions or provide whatever answers he may have that are related to any of the topics we've discussed or of course related to my own personal life.

MARISA: He wants to ask one of the guides on the other side what heaven is like.

WILLIAM: He wants to ask?

MARISA: Yeah, he is asking. He says, "What's heaven like?" He's still here. He hasn't gone all the way over.

WILLIAM: He's still here. He hasn't done his complete transition?

MARISA: Yeah.

WILLIAM: Well, I think, well—

MARISA: But he's in more of a heaven than here, I mean, where he's at he can get whatever he wants, manifest whatever he wants, do whatever he wants. But he's very attached to here. He says, "What's heaven like? Really, I thought I was in heaven. I feel like I'm in heaven."

WILLIAM: That would be my dad!

MARISA: And he says, "So what is it like? So tell me." Yeah, so let's see who comes forward. So we've got Jesus, Mary, Abraham. Okay.

WILLIAM: Abraham or Saint Germain I think he'd like.

MARISA: Yeah, Abraham. Yeah. Abraham is here. So Abraham says, "The utopia of the soul. What you must imagine is that heaven..." He's saying quote/unquote. "... is like an endless sea of opportunity, an endless see of ideas, and an endless sea of that which we are. For know that you may in heaven hang out with yourself. You may have yourself from the earth plane at that time, the piece of you that you miss, you may manifest that with your mind and talk to that self. You may heal in heaven, you may have fun in heaven. Heaven is a state of mind once you are completely unencumbered from that which is the human emotional and mental bodies. For you are entering into a plane where you are consciousness, but you also have a light body. This is very important to understand. You still have a body. You still have something that will enter back into the earth plane. Many people while there in heaven will heal their light bodies. They will heal their light bodies, they will work on many issues that they had in between, but not painful issues. It will be things like, 'I must get closer to this person because I want to feel closer to them, I want to get to know them more.' So there are many people who congregate in these heavenly realms by their religion. And it is really quite entertaining indeed to see that there are all these different heavens for all these different religions that believe that they are the only ones that go to heaven. So understand that people are still people are still people are still people there. They are still in the belief systems that they carry. This is why many people will be raised... let's say somebody is raised Muslim but they feel drawn toward Christianity. It is because maybe they were a Christian in lives past and know they are not coming into this world to be a Christian, but there is a semblance within themselves that have a belief in this. There are many people who are drawn towards Hinduism. There are many people that are drawn towards other religions and it is because they've had these beliefs in other lifetimes. These heavenly realms are quite utopian indeed in which we can create whatever we want. The fun thing about these heavenly realms, the fun thing about these fifth-dimensional realms and the upper fourth-dimensional realms, is that you may create something and send it to yourself in a life that you have just experienced or a life that you are going to experience, because there is no time, and you may see how that affects you. So you may look at yourself, quite frankly you may look at your higher self as a piece of you that's in heaven and playing with you. You may look at them as sending you thought patterns to see what would happen. So understand that anything that you can quite possibly imagine doing, you can do here. So this is why we suggest to you..." They're pointing at your dad. "... that you come here because you could really, really, really have so much fun with the thoughts that you have in your mind because of the creativity which you carry on the earth plane, because of the creativity that you dreamed of having but were unable to unleash at times. This would bring quite amusement to you indeed. For there are the creation rooms which this channel has spoken of, but there is the creation process that you begin to learn about in these heavenly realms if you can break free from the understanding that you are in the right heaven, you are in the wrong heaven. And these are fourth-dimensional realms that people believe that they are in heaven. The fifth-dimensional realm is what heaven... heaven... would be, if you want to give it a definition."

WILLIAM: Would my dad still be able to assist anyone he wants on this three-dimensional earth plane?

MARISA: "Yes, yes indeed. And this is why we speak of this because he is staying here because he wants to help, he wants to help. He wants to help great-grandchildren. He wants to help people

learn. He wants to help people grow. But what he is not understanding…" He's pointing at your dad and saying, "What you are
not understanding is that you can manifest more in these upper
dimensional realms and send them down as packets or you can
send pieces of yourself down as packets of information to bring
this information to people. This is why when one is driving in a car
and a song comes on that reminds them of somebody and then
they can smell the perfume of the person, it is because our minds
are linked up on a telepathic wave between heavens and physicality, and when one is thought about, they are notified that they are
thought about, and they can come immediately down to the earth
plane if they would like. It is much harder to enter into the earth
plane if you are in the fourth dimension unless you still are resid-
ing closer to the egoic frequency. When you are entering in from
the upper heavenly realms then you are able to bring in so much
more information. Especially with the way that you are evolving,
Bill, you would be able to get information much easier from your
father than from him being in the fourth dimension because you
do not resonate with those realms as much as you resonate with the
fifth dimension."

WILLIAM: Wonderful.

GAYLE: Cool.

MARISA: Yeah, so he can send in information and… they are showing me… "In the fourth dimension many will be awoken at night
time by those that are in the spirit realm and that have either crossed
over or have not crossed over. When one is in the fifth dimension
they may project themselves through the astral plane and visit physically with those that are dreaming, so to speak. So they can astral
travel together. The only way that a fourth dimensional being that
is still in the astral plane can communicate with somebody in the
astral plane in their dreams is if they stand within their field while
they are sleeping and project their thoughts into their mind." So it's

showing like people get, "Woah, what's going on?" in the middle of the night, you know? So they actually have to... he has to... come over and be like, "Hey, what's going on? Don't forget to change your tire tomorrow..." you know, like tell you? But if he's up in the fifth dimension he can communicate with your fifth-dimensional self and meet you and go on journeys and do all this stuff.

GAYLE: Hang out.

MARISA: That's cool.

GAYLE: Really cool. Worth going.

WILLIAM: So my mom must be very happy...

MARISA: He's actually going towards the stairs. I think he's going to cross.

WILLIAM: Like hey, I've got no downside.

GAYLE: I can be with my wife and—

MARISA: She's got really pretty nails. Did your mom have real nice nails?

WILLIAM: She painted her nails, yeah, she wasn't overly—

MARISA: Yeah she's not like ... but she's made up?

WILLIAM: Yeah she liked—

MARISA: She's wearing like a black and white dress like she just, kind of like the '50s mom...

WILLIAM: Very much a '50s mom.

MARISA: She's got like the red nails and the black and white dress. She's got her hair all done like perfect. She's got her makeup. And your dad is like, "Alright, alright," like he's not going to admit he was wrong.

WILLIAM: Oh he's never wrong.

MARISA: No, no he will not admit he was wrong.

WILLIAM: What he'll be saying is, he says, "Yes I'm ready now but you know I really learned a lot here. If I transitioned any earlier it would have been too soon. I made the right decision."

MARISA: That's exactly what he's saying. He's going like, "Alright, alright, alright. They brought up the point about me being a creator. They need a good creator over there." And he's like…

WILLIAM: "Well I'm doing it for Bill! You know he needs a little better communication. He's kind of slow sometimes. And it's really for Titus, my great-grandson. I mean, you know, if I can get through to him faster, it's worth it…"

MARISA: That's funny. They actually share like a sixth-dimensional self, so they share a higher self. Which is cool.

WILLIAM: My parents?

MARISA: Titus and your dad. Different spirit bodies, different souls. But they share a higher self. So that's really interesting because that means that anything that your dad did not learn, or anything he did learn, Titus is already going to know, you know? As far as like emotional maturity and all that stuff. But he'll probably be a little know-it-all. But no, your dad just crossed. That's awesome. Yay!

WILLIAM: This is amazing.

MARISA: He's like walking up the stairs.

GAYLE: He's probably pounding up them like—

MARISA: He is! He totally goes, "Argh" and your mom is like, "Yay!" She like worships him.

WILLIAM: Yeah.

MARISA: She loves him. Oh my God that's so cute. She's like giving him a kiss and her toe went up. You know like when they kiss and the little knee bends. I love it when people cross over. That's my favorite thing. When they're over on this side it's fine. When they're in purgatory and they cross over, that's like huge because they're bringing… like, say he was over there because he was scared and he died of say, pancreatic something, like you could end up with that pancreatic… I've had people that I cross over a loved one that's in their field and the person loses all the symptoms. The last girl I did, it was Crohn's disease. She thought she had it. She was going to get radiation and all that. And then I crossed her dad over. A medium had told her, "Oh, your dad is in heaven, he hangs out on your couch at the house, and he loves you, and just call him in anytime." And the dad was like stuck in purgatory, and like hell because he was super religious and he died, and he said, "Men don't die first, I don't forgive myself." He's a Filipino guy. So anyways, I crossed him over and all of her symptoms left for Crohn's disease. She was healed. So a lot of people are sick because they have spirits attached to them–

GAYLE: And he was in peace.

CHAPTER THIRTY-FIVE
WHY WAS MARISA GIFTED WITH HER ABILITIES?

WILLIAM: So now I have a question for you, though maybe the channels will get involved. But so, I've been around a lot of highly evolved spiritual masters and teachers. At least they've been regarded as such on this planet. Not necessarily ascended masters. And I would say of all the people that I have been with including the Dalai Lama, and some amazing, amazing human beings, you have a greater awareness, at least by channeling, than any human being that I've actually spent time with. And your journey–okay, you felt suicidal for a year—but by conventional standards, pretty easy. You know, you didn't have to go through 40 years of solitude in a cave. You know, I'm just comparing you to some of the people that have had spiritual awareness. You didn't have to live in poverty for years and years. You actually had a loving family. Why you?

MARISA: Let me ask them. Let me get out of the way. My grandma says, "Because she deserves it!"

WILLIAM: Okay. Who says this?

MARISA: My grandma. That was funny. She stuck her head in... I never knew her, really. "Because she deserves it!" That was funny. Let me see here. Let's see Abraham...

WILLIAM: I actually like that she deserves it, but then my question would be, why? Why does she deserve it?

MARISA: So Abraham says, "We needed to bring forth somebody from the soul family that was someone who would be recognizable but understandable by all humanity. For when one meditates in a cave for 40 years the naysayers will say, 'I do not want to sit in a cave for 40 years so I will worship this person instead. I will say, oh they are wonderful, they are godly. I could never be like that.' For understanding and knowing that there are many coming in at this time from this particular soul family..." This is our soul family with Abraham. "...from this particular soul family, that they are bringing in practicality to spirituality, practicality to that which is the understanding of the mystery schools, the understanding of the higher sciences, the metaphysics, so that the world can shift, so that the world can change. Everybody has a choice. Somebody can choose to be a famous author, somebody can choose to be Michael Jackson. Somebody can choose to be a famous singer, dancer, writer. All of these things. Each soul just decides. But understand and know that there is a council for each soul family that will ask for volunteers to enter into the earth plane at certain times to play out the chess game which they are orchestrating. For the earth is going through shifts, the earth is going through changes. So understanding and knowing that this soul..." They're calling me something weird... Annasalisa...? I've never heard them call me that before. "...this soul chose to want to incarnate at this time in this lifetime and go through what was considered a childhood that was normal, and enter into a depressive phase and enter into a drug state, and enter into all of these things so that people could understand, so that people could understand with the keen awareness that this would help shape the world. But understand and know that this soul cannot do this without the team of eight which have entered into the earth plane at the same time and the team of eight includes the people in this room. Understand that there are many that have come to change the planet. Those that are able to be understood by others are the ones that are going to be understood by others, and people will change. They will not change if somebody demands to be worshiped because the world is moving out of a phase of worship and into a phase of understanding and following, following and understanding and knowing that one can be greater than the next. Just as we said. Somebody runs a race in a certain amount of time; another person is going to do this. So understand that the human race needed to be led by example, and this is something we are incorporating in and using the divine beings that encircle this soul family to help to move this forward. But understand and know if this channel was to say, 'I don't want to do this anymore, I want to go do something different...' there would be another person from this same soul family that has the same template that would take over this mission. There are many backups, many backups. There are three backups for this channel within the same soul family, but prior to incarnation, there is an order set in place."

CHAPTER THIRTY-SIX
THE SOUL FAMILY FOR EDUCATION THROUGH MEDIA

WILLIAM: So we are all part of the same soul family. How many members are there in our soul family?

MARISA: One thousand one hundred and eighty-three. Three hundred and twelve that are incarnated.

WILLIAM: Three hundred and twelve incarnated on the planet at this time?

MARISA: Mm-hm. No, 250 on the planet. The other ones are in the ascended master realm.

WILLIAM: Ascended master realm? Okay. How many on the planet did you say?

MARISA: Two hundred fifty.

WILLIAM: Two hundred fifty of us on this planet? How many other soul groups are on the planet at this time working with us?

MARISA: "Eleven."

WILLIAM: Eleven other soul groups? And how many people collectively are there on—

MARISA: In those 11 that are—

WILLIAM: On the human being realm, of those 11 soul groups?

MARISA: Eighty-three.

WILLIAM: Eighty-three people?

MARISA: "Eighty-three people that are working with us in this divine plan."

WILLIAM: From those 11 soul groups?

MARISA: Yeah, from those 11, yeah.

WILLIAM: So that's less than 350 human beings currently on this planet—

MARISA: "But understand some have very menial tasks. One's task may be, 'I went to this great girl and I had a session, you must go do this.' And this extends to another person that opens up something that opens up something, that opens up something. So some are very small pieces."

WILLIAM: Well that makes it even smaller. That's the point I'm getting at. This is not a big group.

MARISA: No.

WILLIAM: I mean we're talking about seven billion plus human souls. And you know, maybe there's 200, maybe 100 with meaning-ful roles right now. Is it enough? Are we enough? Do we have rein-forcements coming?

MARISA: "There are reinforcements within the astral planes. There are reinforcements within the astral planes, indeed. And understand that this is your journey, this is your mission. There are others that are singers, songwriters, dancers, but what we are speaking of is the multi-media. This is what's going to save the world. And there are others that do things like sing, that dance, that do all of these things. But understand in the spiritual community, yes. We speak of 250 souls within this soul family are integrated into the earth plane at this time. But only 83 outside of the soul group. For the soul group from which you are from are ministers, teachers and healers. It does not mean that you must minister. But you are a minister and a teacher. This is the role which you carry. A minister and a teacher. It does not mean that you need to stand up on a pulpit with the minister's robes on, but you are ministering to others through the work which you carry. So understand and know that there is, yes, there are very few. But understand and know that if there are so many that could do all of this it would not become extraordinary. People would not want to change. People would just say, 'Oh, that person plays baseball. I don't need to play baseball.' But if people see this as something that they can say, 'Ooh and ah' about, 'Oh look, she didn't know how to do that before,' or 'Look, he didn't know how to do that before and now she knows how and now he knows how. I want to do that, too,' then it becomes exciting, it becomes something that is fun. And when it's something that's fun, that's what people want to do. They do not want to go to church and read a Bible. They do not want to kneel, they do not want to do these ritualistic things. They want to do something that is fun, they want to do something that is fun."

WILLIAM: Okay. So I didn't really present the question properly. More what I was getting at was not just... I mean, that's our unique element in the mission. The larger mission is education at every level. And so what my real question is, how many human beings on the planet right now are part of soul groups that are sharing this larger mission–not our specific mission—but are working in unison to raise the vibration of the planet and prevent what otherwise would be the de-evolution into chaos and madness?

CHAPTER THIRTY-SEVEN
THE LARGER MISSION

MARISA: "There are 12 soul groups that are integrated onto this planet. We would say that a combination of all of the soul groups, because we will give it to you in percentages because we cannot say the amount of people, because there are also people in the astral plane, just as your father was still in the astral plane. So there are still people in the astral plane, there are fragments. So it becomes too abstract in trying to understand this. But understand that 32 percent of the souls in all of the soul groups combined are on this mission. Believe it or not, there are souls that are against this mission. There are souls that don't want this."

WILLIAM: Well, that's what I was going to get to. I was going to get to evil. That's the one thing that we have not really discussed. Are there councils of 12 counseling evil—

MARISA: "Yes."

WILLIAM: To prevent the positive energy?

MARISA: "Four of the oversouls, four of the soul families within these oversouls have councils of 12 that do not see it as evil, but they see the destruction of earth as a way to start over, they see it as a way to get all of the fragmented pieces of their souls that they created out of the astral planes, out of purgatory, out of these physical planes, re-merge them with the greater pieces of them and send them to other worlds to learn. Because pieces of them are fragmented within the astral planes, and these pieces are the ones that are attracting people, possessing people, taking people over and causing people to be evil. For human beings are not evil. And this is what we disagree with when it comes to many people's belief systems, is that human beings were born evil. People are not born evil. Nobody does anything to do something evil. They are doing it because they believe that it is good. They are doing it because they believe God will love them. They do it because their father was violent—they saw that their father liked that, so now they are violent because they think they are making dad happy. So everybody is always trying to please something. So there is no technical evil. But there is evil in the astral planes in the sense that there are beings that take over beings in the physical and take over their thoughts, take over their thought patterns, their minds, their emotions, and cause them to do things that they would never do without these attachments. So these councils of 12 are not necessarily evil; they are people that want to start over. But understand that there are other councils like your own that see the innate goodness of the divine and the knowledge and the wisdom and the education of the human beings. They are at a point in their consciousness, they are at a point in their understanding, and bringing in awareness to the human mind, that they can beat this. And these are, we might say, the more competitive souls that want to see the earth succeed. They do not want to see it destroyed and taken down. Understand that there are many that are in religions that are killing other people, the extremists that you spoke of earlier, that are part of these soul groups where the councils want the earth to be destroyed."

WILLIAM: So, on a percentage basis, it sounds like we've got 12 positive soul groups, we've got 32 percent working for. It sounds like the weight is on the positive side. I imagine there's a significant percentage—

MARISA: Some that are just "eh..."

WILLIAM: That are kind of in the middle that are going to go, "Well, whatever way, you know, the majority goes, I go..." So my intuitive nature suggests it's like 32 percent to something between 12 to 16 percent going for the evil, with about 50 percent in the middle.

MARISA: Yeah, exactly, exactly. It's right in the middle. And it's nine of the soul groups, nine of the councils are...these two councils. Yeah, nine of the councils are kind of good...eight. And then the other four are like "blah" but it doesn't mean that all eight of these things are wanting to do something about it. They're just kind of like, "Eh, whatever..." You know? But we're like on a mission.

WILLIAM: So ultimately it's like a super hero movie about good versus evil, with different strategies, and it just goes on infinitely?

MARISA: Mm-hm. Exactly. "This does go on infinitely but understand that we love to look at life through the 5-D perspective. Because the 5-D perspective is still instant manifestation, but there is still duality. Many people believe that the fifth dimension is the Christ consciousness. Many people believe that the fifth dimension means you've made it and that you are in no more duality. But this is where the fun just begins. This is where the creation state beings and extends out to all the 4-D pieces within the earth plane. But this is fun, this is fun indeed. And souls would not enter into the earth plane unless they found this as being something that is enjoyable. Nobody enters in the earth plane against their will. Many people, religions, Buddhism, other religions will say, 'I hope this is my last lifetime, I'm in hell, I'm serving out a sentence...' Things like this. This is not the exact way that they put it, but this is the attitude that comes forth from some that are less educated within these different religions, within these different beliefs. And this is something that we say, and we must say—if you are there, you wanted to be there. If you are there you fought to be there. Because there are not enough earth beings on the earth to inhabit all the souls that wanted to be there for 2012. There were not enough that wanted to be there for that time to feel and know and shift within the consciousness and see what a baby earth would do right after December of 2012. After this time, the consciousness shifted and all of the souls sang, all of the souls celebrated and said, 'Yes, we are not cavemen anymore, we are not cavemen anymore, we can finally, finally, finally begin to integrate bigger pieces of ourselves into our human capsules and understand and enjoy the earth plane.' Because this truly is an instant manifestation world and people did not understand that, did not understand that indeed, but now they are beginning to."

WILLIAM: Well, I think this is a wonderful place to end our conversation. It's interesting that you chose this information because I know you, as an individual, have not even read my novel *The Twelve*. That's exactly the way the novel ends.

MARISA: Na-ah!

WILLIAM: Aha!

MARISA: That was Abraham I was channeling. That wasn't me.

WILLIAM: Well, I was told by the Mayan–I don't communicate, Gayle did—and the Mayan calendar is a pre-Mayan calendar. The Mayans were just popularizers, they didn't create it. And the entities that did create it through different communication after I wrote the novel communicated that I had in that novel accurately portrayed the true message of the calendar. And this is what you have just said, the true message. The world really did end on December 21, 2012, and a new world really did start. And even in the novel I said of course many people had no recognition of this change because they weren't sensitive to it. Those who were, realized that the world had ended and that a new world had begun.

So we'll end on that note and I think we've got a great course and we've got a great video.

GAYLE: Thank you so much.

WILLIAM: And this will be a great book.

MARISA: I think so, too.

PART III
GOOD FRIDAY

CHAPTER THIRTY-EIGHT
BILL'S BOUT WITH GOUT

MARISA: The guides are saying, "We wanted you to experience that which is the miraculousness of instant healing from the spirit realm, but understand and know that the human mind trumps all spirit. And this is the thing that people don't understand, is they'll say, I had a miraculous healing, but just like your friend Richard..." His name is Richard, right? I thought it was Robert. But anyways, the guide is right, not me. "...just like your friend Richard, he will continue to manifest the same physical injuries or the same physical ailments over and over and over and over until the emotional need for those is gone. So he may be healed miraculously a zillion times, but unless he works out his humanness he's going to continue to attract that in his life."

WILLIAM: One of the questions that arises for me is just like Richard, I'm not aware that my mind is resistant. I mean, on a practical level we all want miracles, we all want instant healing, so it must be a deep-level program that is saying, "No, that can't be, no that can't be."

MARISA: Exactly. And the way that... Okay so Abraham is here. Saint Germain, he's hanging out over there. It's funny. He's like with Jesus. They're like kind of standing there. Jesus looks more man-like. Saint Germain looks more like a hologram, or something like that.

WILLIAM: Big time of year for Jesus. This is Good Friday.

MARISA: Oh yeah. That's when my dad wanted the book to come out, or the ad to come out this week. But anyways, so they are here and yes... here's Abraham. He says, "We started you out, Bill, on this path 18 years ago. We started you out on this path towards spiritual freedom, towards emotional freedom and towards the ability to bring in the energy that is Source into the life which you are living, and fully experience it, and fully manifest it, and teach it to others. For understand and know that even if somebody does not have karma, so to speak, even if somebody is a higher level soul, it does not mean there will not still be piddly, so to speak, little human issues that one will have to deal with while in the physical body. And when we say piddly we say this sarcastically in a sense because these little tiny things are the biggest thorn in any soul's side when they are living in another human being. When other human beings disparage another, like the women in your past, they are placing energy in your field that is keeping you stuck, keeping you stuck and keeping you in a repetitive cycle of continuing to attract the same thing over and over and over again. So even if a soul comes down to experience certain things in their life, others can affect their soul path, too. So know that when one gets an instant healing, they may still have something within them, deep down inside that will attract the energy of somebody that wants to victimize the person or talk bad about the person, or attach onto the person, or impinge upon the person's energy and drain them, and this is something that a healer must see and release this need to allow people to do this."

So there is a piece of you that needs to be needed, but there is a piece of you... and it's an innocent need to be needed. Like, oh yeah, you know, I'm needed, people love me, I feel helpful, blah blah blah. But there's also the ugly side of that where it kind of leaves a little door open to vampire-type energy, and that's that woman. I mean, it's like she watches every move you do, and, "Oh look what he's doing now," and blah blah blah. It's almost like she's taking notes and making little check marks. And it's very draining. So that's your ex-wife. Okay so I'm going to cut her off from you.

WILLIAM: So that was the one 33 years ago?

MARISA: A-ha.

WILLIAM: Connection originally, right?

MARISA: Yeah. Okay, so that's what I thought.

WILLIAM: About how long I've known her.

MARISA: And there's past life stuff. There's past life stuff that you literally, what I saw was, you have like a lock around your ankle and the energy—

GAYLE: A shackle.

MARISA: Yeah. It's kind of like you're shackled to her, or some-thing like that, because you feel this—

GAYLE: You can see it when they're side by side in the same room.

MARISA: Oh really?

GAYLE: Whoa. It just goes like this.

MARISA: And I don't even think that it's a conscious... I mean, it's a conscious thing but at the same time she doesn't know any better. So it's kind of like getting upset with a seventh grader for being petty.

GAYLE: That's how her age seems.

MARISA: Seventh grade.

WILLIAM: Yeah, I have a lot of data on her. She was arrested devel-opment at 13. And it's interesting because my other good friend, who is also an intuitive healer, Dr. Uwe Albrecht, saw the same thing and did remove some of what he called energy cords. But it's, you know, obviously a big recurring issue for her and so, you know, we can't clean it enough. So the more the better.

MARISA: So what's interesting is a lot of healers will work in the fourth dimension. The fourth dimension is the cords, the emotions, the feelings, memories from this lifetime, and it's also where earthbound spirits are, and then spirit fragments. So you guys have spirit fragments. It's almost like a past life version of her is almost haunting you. I'm going to see where the foot is leading us. Gayle, if you go to the energy center where the gout is and you follow it up into his body, where does it end? Where do you see it ending?

GAYLE: Well, I haven't in a while, but I saw around the thyroid area.

MARISA: Okay. I saw it like right—

GAYLE: Oh in his solar plexus.

MARISA: Mm-hm. I see kind of like a cord going up and I see a cord to her and then I see a bunch of fragments of her. So it's not even necessarily… It's more of a shamanic thing and he needs almost a shamanic healing because she has fragments of herself that are attached to you. I had past life regression one time. Went out to a medical intuitive and she ended up doing a hypnosis. And she ended up taking me into a past life regression and I had my mom from a past life stuck to me. And in this life I kept seeing her as a demon, as a demon. But then when we went into the hypnosis I saw it was my mom who is now my sister in this lifetime. My sister has brought me my biggest lessons in this life, you know. But apparently she was in the last life, too. So it's like we can have pieces. So you have past life pieces of her. You know, when you meet somebody you're like, "Oh I just feel like I know them…" It's because there are pieces of them that are in your field and it brings you guys together. So it's

194

kind of what brings you guys together. Yeah, you just have a ton of cords attached to her but then all the way back to... I saw you at age seven. Age seven you're kind of sitting there and you were like, "I'm just going to be the smartest kid around and I'm just going to, you know, ignore everything." And I see you in this room going, "I'm just going to learn and I'm just going to grow and be real big, and be real strong." It was just kind of like this like, you know, a seven-year-old kid, super cute, just trying to deal with the life that he was dealt. And the cord that I see is your mom going like, "Oh he'll be okay." Was she like, "Oh, he can take care of himself" about you?

WILLIAM: Not so much. I mean, she loved me and she doted on me.

MARISA: Oh yeah, but—

WILLIAM: And she was relieved, probably, when I was seven to find out I wasn't retarded. They all thought I was retarded because I couldn't speak. I was probably traumatized by my older brother. And it wasn't "He'll be okay..." She just was not able to control my older brother.

MARISA: Or maybe it's more "He's okay!"

WILLIAM: That was more... he's not—.

MARISA: And that's "I'm going to be smart" because you're not retarded.

WILLIAM: Yeah, and then...yeah, I consciously, but more around the age of 12, realized that I was smarter than everybody else and that was a great tool to protect me. Because as long as I was the smartest kid in school people would leave me alone.

MARISA: Got it. Okay. So, yeah I was seeing the cord attached to your mom and that was also allowing other energies into your field, like from these other women where it was kind of like you allowed them to get away with a whole lot more than you should have let them get away with. You know, treating you in different ways and so forth.

WILLIAM: Oh yeah. All of them. I just ignored them. If they weren't doing what I wanted, I just ignored them.

MARISA: Yeah and that's kind of like what I'm seeing you doing at seven. Kind of like, "Okay, I'm just going to ignore what's going on around me." Your mom's energy is like, "He's okay." And you're just kind of like, "I'm going to be smart and I'm going to be big and tall and strong, and I'm going to take care of myself." So it's almost like when you're not getting the emotional needs that you wanted from the women, it was just kind of like, "Well then, whatever, I'm going to stay in my little thing right here."

WILLIAM: Well, what's interesting is the first seven, ten, twelve years of my life, all my emotional needs that were fulfilled were fulfilled through my mother, because my father was very distant. He was hardly present at all.

MARISA: Now he's always here. But he was distant and then she was the one that took care of you more emotionally?

WILLIAM: Yeah.

MARISA: Yeah, well, once I removed her energy from your field just now, it blocked those other women's energy from coming back and stealing your energy. Because you carry a lot of chi for somebody that doesn't meditate. There's a chi center down here and I call it our gas tank. I do meditations where I teach people how to fill their gas tank, enlarge their gas tank. And you just got a lot of chi, or life force energy. Which is what makes you a healer and easier to connect, because it makes your energy brighter, so your frequency is higher, so you can connect with stuff that has a higher frequency over there. The problem with that is people will take it and drain it. But your energy is so high that you can still survive. If somebody was tied onto me like that, Jeff's dad or someone like that, you know, just any standard person that's not really aware of this stuff, they'd probably go crazy because they would be kind of feeling that person on them all the time, they'd be obsessing about the person. But you don't obsess about her even though she is so in your energy.

WILLIAM: Unless somebody is actually coming into my field, I forget they even exist.

MARISA: And that's that thing where you're seven and you know how to block it out.

WILLIAM: I consider it a privilege for somebody to be in the same universe as me.

MARISA: There you go. And that's what the seven-year-old is doing. He's like, "I'm in my own world."

WILLIAM: They're done, they're done. They're not part of my world anymore. I don't care what they do or what they say. They don't exist.

MARISA: Except women had a way in so I'm getting rid of them.

WILLIAM: Well, obviously I was a little bit arrogant. I mean, that is my Achilles heel or toe. I can't control everything. I can't just say they're not in my universe because they obviously are.

MARISA: Well, what the guides are saying is, they're saying, "This is a lesson to bring into you to show and understand that when one is connected to Source, when one understands Source, this is one thing. For there are many people that are intellectually...spiritual."

It's Saint Germain... "There are those that are intellectually spiritual. There are many who will use big words. There are many that will talk so that others cannot understand them about their spirituality when really it is not their spirituality; it is their knowledge of spirituality. Many people that you spoke to with *Tapping the Source* were intellectually spiritual, for they understood it with their mind, they understood it with their mind and they would explain it. But they did not understand it with their core. They did not understand all of the different aspects that come into the divinity which we are. For many people do not see that the ego is divine. The intellectual mind is divine. But when one is speaking in terms of being spirit, being their higher self, ascending through all the layers of consciousness while they are still within a human body, that is when one must completely understand and learn how to recognize and see emotions for emotions, ego for ego, intellect for intellect, and to see all of these things, and see when they are holding one down. For understand that you are being accelerated through the last 18 years from a—" Just one of you. If it's Saint Germain, it's Saint Germain. He's such a troublemaker. Seriously is. Is it going to be him? It's Abraham. Him? Okay. Saint Germain, fine. He says ha ha ha.

CHAPTER THIRTY-NINE
SAINT GERMAIN EXPLAINS THE
DEEPER HEALING

WILLIAM: He's a showman, I can tell.

MARISA: He's like clapping his hands. He says, "Eighteen years ago we brought this energy upon you. Eighteen years ago we accelerated you to a point that you had not been accelerated to from a soul level. Please know that this is not something to be proud—'Oh I was accelerated up to a higher level'—because we hear the mind that says this still. But understand and know that we brought you to this level because we have all contributed to the learning and the acceleration of the soul which you are, which I am, which we all are. For understand and know that as you begin to embody this larger piece of you, so to speak, you will begin to purge old behaviors, purge old people, purge old places. You may not even want to be doing the same thing with your life. And you will say, 'How was I doing this for so long and now I have no interest in this?' This can be little things or this can be big things. Understand that we are not coming in to change your life and take away your old life. We are coming in to bring a higher frequency, a higher state of knowledge to you. But we are trying to remove the intellectual spiritual person inside of you, because there is a Bill that is intellectually spiritual, that understands how to be spiritual within the mind, but does not allow us through at certain points. And this, this was proof for you. The skepticism is what was blocking. And we do not say go and be a fool now and believe everybody and say, 'Oh wow this is amazing' and then look like a fruitcake and lose your reputation as somebody who can be trusted, somebody that is knowledgeable. We are just saying with discernment, we are showing you that skepticism can be removed from your field when things like this happen because you are a 'see it to believe it' type of guy. You always have been, always will be. And we realized this so we knew we had to deal with something, something to show you proof. For the first healing which you received with your friend with the bubble wrap, so to speak, as this channel will call it, you received instant relief of the pain you had, but it was not healing of the disorder, healing of what was truly wrong. What we encourage you to do later on when you are by yourself is play a little game with yourself. What you must do is when you are laying in bed or you are in the shower, or something where you are alone with no interruptions, imagine yourself dropping from your mind, which is where you are, down into your toe, and imagine who's in there, what's in there, what's around there. Imagine this cyst that is on your foot as a room. Who is inside that room? For at this time, your ex-wife is in this room. At this time there are many aspects of you that were abused in this room when you were a young child that you have repressed and pushed away and pushed away literally down to the bottom of your body, as far away from your mind as they can possibly go. For you say, 'I am a different person. I am a new person.' But this is still part of you even though the soul that is projecting down into your spirit is a different one than it was when you were a child. So know that you switched oversouls about 18 years ago when your soul accelerated up into a higher level of ascension. But please know that the physical body still carries everything. The physical body is like a tape recorder. It records everything. So we are releasing from you today 1,162 spirit fragments of the young boy which you were from age 18 months to 12 years old. Every single time you were abused, every single time you were violated, every single time somebody did something to you and you were not allowed to stick up for yourself, and it was unfair and nobody allowed you to get the last word, a little piece of you, a little piece of you that knew who you were, knew why you were down here, said, 'I am done with this, I'm leaving,' and would split off and leave. These pieces cannot leave so they are little imprints of you at that time. So it is technically a ghost of you at that time. Those pieces of you got pushed into the background when you accelerated up to a higher soul level and have not been dealt with. So these things, these energies are pieces of you that are defensive, that will not let anybody push you around, that are not going to deal with anybody doing anything that you do not like, and sometimes these pieces of you surface. We are releasing these at this time. For understand and know that the path which you are taking at this time, there is going to be a fear of failure that will come in, for you have not failed at anything in your life. You always achieve. You always achieve everything that you want to do. You excel at everything that you want to do. But what about the things that you do not want to do, that you would be okay at? Some of these things are the things which you are going to be doing over the next six months and you may feel—when we say 'you' we mean the fragments of you that needed to succeed—may get in the way. They may step in front and say, 'No, we're not going to do this because we're not going to be the smartest, we're not going to be the brightest, we're not going to be the greatest, and there's a possibility that we may fail.' So they will block. What people don't understand is that with manifestation and with asking for things in our lives, on a human level there are so many things that are blocking humans from achieving what it is they want to achieve. For understand that your mind, your spirit, your soul, everything may say, 'I want to have a production company, I want to be a teacher, I want to be out in the public eye so to speak, and I want to share the knowledge that I've worked my entire life to achieve. But I'm not sure that I am going to be extremely successful at this. But that's okay because I'm going to bring in the energy of Source, because I understand intellectually, understand spirituality and understand how to bring energy in, and I'm going to manifest.' In a perfect world without a fourth dimension around us, this would be successful. You would instantly be successful. There would be no fear. You would achieve everything you want to achieve instantly. But the fourth dimension surrounds us on this planet and that is the emotions, the feelings, the memories, the fragments, the ghosts, the entities. There are many beings that are up in higher dimensions that project through to the fourth dimension that cause trouble in the fourth dimension. But the only trouble that is in your field is you. Old you. The young you, trying to protect you. And with what we have planned—and when I say 'we' I mean you and I, I mean the soul which we are—with what we have planned, these pieces of you must go. But you must understand why they are going, and you must understand, otherwise they will come back. Because there are little pieces of you inside of you. If you look at yourself like a motherboard, if you look at yourself like a circuitry, you will see that there is a little thing in there that says, 'Victim'— 'Must achieve or else I will not do.' There are little behaviors in here that are logged into you so that you would be who you are in this lifetime. So we are releasing these from you. You will feel much lighter. Things that you say do not bug you within your mind will really not bug you now. Many times you will say, 'Oh, I'm not bothered by that, that's okay.' But that's one of the 'We're not bothered by it, we're in our little room, Mom says we're okay, we're going to be smart, we're going to be talented, we're going to be strong.' This is the seven-year-old inside of you that keeps things tight when things aren't going your way. So understand and know that we are releasing this and this will relieve much pain from the foot and this will also relieve many of the needs to be plowed over and walked all over. For understand that you were walked all over when you were young. You had to be. There was an excuse for it. Others had excuses for it and this is something you had to deal with. So it was imprinted into your physical cellular, crystalline structure. So this will allow others to walk all over you unless you become very defensive and very protective, and you always have to be on guard. And this is not going to be necessary anymore because things will just start going and you will not feel the distractions because those pieces of you are going to be re-absorbed back within the soul which we are, and you will feel a difference. Gayle, you will feel a change. You will feel a change in yourself as well. For many pieces of you react to the pieces of him that are not him, so to speak. Does this make sense?"

GAYLE: Yes.

Chapter Forty

Lessons for Gayle

MARISA: "So these young pieces will say, 'You can't do that to me, you can't do this to me,' and you will feel that energy so you will say, 'Well, I'm not trying to do that to you,' when really the two of you as human beings are not even talking about anything. These little pieces of you are arguing with each other. So there is a little bit of a tension between you that you don't quite understand when both of you are perfectly happy. So understand that you will feel a shift, you will feel a change, and you will say, 'Is he really that calm, is he really not offended by this?' And almost a need to want to poke the bear to see if he is really not upset about something. But understand and know that much relief is being released at this time and we would not allow the channel to do it until we are here to channel the information so that both of you can understand it and see it and know that the frequency of both of you will be raising up and the ability to connect with spiritual spirituality, energetic spiritually, will be much more free flowing. The fear which you have had, Gayle, the fear which you have had of not achieving, the fear of not being seen, the fear of not being seen by the angels, the guides, all of these things. You have felt away from them. You have felt you have been away from them for quite some time. And for 11 years you have felt a separation that you did not feel prior to that time in your life. For as you were a young child you always felt a random connection to that which was us, that which was the angels, that which was the guides, but it was a very haphazard connection in the sense that we had to be extraordinary in order to get your attention. We had to really, really, really get right up there so that you would accept what was being seen, because the little things, the little things... You are a skeptic as well. You are a skeptic because you are extremely brilliant, you are extremely intelligent, and the intelligence within your brain says that does not make sense, does not compute, and would block many of the messages coming through. So we are releasing, we are releasing the blocks at this time so you will feel more of a free flowing energy coming in from your soul's consciousness. This is the soul which you share with Mother Mary. And this is why you feel such an affinity towards Mother Mary. But you will feel this need to want to help children. You will feel this need to want to get out into the world and to be seen and to know what you do, and to not be ashamed of it. For there is a piece of you that was in the clergy, a piece of you that was a nun. Bill, you were a priest. Understand the two of you lived a lifetime together in the Roman Catholic Church where you were a part of the church. So there is a piece inside of you that says, 'Do not be seen, do not be heard, be within my faith, raise my frequency, raise my vibration, pray for others, but do not be seen.' And Gayle, you carry the imprints for this. Bill released his imprints prior to coming into this lifetime, but you carry the imprints of the humble servant. You carry the imprints of the one that does not need to be seen or heard, but there is the human piece of you and the spirit inside of you that knows that you are going to be known. People are going to know you. So there is a conflict. Do you feel this conflict?"

GAYLE: Yes.

MARISA: "And this is the most important thing, is accepting and acknowledging it. For many times people will not be aware enough to accept this. They will say, 'I am not conflicted, I want to be seen,' and, 'Because you said I want to be seen, yes, I want to be seen. No, there is no conflict...' And this is the ego. So by accepting and seeing there is that conflict you can allow us to come through and allow you to be seen, allow you to be known, allow you to take credit for that which you have done in your life. For understand and know, both of you have achieved so much in this lifetime that it is very hard to truly, truly, truly accept and honor and see what is coming ahead of you because you have achieved so much already. And you say, 'I have already achieved so much, how could this be the pinnacle of my life where everything is going to just open?' Understand that this is how it is. And yes, as we have said in past sessions, we always say that things are going to be great, everybody is going to be famous, everybody is going to be fabulous if they talk to me, if they talk to Saint Germain, if they talk to us over here. But understand that we are going about this in a different way. For understand that I could come to the two of you, which I have done, Mother Mary has come to you through me and spoken with you, Raphael has come to you, Gabriel, Michael comes to you, they come to you in your dreams, they push you in a direction to do certain things, but by bringing the aspect in, the trinity so to speak of the three human beings in this room, three adult human beings in this room, understand that the blocks are being removed, the blocks, and people will be taught about that. *Tapping the Source* was not a mistake. Seeing and understanding and knowing all of these people that see that they are Source, they see there is a connection. They are tapping into it, they are pulling into it, they are manifesting their dreams, but we can guarantee if they have 20 dreams, they only experience two. And they are talking of the two, which is fabulous. But in their mind there is something saying, 'But there's those other things that I want and I just can't get them. And I know that I say that I believe in this source, this energy, and that I can get them. But why can't I get them?' Those people are going to be interested in how those doubts can be removed. Will they admit they have doubts? They are not like you, Gayle. They probably will not. But understand that when they read the words which we bring through and teach them how to remove these blocks, they will read them. And then they will be proud that they read them and they achieved even more success through understanding that you can tap into Source but you also have to tap into this. You also have to release blocks. You also have to release past pieces of yourself because the emotional body, the ego, the intellectual mind trumps spirit. Remember this. The physical trumps spirit every single time. It doesn't matter how much your spirit inside is calling out for your higher self above you; if there are human aspects of you that are blocking it, they will block it. Some will come through, and that is a lot for many, but after a while it plateaus, it stops. Nothing more comes in because there is work to be done. We are sorry to ramble on and on and on. We could go on forever because that's we do, but we will allow you to ask questions if you will like." Oh my God. I just… Whoa! Where am I? Oh my God. I was not here.

GAYLE: That was phenomenal.

MARISA: I haven't done trance in so long. Oh my God, I left. I was running around with her somewhere.

GAYLE: Wait 'til you hear it.

WILLIAM: Everything they said resonated as truth and I have to admit that there's part of me, and maybe it's lifted now, that ever since, you know, being on this planet in this body, has felt completely unsafe in every moment, and that every human being with whom I would have an encounter was potentially my murderer because that was my experience from birth with my brother. So yeah, there's part of me that, yeah, okay, insulate myself through getting better grades than everyone else, being the best athlete, making a lot of money, being acknowledged as a major publishing guru protects me. But deep down it's kind of like the old, "What makes Sammy run?" Well what makes me run is that deep down I feel that my life is constantly in danger.

CHAPTER FORTY-ONE
THESE LESSONS ARE EMBEDDED
WITH UNIVERSAL TRUTHS FOR
EVERYONE

MARISA: "And this is something that you actually imprinted your-self. Which you must understand, and we must explain at this point, and this is what we wanted to explain to be added to the transcript, is that understanding of how the spirit is programmed. For this chan-nel does not even truly understand this, for she is obsessed with this and this is why we continue to knock her out of her body at this point..." Thanks guys. I just got back in. Hey! "...so that her intel-lectual mind could be removed from this. Because what many do not understand, nobody understands on this planet—and when we say nobody we mean nobody understands this fully— and the three of you will not understand it fully, but as we develop through and as we can continue to channel and as we continue to put the channel into trance, which she has not done for some time, understand that we will be bringing through information that has not been brought through, but we are bringing through practical information. We are not bringing through information where you will tell people and they will say, 'Yeah, so what?' There is so much information that is so true, that is so astounding about the universe, about the soul, about the journey, and people just don't care because it has absolutely no practical use in their life at this time. It's a sci-fi movie to them. It's something that is just, 'Oh that's great fantasy but how's that have to do with me getting a job, how does that have to do with me raising my kids? It doesn't have to do with anything…' So know that there are many that are curious about the mysteries of the universe and we are going to go into the mysteries of the universe, we are going into the mysteries of all of the things which you studied with the Mayan calendar. We can talk about these things. There are many undug-up facts in which you are unable to see because nobody can see them. So know that we are bringing in all this information. But what one must truly understand, and we will get back to the point of the spirit, is that you must look at, just as we have said seven minutes ago about the circuit board, about the mother board, what one must understand is your consciousness is something that is living inside of a spirit body right now, a light body, that was sent down to live within a layered human body, a physical body, a mental body, an emotional body, a spiritual body, an astral body, an etheric body. This consciousness is living within this human, but there is a spirit body that your consciousness lives in. Understand that your consciousness is not programmed, but the spirit body is programmed. So many people will say, 'I need to tune into my spirit so that I can know all.' Your spirit does not know everything. Your spirit… your spirit… is programmed to allow people to attack you. Understand that this is something that will go against spiritual teachings because nobody will want to say, 'Oh if you tune into the divine piece inside of you it will be a piece that is making you be attacked.' This is not how people want to see this. But understand with the multi-dimensionality of all the layers of self, what people must truly begin to understand is, as we begin to understand these lower senses of self, the bigger pieces of us, the higher dimensions of us begin to drop down into physical body. The physical body can access all layers of consciousness. But understand that your spirit, your spirit was programmed to be this way so you say that you feel that there is an attack on your life, you feel as if you are in danger. It is because your soul programmed your spirit to feel that way. So understand that many people will look at themselves as human beings and they will not be as open. They will not be as humble as you and say, 'I feel as if I'm being attacked my entire life, there is a piece of me inside of me.' They will be too proud to say that. 'That's a wussy thing to say, I'm not going to say that, because that doesn't sound calm and collected and cool. I'm not going to say that.' But understand that that's not Bill. It's the spirit that's in Bill that is programmed within the motherboard that is inside of you. So know that as we release this at this time, spiritual healing can be done on these aspects of people. And all of the things that have come from being attacked in your life will begin to subside and fall away. All of the cords, all of the people, all the places, all the things. All of the things which you have experienced in your life because of this programming, like a computer, will fall away as if they never existed before. But your soul that sent the spirit down into this body will have learned the lessons it needed to learn by having a spirit that felt it was going to be killed or attacked, or its life was going to be threatened up to this point in your life. Does this make sense?"

WILLIAM: Not only does it make sense, it seems very timely because if you look at the terrorism going on around the planet right now it's increasingly real that many people should feel that their life is in danger, because it actually is. And by having had this imprint from birth, I have much more awareness and understanding of the kind of determination and possibly over-reaction to protecting that the planet as a whole in terms of mass consciousness is experiencing. So I think it will make me a more effective spokesperson in dealing with these very serious and important issues about the balance between kindness and protection. Because we want to be kind to others but we must always protect ourselves.

CHAPTER FORTY-TWO
SELF PRESERVATION

MARISA: "Absolutely. And self-preservation is the key in the human game. Self-preservation is the key. And many will say, 'Help others, help others.' Yes, this is great, but preserve one's self first. Love one's self first. Otherwise one cannot love another. One will love another the way that they love themselves, the way that they were loved. Abusive energy will be love so they will abuse others. This is how things go. So understand that these people, this terrorism out killing... many of them are sheep. Many of them are human beings who do not know or understand or... Let's use children that join gangs as an example. They don't feel a connection with other humans so they find a family, they find a connection that works with them so that they feel wanted, so they feel needed. Many of the people that are joining these terrorist groups are people like this. And then children are being raised within these terrorist groups. But the core of much of the terrorism that is going on in this planet is a soul group gone rogue. A soul group that has decided that it's going to take the planet down so that the planet can start from fresh, and that the souls, the souls that are incarnating down here can start with a fresh new planet because of the corruption in the fourth dimension. The fourth dimension has so much corruption that the soul group says, 'There is no repairing this, no healing this, so we are going to just take it out completely.' But yes, you understand the fear of having one's life threatened. You understand this so you have the compassion for the planet at this time. So, many times when you have an emotion or feeling inside of you that was singular for your life and it resonates with something that the mass group consciousness for the planet is experiencing, your life will be affected by that. Your life will be affected. There will be the resonate energy of being harmed here in you and then in the mass consciousness of humanity up here, and you will get connected to it. So if you are feeling ups and downs, ups and downs in your days, and you are just not quite feeling yourself, please ask us, please ask your higher self, please ask me, to come in and release any energetic ties that you have to the mass consciousness of this planet. For understand that much of your energy is E.T. energy. You have lived on many other planets but you love Earth. You love Earth and this is why you continue to come to Earth. And there is much, much, much elemental energy within our soul group so there are many fairies and gnomes and magical creatures that are within this soul group, and they are tied to the earth. So much of your mood and emotions and feelings will get tied in with the earth. And since the earth is going through something so traumatic at this time, especially over the next 10 months, you will begin to see that your moods may be tied in with this and it's a very easy fix. Just ask us to release you from the consciousness of the planet. And it will not release you in a bad way. It will just release the cords that you have connected to those who are suffering. For when you see something on the news and you see people suffering, this channel may watch the news and say, 'Oh that's too bad.' You may see it and hurt inside and know what they feel like, and it will affect your day. Does this make sense?"

WILLIAM: Yeah. And one of the things that I think is very important when you talk about the rogue soul group that thinks that a better strategy is destroy human beings and start over, it's impossible. Because the imprint of everything that the human beings on this planet have experienced will remain even if every human being is destroyed.

MARISA: "And this is why they want to destroy it because it will take the planet into the fifth dimension and leave the fourth dimension behind. So it will take the awareness above all of the pain, all of the hurt. For the fifth dimension is where all the souls reside. So they will say, 'Leave all the fragments behind, leave all the emotions behind, leave all the stories…'"

WILLIAM: It's a short sighted solution because—

MARISA: "Absolutely."

WILLIAM: It's trying to get a quick fix—

MARISA: "Yes—"

WILLIAM: That ultimately will be self-defeating. Because it's only by unifying from the bottom all the way up through all the dimensions that you can achieve the true purity of the higher dimension existence. And so it's just misguided. It may even be well-intentioned. But that's why I think that we can be unambiguous because when you raise this issue, there are many people out there who may think, 'Ah, we're so terrible as a human species, let's destroy ourselves and start over.' You can't do it. It's not the most effective solution and so no matter how much you may fault what humans have done to date, it is better to work with humans and to ameliorate our mistakes in the best way we can as humans to raise ourselves to the highest level we can, so that we can in fact emerge into a higher dimension in a unified, integrated way as human souls connected to our higher souls, connected to the higher dimensions.

MARISA: "Exactly, exactly. And—" Here comes Peter. You know Peter is part of Saint Germain, that's why he feels so familiar to me.

WILLIAM: Is this Saint Peter?

CHAPTER FORTY-THREE
THE NATURE OF GOOD AND EVIL

MARISA: I don't know if he's Saint Peter, but he's Peter from the Bible, but he comes in. He's a total goofball. He's one of my guides. But he just came in and he's right under Saint Germain. So he must be part of that... Yeah, he says, "I'm part of the soul group." He says, "But I'm here to say—" He likes to talk trash... not talk trash, but he likes to expose the truth about other soul groups and things. He's kind of like, as my mom calls it, "chisme." He's the gossiper, kind of. But he says, "There is talk on this side that this rogue soul group wants for the earth to start over for the fifth-dimensional souls to start over somewhere else, so that that soul group can rule the planet. So they will rule the lower dimensions. And this is what's happened in the past when beings have fallen, so to speak. This is not necessarily 'fallen.' For what is good and what is bad. The fallen beings will say, 'We're doing what we want to do, that's what God made us to do, so we're not fallen, you guys are the ones that are fallen.' So there's really no fallen. There's no good, there's no bad. There's no evil. There's none of that over here. There's just energy. There's just different layers of consciousness. There's just beings. And understand that this rogue soul group has three beings at its head and there's over 3,000 souls that come from these three beings that create this soul group. And there are souls that are interspersed throughout soul groups and then there's a majority of them on other planets in other places that do not live on Earth, and this is why they do not necessarily care about Earth, because it is not their primary planet, it is not where they are from. It is a place where they say, 'Oh, we can take this over with our low frequency energy and these human beings that were oh so happy will not be happy anymore. They will begin to kill each other, and then they will start fresh. The souls that were living there will go somewhere else or they will go to a higher dimension and live in other places with higher dimensional consciousness and we will be able to inhabit the earth and do with it what we will.' "

WILLIAM: Well, this makes me believe that there really is good and evil in the universe because it seems to me quite an evil plot to not care, not have compassion, and just want the solution that is most convenient for that particular soul group, without taking into account the larger interconnectedness of all energies.

MARISA: "And look at when you walk over and you see an ant hill. You see an ant hill. These beings have consciousness, they have colonies, they work together, they create together, they carry massive amounts of weight load, they are hard workers, they get together. They are on a group consciousness together working together. And one will just come and step on it. This is the way that they look at the earth. Just step on it, it doesn't matter, it doesn't matter. It does not matter because we know that we are spirit, we are consciousness, we are just living in these little things down there. It does not matter because when we step on it, those pieces that we have created to live inside those human beings will just come right back to us. Because it's not real. It's not real. So they look at it as if it's not real, but we look at it—those of us who you may say are the good ones, the good ones, the soul group that is ours of those that are sitting in this room right now, and we are all part of this group—it's the group that is coming to this planet because we see the human beings as us. Because the human beings are who the human beings are because of us, because our souls have lived in them and reincarnated through them, and left our spiritual DNA, our energetic DNA, our physical DNA for generations and generations and generations. It's like playing a chess game and just taking all the pieces and throwing them on the ground when you're almost done and how are you going to start all over? Who wants to do that? That is something that is absolutely ridiculous and our soul group, the good ones, so to speak, are the ones that want to keep earth the way that it is. But yes, there is good and evil on earth. Yes, there is good and evil. But as you go into the upper dimensional planes there is not good and evil, there are just different energies. Sometimes evil creates good. Sometimes good creates evil. So it's very hard and many human beings want to judge this, and this is nobody in this room, but there are many human beings that are more religious, they are more structured, more organized and want to say this is good, this is bad, because it helps the human to stay on track because they feel lost. But understand that when you begin to remove the good and evil from the consciousness, from the mind, you begin to see much good in evil, and evil in good. But this is besides the point. So understand that as we come in here today we are bringing this understanding that, yes, there are beings that could care less about human beings."

WILLIAM: Well, it's like treating human beings as if we're just a colony of ants—

MARISA: Yeah.

WILLIAM: And who cares if we die or not. Who cares if we evolve or not. The reality is, at the perspective of the human beings with whom we are intending to communicate, there is good and evil, and it's important to be aware that there is good and evil, and to as much as possible, operate from the good. Now, I'm not disagreeing with the higher level reality that at the highest realms there is no good or evil, because it's just energy, and energy creating energy, and sometimes it's what we would call good, and sometimes what we would call evil, but since we're living at this dimension of humanity, and whether it's third or fourth dimension earth, we need to play by the rules of third and fourth dimension earth. As I always say, "If you're playing a little league game, you play by the rules, and during the game that game is the only thing that matters." It's the same if you're a human being and you're on this planet in the year 2016—the only thing that matters is the human realm that we're trying to project into the future in the most positive way possible.

MARISA: "Absolutely, absolutely. And that is 100 percent correct. Very well put and yes, yes, this is it exactly. We agree 100 percent." That was Saint Germain and Peter. It's funny. They keep melting into each other. That's interesting. No wonder I love Saint Germain's energy so much, because Peter has been one of my guides before I knew he was Peter from the Bible. He would just come in and say, I'm Peter! And then when we started doing those books it was like, oh, that's who Peter is.

CHAPTER FORTY-FOUR
JOY

WILLIAM: The other final observation... and this has been a great session... I think we should just add this to prior sessions and we have a complete book now... and my observation is, that it's the unique human personality that makes this worthwhile. The information that I have received I may have already known in my higher self and through my communications, whether they were in my awareness or not, with all these other wonderful soul beings and soul groups. But what makes it unique is the personal journey that I, as William Gladstone, a human being, have had, which enables me not to talk in the abstract but in terms of the specifics. Whether it's suffering from gout, or having had an older brother who is paranoid schizophrenic choke me from the day I was born. But having these experiences... and the positive experiences as well of seeing the joy of having a grandchild, seeing the joy of having great success, having disappointments—that allows this information to be manifested in a unique one-time-only way that is my experience, and at a higher level, a unique one-time-only way for the human souls that happen to be on the planet at this time. Even though there's over seven billion of us, seven billion experiences that we currently have had and continue to have are unique in this time/space moment. And yes, from the infinite perspective, seven billion is nothing. We have infinite time, infinite space, we can just destroy the earth, recreate it. It can go on billions and billions and billions of times beyond knowing. But what makes it uniquely pleasurable at even the highest levels of knowledge and awareness from the highest level spirits is the uniqueness of the time/space moment. Because even though there's infinite numbers of these, each one is what gives the true existence experience to the highest level of collective consciousness the unique flavor and joy of constant existence.

MARISA: "Yes, and you may look at each different world, each different earth, each different planet, for there are over 200,000 planets that carry a third, fourth, and fifth-dimensional consciousness where souls can say, 'I would like to live there because this is the consciousness in which I want to live in,' understand that each different planet, each different place, each different universe is sort of like a different amusement park. It is like a different amusement park. And look at it as souls will choose to build the amusement park. They will build, say, a Magic Mountain. And they will put in different roller coasters. They will put in different rides. And then after they ride them for a while they will say, 'Oh gosh, it's getting a little tiresome and boring here, let's put in some booby traps between each ride so that it will be a little harder to get to the ride, and then we will put some people in there that will distract us and tell us that the ride is not going to be fun, and that we should go over here, go over this place, or just leave altogether.' So look at each one as, yes, just as you have said, a collective experience where those who have created this planet are experiencing the fun of living on it. So understand that lessons are being learned while on this planet, but also souls are learning about new ways to make it a more pleasurable experience to live down here by putting contrast in. So this sounds kind of silly, but if you were to have a buffet of food that you loved every day, you would get tired of it. You would get tired and you would want to add something different, or you would want to add a challenge in getting to it, so you would feel rewarded for being able to get through this trap so you could get to the food that you enjoy. So, know that everything that goes into the creation of this planet is devised so that a soul can have fun. And yes, this sounds very silly because many people are suffering, many people have horrible lives, many people do not want to be here and they think their life is horrible. And even if they have a good life, so to speak. Even if they have people that love them, children that love them, pets that love them, a job that they enjoy, there is still always that missing piece inside of them. And that missing piece is the joy, the joy. Because they feel that life must be hard. They don't see that the challenges are actually fun because they don't see it from a soul level. So many people on this planet see it from a human level, which of course, we're humans, that's why we see it as humans. But understand as one can begin to see life from a soul level..." I just asked them in my head, is it of the spirit, the higher self, the soul, the oversoul? They said it doesn't matter. Just whatever is not the human. "...from a higher state of consciousness, we will say. If people can begin to see this from a higher state of consciousness they will see that the challenges are actually challenges so that the soul can have fun in learning and growing and expanding. So as we come in and do these sessions with the two of you, with the three of you, with the four of you, you will begin to see that we are bringing joy into people's lives. We want people to see that this life is joyful, it is fun. Because the root of everything, the root of everything, the seed of the soul carries an internal GPS system that will lead you. It is God. It is the zero point. It is Creator. It is Source. Whatever you may call it, but there's a piece of that oneness, that Source of all creation within every single human being because it is inside the spirit when the spirit enters into the physical body. So know that everybody is guided and led by joy, but many people are programmed to feel guilty by joy, to feel guilty if they are having too much fun, to feel guilty if they make too much money, to feel guilty if they eat too much good food. This is just how human beings are. And this is the challenge. It is not like, 'Oh I can't believe this person feels guilty and they can't make any money.' It's like, 'Oh, ha ha. Look at the contrast that they placed within their field so that they would be challenged in this life. Now they know that they do not have to feel guilty for this. They released this block and now they can be successful. So there are many challenges in this life and we see them as fun, we see them as fun. If things are not fun we do not do them. This is the way that we look at it from the fifth and higher dimensions. We do not do things unless it brings joy, unless it is fun. And even the deepest darkest hour on the earth plane is still an enjoyment to the soul that is experiencing this because it is learning, it is expanding, it is growing, and learning how to create, create, create. Because all souls want to eventually become creators themselves."

WILLIAM: This is music to my ears. I've always, I think even the original ending I had to my novel *The Twelve* was so that the one could go back to the artist that she or he is, of creating infinite pictures of ever-greater aesthetic complexities. Because my own intuitive knowing has always been the only real reason to exist is to experience joy, and that the ultimate divine recognition that each and every human being can make to his or her god, oversoul, whatever they're calling it, is to experience joy. Every moment that an individual is in their joy is a prayer to their higher self.

CHAPTER FORTY-FIVE
READING THIS BOOK WILL RAISE
YOUR FREQUENCY

MARISA: "Exactly. And one of the things that we want to make sure to feature in this compilation in which the two of you, the three of you, the four of you..." It's funny they keep saying the two, the three, the four of you. "...are bringing together, for all of these energies are combining, even the child's energy is combining within this session. This is why this channel is able to leave her body. For the child is acting as a guardian for the energy. So know that we are able to enter into her field to speak to you at this time for she has never trusted to do this, but the child, is protecting the energy and allowing her to leave. But know that what we would like to feature in these books is a short lesson so there may be a conversation and the reader may be reading through saying, 'Oh, this is very interesting about the higher self, this is very interesting about the soul groups...' What we would like to do is we would like to put little exercises throughout the book where the person can learn to connect to their higher self. If somebody is not connected to their higher self, if somebody is not connected to the joy that is not their human, so they're feeling their human, they are feeling their emotions, they're feeling their feelings, they are feeling their mental body, their emotional body, their intellectual mind, their ego, all of the things which they have experienced in this life, when a human fully experiences letting go and allowing themselves to be connected to even just a tiny piece, a tiny piece of their higher self, their life changes, their life shifts. And this is why spiritual awakenings are so life-changing for people, because just a little tiny bit, the higher self dips its toe into the pond that is the human existence. It dips it in, makes some ripples, and things change. And then as the higher self begins to integrate itself more into the human life, that's when the a-ha moments aren't so exciting anymore. It's, 'Oh, that happened before.' But in the beginning it's just so exciting. And those are the people who are going to be gravitating towards these teachings, towards these channelings, towards these books, towards the videos, towards the movie, towards the TV shows that you will be doing on the computer box. So understand and know that the people gravitating will be people that are already into spirituality. They are intellectually spiritual. They've read the books. They understand the books. They think they are spiritual but they don't know how to be spiritual because their mind is in the way. So three or four short exercises which we want to place into the field where somebody can meet their guide, they can connect with their higher self, they can clear their energy, and they can protect their energy. These are the only ones that we ask for this channel to place into these teachings in strategic places in which you would like them to be placed, Bill, so that it will flow with the material. But the reader will also be able to not only get the intellectual spirituality, but they will be able to stop while they are reading, close their eyes, and it will be as simple as imagining themselves connecting to their higher self and that is it. And they will feel shifts, they will feel changes. And this is what will draw them back to the teachings. It is not the intellectual spirituality that draws people in. People will go, 'Ooh, ahh, that person is so brilliant, that person is so smart...' It's how they feel after they read a book, how they feel after they hear a teaching that makes them want more. Because it's experiential. And the two of you in these books will bring experiences to these people rather than just the knowledge. The knowledge is fabulous; the knowledge is wonderful. And this will help others to believe and even humor themselves into doing these exercises. But know that we will be bringing experiential energies to them. And know that also we are setting up the codes within the field of the books that when they read them, their higher self and their guides will come in, so it is like an ON switch. When they are reading this book their higher self, their guides, are coming in—their guides only from their soul lineage, so there are no outside rogue guides that will be coming in—but when they open this book, when they read this book, when they are reading the teachings, their soul lineage is activated and it is coming into their field, and their life is changing. They may not understand why. And that is why you may place something in this book: 'By reading this book you were drawn to this book, you were brought to this book in some way, shape or form. You may be skeptical, that is fine, but by moving forward and understanding this you are opening up your awareness to a higher aspect of you, a larger piece of you, a piece of you that knows your life, a piece of you that knows your soul's purpose, a piece of you that knows the plan. So humor us and in reading this allow this piece of you in, allow the beautiful things in life to happen.' When you begin to see the same time on the clock everyday, you see 11:11, you see 12:12, you see 2:22, or you see the same word over and over, or you hear the same song over and over, allow yourself to begin to know that this is the higher pieces of you trying to get its way into that human dense consciousness that has blocked it out for so long. For there is a piece of every soul in the soul plane inside human bodies and they are sometimes blocked by brick walls. There is no communication between the two of them. It does not mean that God is not inside each spirit. It does not mean that God is not leading. God is in a sense leading each human. But the higher self wants to be a part of this, and this is the whole meaning behind living a multi-dimensional life within a physical body. It is allowing the spirit to connect with its creator, the soul, the higher self, whatever you may call it, and allow that information in to live a fifth-dimensional life on a third-dimensional planet. This is the way that the world is going and we want to bring joy to people, and this information we are bringing through will bring joy. They will feel it and they will know that their life is changing. And they will not say, 'Oh, you two changed my life.' It will be, 'My higher self is changing my life.' And that's the key. All of the spiritual teachers on this planet at this time, to a certain extent, want the pat on the back. And then there are the spiritual teachers that say, 'It is all spirit, it is all spirit,' and they take no credit, so they do not succeed either. So there is a good combination between 'Yes we are taking the time, we are channeling, we are writing, we are editing, we are putting the money into this, we are taking our time, our valuable time into doing this as humans allowing this energy through,' but also allowing the readers and the people that are reading to turn this over to spirit and allow them to know that it is their higher self coming through that is helping them; it is not the two of you that are helping them. And many teachers are like that. We will not get into names. We can go through and list many, many off the top of our spiritual heads here. But know that there are many that take the credit and this is when they get blocked, this is the downfall with spiritual teachers and the integrity of spiritual teachers. Not that they are out of integrity, but they begin to feel way more important and then we can't get through anymore. So this is why we have chosen this channel for the humility and the fact that she has been knocked down so many times in her life, that for the most part she does not even believe she is worthy of the information coming through her, and this is why we can get through. We do not say that we want her to feel unworthy. But this is why the information is able to come through. If she begins to feel self-important and feeling as if everybody is changing their life because of her, this is when we will not be able to get through the way that we are able to get through. And this is why we have been successful in continuing to get through her energy, because she does not remember the information that comes through, either."

WILLIAM: I just would like to make one comment since we started this book before Madison, Marisa's infant daughter, was even born, she was I think three weeks away from being born, and I think it's also important in terms of Gayle. Gayle has been present for all these conversations. And I think this is also important in terms of the way the world looks at the creative process. The reality is, the information is coming through our wonderful friend Marisa. She is humble because she doesn't even know what she is doing. I'm not necessarily so humble. I've got a pretty big ego about the things that I do know what I'm doing and that I've accomplished. In this particular space, however, I am in fact humble because this is all new to me. I don't consider myself a spiritual teacher at all; I never have. I'm okay with it if that's something I'm supposed to be in addition to other things. But my point is, that this creative process in this book includes… and when the guides are saying "the two of you, the three of you, the four of you," they're not saying it just to say it. The reality is, the energy that Gayle is holding, the energy that Madison is holding, are just as important. If they were not in the room at this moment, I don't think that the information that is coming through would be the same. And so I think that it's actually—I'm not going to list them as co-authors because they're not adding words—but they are part of the creative process. And the quality that is most striking with both of them is humility. Neither one of them, Madison particularly, since she's only six weeks old, or four weeks old, has no ego in this at all. And Gayle has never… you know, she's always behind the scenes. So I think that the fact that this information is brought forth with true humility and from a group, and that yes, we want to make our million dollars in royalties, and you know, we're going to enjoy that money, but that's not the primary motivation why we're doing this. I have other projects. Marisa has other ways of generating money. We're taking away from those other opportunities to put our energy here. So it's only appropriate that we are rewarded on a material level. But that is not our motivation. The motivation truly is selfless and humble. We would like to see a world of greater joy. We would like to see a world in which my grandson and Madison, you know, 70, 80, 90 years from now, are going around and having a great time and you know, recreating a great world for their grandchildren that they'll have at that time. So there really is a selflessness about this project and about this book. My feeling right now is that let's go straight to the exercises that we want people to learn so they can get in touch with their higher self—they do have some very specific exercises they can do. And I think just adding those exercises to the material we've already created will create the final book that hopefully we'll be able to start sharing with the world relatively quickly.

MARISA: "Absolutely, and this will complete this. Understand that, yes, Gayle's energy is a co-creator in this, for the two of you come from the same soul group. She carries the divine feminine; you carry the masculine. For the channeling which you are doing in bringing through the information from your higher self is being catapulted by her energy and connecting with you as a battery. She was acting as a battery for you each and every time and accelerating your vibration so that you can stay focused within the higher self. So yes, the information coming through would be completely different in the sense that the totality of that which I am..." This is Saint Germain. "...would not be able to come in. The lower aspect of me would be able to come in, but not the aspect which is coming in at this time would be able to come. Abraham would be able to come in. Others would be able to come in. But with a battery, so to speak, in this room to accelerate the energy—which is Gayle and her spiritual abilities, her spiritual gifts—raises the vibration of the room so that all of you can connect to that which is the higher dimensional planes. Yes, yes, and Madison has been, her soul has been accelerating the soul that resides within Marisa since two years prior to pregnancy. So she has been acting as a battery in the spirit plane without Marisa knowing. And this is why her abilities have shifted. This is why her abilities have changed. And this is why we have begun to—we will not say entrust—but we have begun to bring in more energies to catapult her into the eye of the public. For prior to that, prior to having this backup, so to speak, she was afraid. She was afraid that she would fail. So this fear of failure kept her in her office, kept her doing sessions so much that she could not get out and have classes any bigger than five, ten, twenty, thirty people. But we are now working with all four of you so that we can bring this information into the light. But everything has happened exactly the way that it needs to happen. Everything has happened in the steps it needs to happen. And understanding and knowing that all four of you are the creators of this, along with this, is something that is very important indeed. And thank you for bringing this point up because it is very, very important indeed. The exercises which we want to bring together, would you like us to bring these through at this point? Or would you like to—" Oh my God, there are so many guides coming in.

WILLIAM: Take a five minute break and then let's go straight to the exercises.

MARISA: Yeah, five minute break because there are so many guides coming in. Oh, they're not guides. They're spirits. Oh, Gayle, I connected with your energy. We need to clear these guys. They're just after you.

GAYLE: They always have been.

WILLIAM: Well, see I've always complained that Gayle is too kind. By being too kind you open and then you get distracted, and you can only save so many souls at a time. And you have a higher purpose which is far beyond the need of any single soul or spirit. And so you need to be protective of your energy and contain it, so you can direct it in a way that reaches billions of people rather than just a thousand or so.

CHAPTER FORTY-SIX
QUANTUM HEALING

MARISA: So in quantum healing we can go up into the soul level and we can ask why. So I'm asking why are so many souls connected to you, and it's because you were a shaman. You were a shaman in 18 lifetimes and the shaman... the shaman vowed for eternity to take on lost souls, cross them over to the other side, send them back into the earth, do whatever with them that they needed to do to send them back to Source. So you have this soul contract. So your soul thinks that's its job. It is not necessarily your spirit or Gayle. It's your soul believes that it's its job to cross these spirits over, which it's not, because it interrupts your life. And the only thing that spirits really affect in a human lifetime are our emotions because they can see our emotional body. So they're going to affect us emotionally. And then when we're affected emotionally, then our life goes to crap because we can't enjoy it, or we start attracting more negative energies because we're in a depressed state and we don't' realize it because our mind is saying 'I'm not depressed,' but really your body is in a depressed state because you have all these depressed spirits around you. So what we can do is... let me ask Mother Mary to come in. We're going to ask Source. Okay, so we're going to ask that a seal be placed around Gayle. The seal is going to be programmed with... any spirit that sees you is just going to get crossed over. They don't need to enter into your field. Okay, so they're putting a field around you. So we're going to ask God to go ahead and program your energy into understanding that it can have purpose without the need to cross over spirits, that it's still wanted, that it's still needed, that it's still accepted, that it's still important, that it's still revered, that it's still worshiped without, or free from, the need to cross spirits over. Your soul is getting a lot of like "oh I'm needed" by these souls coming to you. And it's not you. I mean it is you, but you know, it's a piece of you that really, it's not Gayle. It's your soul. So your soul is going, "Oh but I'm taking them all in, I'm taking them all in," but it's affecting you on a human level to a certain extent. So let's see here. So we ask that all spirits be removed from Gayle's energy unless they all be crossed over. Source energy is coming in and we ask that Source ask that any time a spirit sees Gayle it be crossed over to the light, sent back to where it came from, whether it's a fragment of spirit, an entity, earthbound, totem animals, fairies, anything. There's so much stuff, oh my gosh. And we ask that Gayle's energy be taught what it feels like to know and understand its importance in life, that it knows and understands that whether she is seen, she's important, whether she is seen, she's important. Understand and know what it feels like to feel fully accepted, fully loved and fully treasured at any time, anywhere, regardless of circumstances outside of her. There we go. Just pulled a big black plug from your back. Your ex did a number on you. And when you were 12 something happened. What is that? What happened when you were 12?

GAYLE: My brothers.

MARISA: Pushed you around, pushed you around, pushed you around?

GAYLE: Tied me up, played with me.

MARISA: Okay so let's release Gayle's need to be victimized, Gayle's need to be attacked and Gayle's need to have offenses brought against her that nobody else could possibly handle. Let's teach her soul what it feels like to feel strong and needed and worthy without having to go through these battles of people doing atrocious things to her. Because there are things that people have done to you that are just nasty.

GAYLE: Still.

MARISA: Yeah and it's still coming in and that's why they were wanting to remove it. So let's see. Here comes Archangel Michael. Oh you have the same guardian angel as me. We have an angel called Michael. It's not Archangel Michael. He's just an angel named Michael. He's a big blue firefly. That's how I see him. And he's coming in and he's infusing you with the energy and releasing the need to be attacked. Your spirit has the need to be attacked. Kind of like Bill. You guys attracted each other. You have the same energy there, which is funny because it's like two people that have been attacked, and you guys are like, "Put 'em up, put 'em up." But you're not the attackers. Neither one of you are. But you're both kind of defensive because you've been attacked so much.

GAYLE: Well, so actually it was a good thing because we recognized each other.

MARISA: Exactly. No, exactly because you're perfect mirrors for each other. Perfect.

GAYLE: I mean it served a purpose.

MARISA: Let me seal up the veil. There's a big huge rip in your field in the back where they get in.

GAYLE: Thank you. Thank you so much.

MARISA: Do you feel lighter?

GAYLE: Yeah, I felt a big sigh a little bit ago.

MARISA: Good, good. Yeah, they pulled the plug. It looked like a plug with tar coming out of your back and that was, I saw your brothers just like pinning you down and punching your chest and like tickling you beyond belief and like slapping you, and I saw a man. I didn't know it was your brother. That's why I asked who was that when you were 12. And then you know, the spirit inside of you, you have lots of fragments. So we just kind of reabsorbed… let's pull in all her fragments. Replace all her fragments. There we go. Ah there you go.

GAYLE: Yeah, and I think that Europe thing brought in a lot of spirits too.

MARISA: What Europe thing?

GAYLE: Where they had the big bombing a lot of people crossed. Because a boy… I don't know if that's it but I'm sure feeling a major event—

MARISA: See, we want to bring… you brought up into kind of like a… brought up off … Like they were saying with Bill is he's tied in with the earth's consciousness, too, so when you're starting to feel down and low and all those things… I mean these people can cross over without us. They don't need us to cross over.

GAYLE: Yeah, I'm not down with that.

MARISA: They need to find their own way. And the cool thing is, with the quantum healing we can program into your field. It's almost like "Oh, I see that. I'm crossed over." So it's like they're just crossed over from them even seeing you, you being in their awareness. They're crossed over so they don't have to enter into your field at all. So you'll feel a lot lighter and a lot less like frazzled. They're making you feel all ungrounded and frazzled. And remember I said I could feel you guys heading my way because all these spirits were in the house.

GAYLE: They were all coming in?

MARISA: Yeah. So now they're not here anymore. Yay! They're all gone. It's just you and Mary and then who's this? Annabel? Was she here last time?

GAYLE: She was.

MARISA: She's yours. Annabel is one of your past lives. She's like Rosemary.

GAYLE: Oh okay. So I hope she's a good one.

MARISA: No, she's… Is Annabel your soul? No, she's an aspect of your soul. She was a priestess in one lifetime. But she likes incarnating as the humble woman of a great man. Kind of like was her thing. And in this lifetime she kind of brings the appreciation of being able to relax and not have to be like "I gotta fight, I gotta fight, I gotta fight to succeed and achieve." It's more kind of like "I'm here to enjoy this life." But then she has all these other lifetimes where she was like a healer, she was magical, she ran all these circles and would heal all these people. So she was the aspect that was the oversoul over you when you had your center and you were healing people. And then she kind of took a step back. But now she is coming back in. Oh, she's your soul, she's your soul. Annabel. I mean you have Grace. Grace is like your oversoul, which I see as like, you know, there are 12 oversouls. Mine is Sofia. And I call yours Grace. But Grace created a bunch of souls. So Annabel is the name that all of us would recognize. She says, because we all lived a life together when she was Annabel. And all of us have this together, including Madison, including Jeff, including Bill, including Bill's son.

GAYLE: Good. That's why it's so familiar.

MARISA: Yeah, so we're all like "Oh hey, what's up?" And we were all part of the same village, and you and I ran in the same spiritual circles healing people with like crystals and stones and plants and herbs, and things like that. And Bill was a clergyman but he was like a corrupted clergyman and he had us killed. He had us dipped upside down in a well and drowned. Our feet are tied up and he's going "The world must abolish this nonsense...or this abomination..." And there are all these women lined up getting dunked.

GAYLE: Because we're all doing this spiritual—

MARISA: We were witches. Yeah. But he's like a clergyman. I don't know if he was corrupt. But he just thought what we were doing was really wrong.

GAYLE: He was just doing his job.

BILL: I'm sure I was corrupt back in those days. All the priests, there's a license for sex and—

MARISA: Yeah, I know. Exactly. I think that's hilarious. And then we live in this lifetime and he's part of our little clique. Who would have ever thought?

GAYLE: We've all cleared our stuff.

MARISA: Yeah, I know. It's hilarious if you look at it from a soul level.

GAYLE: We're not doing the witch thing either.

MARISA: I know. Well, they would have called this witchcraft back then, too, and all that. So it's just funny how the world has changed, and our souls just must think it's hilarious looking down and going like, oh my God, remember this? Remember that? But we don't remember and our spirits have amnesia.

BILL: Let me remind you, the world has not changed that much. There will be people who read this book who are going to say this is witchcraft and are going to totally reject it. And I do suggest that we keep a low profile and high security.

MARISA: Exactly... I'm going to go ahead and hit Stop on here. Oh that was good.

GAYLE: That was great. Thank you to the guides and thank you for the healing. I totally recognize what you said and what they were saying to me.

MARISA: Good. I don't remember anything I just said.

GAYLE: I appreciate it because I feel things coming in that are very distracting.

MARISA: You're a fourth-dimensional magnet and that's the shamans, they deal with the emotions and feelings, the spirit fragments, all that, and you have very shamanic energy. And so do I. That's why I feel it.

Part IV
Easy and Powerful Exercises

CHAPTER FORTY-SEVEN
GROUNDING AND CONNECTING TO HIGHER SELF

1) Find a quiet place where you will not be interrupted. This process can be done very quickly with your mind and imagination or you can take your time and enjoy the feeling of connecting with the magnificence of synchronicity by aligning with multiple layers of self and the divine.

2) Close your eyes and imagine that there is a brilliant ball of light surrounded by mist one foot in front of your face...

3) Breathe in this light mist through the nose, allow it to fill your body, and breathe out anything that is not for your highest and best good. Do this 5 times as you allow your body to relax.

4) Now take your attention to 2 feet above your head and imagine that a big bubble of light is there. This represents your higher self and it can be any color.

5) With your mind, imagine this bubble dropping down into your head where it will absorb your consciousness. You can see your consciousness as a little version of you, that looks just like you standing inside this bubble that will now continue, like an elevator, to drop down through your head, down through your neck, and into the heart where you will connect with your soul center.

6) Continue to drop down through the torso and down through the hips, the legs, and out the feet and into the earth where

you will continue to drop down through the soil and into the center of the earth.

7) There is a huge ball of light in the center of the earth that you will merge with. Take a deep breath in through the nose and out through the mouth. Do this twice.

8) Move back up towards the surface of the earth, enter back in through the feet, up through the legs, through the body, and back into the brain.

9) You are now grounded to the earth and in full alignment with your higher self and Source.

10) Say thank you to your higher self and go about your day or go onto the energy clearing and protection exercise.

CHAPTER FORTY-EIGHT
ENERGY CLEARING

1) Now that you are connected to the higher self say in your mind, "I now ask my higher self to remove all energies that do not belong to me, and any energies that are not for my highest and best good and send them to the light.

2) Imagine energy lifting away from your body and aura and leaving the room. Watch as the energy is swallowed up by a big portal of white light that represents Source.

CHAPTER FORTY-NINE

PROTECTION

1) Take your attention to the portal that represents Source energy. This may be above you, to the side, or in front of you, it does not matter where you see it.
2) In your mind imagine a golden sphere of protection coming out of the portal of light, dropping down into the room, and around your energetic field that spans about 5 feet above, below and to the sides of your physical body.
3) Allow this golden sphere to merge with your field by taking 2 deep breaths in your nose and out your mouth.
4) You are now grounded, cleared, protected and aligned with your higher self.

You may visit our website www.discoverintuition.com for a 5 minute free instructional video walking you through these exercises.

PART V
THE CONVERSATION CONTINUES

CHAPTER FIFTY

LIFE PATHS

MARISA: Saint Germain says that you have seven life paths, Gayle has three; I have four.

WILLIAM: Okay what does that mean, life paths?

MARISA: Let's ask him... Okay, Saint Germain says he wants to answer the first question about the astrology signs and he will make it quick, but he says, "Each soul chooses and decides what kind of make and model they would like to drive while on the earth plane. They choose life paths, they choose different soul mates and they choose different life partners. Life partners are not always of the opposite gender for love. Life partners can also be best friends. Life partners can also be business associates. Life partners are game changers for souls who have fallen off their path. These game changers will bring the soul back into the game. So, many times a soul while in a human body will meet somebody and their whole life will change. This is because that somebody is coming into their life to get them back onto their path, one of the lives in which they have chosen. For understand that the different demeanors that human beings have based on the way that the stars, the planets, the sun, and all the energies within the universe reflect upon the earth, these energies affect the mind of the human being. So if somebody wants to be born into a human being with a hot temper, they will be born into an astrological sign that has a hot temper, because this is something that they may want to work through in this lifetime. They may have been very passive in another life, and in this life they want to have a temper and they want to learn to get through and understand how to control their temper in a satisfactory way so that they can in essence check it off their list. But this is one of the human behaviors that they have learned to master. For you must see the earth plane as a game board and understand that each different human behavior, each different human experience is something that is within a checklist the soul wants to experience and they want to master." He says that you have seven life paths. Gayle has three or four. Is it three or four?

WILLIAM: You said three before.

MARISA: Yeah but it's like there's a fourth one kind of like… that's weird. Okay so here is Saint Germain. We'll start with Bill. He says, "The seven life paths are very, very similar to each other. For understand that one of your life paths is very, very, very different from that which is the life paths that you have now. For there is one life path in which you would have never gone into publishing. You would have gone into teaching. Teaching only. There is another life time where you would have gone into film. Film only. There are other lifetimes. All the other lifetimes are where you entered into publishing at the age that you entered into them. Each of these different life paths have ended you—" Hold on. You have so many guides here. Let me just talk to Saint Germain. C'mon, just Saint Germain. Your higher self wants to talk. Your higher self actually has stronger energy than Saint Germain's energy. It's very, very strong. I've never seen your higher self come in this strong before. He says, "If somebody's going to ask about my life path, I will share my life path. For I am the one that created these life paths. He does not know about my life paths." And he pushed him aside and he flew.

WILLIAM: Saint Germain we're pushing aside?

CHAPTER FIFTY-ONE
BILL'S HIGHER SELF SPEAKS

MARISA: Yeah, you pushed... but it's you and you're about 40 feet tall wearing all white, kind of like a yogi or something like that. You know the pants, the button up shirt and the linen... "I am the one that chose the life. I am the one that chose the path. I am the one that chose this time. For what you must understand and what this channel does not understand is that—" He says, "May I? May I step into your energy?" And I said, hold on, let me ask my guide. And Jesus just popped in up here, and he says, "Yes, you may step in." "For I have chosen this lifetime indeed and I have chosen this time. I have chosen this time and space. For what human beings and what this channel does not even understand and the teachings which she has brought through to students, to herself, and to her own understanding, is that we can choose a time, a time on the earth plane. Time does not exist on this side, so in essence one can be born into the past. This does not make sense. It does not make sense within the human mind. The human mind will say, 'Well, what if I am living in the future and then I am born into the past, the past has already happened, the future is already happening, and then I change something, then everything will change?' What one must understand is that no, this is not an illusion, but the timelines are illusions indeed. For there is a soul living on the earth plane." He says, "Hold on, let me start this over, let me explain this in my words." I'm just going to channel him directly. I'm not going to do trance. They're going to let me leave. Nice. Okay. "As a soul decides to take an incarnation on a planet, one will first decide what do I need to learn, what would I like to learn, where would I like to go? There are many different planets, 63 in fact, that are local to this universe. Sixty-three planets that serve up some of the experiences that the earth plane serves up. Understand that the earth gives duality. The earth allows a soul to experience life in a fairly civil being, a fairly intelligent being, but also deal with having something within them that makes them want to destroy their life, that makes them want to get in their own way. This is the human mind, the human ego, the human emotions. Please know that the earth plane is a very, very challenging planet to live on. Many will say that earth is the hardest planet to learn on. I believe—" And this is your higher-self—"I believe that earth is the most intriguing, for I have lived on many planets, many places, and I have been many things. Earth to me is the most intriguing. For you will look and you will see many different creatures, many different types of beings, many different types of energies all living in the same type of being. For other planets there are beings that are not the same type of being, but they can communicate. It would be like a human talking to a dog in the same language, or a dog talking to a hamster and then having tea with a human. This is how other planets are where the souls are born into different creatures but can all communicate. On the earth plane, creatures communicate with other creatures like themselves but many different types of souls can incarnate into the same creature, so you may look upon someone and they are from another planet, another place, they are an elemental or fairy being, or there is an angelic being living within a human being, or there is just a human soul that was created to be a human living in a human. For there are all different types of creatures living in human beings. And this is why I find it quite intriguing indeed. For each lifetime that I have lived, I have been a seeker, I have been a seeker. For I know the answers on this side. I know the answers on this side. But when I enter into the earth plane—this is the most interesting thing indeed—I do not allow myself to remember. I do not allow myself to remember pictures, I do not allow myself to remember past things which I have done in other lifetimes, for I have lived this same life that I am living right now six times. I have lived it, because

I find it so amusing, I find it so fun to find out the mysteries of the universe. This is my favorite thing to do. My favorite thing to do is to find out things that other people don't know, and I find these and it is very satisfying. This brings an emotional freedom to me in a human being that others may not find in figuring out mysteries, or finding out knowledge that one has wanted their entire life. For I was born with wanting knowledge, with wanting to be intelligent, with wanting to be smart, but also with finding clues and discovering things that other people cannot or will not ever know. Please know that all of my life paths lead down ..." One of your past lives just came in. Hold on. Okay, go. There we go, okay. "... All of the paths lead to this point, all of the paths which I have created lead to this point right now at this point in our lives. Please know that this life is very satisfying for me at this point because I am able to connect with the human aspect that is me, that is Bill. For I am not Bill; I am the energy, I am the self, I am the soul that created the spirit that is Bill living in Bill. But as he ascends and as he, as you, allow for the higher aspects of yourself to enter into the physical plane, you are now bringing in so much information, so much knowledge that you have been wanting, that you have been needing your entire life..." Saint Germain just came back in. He's basically going on about how... hold on. "... Last time we incarnated we incarnated in the year 2364. We incarnated in this time because this is when the world comes to a point where all of the consciousness, all of the awareness, all of the human beings on the planet are able to connect with the upper dimensional aspects that are them and bring in energies from upper dimensions, but it just is not as fun, it is not as fun to live in a planet where you can connect with all the knowledge that you've ever had. There is just no point. This is the way that I see it. Others may not see it this way." He stopped. Do you have a question for him?

CHAPTER FIFTY-TWO
CONFIRMATION FROM 2016 BILL

WILLIAM: Some observations. One, it's very interesting that I wrote the novel *The Twelve* in which, at least at the time, I was not aware I was being divinely guided at all. And I created a character who represented all of the knowledge and the creative force of the universe who incarnated and had no memory of anything. And this was the path that had to be followed in order to unite the human beings which happened to be the twelve, so that they could bring forth the energy and the awareness that was prophesized by the Mayan and other indigenous cultures to ensure that the end of the Mayan calendar, the end of the 26,000-year period, would bring greater awareness and a higher vibration; not the destruction, not the physical destruction of the planet. So number one, yes, I totally identify with this higher self and it's reflective of my personality because I never want someone else to speak for me, even someone as noble as Saint Germain. So I'm very comfortable with my higher self coming in and it resonates with me that I could have seven pathways in this life and it wouldn't have really mattered which one I chose because I'd be exactly where I am at this point. And what was reflected by the higher self I respond to. I did consider very seriously being a teacher and being a college professor and I was actually on that path. I went to Harvard University to get a PhD in anthropology and that at the time was the only possible use of a PhD. I also took a position in Hollywood at a very young age after making *In Search of Ancient Mysteries* and could have easily have had a very, very lucrative film career. And for reasons having to do with ethics and goodness, at that time Hollywood was not a place I wanted to be. So the comments about one life path would have been film, one would have been teaching, one would have been publishing at a different time— they all ring true. And I think that the guidance that even had I made one of the other choices, which I could have made, and another Bill would have made, would have still brought me to this place. So I'm very comfortable with where I am. I do feel my life is blessed. I also respond to the observation that this is a more interesting time than 2364 because it's more challenging, it's more intricate. The mathematics that need to be parsed to achieve total unity of communication is much more problematic and difficult, and therefore much more rewarding. It's like playing a golf course that's very difficult when you're a very good golfer. There's much greater satisfaction in getting a birdie on a really difficult hole than a really easy hole. So I totally resonate with my higher self, and confirm that this is ringing true on every level.

CHAPTER FIFTY-THREE
FREE WILL RULES

MARISA: And there's no way I could have known that you would have been a teacher or worked in film. There's just no way. That's amazing. I'm going, "Whoa!" And what they're showing me is... so the higher-self is stepping forward and showing... and he looks just like you, which is a crack up. He's you but he's huge, tall. And he keeps looking down right in my face because what they do is they touch my energy and then I'm allowing them to take over and kind of talk. That's why I kind of stutter. Because my consciousness keeps trying to whip back, and I'm like, "No, stay out." So, anyways he's saying, "Imagine this and you will be able to relate to this. You will be able to relate to this because this is part of your soul grouping. Your soul grouping is that with Saint Germain. And understand that when a soul looks upon the earth one will look and say 'All of these things happened on the earth but what if I went down and I discovered something. How would it change, how would it change indeed?' For there are many, many very wise, very intelligent beings that work with and understand different theories such as string theory, such as quantum mechanics, such as quantum physics, where the act of observing is what makes something happen. Perspective is what the world is. The soul is perceiving through that which is a human being. But understand if a soul can perceive prior to incarnation something they can in essence create a split, a split. So let us try to keep this very basic, for we can speak in very complicated terms but this channel is asking us to keep this very simple. So, imagine that there is a movie, there is a movie. Everything that has happened, has happened, and that is how it is. There is the beginning, there is the middle, there is the end, there is the plot, there are the characters. Imagine if you could watch the movie and say, 'But what if somebody discovered America right there? What if they discovered America? What would happen?' And a soul can choose to incarnate into that story and go be the one that discovers America and see what happens. There are so many different parallel alternate universes, there are so many different 'this' happening in many different places, and many different places all happening here. This is a very hard thing for a human mind to understand, but if you look at life as a movie, you may see that a soul can look upon this and incarnate at different times. For the soul which you are from discovered America. This is Christopher Columbus, indeed. This is what the channel and Gayle were speaking of yesterday. So when one soul decides that it wants to discover something, it does not mean that it will discover it for sure. It does not mean that it will happen for sure. But there is a chance, there is a gamble that the soul will stay on track and this is why guides, this is why angels, this is why us as higher selves are so invested in connecting with the aspect of our self that we create that is living in a human body. You may look at it, you may look at it as the soul that we create, just as we have said in other conversations, is like a clone of us. But this clone does not know everything that we know, as this channel has thought in the past. For understand that the clone is made to only know what we want it to know. It is made to have beliefs, it is made to have flaws, it is made to have things within it that will cause it to do certain things while it is in the human body. For we cannot make the human that the aspect of us lives in do anything because of free will. Free will is the biggest rule, for the lack of a better word, on the earth plane. Human beings have free will, and we cannot make our human counterpart do anything. So understand that we can plan these lives, and we set our clone free, and then we wait for the clone to come back and discover that we exist, so that we can plug in and say, 'Hey, you were supposed to be over here' or 'You were supposed to be here' or 'You were supposed to be over here.' And this is why miracles happen. This is why people have spiritual awakenings. This is why things happen in lives where people just do not understand, and then all of a sudden their life is completely different, and it's because they finally plugged back into the source that created them, and that is the higher self. For many will think, many religions think that God is their higher self. Many religions believe that when their higher self... many characters that created religions believe that when they were visited by their higher self or reconnected with their higher self, they were connecting with God. There are many layers, many layers of us and the true goal of a higher self is to reconnect with its spirit fragment that it has created to make the life that they want created."

WILLIAM: I have a question to my higher self. You're with the Council of Twelve, or you are reporting to one of the members of the Council of Twelve? I'm talking about the ultimate Council of Twelve that have responsibility for the creation of the universe.

MARISA: "We are definitely part of one of the council members. You may look at the council members as oversouls, as energies that are able to create other energies, and we are part of one of these energies. For we are part of one of the original creators of the souls that were on the earth plane. Understand that we have not lived many lives on earth in the recent years, in the recent 2,000 years, because of the fact that we do not enjoy the consciousness level of the human beings for the last 2,000 years. We enjoy it a little bit in the future, and we enjoy it much, much, much in the past, but we enjoy Sirius very much. We enjoy living on other planets very much. But yes, you can say that we are a part of that council if you want to say that what created us is one of the council members. There are also many other councils, though. There are many other councils and you have seen one of the councils that will come into you. There is a council of three that helps to manage your life path, your specific life path. So this council is for the spirit that lives within Bill. So let's call this spirit Bill. This is Bill. So when Bill's physical body no longer exists, Bill's spirit will be here. We will still be separate

261

but the same, and then Bill will eventually re-emerge with me and become one with me. So I am him, he is me, you are him, he is you; we are all one. But we are different aspects. And there are many councils, many councils that live within the ethers, that live within the astral planes, that live within the universe, that will help to dictate and help keep souls on their path."

CHAPTER FIFTY-FOUR

BILL'S RELATIONSHIP TO SAINT GERMAIN

WILLIAM: And what is the relationship between my higher self and Saint Germain?

MARISA: "We are of the same soul. So you may look at a soul as a being. You may look at this as a being, as a creator being, and this is a highly advanced soul that made it to a point where it could create souls of its own. So you may look at Saint Germain as, in human terms, your brother. You are brothers and you are very similar in the paths which you take. The two of you resonate very much so with each other, but the energies, the energies which the two of you are, are not the same being but created by the same being. So like brothers. But understand that when tuning into higher aspects of yourself as myself, the two of you are tuning into the same thing. So this higher self that we're talking to is also Saint Germain's higher self." So what they're doing is, there's a higher self of Bill here and then there's another one, and they're kind of going back and forth. I think the one that I'm talking slower with is the one that's up higher, and then there's one right here. So there's different layers of you.

WILLIAM: So would it be that the second to the highest, highest self is at the same level as Saint Germain as a brother, and there's a higher self of Bill's higher self, who happens to be the higher self for both Saint Germain and my higher self?

MARISA: "Yes. This is the way that I will put it." Let me…the soul's coming in. "I am the soul, I am the soul of Bill, basically. I am the one that remembers all of the lifetimes. I am the one that remembers all the lifetimes in which we have lived in all universes, all places, all the dimensions, all of the parallel universes, all of the lives which we are living right now. I am the soul. My soul brother would be Saint Germain. We exist in the fifth dimension. We are fifth-dimensional beings. There is an aspect of us that is sixth-dimensional, but as sixth-dimensional beings we share this same layer of our body as does everybody in this room. The seventh dimension would be the soul that created the two personalities that are Saint Germain and Bill's soul. So this seventh-dimensional soul is a shared soul by you and Saint Germain. So in essence, if the two of you are standing next to each other on the earth plane in human form, if you were to tune into your fifth-dimensional self, you would have different information, different memories, different resources, different personalities. You go up to the sixth, you would be pulling on the same Christed resource, the same school, so to speak. It would be as if you were in a university and the university had a master hard drive that stored everybody's experiences, everybody's knowledge, everything that every single person that is in that school has experienced and done. It would be like a hard drive for this Harvard University. So there are many different universities throughout the universe. There are many different schools. Each of you in this room share the same sixth-dimensional school, and the two of you both go to this school. The seventh, if you two as humans were able to completely embody your seventh-dimensional self at the same time, you would be the same person. You would be pulling on the same resources. You'd be pulling on the same knowledge. And this is the way that you and your grandson are. You have the same information, resources, that you are pulling in from upper dimensions. And this is why you feel so connected."

WILLIAM: And this reference to 2364, that's a future life where Saint Germain and my higher self soul cohabit and is that a time that is inevitable because of what's happening now, or a time that was inevitable no matter what happens now?

MARISA: "Ah we are getting tricky indeed." Here comes Saint Germain. "Ah, we are getting tricky indeed and asking the questions and understand that, yes, this is a time that is inevitable in this universe, in this time, in this reality. For understand that if you were to step out of your body, come back over here, and plan another life, you could go into a different time, into a different reality where that did not happen. But yes, in this reality it is inevitable. It will happen. It is a time that is coming. For you to choose to be born within the same timeline because you want to play–just as you have said, golf— you want to play the same course because you want to see how you are going to do each time. In the case of golf you remember how you did last time. You remember you hit it into a sand pit and you got a bogie. You remember this. So you say, I will not do this this time. But understand that you are challenging yourself even more where you're not wanting to remember that there's a sand trap there, where there is a body of water there, where the par is almost impossible to get on this one unless you hit it this way with the wind. So understand that you don't remember these things because you want to challenge yourself. But yes, in the future you and Saint Germain in essence are the same being because the consciousness and the awareness of that which is the planet is able to tune into seventh-dimensional aspects of themselves and embody them. Does this make sense?"

WILLIAM: Yes. Though one question that I've always had because of the concept of infinity, infinity really is difficult for human beings to understand. On the basis of infinity and the cosmos and the structure that through this wonderful channel has been outlined, isn't it inevitable that every single human soul will eventually experience every single human experience and share in the sense that we are all one, an aspect—so yes, in this reality that we're experiencing, I'm William Gladstone, I'm Bill; Saint Germain is Saint Germain. But isn't there another level? I don't know whether it would be called a deeper level or a shallower level, but a level on which every single human entity eventually is Bill and Saint Germain?

MARISA: "Yes, yes. And we may look at this as the dimensions in that everybody on the earth plane at this time shares... Well, we will say the souls that are supposed to be here, the souls that are supposed to incarnate here; not the souls that have hijacked auric fields or souls that have incarnated into human bodies that do not understand that they can be hijacked. Understand that the souls that are supposed to be here, that have chosen to be here, all share a ninth, tenth, eleventh and twelfth-dimensional body. For they are all one. So if the human beings on the planet had the capacity, had the ability to open up the auric field and allow that high conscious level in, everybody would be the same person. Does this make sense?"

WILLIAM: Yes, because one of the reasons I asked the question is I personally as Bill am very interested in the destiny of Bill, and the experiences of Bill. But I'm hoping this becomes a book that is of universal interest. And I think it's important for the reader to understand that we're really talking about them. These happen to be the circumstances of this one Bill personality; but it applies to everyone.

MARISA: "Yes. Absolutely. And everybody can see that, everybody can see. And this is the reason why we have chosen to bring all of you together in this room, and we speak of all four of you. We have chosen to bring all of you together because three of the life paths which you have bring this team together and the ability to ground the energy which we are bringing in through this channel, the ability to amp up the energy so that we may connect with this channel, is something that we will be able to bring information in for everybody. But understand that when many people learn about things, they learn best through example, they learn best through other people's examples. So yes, this is speaking of everybody who would be reading this material. Understanding and knowing that yes, they have many different layers of themselves and they are in essence a clone or they are in essence a creation of their higher self which is who we are speaking to at this moment that is Bill's higher self. So they may know that they have many life paths and if they see or feel as if they are completely off their path, all they must do—and we make it sound very simple, but understand that simplicity is key here, simplicity is key—all they must say is, 'If I am not on my life path, I now give my higher self permission to facilitate this.' Be ready for changes, though. One must be ready for changes. For many human beings will say, and this is what they sound like when they pray, they say, 'Dear God, dear God, I really want this job, I really want this job really bad. But if I'm going to have to sit next to somebody that smells and I'm going to have to sit next to somebody that whines and complains, then I really don't want the job. But I really do want the job, but I don't want the job. But then I don't want to have to be gone from work and I don't want to be gone from home, and I don't want to not see my kids, but God I want the job.' So this is what many of us higher selves have to listen to all day. This is what we listen to. So understand that the prayers with which each spirit pleas to God go through the higher self and into universal consciousness which is God, Source Energy attaches onto the prayer, it's shot back down into the auric field of the human as a delivered message. 'I want a car' goes up through the higher self, higher self decides if this is part of the life path. If this is something that is going to fit, goes up to God, comes back down as an energetic signature into the field–so once it's 'I need a new car,' now it is projecting out to the universe that a car must be manifested. So this is the way that the energy works in very, very simple terms. But yes, human beings for the most part do not know what they want, and if they do know what they want, usually if they are within most of their humanness, they think that their plan is better than the higher self's plan, even though they are their higher self and the higher self was the one that made the plan—and the human beings will sometimes sabotage the plan that is trying to come through them."

CHAPTER FIFTY-FIVE
THE DARK NIGHT OF THE SOUL

WILLIAM: Very interesting because I did go through the dark night of my soul in my mid-twenties where I had come back from Hollywood where I had been asked to procure cocaine as a part of my assignment, which I did not feel was appropriate, I had left Harvard University because, although everyone loved my PhD thesis they said I had to go back and put in footnotes, which I thought would be a big bore, and I left publishing because my father had sold the company to a company that I found very boring to work with. So I was between things and not sure what to do and started to write a novel, *Suicide Plus*, which may someday be published. And it's called *Suicide Plus* because I was definitely having suicidal thoughts. I really was very unhappy at the time and I do remember during that time someone leaped from six floors above my apartment to their death and I kind of felt guilty in a way that they had caught my suicidal urging, or maybe I had just been empathetic with their suicidal urgings, but what I did, and which totally got me out of the funk—not in that second but over a period of weeks or a few months—was I just wrote next to my typewriter—these were very old times before we had computers; I was writing a novel on a typewriter—and I just wrote "Thy will be done." And I just let go of any... Because I was so confused. I had no idea what I really wanted anymore and I just turned it all over to my higher self. I didn't think of it as my higher self. I didn't necessarily think of it as God either, just as a higher source of energy, the universe, because I wasn't particularly religious.

MARISA: That was your guide Michael. "That was your guide Michael that spoke those words to you over and over and over for 19 days. Thy will be done. You wrote these words and this was an energetic signature that allowed us to enter into your field and make changes. This was quite a beautiful time indeed because in essence we had been entering into your field for nine months prior to this, and as the energies got stronger and stronger and stronger coming in, trying to change things, trying to get things back on track, this is when many people listening to this or reading this begin to feel such a struggle inside… People can be unhappy, people can be happy. When you are unhappy and happy at the same time, this is when human beings begin to say, 'There must be something else. Why am I feeling two ways, why am I feeling two ways? I'm going crazy, I'm feeling crazy.' And this is when the higher self, the guides can be used as a resource to remove either the happy or unhappy to get the human being back on track. And yes, this began to get you back on track. It took years, it took years and much assistance from us on this side, but understand also that this dark night of your soul that you speak of was part of four of your plans."

WILLIAM: Well, they say it's a beautiful time from the perspective of the higher self, but I can tell, so that other people won't think that they're crazy either, that the actual experience when you're going through the dark night of the soul is not a happy or fun time or beautiful. It's very painful. And I can share that when you come through it, life is lighter and more beautiful. But going through it in and of itself from the human perspective is painful.

MARISA: And Abraham says, "And each person must go through pain in order to succeed in a sense on the earth plane. But what we want readers to know is that pain is not necessary to learn, and pain is not a test. Many people believe that God is testing them. Many people believe that they are being tested. So things like the death of a child, things like losing your job and your family going poor and the kids not being able to eat, that this is God testing, testing to see if you can make it through, to see if you can do this. No, this is not God testing. This is the higher self, you, planning to go through these things to experience how to get through them, or to just experience them, to just experience them. Imagine being, place yourself in the mind of your soul, and see that each thing is just an experience. And yes, just as you have said, things are very complicated while in the human body. But when you can look from the soul perspective and see all of the things that come from it like hardworking, humility, new ideas, new passions, new emotional understanding of things, this is something that you will be able to see the soul is succeeding within. And this brings us with..." This is Abraham and Anabel "... This brings us to Gayle for just one moment, if we may. For the three life paths which Gayle has lived, they are all exactly the same. The reason why we show, and many people that may be reading this will understand, that sometimes when they are feeling conflicted about things, many times the soul will begin to bring in a separate life path because it will choose to change the life path once the soul is within the human body. So there are many people who you will see who are living a life. It is a good life, it is a fine life. And all of a sudden they just change. They may even change their name. They may change their hair, yes, they may change the way they dress. But they will just completely change the person that they are because the soul will say, 'I learned the lessons faster than I thought I would, now I need to create a different path.' And this is what the soul is choosing to do at this time for Gayle in understanding that many of the lessons that needed to be learned on the paths which you chose were learned three years ago, and a new path is being created now with more complicated lessons, so to speak, but in a sense they are not more complicated. The soul is more advanced at this time. But understand that by choosing to create this fourth path in essence, all the things which were unresolved from the other paths are going to enter into this path and sometimes can seem quite overwhelming. So what one must fully understand and recognize within one's self is 'I am flawed, I know that I am flawed, and when I'm flawed it is my human, it is not the spirit.' Because many insecurities may pop

up over the next nine to ten months as this new path is being created. For the soul decided that it wants to understand and feel and
be within the healing energies of other humans, within the healing
energies of children, within the healing energies of animals again,
whereas with the other paths this did not exist anymore."

GAYLE: Thank you.

CHAPTER FIFTY-SIX
UNDERSTANDING PAIN

WILLIAM: Just a comment on the pain. I'm not one who ascribes at all to "no pain, no gain." I think that's very silly. I don't think pain is necessary at all. However, I do observe that the majority of human beings can't seem to escape significant pain in their lifetime. In many cases it's towards the end of their lifetime with illnesses and with reduced capacities. Dementia is certainly very painful, lung cancer. Things that are quite painful. I know that I'm still experiencing a little bit of this gout, which on a big scale is not a big pain, but I'm still wondering why it's lingering so long and what we talked a little bit about the lesson of the gout, but I'm still a little bit wondering. And I do see the dark night of the soul that I went through was really on a wider human scale not much more than just a little bout of gout. It wasn't a severe amount of pain, relatively speaking. But I do wonder about the role of pain and you mentioned that the higher self chooses the experiences just to have the experience. So is it so that a human being can be more compassionate to other human beings and more empathetic with the pain that seems part of the human experience? So if they could just explicate a little more about whether in general the purpose of pain, or the specifics of my gout.

MARISA: "With pain there may be many different types of pain. There may be many different types of pain and everybody in this room has experienced pain, even the child. So understand that pain, yes, exists in all different layers of the human existence, whether it be the mental body, the emotional body, the etheric body, the physical body, the astral body. All these different layers experience pain, so to speak. So Bill, you have come to understand the human experience, yes. Gayle, you have come to understand the human existence but also the coming of the human experience—what one wants to understand while they are in the human. So on a vaguely different level you want to understand this and have had experiences your entire life to draw you towards this. Now, pain in the physical body such as what you are experiencing at this time is brought upon by the pain not being released from the other layers, not being caught in the mental layer, not being caught in the emotional layer. So many times lessons, emotional lessons, are programed within the spirit that they must learn in this lifetime or there are things that were experienced in another lifetime that the soul or the spirit wants to work out, and these things will start to rise up within the field as if they are a computer program. It will say, 'The spirit, the human is at this certain vibration, this frequency. The human will be able to survive through this gout through the anguish of this right now, and they will learn humility, they will learn about healing, they will learn about emotional release, they will learn about not letting others take advantage, not letting others stab one in the back, not letting others take advantage.' This is the energy that surrounds you, energies of women as we have talked before, taking advantage or demeaning you in some way, and coming at your energy in a way that you have allowed in the past. And at this point in your life, now it is not okay. And it does not mean that you lash out upon these people, but this is just an old resonate energy that is being released at this time. So this is happening so that you can see it and then in the future it will not be an issue. So understand that pain comes from not being released, and the pain usually comes from a life lesson that was very important for the soul to learn. So you are learning this lesson, you are learning this lesson and allowing to release it by seeing that the pain is there. Does this make sense?"

WILLIAM: It makes a lot of sense, particularly given that just recently a former employee is trying to take advantage of me and in the past I might have allowed it, just because I don't care about these people. But I'm taking a very firm stand and not allowing the abuse, the disrespect, and the unfortunate consequences of giving people things they don't deserve.

MARISA: "Exactly, and many times, many times in your life, both of you, many times in both of your lives, you will give unto others when they do not deserve. And this does not mean that you are God and you are the judge of what they deserve and what they do not deserve, but you are the judge of what energies you are willing to give away of your own to others without them deserving them, so to speak. So this is something that was a lesson which you are continuing to learn. And yes, you are beginning to put your foot down, and this is the beginning of the end of the energies which you are releasing at this time. For this is a lesson, a very hard lesson which you have had to learn throughout this lifetime. Allowing others because you just don't want to put your emotional energy into it, like you don't care or 'I just don't care about this,' so you shut down and say, 'I'm not going to deal with this,' but then they get their way. So understand these are energetic cords which you have connected to the root chakra so this became physically aware to your mind. You became physically aware of this through the gout. The energies will continue to release over the next few weeks, but understand that there is a party, a party that became connected to you 18 years ago that causes the flare up to continue, and it's connected to you, too, Gayle."

GAYLE: Eighteen years ago...

MARISA: Well, Gayle your —

WILLIAM: I didn't know Gayle 18 years ago.

MARISA: No, your 18 years ago person—

WILLIAM: Is a different person?

MARISA: Is a different person, okay. And then somehow Gayle, your energy is mixed in with it somehow. So I'm cutting it.

GAYLE: Well, that would probably be the divorce at the time. Or maybe someone who passed over when I was in the music business.

MARISA: It's just an energy that you have that's similar to their energy. Not that you're like them, but like, say it's like your energy gets reminded of that, and then it causes a flare up of the connection over there, and that's just a cord. It happens all the time. Like if Jeff, my husband, does something that reminds me of my ex, then an old cord to my ex may flare up or something, you know. So there's something there… I don't know. But they just cleared it, which is cool.

GAYLE: Oh, thank you.

MARISA: Yeah. So it's Bill's 18 years ago. Not your 18 years ago. There is some energy in your field from someone or something that basically brought attention to that. It's very strange. It feels very catty, gossipy-type energy that's connected to him.

GAYLE: That may have affected our relationship?

MARISA: That may be affecting you guys, yeah.

GAYLE: Yeah, absolutely. Yes, I know what you're talking about.

MARISA: Oh, okay.

GAYLE: That would be an old energy bringing suspicion to our energy.

MARISA: Okay, got it, yeah. And that's what's attached to his foot right now. It's like "plunk" on his foot. Poor foot.

GAYLE: I actually feel it, too, that connection, but it has to work itself out through his discoveries, I would think.

CHAPTER FIFTY-SEVEN
THE KEY TO THE UNIVERSE

MARISA: But the thing is... here's Saint Germain, he says, "But once you have the key to the universe, once you have this key..." It's this big key and he's spinning it on his hand. "... Once you have this key..." And he's tossing it and kind of juggling it, turning it into three keys. "... Once you have this key to the universe, what you must understand is that you can cure yourself with the snap of a finger, you can cure yourself with the blink of an eye. And this is the information which we love to bring to human beings. We love to explain to human beings, but human beings need to be willing to look at their stuff, they need to be willing to look at it and not get so upset or so defensive, or so offensive, at the fact that they are flawed, and the fact that other people see their flaws. For I work with many beings, many beings, and they say, 'I am spiritual, I have ego—' "

WILLIAM: Well, Saint Germain tell us... we won't resist. We're listening.

MAIRSA: He's like what my mom says, he's in here ready for the "chisme." That's like the gossip. He's like, "Many human beings, many human beings will say, 'I want to be spiritual.' They will tell everybody, 'I am spiritual.' They will tell everybody, 'Yes, I have ego and yes I will let this go, and I will do this,' but they look in the mirror and they are not happy with themselves. But then they look at others and they say, 'I am happy with myself.' So there are these two conflicting ways that human beings are, and it is very hard for us to

WILLIAM GLADSTONE AND MARISA MORIS

enter in and remove energies if one will not admit that they have them. So when we enter into the planes of existence of a human being and we want to help a human being release something, they have to be willing to let us release it, and they have to say—and this is why prayer sometimes works when people say, 'God please release my flaws' but it doesn't work if the person doesn't know their flaws and they are not able to admit that they have flaws. Like this channel will admit, 'I need to be right, I need to be right at all expenses. I will argue because I need to be right.' And this is the human aspect of this channel. But then when she begins to feel this rise up she can laugh at the human and say, 'Hey, look at me, I'm trying to be right, right now.' And this is a human being calling themselves out on their stuff, and this allows us to come in and release the energy that is causing the human to be the way the human is being. Does this make sense?"

WILLIAM: Yes.

MARISA: "So there are many energies that humans may be reading about this they have within them and they may say, 'Me and my husband fight all the time because he needs to be right and because I know it all, I know it all.' And they know that's there, but the husband will say, 'You are a know-it-all!' And they will say, 'I am not a know-it-all!' And they will say, 'No, I am not.' And they will work the whole day to prove to their husband that they are not a know-it-all. So much of their day is completely wasted trying to convince someone that they are not something that they know they are inside, if only they could just say, 'Saint Germain, Mother Mary, higher self, Archangel Michael—whoever it is that this person works with—please come in and release from me on all levels the energy that is causing me to feel that I need to know it all.' And actually allow this energy to leave. This will make human beings happier because it will release the energies, not only from this lifetime but from other lifetimes, and it will release energies from past people, places and things, and cords. For one may feel as if they need to know it all because they had a parent that was like that. So if one can say, 'Higher self, please come in and release the energies that are causing me to feel I need to prove that I am not a know-it-all, because I am one, please release these energies...' These energies will be released, most likely a cord to a parent, most likely to kids that may have teased one because they didn't know it all, because they were dumb in second grade, or in their mind they were dumb. So many of these things will be released and people will change. But people don't like to change because they don't like to admit that they need to change." Mother Mary just came in because he said Mother Mary. So Saint Germain is in here to play now. He's like, "I am here." He says, "I am sending down energies to each and every single person in this room because we are here to talk about the plan for the planet. The plan for the planet is that each human being becomes self-aware. Each human being becomes aware within themselves that they have a path, a path that they may follow, but they also have a higher aspect of themselves that can put them back on this path. Once the planet knows this, once people can be aware of this, that is when the planet will change. Many people will be able to relate to 'I have a bigger version of me somewhere that is helping me and guiding me,' rather than 'God is guiding me and leading me.' Because the biggest question that I am asked by individuals through their subconscious or individuals that channel or individuals that can see me and hear me is, 'How are you in all places at the same time? How can everybody talk to you and how can you hear everyone?' And sometimes I will kid and say, 'I only listen to the ones that I want to,' but that is not true. That is not true indeed. For understand that the aspect of me to which you speak, there is a human aspect of me, there is the spirit that is me which this channel is able to communicate with and which is the more playful, rascally as she will call it, piece of me, this is the fifth-dimensional aspect of me. But there is a field, a morphic field that is in essence a hard drive, of all of the information which I know, which I have, and many people are communicating with that. It is like talking to the artificial intelligence within the iPhones, the Siri. It is like talking to this. You ask it a question; it answers back. How is Siri everywhere? Siri is in all of the phones, but there is a consciousness that is Siri. So understand that every single being on the lower dimensions has a consciousness, has an aspect of them that can be communicated with and that people can communicate with, and this is the consciousness that you may call my higher self that comes into my field, and I am able to communicate with. So we have described our frequencies as radio stations in the past, and this is the best way to put it. Everybody can be listening to the Saint Germain radio station and everybody, no matter how many people, can be listening to this, will hear the same thing, but they will hear it differently. Based on people's understanding and experiences and their perspective on life, they will hear the same message differently. But I may be in up to 1,288 fields at one time. I am working my way up. I am working my way up, indeed, but in 1,288 fields I can be present. Otherwise, you are kicked over to the hard drive, so to speak. Does this make sense?"

CHAPTER FIFTY-EIGHT
THE MAYAN CALENDAR AND THE
NEW VIBRATION

WILLIAM: Sure. Now, let's get into some of the specifics that have been bandied about by other spiritual teachers of late including the belief that at the end of the Mayan calendar, December 21, 2012, the planet entered a new vibration, and how this relates to what other spiritual teachers have been talking about in terms of the earth has averted the prophecies of Nostradamus and other spiritually aware individuals and that we are moving from the third dimension to the fourth dimension to the fifth dimension. And what does this really mean on a practical level, since for the majority of human beings there was no difference the day after December 21, 2012 and the day before?

MARISA: "The practicality behind this is that thoughts are more powerful. This is a very simple, simple answer to a complex question, indeed, in that as the dimensional aspects of a human being are shifting into a higher aspect, imagine a hard drive on each dimension, and each hard drive as the dimensions go up exists within each other, so the fourth dimension exists within the fifth, the fifth within the sixth, the sixth within the seventh, all the way up into the upper dimensions. So understand that as human beings are given the ability to tune into higher aspects of themselves, not only is more information coming into the subconscious mind without them realizing it, not only are new talents from other lives past that their spirit's hard drive may not have had in it, they may be accidentally tuning into their soul's consciousness that remembers how to play the piano, that remembers how to play hockey, that remembers how to run a marathon. So people will get different interests and they won't know where they came from. But the most important thing about this shift, the most practical thing about it, is manifestation. Because the higher the dimensional aspect of a person that they are able to embody, the higher their frequency, the higher they are able to exist within their chakra system, and the more they are able to manifest. But this is not just for good. There are people that say, 'Oh, my life is horrible. I'm just waiting for the other shoe to drop. Things are so good but I'm just waiting for something horrible to happen like my dog's going to die, or something.' And then the dog dies. And this is their own making. Some may say, 'Oh my gosh, I just knew this was going to happen,' and it happens. This may be a little bit of intuition on some people's part because in addition to manifesting negative or positive thoughts that are within the human beings' mind and subconscious mind, and these things manifesting much faster than they were even a year ago, these things are manifesting much quicker. But understand and know that people are more intuitive, people are more tuned into the upper dimensions, and understand also that practically— and this doesn't sound practical because we speak of spirits—look at spirits as energy packets, as little packets of energy and emotions and hard drives floating around with all the life experiences of that person that is now no longer in a body. This is floating around in the fourth dimension. If a human being was only third-dimensional but now they are ascending through the higher dimension, now that the Mayan calendar has struck, so to speak, and the earth is shifting and the consciousness is changing, it is because the human beings are plugging into a different higher consciousness. But now many people who were not visible before to the spirit world are visible. And they are being affected emotionally. There are more suicides today than ever. There are an increasingly large number of murders. There is more domestic violence. There are more things going on, on the planet at this time, that are emotionally fueled from people who were not emotionally fueled even a year ago. Many of these things are, yes, spirit-possessions, so to speak, for the lack of a better word. This is a church term in essence. But the hard drive of someone who is not alive anymore is entering into the field of a living being and their hard drive's information is getting all mixed up with their information, so people are confused about who they are. There are many beings on this planet now who believe that they were born a girl and now they need to be a man, because they have the hard drive of a man that has entered into their field, because they are now visible to the fourth dimension. There are many, many, many things that people will diagnose as things that are becoming more and more accepted, but these are actually the byproducts of the dimensional shift on the planet and people being open to the energies that have always been around them, but they have never felt or they have never consciously been aware of. And this is part of the mission of all of you—to bring an understanding to the unseen. Not in so much of a spiritual way, not in a woo-woo way, not in a religious way, but just in a… there are energies that are unseen. There are energies that are unseen that are affecting everyone, whether they are spiritual, whether they are religious, whether they pray, whether they don't pray. Whether they are completely unspiritual, un-energetic, they are being affected by these things because if they are not being affected directly, one of their family members is, and they are connected to that family member and the energy transfers between the two of them."

WILLIAM: Well, so raising to the fourth dimension enables manifestation to the unseen energies. But is it necessarily good from the perspective of the human being? Is the fourth-dimensional planet a better planet than the third-dimensional at the lower frequency? Because just as you have mentioned, the evil gets manifested much more rapidly. More suicides, more murders, more horrific behavior. So is this progress? Is this an evolutionary step forward, or is it neutral? Or is it even a step back?

MARISA: "It is a step forward. Let's use an example, indeed. Let's imagine that there is a maze and there are human beings that want to go through this maze. In the third dimension they would go through this maze with their eyes open. They would be able to see if you need to step over a puddle, if you need to step over a trap, if you need to turn left instead of right because you're going to hit a wall. The eyes are open. This is the third dimension. This is physicality. Human beings enjoying, the souls within these human beings enjoying this maze that they are going through. It is a game, it is fun. They say, 'Oh, I was here before. Oh let me do this, I'm going to go this way and I'm going to get to the end and it's going to be lots of fun.' It's not just about getting to the end of the maze. It's about the experience of being in it and the challenges that come with it. If there are creatures or there are people that are within this maze that are made to confuse the people and say, 'Oh, go this way. I think you're supposed to go this way,' and the person falls for it and they end up in a dead end, these would be considered maybe like spirit beings, earthbound spirits that are confusing people. But they can see them, they can see them so they just avoid them. They do not experience them. They go, 'Oh, that's someone that's messing with me. I'm going to go this way.' Now understand that fourth-dimensionally the human beings in essence are kind of blind, so they do not know that those people are there tricking them. The people that are there tricking them are saying, 'Go this way, go that way,' and it sounds like their own mind. Their eyes are closed and they go, 'Okay, I'm going to go that way.' So they get confused. They think it's their own self getting lost, but they are blind, they cannot see. So understand that in the third dimension everything that was affecting the spirit within the human body was seen. It's able to be seen. The fourth dimension is unseen. It is not something that most human beings can see. Many can feel it and they are affected by it, but they cannot see it, and many will not even admit that it exists. So understand that things like emotions, feelings, spirits, entities, all sorts of spiritual beings can affect the person in that maze, cause them to just stand still in fear. Because all of a sudden they are scared for their life because something is there threatening their life or something is there making them depressed or making them sad, but they cannot see what it is, and they will not even admit that it's there. They just think it's themselves, so they are standing there in the middle of the maze and they will never make it to the end. The fifth dimension would be: There is a little silver cord that leads each person through the maze to the very end to where they will be reunited with their higher self. So the higher self is in direct line communication with the human being the entire time. The human being knows, the human being allows the higher self to embody them and to live life through them, but it is just not as exciting when you're living on a planet that requires density to have all of the challenges. So the third and fourth-dimensional worlds... it is not as exciting for the souls that enjoy that type of experience, where they want the challenge. Like yourself, like all of you in this room. There are planets that are fifth-dimensional where many souls will go to create inventions, to create music, to create things for third and fourth-dimensional planets where those things can then be channeled into the souls and the spirits that are inhabiting the human beings that they belong to. And these beings will say, 'I've come up with an invention to get me through this maze, it's an epiphany. I've just come up with this amazing invention that will lift me up over the walls and I will make it to the finish line before everybody. And this is an invention that I just came up with...' But really it may be a higher aspect of them that has created that and is channeling it down into the human being for them to discover, so to speak, to help human beings make life easier. Does this make sense?"

CHAPTER FIFTY-NINE
THE TIMELINE

WILLIAM: Yes, and I want to help the readers a little bit here with a time line. So let's start at the beginning, the creation of Earth. We start out, I assume, would call it dimension one, the Earth, just as a planet without any human consciousness?

MARISA: "In essence, yes."

WILLIAM: I mean it's a barren rock and life just sort of starts. So we start at what I would call the level of the microbe, perhaps.

MARISA: "Yes."

WILLIAM: And that could be dimension one. So at a certain point as we have the development of animals, that I assume would be the beginning of dimension two when we have creatures and plants, but with limited intellectual abilities? Would that be correct?

MARISA: "Yes."

WILLIAM: And the time line for dimension one was how many billions of years?

MARISA: "Three hundred and sixty-two billion years."

WILLIAM: Three hundred and sixty-two billion years was dimension one? And dimension two, before the emergence of intelligence, cognitive self-aware life on the planet, was how many billions of years? Or was it only in the hundreds of millions?

MARISA: "This is an interesting question in that there are many different phases to this in understanding that there are many different parallel dimensions within themselves. So do you speak of creation of consciousness, or do you speak of physicality?"

WILLIAM: Physicality. Consciousness within an ape or a relatively more self-aware creature.

MARISA: "One hundred eleven million years ago is when this first was established on what would be considered the earth plane. But there was physicality on other planets in other spheres within the universe, and even worlds that were very similar to Earth that were created much longer ago."

WILLIAM: Okay. For most readers, because many of our readers— and I want to be as inclusive as possible—I'm assuming that many readers really can only fathom Earth as their environment and not complicate it with the interactions with life on other planets, alien interaction. And I'm not asking readers to necessarily accept that any of what the guides have been telling us is specifically quote "truth," though I'm beginning to trust it. Now so we have...? What was the number again, for the dimension one, was how many billions?

MARISA: "Three hundred sixty-two billion."

WILLIAM: Three hundred sixty-two billion years? And for 111 million years we had the evolution of evermore self-aware complex life forms.

MARISA: "These beings would not... the first ones would not be self-aware. They would be more as consciousness testing itself to see if it's able to live within density."

WILLIAM: More like a plant or an amoeba?

MARISA: "Yes. A plant, yes."

WILLIAM: Which is why it would take so long. So when we have the emergence of mammals, I would imagine that's the beginning of dimension three?

MARISA: "Yes, the mammals, yes. Dimension three would be mammals. There are aspects of the mammals, so to speak, that are part of the second dimension, but this will get fairly confusing if we go into this because part of the consciousness in each human being is also part of the earth, is also part of the second dimension–"

WILLIAM: Right. You bring with you—

MARISA: "Exactly. It's housed within."

WILLIAM: The experience which was inanimate, which was dimension one, the animate which was dimension two, and then the ever-increasingly self-aware human which is dimension three.

MARISA: "Exactly."

WILLIAM: So, I'm getting—I'm trying to keep this very simple. So, dimension three started approximately how many millions of years ago?

MARISA: "Sixty-four million years ago."

WILLIAM: So it is millions? Because, as you know, the archeologists, and I've studied at Harvard in this field, have not documented human life more than 10 to 20,000 years ago, and even when they go back to the Australopithecus and the pre-human hominids, it is less than a million years. So explain how it can be sixty-four millions years?

MARISA: "Sixty-four million years ago is when the first…" I'm doing a teleprompter. Is it homo sapien?

WILLIAM: Homo sapien.

MARISA: "When the first…" I'm reading what they are saying here. "… Sixty-four million years ago when the first homo sapiens were tested on the planet, this is when you may look at… we are going to make this very human, very linear. We are going to make this very easy to understand. You may look at the Council of Twelve that sit upon the planet and say, 'We will see if the consciousness which we create that is us, the awareness, like it is in these physical beings.' For sometimes the frequency is too high of a consciousness or awareness to exist within a physical being. It just does not work. There is no sync or rhythm. So sixty-four million years ago many will say the human body is so magnificent, it is so magnificent. It works on its own, it thinks on its own, it breathes on its own, but many things had to be tinkered with. So, sixty-four million years ago, this homo sapien type being was not what human beings are at this time. You may look at it as though these are cars. You create the first car and it's not anything like the current cars now. So the human bodies have continued to get better and better, but not because of the common thought of many thinking 'apes became humans and humans are evolving.' This is not necessarily the case. This is a lot of the changes, a lot of the tinkering, so to speak, is done from the consciousness from the Council, from the beings that created Earth and that created human beings."

CHAPTER SIXTY
THE LIMITATIONS OF THE
DARWINIAN PERSPECTIVE

WILLIAM: So let me ask this question. Number one, this puts Darwinism and evolution into a relatively minor category of relatively minor adaptations, and nothing truly significant in terms of creating the great chain of being. More importantly, it also would explain the gaps in the archeological record of great civilizations that may have existed tens of thousands or even hundreds of thousands of years ago, which disappeared and no record was left. If we have a sixty-four million year time span, if this is correct?

MARISA: "Seventeen times the earth has destroyed itself. Seventeen times."

WILLIAM: When you say the earth has destroyed itself, the human consciousness element destroyed itself, because the physical earth, I assume, did not destroy itself?

MARISA: "A couple of times, and we say a couple we mean two, there were major plate shifts within the earth and the earth did in essence become a big pile of lava using this channel's vocabulary. Understand it became molten lava. The planet became very hot, indeed, because the inside came out upon the surface. This was twice. This happened twice. The last time was a little under 10 million years ago. So know that between the 64 and the 10 million years—"

WILLIAM: There's no trace of anything.

MARISA: "Exactly. So it is like starting completely fresh. From this time forward the earth became what the earth became now. So you may say that the archaeologists may find things that are going back, but they do not have the ability to carbon date, so to speak, these things yet because they have found things but they can't process them as how old they really are, if this makes sense."

WILLIAM: Yes.

MARISA: They're trying to use my brain. They're using really big words that I don't understand. So they're showing these machines and they're showing rocks or physical matter that they're putting in there, and it's like 32 million years old but it says three million or something. It's like cut off or something. Like they don't have the ability to differentiate between this old and this old. They just come up the same. Oh, interesting. They're showing the ice caps. Is that like Antarctica, up there, the North Pole? The ice caps have ancient civilizations within them. "There are many that are frozen within this, for the earth was the other way. So what is cold was hot, what was hot is cold. And many things shifted. So there are, if one was able to melt many of the ice caps in the most frozen areas of the world, there would be temples, there would be castles, there would be homes, there would be structures, and humans would be able to see this. And it's very quite fascinating, indeed."

WILLIAM: Well, since we are experiencing global warming it seems to me that it's only a matter of time before archeologists will discover such structures.

MARISA: "They will discover some, but they will never discover all of them, for there are many that are very deep down within the seas, within the waters, and there are many, many, many places where there were structures, where there was humanity that are under the oceans now. And this is why they are undiscoverable, because it is too deep for people. It is much easier for humans to go into space and find things than it would be to go into the depths of the ocean where there was civilization prior to there being water there."

CHAPTER SIXTY-ONE
THE CIVILIZATION OF TIAHUANACO

WILLIAM: Two of the most famous civilizations of recorded human history are the civilization which is in Tiahuanaco, which is near Lake Titicaca in Bolivia. (And there was an investigator who felt that that was actually the oldest civilization.); the other one being, of course, the Egyptian, where we have the great pyramids. Is there any information that can be shared relating to these two civilizations?

MARISA: "These civilizations are true, have existed..." Do people question that they didn't exist?

WILLIAM: No.

MARISA: Okay.

WILLIAM: The question is, which first? Which one is older and was there communication from one to the other?

MARISA: What are the two names again?

WILLIAM: One is Tiahuanaco in Bolivia and the other is the pyramids of Egypt and the Egyptians. So one was in South American and one was in the Middle East. So it's really was there—

MARISA: They are exactly the same.

WILLIAM: They are the same civilization?

MARISA: They're like the same, yeah. Because I'm asking what one was older, and it looks like the – what is the Titicaca one?

WILLIAM: It's Tiahuanaco.

MARISA: Yeah. Tiahuanaco. That one looks a little tiny bit older. They're showing it to me on a map, like a chart. They're showing me the earth. And they're showing that it's like a little tiny bit. But they existed at the same time.

WILLIAM: And what approximate time frame was that?

MARISA: They're showing those... I'm seeing 32... there's no way that's 32,000 years.

WILLIAM: Yes, it is possible.

MARISA: They're showing 32,168.

WILLIAM: Yes, that would have been the Tiahuanaco in the plains—

MARISA: And then the Egyptian comes in a little bit after that, but they existed at the same time. It wasn't like Lemuria got wiped out and there was Atlantis. It looks like they existed at the same time. They could fly back then.

WILLIAM: Yeah. Well this is very interesting—

MARISA: Oh my God. They could fly back then. They're showing planes flying cargo between them.

WILLIAM: Yeah. Well, because in my investigations I had found similarities. I discounted— I have to give props when I'm wrong—Zecharia Sitchin, the great scientist philosopher, who wrote about Tiahuanaco and who claimed it was older. I questioned it because he also said a lot of other things that I never believed, so I discredited him when I shouldn't have. But in any event, I visited as a young man, and there's certainly elements of that civilization that prompted me to explore in greater depth the Mayan calendar, because it was my intuition, or perhaps it was my higher self, telling me that what is popularly known as the Mayan calendar was actually developed at that time because why would you have a civilization develop a calendar of 26,000 years that had the calendar ending in less than 2,000 years? It wouldn't make any sense. So I've always postulated that the Mayans were the popularizers of a calendar that had been created by a more ancient people and my assumption is that the roots of those people are the people from Tiahuanaco.

MARISA: "Yes, and they were the channelers of this information. For understand that the calendar which was the Mayan calendar is a consciousness calendar. It is a calendar that brings about shifts and changes within the frequency of the planet and this is what it was based upon. But understand that this was brought in from higher aspects of the souls living on the planet at that time. So you may say, and I know we are keeping this very earth and human and linear and human, but it is other-worldly. It is otherworldly in which this information... it is all mathematics. It is all mathematics. It is all numbers. It is all ratios and equations and all of these things that make the world tick in terms of frequency, in terms of time, in terms of consciousness. So this information, yes, was all brought in 42,000 years prior to the Mayan calendar ending. This was information that was brought in on what you would call scrolls or parchments of information that were kept within pyramids that were kept within thrones. There was the original information that was entered in from the higher self of the founder of the original idea of this calendar, and the scribblings of what the calendar would be were placed within the throne of that king. For it was a king who was able to speak and communicate with God."

WILLIAM: This actually makes a lot of sense because I've known that it was impossible for pure observation of the stars, which is what proponents of the Mayan calendar have maintained, that it was because of great focus on the constellations and great observation that they were able to develop the Mayan calendar.

MARISA: "It was proven because of that but it was not based on that."

WILLIAM: Well, that's exactly my point. But there's no way the calendar itself could have been created based on those observations alone unless you had extraordinary instruments of observation, and if you had such extraordinary instruments of observation you would have had to have a much higher civilization than even the Maya, which is why I thought it was from a prior civilization. At the same time, the ability to communicate directly with higher souls would be the least complicated explanation for how that calendar could have been created. And as I believe it was Einstein and many other scientists have stated, the best explanation to hold is the one that is simplest and requires the least amount of complication. So this rings true to me and does help resolve some of the mystery surrounding the Mayan calendar. The other question that is related to this, and why I mentioned the Egyptian civilization, is the role of the pyramids in the development of human civilization, and the role of the pyramid today. How old are the actual oldest pyramids on our planet?

CHAPTER SIXTY-TWO
THE PYRAMIDS AND ANCIENT TECHNOLOGIES

MARISA: "There are many different pyramids, many different civilizations. There are many different pyramids that are covered by water. There are many that have not been discovered and there are some that are underground now due to shifting of the planet. There are even some that have been grown over with forests. This shows how much the climate has and will continue to change, going from desert, going to growing rainforests over what used to be desert, what used to be sand. So the earth has shifted very, very much. So… Eleven thousand years ago brings about one of the pyramids which has been discovered, one that is studied very much. But understand and know that going back to the Mayan calendar it was not the Mayan calendar. The Mayans were the adopters of this calendar. This calendar is very—and again, we will try to keep this as human as possible—but brought in by other-worldly beings. But they were not aliens with antennas and five eyeballs around their heads. This is not what they were brought in by. They were brought in by humans who lived somewhere else. It is like bringing in a way of thought from America to China, and then China saying, 'Oh, we really like baseball and hamburgers and hotdogs. We're going to adopt this as one of our own cultures.' So this was taken on by the Mayans and we only understand the Mayans so we call it the Mayan calendar. But this is something that existed before. There were also—and we must say this now—there were also instruments that were great and that were greater than that which we have now in the earth's history, but not at the time when the calendar was created. We just wanted to clarify this because there were two statements made in one question in essence because there were the telescopes, for the lack of a better word, but they were not used to make the calendar. But they did exist prior just for those who are interested to know if there was technology prior to our technology age. We sometimes chuckle at the technology age that is on the planet at this time because it was technology that destroyed the planet last time—it destroyed the humans and many other creatures upon the planet last time. It is the technology that got out of hand and the humans that used the technology fueled by the human emotions to destroy the other human beings. So technology has gotten out of hand in the past. And this is something that we hope will not happen in this round. But as the world plan goes—because not only do humans have a soul path, the earth has a soul path—this is not something that is planned for the humans to destroy themselves any time soon."

WILLIAM: Well, this is very good news. When I was doing my research for *In Search of Ancient Mysteries*, I came across samples of what looked like laser surgery performed at least 400 to 500 years ago in the Peruvian Andes. Was I correct in confirming that it was some form of very sophisticated surgery, or was I mistaken?

MARISA: "Yes, you were correct. There are many technologies, many technologies on this planet on this world that many people do not know about. There are many who can communicate with upper planes. There are many who can communicate with the outer planes and bring through technologies that people would not believe even existed prior to 10 years ago."

WILLIAM: One of the other mysteries that we investigated was the creation of Sacsayhuaman in Cusco where you have enormous rocks weighing in some cases 10 tons fitted together so that even a razor blade cannot be inserted between the rocks. My assumption at the time was there had to have been ancient technology that allowed this and it was not just human labor putting it together.

MARISA: "What we would like to bring in is the abilities that a human being has that maybe nobody in this room..." The person that we're talking to right now is Thoth by the way. Thoth. He's in here. He's the one that started talking a little bit ago. "... What human beings don't understand fully is their ability to move things, their ability to walk on water, walk through walls, and see this as a matrix. There is a famous movie called *The Matrix* where the human beings realize that they can defy gravity, they can move at hyper speed, they can dodge bullets because they realize that their full alignment with their upper-dimensional body allows them super human powers. So know that the planet was an upper-dimensional planet at one time and this is when the structures were created. So know that many beings from other worlds, many beings from other planets came to inhabit Earth because Earth was in essence a new planet. There were creatures called humans on it, just like their planets had humans. And they decided as souls to incarnate on this planet. At that time Earth was created as a fifth-dimensional planet. At that time if you thought about something, it appeared. If you thought about a place you went there. You could move, you could manifest instantly, and that is the direction in which we are moving at this time. But human beings have so many beliefs and so many beliefs that gravity is real. You cannot float, so this belief is much stronger than 'I'm a fifth-dimensional being living in a human body. I'm going to float.' This does not work. But Jesus Christ was able to walk on water, yes, he did, because he was able to embody his upper-dimensional body within his human lifetime. Anybody can do this and this is why he came—to teach people how they could do this, but they worshiped him instead. So understand that back, back, back millions of years ago when the planet was fifth-dimensional, these rocks could be moved with the mind, these rocks could be placed together when human beings would get together and all focus their attention on moving this or placing this, or building these pyramids. This is how they were built, because of the dimension that human beings had access to. Human beings were still third-dimensional. Many people who study the dimensional effects on the pyramids, on history, will say human beings were fifth-dimensional, human beings were spirit bodies, human beings were higher selves living on a planet. No. Human beings were still third-dimensional just as we, you began to go through the different dimensions. The human beings were third-dimensional. They had access and were able to embody their higher bodies to move things, to manifest, to do things the way that we would think would be magical at this point, like walking through walls or floating or levitating. There are many people that are able to embody higher aspects of themselves and levitate at this time. There are many people that can do many things that the human mind would not understand as being realistic, and it's because they are embodying higher aspects of themselves. And this is where the world is moving in the direction of. But this is how things were created in the past because there was a higher dimension that we had access to as human beings."

WILLIAM: Well, from an evolutionary perspective then, are we really going forward, or are we going back?

CHAPTER SIXTY-THREE
THE GREAT FALL

MARISA: "We fell, we fell 23,000 years ago, we fell very, very hard, very hard. For understand that we were fifth-dimensional. We were able to heal by touch. We were not sick. We were not angry. We were not an angry civilization that destroyed each other for our own pleasure, which is what human beings are like very much so at this time. Even the kindest person in the world will have a day that if somebody that they are close to is having a bad day, and they are having a good day, inside they will be happy that they are the one having the good day—which is how human beings think. Which is fine. This is a human feature. It's survival of the fittest. It is the last man standing. The one who is going to survive is the one who is going to survive that can cut others down and that can survive on their own. This is the way that the human consciousness was brought to this planet 23,000 some odd years ago, and was brought to this planet. And the humans at that time were affected by this and began to destroy each other. As they began to destroy each other and take on more third-dimensional aspects and began to develop more of the ego personality, this as a group consciousness, as a whole—just as we have discussed in part one of this book, the saying that there are 144 people and half of them are the higher consciousness, half are not, and as soon as more than half of them get at a higher consciousness, everybody will rise—what happened was the earth's consciousness dropped. It is not that the planet went from being fifth-dimensional. The planet is still third-dimensional, it is still physical, people are still third-dimensional. It is what they had access to. So what happened in essence was a burlap blanket of misery got thrown over the third dimension and the third-dimensional beings could not see the fourth, fifth, sixth, seventh, all the way up to the upper dimensions. They were not aware that they were gods living in human bodies, experiencing human life for fun, to enjoy, to create, to manifest, to build, to intermingle, to have physical relations, to have a human experience just to experience. This cloth was thrown over civilization and this is the void in which we are living in at this time. And the cloth is slowly but surely lifting higher and higher so humans are able to tune in. The three of you have got the understanding almost as if you have cut a hole in the burlap cloth and you are sticking a probe through, getting information from us on this side, on this side indeed, sending it into you so that you can expand with knowledge and push the veil up, so to speak. So we are moving in the right direction, but we fell prior to this."

WILLIAM: Very interesting. Because if you look at recorded history, recorded history has only recorded since the fall of the higher level human, and we have to resuscitate the prior-to-recorded history in order to provide a model of what the future might be.

MARISA: "Yes, yes, and this is very important and this is why channels such as all of yourselves that sit in this room are very important indeed. There are many channels, many channels indeed that are channeling information from under the cloth. They are channeling from under the cloth because just within the third dimension there are all of the thoughts, the emotions, the stories, all of these things that people will have made up, all of these things that are true, all the things that are untrue, all being mixed. So many people are bringing in untruths through channels, and people are saying, 'That is truth, that is truth.' And what must be told is not anything really in particular be told. But the feeling of knowing that there is a connection to the upper dimensions and once that upper-dimensional aspects of everyone on the planet—we do not say that everybody on the planet has to be connected. But as people become aware of this, the information will start to flow, because the information is there. And once the information begins to flow, it becomes possible within people's minds and they will just find it. It is like looking all over the house for something. You are looking all over the house for a key, you are looking all over for this key to a safe. And in your mind the key has a plastic black handle, a little silver key coming out of it. So you are looking everywhere for this key. You cannot find it, you cannot find it. And then one day all of a sudden the thought comes into your mind, 'The key is pink.' And you look down and it is in your pocket. So this is the information about the earth—it is in your pockets. It is here. It is on you. All the information, all the earth's history, all of this is here in the human beings' pockets. But it's not in their awareness, it's not in their consciousness. So you will be bringing through information for them to say, 'Oh, I can look to that information. Oh that information coming through is something that may be real.' And people will begin to share and major discoveries will be made in bringing ancient civilizations to fruition. There will be many, many ancient civilizations discovered in 30 years because of the rainbow children coming onto the planet at this time and their ability to stay tuned into their fifth-dimensional self."

CHAPTER SIXTY-FOUR
FINAL THOUGHTS

WILLIAM: Well, I think this is a good place to end. What I think we should actually add this as a final chapter to our first book because this is the beginning of the discovery of the unexplained mysteries of the universe. It's specifically the unexplained mysteries of the planet Earth, and in our next books I think it's going to be very important to explain how readers can differentiate between pure truth or a high level of truth, and adulterated truth. Because in my own experience as a literary agent representing many great writers, I have observed that adulterated truth has been much more popular in the last 50 years on this planet than pure truth. And I think that a challenge facing us is finding ways to present these deeper truths that will resonate with as many people as possible so they in turn will want to write their own books, create their own films, their own websites to share these truths, and to explore new truths that are beyond those that we might seek to learn ourselves. Because we're limited not by our guides but by our own awareness so that we can ask the questions that are most pressing and most relevant for the human species at this time. So I just want to thank you as the channel and thank the guides, Thoth, and Saint Germain, and I'm not sure of all the other people... Mary... that had participated. They are truly the co-authors of this first book and we're very, very grateful to all of them. We're grateful to Gayle and Madison for holding the energy and no doubt bringing forth some of this wisdom, and this is just the beginning. This is the first book of what will be many books and much information which will be not only intriguing and useful to humanity but fun to learn about. Because part of the reason we're here is to learn, and so this is on multiple levels an amazing fun project that we hope to share eventually with billions of people.

CHAPTER SIXTY-FIVE
PRACTICAL EXERCISE TO DETERMINE
TRUTH OF THIS BOOK FOR YOU

MARISA: "Yes, and we thank each of you that are here, each of you who are reading this. We must say and leave you with one practical piece of advice, is that what we would like you to, when you're trying to decipher truth, when you're trying to decipher unadulterated truth, just as you have said, some people want truth for entertainment, some people want truth that may not be truth for entertainment, and some want real truth and they do not know what real truth is, and they want that for entertainment too. Everything is entertainment on this planet. But understand that if you want to know a truth, a truth that is a truth within you, you may do something that is very simple, very simple indeed. What we would like for you to do, and this only takes less than a minute and you can do this with anything in your life, you can do this with something that your spouse has told you, you can do this with something that you have learned in school, you can do this with anything—you imagine yourself within a ball of energy. So you can imagine yourself as a snow globe, or you can imagine yourself as a disco ball, or something that is a bright ball of energy. And then what you are going to do is, you're going to ask your higher self that is two feet above your head, ask your higher self as another bright ball of energy, to drop down into the bubble that you are. Just imagine this with your imagination. You do not need to be clairvoyant to do this. Imagine the bubble of light coming into you. This is downloading all of the knowledge that your higher consciousness has. This is downloading all of your fifth-dimensional, sixth-dimensional knowledge into your field at this time. And then all you must do is imagine that whatever the truth is that you're asking about is an item. You may see it as a book. You may see it as a box. You may see it as a number. As anything. And place it against you. Place it against your heart. And when you place it against your heart, if your bubble gets brighter, it is truth. If the bubble gets less bright, it may not be pure truth. But it may be okay with you. So you may say, 'I am being told that A, B and C exist.' A, B and C existing, place it against your heart, you get brighter. This is a truth within you. It does not mean that you need to run out to everyone and say, 'I know the truth, I know the truth, and this is my truth, and this is everyone's truth.' This may not be everyone's truth. This may just be your truth. It depends on the question being asked. So just know that this is one way that we would like to give to you as the students of truth. We would like to say, as the new students of truth, or the ones that have been students of truth their entire life that are just finding this book, that are just finding this material, a way that you can communicate with your higher consciousness that we speak so much of, so easily, so quickly, in such practical ways. 'Shall I take this job?' Imagine taking the job as an item, place it against your heart. Is it bigger? Is it smaller? This is a way to communicate with your higher self. And we wanted to leave you with this practical piece. Because the thing that will make this information useful is that it will not just be another metaphysical or spiritual book with rantings of a channel and rantings of a mad scientist, Bill, that wants to find the mysteries of the universe. No. This is practicality, practicality brought to you with information that will spark your interest in who you are, where you came from, who are you, why are you here, what are you doing here, where are you going to go, what's driving you, what's driving the planet. Why, why, why, why? And these are the answers to all of these why's in which we will be bringing to each and every one of you. Whether you are interested in all of the information or just some of the information in the book, it is okay, because every word that you read, every second that you spend engaging in the material which we are bringing through, you are experiencing the energies that are existing in this room at this time. You are experiencing the ascension process. No, we are not propelling you into ascension and you will not be god-like tomorrow because you are reading this book. But what you will feel is that your higher self is engaged within you while you are operating with this material, because this is how we have it set up. This book is an ascension tool. Knowledge equals power; power within one's self equals the ability to reach out to more powerful aspects of one's self, which are the higher-dimensional aspects. We bless each and every one of you, and thank you for being a part of the earth's evolution. We bless you and leave you with that."

WAR AND SOCIETY IN
REVOLUTIONARY EUROPE, 1770-1870

War and Society in Revolutionary Europe 1770-1870

Geoffrey Best

ST. MARTIN'S PRESS

NEW YORK

Library of Congress Cataloging in Publication Data
Best, Geoffrey
War and society in revolutionary Europe, 1770-1870.
Bibliography: p.
Includes index.
1. Europe — History — 1789-1900
2. Europe — History, Military
3. France — History — Revolution, 1789-1900
4. Social classes — Europe — History — 18th century
5. Social classes — Europe — History — 19th century
I. Title
D299.B484 1982   940.2'8   82-3261
ISBN 0-312-85551-6   AACR2

Contents

EDITOR'S PREFACE

The term 'war and society' has recently been so stretched and overworked that it cries out for definition. When it entered common historical usage, ten years or so ago, it had at least this strong meaning: that, just as some thought war too serious a matter to be left to the generals, so the history and scientific analysis of war seemed too serious a matter to be left to the military men and war-enthusiasts who did most of the writing about it. Not that they held the whole of the field. The study of war has attracted, as it still attracts, the attentions of scholars of the finest kind. But such men were to be found, no doubt reluctantly, in company with a proportionately huge crowd of narrower-minded writers, for whom 'military historian' was the most complimentary title that could be found, military enthusiast or even war maniac often the more apposite. War and society studies began largely in reaction against that kind of stuff. Sometimes sinking to uniforms, badges and buttons, it rarely rose above campaigns and battles; it viewed them from the professional soldier's angle; it tended to extract the fighting side of war from its total historical context; and it usually meant a view of an army, navy, or air force from within, little concerned about the nature of their connections with the society on whose behalf war was, nominally, being fought. Much might be learned from such books about the way an army did the job set for it and, especially from between the lines, about the ways soldiers viewed themselves; little, however, about how soldiers got to be like that, and nothing at all about how armed forces fitted into, emerged from, and perhaps in their turn made impressions upon the societies to which they belonged.

The recent vogue for war and society studies has undoubtedly had much to do with the desire to put back into history the whole 'military dimension' of war-readiness and war-conduct. It also, no

7

doubt, was to some extent a civilian reaction, connected with a belief that war and soldiering – ancient, admirable and 'normal' though they may seem to be – were worth more critical inquiry than military men and their myriad admirers seemed likely to undertake, and with a recollection that war and peace were, after all, two sides of the same medal. For 'war and society' may just as well be read 'peace and society'. Best of all would be 'peace, war and society'. That alone comprehends the two poles of moral and historical interest between which 'war and society' studies oscillate. Why do wars happen at all?, is a question much more likely to be in the mind of a historian now than it was before the Second World War (or, *a fortiori*, before the First). Like the boom in 'conflict analysis and peace research', it is related to the preoccupations of the generation born under the shadow of the mushroom-shaped cloud.

But it is nothing new, that the more reflective of men should ponder upon the idea of war itself. War and the imagination of it are the ultimate link between armed forces and society. Human society, politically organized, becomes a State; and States distinguish themselves from other States, to put it bluntly, by their abilities to fight or protect themselves from one another. Whether there is something congenital in the natures of men and States which compels them towards conflict, is an enormous field of inquiry which has for long engaged the attention of some of the most thoughtful and responsible of our kind. The idea of war may, to many living now, have become repulsive, unnatural and essentially destructive. The historian has to note that this marks a big change. War appeared in quite a different light through the greater part of history. Wars may not wholly begin in the minds of men but an excellent case may be made for saying that they begin there more than anywhere else. The idea of war, therefore – the place of war in what the French call *mentalité* – is of itself a matter of giant historical importance: how at particular epochs and in particular societies it is diffused, articulated, coloured and connected. Only by way of that matrix of beliefs about God and man, nature and society, can come full understanding of the causes and courses of wars that have happened, and of the armed forces that have for the most part conducted them.

Ideas, then, are not the least of our interests; the social and economic history of war and of preparation for war fill our middle ground; and naturally conspicuous upon it are armed forces themselves, about which something further must be said. Armed forces are a very special sort of social organization. They are more nearly 'complete societies' than any other of the 'secular' associations and interest groups which structure society within States so far as governments permit. Their internal life is by nature peculiarly structured, tough and ritualistic; their business – force, violence, war – makes them exceptionally formidable; by definition they subscribe to codes of behaviour – honour, loyalty, obedience, etc. – which emphasize their solidarity and reinforce their apparent differences from the societies beside and around them. It is not difficult to understand why so much that has been written about them has treated them as if they were absolutely different and apart. But of course they are not so. Except in cases where an armed force or a coalition of armed forces succeeds in *totally* militarizing society or where a 'war-minded' ideology possesses a whole society to the extent that every citizen is as much a soldier as any other, there are bound to remain differences and distinctions between armed forces on the one hand, and the societies they spring from on the other. And yet, while there are differences and distinctions, there must also be relationships and interactions. So they can and to some extent must be studied 'on their own', because in their own right they tend to be so remarkable and influential; but in other respects their history, nature, and influence demands that they be studied in their relationship with the world they belong to. A good many social scientists and historians nowadays devote themselves to this quite distinct area of study. A glance at the periodicals *Armed Forces and Society* and (one which monitors periodical publications and research in progress) *War and Society Newsletter* shows how many they are, and what kind of inquiries they undertake.

Such is our case for picking out of the whole 'seamless web of history' the scarlet warps of war, for putting them under a magnifying microscope, and for writing about them in a way that the general historical reader – not normally a military buff – will understand; as was brilliantly done, for example, in miniature by Michael Howard in his *War in European History* (1976). 'War and society', historically considered, comes to much the same thing as 'war in history'. War is a unique human interest and activity, with its own character, its own self-images, its own mystiques, its own

9

forms of organization, and, to crown all, a prime place in determining the standards of national societies and their political viability. The traditional campaign-conscious military historian cannot contribute much towards the study of wars thus conceived beyond (a priceless contribution indeed, when well done) the demonstration of how the fighting part of war, once begun, turned out the way it did. General national and regional histories (for instance, the Fontana History of Europe, which our series is designed to support), while of course amply registering the political and economic results of war, rarely give the military dimensions of society the specific attention it usually deserves. And beneath all that, lies the as yet hardly touched field of study of the place of war, and of readiness for war, in men's hearts, minds and daily lives as producers, consumers, subjects, citizens and spouses; a study of something more important to men from time to time in history than anything else except perhaps that even more perennial problem of keeping body and soul together – the other great matter of life and death.

Geoffrey Best
University of Sussex

AUTHOR'S PREFACE

I have tried to do justice to a big subject within the limits of a rather small book. This has meant much summary and selection. Any historian has to do this. Whether he does it well or not is for his critical readers to judge. To save them time and to advise them of what they will not find here, let me say at once that I have stuck to what seem to me the main dynamic lines of the subject – the societies whose development of their military capability and whose use of it in armed conflict prescribed pattern, limits and examples to the rest. I have written mainly about the great powers, and (for obvious enough reasons) more about France than any other through the first half of the book. I have not thought it necessary to say much about Spain in the *ancien régime* (perhaps a misjudgment; Britain believed the Spanish fleet to be the next most formidable after the French), about Piedmont/Savoy before the 1840s, or about Sweden, Denmark, Switzerland, Holland, or what went on in the Balkans. I have indulged in a little overweighting of my own country, the United Kingdom, partly because it is only to be expected that this book will be most read within the British Commonwealth and North America, partly because the British part of the story is so unusual.

The spellings of foreign names are not consistent but will all be, I believe, intelligible to English readers; where originals possess resonance lost in translations, I sometimes give both. I have used such common European language phrases as come naturally to an English writer who is, at the time of writing, Dean of his University's School of European Studies; for readers to whom they are unfamiliar a glossary is provided (p.317–19). I have made no attempt to use the technical languages of armies and navies. Maritime vocabulary is peculiarly extensive but I have concluded that its systematic use, as by the saltier sort of naval history writers, actually obstructs general understanding. More people

11

understand what you mean when you refer to the front of a boat than when you refer to the bow.

The Guide to Further Reading List and the notes (kept to a minimum) expose my principal literary debts. It is worth remarking that several good general studies of my period and particular studies of parts of my subject have been published since I began work on it, let alone since the series as a whole was planned. I rejoice to see them. My transnational point of view and the judgments proceeding from it cannot be expected to appeal to those who see things through the lenses of national military traditions but it is time for them to realize that the history of armed forces and war can be perceived differently. The history of war and society has for far too long been too little studied, and it must be many productive years before the market nears saturation. Either more bold or more reckless than most, I seem to have operated an unusually wide-angled lens – taking in naval matters, for example, when it has been necessary, as well as those relating to land forces. 'War and society' normally means no more than 'armies and society'. But although those who write mainly about land warfare are bad at looking out to sea, those who write mainly about sea warfare are even worse at looking landwards. . . .

Many colleagues and friends have helped with advice, information, and criticism. Perhaps my largest debts are to John Grenville, a pioneer of 'war and society' studies, whose invitation to help with the editing of another series first introduced me to Fontana; Maurice Hutt and Andrew Wheatcroft; my collaborators in this series, Derek McKay, Brian Bond and Victor Kiernan; its very admirable editor at Fontana, Helen Fraser; and my wife, Marigold.

But I am indebted also at least to André Corvisier, Wilhelm Deist, Eduard Goldstücker, Peter Mathias, Lionel Kochan, Harry Dickinson, Clive Emsley, Douglas Porch, Jim Le Goff, Felix Markham, John Rosselli; and to Peter Paret and Michael Howard for allowing me to cite several chunks of their fine translation of Clausewitz (by kind permission also of Princeton University Press). I am grateful for having been allowed to consult the Bingham Papers in the National Army Museum. I have tried meticulously to acknowledge all borrowings, and I earnestly apologize to anyone whose translation or remark has slipped through unnoticed.

Part I

RUMBLINGS OF REVOLUTION

1

THE MARTIAL
CONTEXT

What did people know of war in the last twenty years of the *ancien régime*? The answer depends on what is meant by people and war. Let us begin with war, in the most obvious and normal definition of it: the organized and controlled use of armed force by one State against another. This was going on in much the same style as it had gone on through the past hundred years, though in diminished degree and more outside the heart of Europe than in it. The greater empires viewed their rivals with competitive hostility and sought to expand at each other's expense; from the conclusion of the Seven Years' War (1763), all Frenchmen who thought much about their country's place in the world looked forward to getting their own back on the British, and between 1778 and 1783 they got some satisfaction. Spain's concern about imperial security led it to join France in 1779, and to use the opportunity to try to recover possession of Gibraltar. Russia was at war with the Ottoman Empire between 1768 and 1774 and again from 1787 to 1791, and when not officially at war with its sprawling southern neighbour was less at peace than in a state of suspended hostilities. Austria, short title for the Habsburg Empire, was not expansionist like Russia, but carried two burdens of worry in facing south and east: what could it take from Turkey without painful exertion, and how much Turkey dared it let Russia take without wanting some equivalents itself? The same concern with equivalents, made semi-respectable by appeal to the principle of the balance of power, caused Austria to join Russia and Prussia in the carve-up of Poland: 1772, 1793 and 1795. Nor was fighting or balancing their imperial rivals the greater empires' only preoccupation. Some smaller neighbours could be a nuisance. Prussia, prudently aggressive as a matter of principle, was a standing nuisance and menace to all its neighbours, large and small alike. France was in an unusually favoured position, needing to keep half an eye only on Piedmont. Russia had to keep a whole eye on Sweden, being actually at war with her from 1788 to 1790.

Defending the frontiers was one thing; maintaining authority within them was another. Our definition of war must of course extend to include this equally normal and continuous use of armed force. With the western European imperial powers' military operations overseas, we need not be particularly concerned; but the British experience in its North American colonies had far too much direct connection with events in Europe and influence subsequently upon them, not to be given first mention. After having to fight the French over there, and the indigenous Indians, the British government found in 1775 that it had to fight its own English-speaking colonists as well. They were clearly, by every sort of law going, rebels; but they claimed to be rebels in a very good cause, and soon defined it as national independence. In the terms of our own day, they were conducting a national liberation struggle against colonial oppression. In the experience of their own, they became only the most conspicuous, as well as the first, of a series of national independence movements which established governments had to use armed force to put down. The British had a permanent problem of this kind in Ireland, where between a third and a quarter of their troops in peacetime was stationed; the Russians were to acquire an even more indigestible one with their annexations of the greater part of Poland. But rebellions with so fine-sounding a cause were the exception. Few of the insurgencies and disorders within States can have lacked religious, linguistic, racial or national animosities to fire them, but class animosity and wretched conditions of existence were their common characteristic. Eighteenth-century government tolerated a great deal of disorder and violence as natural behaviour of society, and was happy either to leave it alone or to leave the handling of it to local officials or *seigneurs*, but beyond a certain point – e.g., killing of the king's officers, prevention of tax or customs collection, endangering of national security – the troops would be sent in. Protecting the State against such threats to vital internal interests was more usual an activity for some armed forces than formal fighting against foreign powers. We shall note in greater detail later the extent to which armies – for it is obviously of them, not navies, that we are now talking – were involved in the ordinary government

16

and administration of countries; for the moment it need only be said that in no major European country during the twenty years before the French Revolution were troops not, at some time or other, engaged in suppressing internal insurgence or riots. Russia and Austria took this sort of thing as a matter of course; their biggest disturbances were respectively the giant peasant rebellion led in the Volga region of Russia by Pugachev in 1773-4, and the rebellion of thirty thousand or so in Hungarian Transylvania, led by the Rumanian Horia in 1784. Things were of course different in more prosperous and civilized Britain and France, whose armies moreover had learnt to dislike and so far as possible to avoid such service. But even here it could not be entirely avoided; Irish happenings apart, British troops were often summoned to the aid of the civil power on occasions of serious rioting, the worst of which in our period was very serious indeed – the Gordon riots, bringing anarchy, murder, arson and looting to the nation's capital for six days in 1780. Paris suffered nothing so bad so soon before the Revolution, but otherwise the French army had to perform the same domestic tasks.

Such, most briefly, were the wars and the other forceful operations in which the armed forces of Europe were engaged between 1770 and 1790. Together, they make up the substance of 'war' as this book will define it. It could mean the classic war of State against State, or it could mean the use of the armed force of the State against the rebel and the law-breaker. When internal fighting occurred because of the activities of rebels and law-breakers, it would of course often contain elements of racial, religious, national or regional hostility; but it was also likely to be some kind of class war. The armed forces of the last years of the *ancien régime* served the interests of the State, but it would be a masterpiece of naivety to imagine that, because that was their proclaimed purpose, theirs was bound to be the only idea of the State going, or they might not also be serving the particular interests of some class or social group within the State, at the expense and perhaps to the detriment of some other(s). For whenever an army or any related armed force (we shall soon see what a variety of such there could be) appears in history, the questions may always pertinently be asked: whose armed force really is it? Whose work is it doing? And to what social group or class's idea is it answering?

17

2

ARMS AND THE MEN

The men of Europe near the end of the *ancien régime* (we need not concern ourselves with the women, who had very little part in our story) knew themselves to be socially ordered in a series of strata, each acutely conscious of its rights and duties and of the rights and duties of the others in relation to it. *Ancien régime* society is usually described as hierarchical, and rightly so. The way in which the hierarchy was organized, and the degrees and kinds of freedom achieved within its various levels, varied from country to country, roughly in proportion with the state of economic development; serf-type 'peasants', for example, common in Prussia, Poland and Russia, were unknown in the United Provinces, Britain, and (virtually) France; and noblemen in France and Britain had for many years been unable to practise the sorts of personal despotism still normal in, for example, Russia and Hungary. But society *everywhere* was ordered in a hierarchy allowing to hereditary aristocratic title, wealth and property, and official status the enjoyment of privileges and rights which were normally denied to the inferior orders; a state of affairs about which the latter, obviously, would tend to feel envious and resentful.

This is not to be taken as implying that there was not much envy and resentment among the relatively privileged classes and groups (I use the word class loosely) themselves. The common rule of stratified and privileged hierarchy made sure that those enjoying one sort or level of privilege might very much resent the sorts and levels of privilege held by others, and even perhaps contemplate political action against them. This was in fact happening through the very years with which we are now concerned. Men of the middle strata, where most of the economic development and intellectual excitement was going on, more and more concluded that though they liked privilege and class distinction themselves

18

– even elevation to noble status if they could get it – the vast privileges and advantages claimed by hereditary title were after all insufferable. Some such men – there were even a few advanced-thinking aristocrats with them – were coming to disbelieve in privilege altogether, and to espouse principles of equality and democracy. So there was plenty of room for a ferment of trouble within the superior orders of society (which together, of course, made up only a small proportion of the total population) and such trouble was clearly brewing up, especially in the more free and economically go-ahead countries, France and Britain at their head. But there as everywhere else the potential revolutionaries, having themselves something to lose from the collapse of public order and the unloosing of the normally suppressed hatreds and resentments of the lower orders, might need to calculate carefully the extent to which they could safely invite men of the lower orders to join them in toppling the traditional order of things, or the extent to which they dared to use the threat of such invitation to squeeze concessions from their superiors.

All this is commonplace enough, being no more than a thumb-nail sketch of the social circumstances which produced, from the 1770s, the liberal bourgeois – R.R. Palmer has even called it the democratic – revolution in general, and the French Revolution in particular. But something has to be said about it here, because the social forces thus in triangular or even polygonal conflict might turn to arms to settle their disputes, and their respective experiences of the use of arms and ideas about armed conflict would help to determine what happened. Above all, the role of the official armed forces of the State would be crucial; how they behaved, what were their relations with society at large, and who ultimately controlled them. Those are big enough matters, and distinct enough, to demand separate attention later. For the moment our concern is simply to see what the principal social groups in the last years of the *ancien régime* might know about fighting.

It seems as if they knew a great deal. Except in well-policed cities (Berlin, Vienna, and the Dutch ones would be the best examples) and unusually orderly countrysides, the common man had little defence against the bandit, the murderer and the thief but his own strong right arm, cudgel and gun, or the collective strength of his own community. The latter could be quite effective within itself but its guarantee of security against internal foes might bring with it commitment to conflict with external ones; feuds, vendettas and private wars against those who belonged to other faiths, denominations, races, clans, families, even just villages or valleys. Such were to be heard of almost everywhere and were quite normal, of course, in the more backward, remote, wild and mountainous parts of the continent, where moreover smuggling – a semi-violent form of commerce – occupied some immeasurably large number of people, by no means all lowly-placed.

How much violence the lower orders did to each other in their ordinary course of life was of less interest to their superiors than that the violence should not spread in their direction. The familiarity in most countries (Prussia and the United Provinces seeming the principal exceptions) with riots and *émeutes*, and the extremes of savagery sometimes reached by both sides on such occasions, show how little was the upper classes' anxiety misplaced. Inter-personal violence, and familiarity with the use of some sort of weapons (scythes and home-made pikes were what came most readily to peasants on the warpath), seem to have been more normal than exceptional among most of the lower orders of the Europe we have in view; while the admired figures of popular folklore were notable robbers and rebels as often as they were national military heroes and mythologized fighting monarchs.

Some of the lower orders, it must be added, had the most direct and formal military experience that was possible: they were, or they had been, in the official armed forces of their own or of some other country. But this was not nearly as common as the twentieth-century reader, accustomed to the idea of national military service, might suppose. As will be shown in chapter 3, dealing with the official armed forces, recruitment from their own lower orders in peacetime was statistically insignificant in many countries. The requisite manpower was obtained from other sources. Prussia stood out with its 1786 proportion of one regular soldier to every twenty-nine of the population, but since something like half of its regulars were recruited from abroad, the actual proportion of Prussian subjects in regular military service was probably only about one in sixty – and that includes the officer corps. Lesser adjustments have to be made for the same reason in respect of the best figures we have for France, Austria and the UK: respectively, 1:145, 1:96, and 1:310. Russia, which recruited fewer aliens, shows about 1:120 in the same chart.[1] We must therefore not exaggerate the extent to which the lower orders of the late *ancien régime* knew about arms because of military service. But it must also be noted that *some* groups of them knew an extraordinary amount about it, because it was their tradition, their basic means of livelihood, and often their constitutional liability or clan calling; groups such as Scottish highlanders, Polish and Russian Cossacks, Breton seamen, Alpine and Pyrenean sharp-shooters, and the peoples to whom was committed the defence of the Habsburgs' long Military Frontier against the Ottoman Empire.

Moving up the social ladder (and remembering that we are dealing in gross generalities) we come to the middling classes, spread out from the more free and prosperous peasants and petty bourgeois types, to the fatter urban burghers and businessmen whose wealth was often greater than that of the titled folk who sat at the top of the social tree. Of the military experience of this, the most varied and indefinite of the three principal layers we are considering, three things at least may be said. First: from the upper levels of this middle layer was coming, increasingly as the eighteenth century wore on, a certain demand for admission into commissioned military service; not only in the navies and the more specialized, 'technical' branches of the armies (above all the artillery and engineers, which needed some measure of higher education and in which middling men were well represented) but also the infantry. Whether because they were driven by ambition to show that they could honourably serve their country just as well as the men of birth and breeding, or simply because the armed forces offered respectable salaried employments in a competitive world where such were at a premium, sub-aristocrats were pressing for easier admission into their country's officer corps, and increasingly resenting the exclusiveness of the social class claiming possession (to which we shall soon turn).

We should next remember that, although there was effective aristocratic resistance to the general admission of sub-aristocratic types into the regular forces, there was none to their participation in the variety of local defence and security forces which were to be found all over Europe, but most of all, naturally, wherever there was risk of foreign assault by sea or land. Constitutionally, these were normally survivals and adaptations from earlier ages when all men capable of it – all 'fencible' men, to use the contemporary

British term – had a duty to turn out armed when summoned by the public authority. In Germany, there were the *Bürgergarden*; in France, the *milices urbaines* or *milices bourgeoises* and the *gardes-côtes* round the littoral; all with some vestige of life still left in them, and the maintenance of law and order by now their only quasi-military activity; likewise the Volunteers of Ireland, though they had a political edge to them too.

Much more significant as military experience was the third way in which these middling sort of people might get it; through engagement in maritime commerce. Trade on land was by this epoch becoming fairly safe from bandits and highwaymen in most of the more populous or economically advanced countries, but trade at sea often added to the ordinary hazards of wind and weather those of armed conflict. Pirates were still a menace in southern or eastern Mediterranean, Caribbean and above all Oriental waters. No modest ship sailing them dared not be prepared for a fight. More serious fighting had to be anticipated when there was a war on or, not less important, half-on, it being the practice among the maritime rivals, when in doubt (and an East Indiaman homing after more than twelve months' absence might well find itself in grave doubt), to fire first and find out about the law later. Then there was privateering, to which the French, the British, the Scandinavians and, less, the Spanish regularly resorted the moment hostilities had begun: a belligerent style typically adopted by men the rest of whose working lives was spent in commerce or fishing, though some official naval personnel might be seconded to it. An enormous proportion of the sea-going populations of Europe was accustomed to sailing armed, whether the times were technically ones of war or peace, and of fighting for their own interests in the maritime jungle.

We now approach European society's highest levels: those where aristocratic title, lineage and rank (which commonly but not always went together) were all in all; levels allowing room for plenty of social discrimination and political in-fighting, but whose ultimate solidarity was cemented by common consciousness of superior social standing, public honour and legal privilege, and the conspicuousness with which they usually enjoyed them. 'Feudal privilege' was to be among the primary targets of the French revolutionaries and their followers elsewhere, and feudal indeed had been the origins of many of the privileges which the later

22

eighteenth-century aristocracy enjoyed. But just as by no means all families with noble title could trace ancestry back that far, so many of the privileges they now enjoyed were of recent origin – conferred by monarchs as part of political grand strategies to strengthen and solidify their régimes and to deprive the nobility of its ancient power to rock the throne. Whether the privileges and their conspicuous enjoyers were new or old, however, the rest of society (i.e., vastly its greater part) was made most aware of them by their common attributes of exemptions from this or that tax burden, and manners which marked them off from 'the rest', and above all by their particular right to wear the sword: prime symbol of their special position in the leadership of society, and their special roles as society's and the State's proper military leaders.

For it was undoubtedly a general rule of the *ancien régime* that the social class most concerned with the armed forces was 'the aristocracy'; and this was even more true in its later years than earlier on. But like all general rules, it contains a variety of contradictions and exceptions, to which, in proportion as they mattered, we must now turn.

First of all, note that this class of the aristocracy or nobility itself, though all its members could wear the sword and all shared a common interest in landownership, horseflesh and blood sports, included a vast variety of incomes and statuses. The duc d'Orléans, with more than two thousand staff in his employment, and the rustic Gascon aristocrat who inherited a rather ruinous little château and drew a smaller income from his land than most Bordeaux grocers got from their shops, were both 'noble', no mistake about it; in pure social prestige this mattered, as we have already remarked, more than anything else in the world; but applied social prestige was something different! The wealth of the one was bound to give him a style of life and a state of mind quite different from the other, a difference which extended to their ideas about their military responsibilities. They would not disagree about their class's special military responsibility as such. The aristocracy's military origins and traditions were well understood, and no born aristocrats (except a few eccentrics and mavericks on the eve of the Revolution) wanted to give them up. They were part of the nobility's distinctiveness. But not everywhere did this mean much in active, persistent military practice; and where it did, as in Prussia and Russia, that was largely because it had been part-driven, part-persuaded to do so by monarchs determined to bind their aristocracies to this particular role. In France and in Hungary, things were different; in France, because the military tradition had become deadened in some families, in Hungary (where 'aristocrats' were amazingly numerous), because the Habsburg emperors had found no way to use all of them safely in the army and because most of them preferred to stay in Hungary anyway. *Mutatis mutandis*, the position in Spain was much the same. The position in the UK was like France, only more so; some aristocratic families – especially Anglo-Irish ones, such as bred Wellington, and Scottish ones such as bred so many of his generals – regularly fed sons into the armed forces, but others, including some of the biggest and richest, had lost all but the most local and sporting sort of military interest.

With this specialized military function, then, which was often obvious and everywhere potential, went the characteristic ethos and manner which marked the aristocrats off from the rest of mankind and gave them to think, and their admirers and toadies to tell them, that they enjoyed moral superiority as well as social. This superiority consisted above all in their characters as men of 'honour', subscribers to a code of conduct which required, above all things, courageous devotion to the armed service of their king (some of them might perceive it as 'king and country') and a readiness to sacrifice their lives for him (and his cause) when bidden by their code of honour and duty to do so; even, perhaps, to sacrifice their lives when bidden by honour alone, for by some contemporary understandings of the concept it stood above even the commands of kings. Whether they were actually fighting men or not, theirs was a fighting man's ethic, and although it left an awkward amount of room for duelling, bullying and insolence both general and particular, the greater part of it had a moral quality which appeared consistent with its social exclusiveness. From the mouths of non-military or demilitarized aristocrats, these assumptions quickly became offensive to persons of lower classes, but when they came from serving officers, they made good sense and sounded perfectly functional. Aristocrats who took their military role seriously argued that men of non-aristocratic backgrounds could not make as good officers – at least, would not *naturally* make as good officers – as men of their own sort, bred with honour in their bones. It was their privilege as well as their duty to show how a man should die.

Such was the general case made for the aristocrat's title to leadership in military affairs throughout continental Europe; a case pressed increasingly from the 1750s on, as the aristocracy found it necessary to defend its interests and reputation against increasingly vocal critics, and to assure itself of a source of income that was consistent with its sense of honour and self-respect. But the aristocracy was not united in this effort of self-defence. Besides the critics from outside, there were plenty of self-critics within the aristocracy itself, and the arguments of the two groups considerably overlapped. From this crossing of class lines has come much confusion. The complaints made by outsiders against the aristocracy's general military pretensions were not more important than the complaints made by the less wealthy or plainly poor aristocrats against the wealthy ones. In both cases, what was being complained about was the extent to which wealth and other social considerations were allowed to interfere with the pursuit of military efficiency.

The crucial fact was that the aristocrats who most coveted opportunities of military service and sought military glory, who were most interested, in fact, in making the army or navy their careers in a modern professional sense, tended to be the less well-off ones, the plainer-living provincial ones who could never dream of cutting a figure at court or in the fashionable society circling around it; in eighteenth-century English terms, the gentry or squirearchy, even just 'gentlemen'. They tended to resent the way that the richer of their class, by no means sure to be the better soldiers, used their social and political influence to near-monopolize the higher ranks and honours, irrespective of their actual talents and qualifications. At least as much did they fear the prospect that bourgeois riches would be able to buy military as well as civil office. The bourgeoisie, to put it bluntly, was trying to take their jobs. *They* couldn't 'go into trade'; why should the man born to trade horn his way into the armed forces?

But besides snobbishness and self-interest, another motive was in play which was not less weighty than the others and may have been the most influential: professional standards. No error is greater than to think of these later eighteenth-century aristocrats' objections to admitting bourgeois to the officer corps as selfish

25

attempts by gentleman amateurs to exclude would-be professionals. What was being principally objected to was the claim of wealth to walk in, regardless of professional standards and requirements; the insolence of mere wealth, whether aristocratic or bourgeois.

Armies and navies, it is high time to remark, were steadily becoming more professionalized as the century wore on. Part of this process was the definition of professional requirements, control over entrance standards, and proper education and training. The development of the technical arms, gunners and engineers was but a particular instance of a general rule. In every country of military pretensions, schools, academies and colleges were founded in mounting numbers to prepare boys and young men properly, in ways appropriate to their ages, for the military career. In the United Kingdom and in France, some of these were more 'private' than public and official; young Arthur Wellesley put in a year at a private academy of this kind in Angers, but he could have got something of the sort in Chelsea. The most imposing of these institutions were royal foundations which came in all shapes and sizes: the Ecole Militaire in Paris, St Petersburg, Mezières, La Flèche, Toulon and Brest, Berlin and Potsdam, Munich, Wiener Neustadt, Woolwich, and that 1776 French batch of 'junior colleges' at one of which, Brienne, the nine-year-old Buonaparte began his vocational training. To what extent non-aristocratic boys were admitted seems to have depended as much on chance (e.g., short-fall of aristocratic applications, or the sudden imperatives of a military expansion programme) as on principled policy, but some policies were clear enough: for example, Frederick II's well-publicized determination, after the Seven Years' War, to reduce the bourgeois proportion of the officer corps to the lowest possible (preferring foreign aristocrats to bourgeois nationals), and the French military reformers' pursuit of his example. By 1789, only about 10 per cent of the 10,000-odd French army officers were of bourgeois origin (the proportion in the technical arms being more like 25 per cent). But non-aristocratic types did continue to effect some entry into armies (not just into their technical branches) and navies, and there was one such type against whom the aristocratic military professional seems to have had little objection: the officer's son, whether the father had been aristocratic or not, brought up in a professional atmosphere, and educated in a proper professional institution. Officers' sons, indeed, were a class of lad for whom most of the royal foundations made particular provision (just as common soldiers' sons, suitably schooled, were found to be a convenient source of military manpower, lower down the social scale).

So military professionalism and aristocratic status merged pretty easily and naturally. At one end of the aristocratic scale there were snobbish aristocrats, congregated mostly in the cavalry and in fashionable, court-focused guards regiments, among whom an amateur, sporting spirit was likeliest to be found. At the other end of the professional scale were the officers of bourgeois or even lower origins (some of them even risen from the ranks), whose chances of rising above the lower rungs of the officers' ladder were very small, who were concentrated in the artillery and engineers, and in low-status garrison companies. In between came the greater part of the officer corps, its spirit and style determined by the confluence of its mainly aristocratic social character with its respect for professional competence and achievement. Since aristocrats were just as capable of acquiring competence and of achievement as any one else, they had little difficulty in dominating the officer corps once they set out to do so, the French case *par excellence*, or once their monarch decided they should do so, which was what happened in Prussia before officer service became the Junkers' second nature. But if this was dominantly aristocratic, it was no less obviously professional, and the two principles had in common one attribute which set much of the military tone of Europe in these years: cosmopolitanism.

Marx was to say in the nineteenth century that the working man had no country. Something of the same was true of the aristocracy in the eighteenth. They were an international élite with trans-national interests and they more readily found common ground with fellow-aristocrats of other countries than with bourgeois fellow-nationals of their own. (The very word 'national' is of course questionable here.) They were not much touched by the rising tide of nationalism; their readiness to fight might have 'the nation' in mind but it also included objects which were distinct from nations and might be incompatible with them: emperors, monarchs, their own international political ascendancy. It was not surprising, therefore, that nothing ill was thought in the professional military world of moving from one sovereign's service to another, as opportunity and career-prospects offered. To the aristocratic mind this was a perfectly honourable thing to do, the laws and customs of war knowing no frontiers, and officers and gentlemen being recognizable the whole world over; to the professional mind, war was war wherever it occurred, and the experienced professional was worth his hire. This happened so much as to be taken absolutely for granted before the French Revolution popularized the notion that the idea of the nation, *patrie* or *Vaterland*, might make a more exclusive and monopolistic claim on men's devotion – and not merely the devotion of aristocrats.

3

ARMED FORCES AND THEIR SOCIETIES

Each country's armed forces of course had their own characteristics and styles of social establishment. Some of these were so pronounced and peculiar that they demand separate description. But before we get to that, we must sketch their common characteristics, which were numerous; not surprisingly, in that pre-modern, industrial Europe of a still prevailing *ancien régime*.

1. They were by far the biggest and sometimes virtually the only branch of State-managed public administration. This was no change from the past, nor was it different from the immediate future, though the growth of 'civil services' (e.g., education, public health, police, revenue) in the modern State would gradually change the balance in some countries and make people realize that 'The State' had a lot more to it than the articulation of a population's military capability. Armies and navies and, when they happened, wars, were also responsible for by far the biggest demands ever made on national revenues; between one-third and one-half of States' incomes normally going to them in peacetime. Except in the countries where the provision of troops for mercenary service elsewhere was actually a means of raising money (the Swiss cantons and some German specialist States like Hesse, Brunswick, and Württemberg), the known great expense of raising and running armies and navies was a factor present in the minds of all rulers in proportion with their consciousness of the desirability of husbanding their resources and the limits to the patience of their tax-paying publics. To Russian rulers' minds, probably, it was relatively the least inhibiting; but even there a direct connection was traced between the costs of their expansionist wars and Pugachev's rebellion. The Hapsburg Empire would have been better able to cope with the Revolution if its war with

29

Turkey hadn't nearly bankrupted it; Archduke Charles found 154,000 unpaid bills in sacks in the War Office cellar when he explored it in 1792.[2] The French State was bankrupted by its semi-victory over Britain in the War of Independence. The British expenditure in that same war cost at least £110 millions. This was the more of a blow, in that Parliament had for a century or more become accustomed to the concept of wars that paid in the sense of directly producing imperial expansion and commercial growth.

Wealthy Britain could stand the unaccustomed shock of a not immediately profitable war. But all wars were like that on the continent. Territorial gains, their normal prizes, might offer long-term profits in manpower, production and taxation, but could not possibly offer immediate recompense for the cost of winning them. All rulers and ruling classes therefore ran their armed forces on the cheap as far as possible and as far as dignity allowed; sending the men back to the labour market in peacetime, strategically planning to quarter the troops in enemy territory in wartime, and so on. Standing armies actually stood down for much of the time.

2a. Recruitment of the criminal, the vagabond, and the destitute was standard practice. The scope of compulsion to military service varied from country to country but opportunity was usually taken – especially, of course, in wartime, but not then alone – to funnel into the army or the navy men considered socially dangerous and undesirable, whether they were convicted (or about-to-be-convicted) criminals, habitual mendicants or malingerers, or just serfs deemed expendable by their lords and masters, who in Russia and the Habsburg Empire used conscription as a means of cleaning out their human livestock. In the rickety Kingdom of the Two Sicilies, Bardin tells us, '*bricone* and soldier meant the same in Neapolitan speech: years in prison and years of military service were interchangeable in the language of the courts'; when war threatened, the convict population became the army, and when the threat had past, the troops went back to the prisons and the galleys.[3] What this sort of thing meant in terms of military efficiency and morale, needs no comment here.

2b. Volunteers were welcome in all armed forces and were

reckoned to comprise their better elements, most likely to attain non-commissioned rank. There was more volunteering in practice than appeared in official recruitment statistics. It was uncommon for any country, not excepting Prussia, to need to call up the whole of the male population theoretically liable to military service in one form or another. The normal thing was for government to specify the proportion of liable men it needed – e.g., 'one in twenty-four' – and to leave the method of selection to the local authority. The man thus enlisted might be forced into it, as he certainly was when the local authority was a landlord exercising feudal rights, or when, as frequently happened in France and Britain, there was a ballot. But it seems often to have been to the advantage of all concerned, to make enlistment worth someone's while by giving him a sum of money subscribed by those who might have been enlisted instead. He was in fact a sort of volunteer. Such payments, which we know to have been quite common at least in France to fill the ranks of the provincial militia part of the army, were an exact equivalent to the bounty (*prime*) offered to proper volunteers as part of the continent-wide military ritual: the recruiting-officer or sergeant with his exciting talk about the glories and advantages of a soldier's life, his height-measuring rod, his flattering of the bold and muscular, his generosity with drink and good cheer, his ready store of money to pay the tempting bounty – and the privileged security awaiting the recruit, the moment he had accepted the bounty, drunk the king's health, and become 'the king's man'. This security obviously mattered a lot to many volunteers. Their motives might be adventure, enrichment (by hoped-for plunder), even a relative degree of freedom and respect which would surpass anything offered by life at home; they also included security from the due processes of civil law and social pressure – e.g., the debt-collector, the unhappy home and, most classically, the pregnant girlfriend's irate father.

2c. All States employed foreign troops, sometimes in vast numbers. We refer not merely to officers, of whose cosmopolitan transferability enough has been said, nor to pure mercenaries (hired by the thousand, officers and all, from a German princely provider or taken on long-term contract from a Swiss canton) but simply to foreigners recruited directly into national regiments or naval vessels. The French royal navy couldn't put to sea in full strength without sailors from Malta, Venice and Genoa;[4] the British suffered badly when its North American recruitment (not that it had been, strictly speaking, 'foreign') finally stopped in 1783. Swiss and German regiments – the latter, however, increasingly drawn from Alsace – were among the best, and best paid, in the French army. As many as half of Frederick the Great's soldiers came from without; recruited either by regimental agents (royal, after 1763) on foreign soil or, after victories, directly from the ranks of prisoners of war; otherwise blandished, bamboozled or simply pressed into the Prussian king's service, and kept there by means described in the next paragraph.

2d. All States used force to get men into their armed services, and force to stop them getting out. Of the major powers', the most conspicuous in this respect were the armies of eastern Europe and the greatest navy of the west. Kitchen has written: 'The bulk of the Prussian army consisted of demoralized men, often the dregs of society, press-ganged foreigners and prisoners-of-war, unwilling peasants and unreliable mercenaries, the whole motley crew held together by brutal discipline and ferocious punishments.'[5] He may be laying it on a bit thick, but not by much; Frederician discipline *was* famously ferocious, the rate of desertion (see para 2e below) was high despite all attempts to stop it, and neither then nor since has the truth of Frederick's dictum been underrated: the secret of his troops' discipline in battle was that they feared death and the enemy less than they feared their NCOs and officers. Much the same, allowing for the mitigations of inefficiency, was true of the Russian and Habsburg's armies, and even more similar was the British navy. This was recruited in wartime principally by impressment (as indeed was the British part of the British army before the 1780s), and disciplined by a variety of torturous punishments of which flogging was only the most familiar. The press gang was as brutal and arbitrary a means of enlisting fighting-men as any in Europe, and it would be a nice question to ascertain whether more lashes were laid on per man in the British armed forces or the Prussian. Yet something has to be said by way of qualification. British crews apparently fought just as well as Prussian regiments, and in neither case can 'fear of their officers' be a sufficient explanation. The mysterious fact is that some alchemy of *esprit de corps*, camaraderie, institutional – perhaps national – pride, pride in strength and valour and the defiance of death, and official indoctrination could convert even the most unlikely and unwilling recruits into enthusiastic warriors; along with which may be noted the other great paradox, that regular soldiers in this age as in many others could actually be attractively straightforward, 'decent' characters, kindly and humane off the battlefield and, so far as circumstances permitted, on it too. As a great contemporary soldier has remarked: 'professional soldiers are sentimental men.'[6]

2e. Unsurprisingly, every army and navy was leached incessantly by desertion. Corvisier reckons that about 10 per cent of French soldiers at any one time were deserters from other regiments or armies; by the eighties, when the French army enjoyed as efficient a system of *contrôles* as any in Europe, there was still an annual loss of about 2 per cent.[7] The figures for armies of less voluntary character were of course much worse. Fortescue found that about one-sixth of the British military establishment in Ireland was deserting every year in the eighties.[8] So many Prussian soldiers wanted out at all costs, that the Habsburgs found it worthwhile to place permanent reception posts for them along the Silesian frontier.[9] Desertion from the British navy was, naturally, as much desired as from the Prussian army. Just as Prussian commanders sought to avoid fighting or camping in wooded, hilly country, and marching by night, so British sailors were not normally allowed on shore even when their ship was in port; the delights of land-life had to come aboard, to them (and did).

3. Losses from disease could be enormous, and went on through peace and war alike. Typhus was a particular bane of camp and barrack life. But nothing on European land (except hospitalization) was normally as lethal as life on ships and in the tropics. About 13 per cent of the seamen in the British West Indies fleet were dying from disease annually around 1780.[10] Ten years later, more than a third of British line battalions were, wrote Fortescue, 'quartered in climates so deadly that a Minister could safely reckon on the necessity of renewing the whole of each battalion every second year'.[11]

4. Armies and navies were, by our years, more recognizably

'national' institutions than they had been earlier on, and more familiar institutions as well. Formerly open to suspicion as foreign bodies within the national organism, as pure instruments of power – a power capable of standing over against the nation – they had become, so to speak, assimilated, needing little further development or acceptance to become the armed forces fighting the battles of the nations ('nations', themselves newly understood) after the Revolution. This developing acceptance and assimilation naturally took different forms in different countries; in Prussia, for instance, uniquely moulding society in the army's own image, and cultivating a military aristocracy to rule it; in Russia, approaching a similar end by equating the civil with the military hierarchies as co-equal force-deployers and status-enjoyers in the service of the Tsar. Nowhere else were the very institutions of government militarized in such stark ways. In France, indeed, civilian control became if anything strengthened; a development perfectly compatible with the growing professionalization of the military, already mentioned. But equally in eastern and western Europe, armies became unsurprising, familiar features of social existence, integrated with society at all its levels; normal, not extraordinary, because in most respects a known and regulated quantity.

The history of military uniform itself now went through a significant development. Each regiment of course retained important singularities of dress, but some assimilations took place between them, emphasizing their collective character as the national or imperial army; they were regulars, 'professionals', decidedly unlike the part-timers, amateurs, freebooters and bandits they had once tended to resemble. They commonly retained a rough and rowdy reputation and were kept so far as possible at arm's length by every social class or group capable of considering itself superior, but there is no evidence that in peacetime they were massively ill-behaved, or that the population as a whole suffered from their presence. The servants, the chickens and the innkeeper's daughter might be at risk; the master and mistress of the bourgeois house were not. They got drunk and behaved badly when drunk, of course; but so did the lower orders generally. And those soldiers in fact lived in among the people to an extent which was to seem quite surprising, only half a century later. Not many lived in barracks. Barracks might be found in the national capitals and in various provincial and frontier towns; a few custom-built, most of them in made-over old palaces, colleges or monasteries. But much more often soldiers were quartered or billeted on the common people or in public houses. The latter, indeed, were their normal habitat in England; as Ian Roy sharply puts it, 'one criminal class, the soldiery, [was] billeted on another, innkeepers'.[12]

Throughout the continent the load of soldiers was spread more widely, and far from being burdensome, was often positively welcome. The rates paid for lodgings and rations might not be much, but they were much better than nothing in depressed towns and regions; and the quantities provided could be colossal. Consider, for instance, the scale of daily requirements used in Hungary, and perfectly representative: for each man, bed, firewood, light and salt, one pound of meat and two pounds of bread; for each horse, six pounds of oats, eight of hay, and half a bale of straw.[13] Local farmers and merchants could do quite well, keeping platoons or companies going at that rate, and the people housing the troops would manage to get a bit of income out of it. The troops might be making a bit of money too – or their regimental officers might make it out of them. Soldiers in peacetime, with nothing specifically military to do for part of the day or much of the year, commonly worked like ordinary civilians. 'If drafted from a village,' wrote Redlich, 'the soldier spent most of the year on furlough working at home; if he was a craftsman, he was freed from guard duties and worked as a journeyman with some master in the barracks; and the unskilled worked in their spare time as handy men or as spinners. In fact, eighteenth-century military barracks in Austria and Prussia were veritable spinning mills.'[14] The normal daily life of French soldiers in peacetime included 'ten hours of free time' which were usually filled by work for civilian employers.[15] The later *ancien régime*'s regular armies generally lived, not apart from the common people, but close to them; and the parts of town or countryside where they lived could acquire a homely military air, as civilian and soldier mingled in going about their ordinary business, with the army's bugle-calls and parades redefining the times of the day.

In wartime, of course, the people's involvement might be much increased; more troops, perhaps marching through and having to be crammed into the limited housing available; the requisitioning (this was absolutely regular) of horses and wagons for the great supply trains, of drivers for them, and maybe of labourers for work on roads or, in the unlikely event of enemy approach, fortifications. And if such an enemy should nevertheless arrive – requisitions without payment, probably, and all the losses, damages and terrors which an invading force would inflict except insofar as its officers chose to prevent them or were actually able to do so.... But we are not yet concerned with what happened in war.

That much said about the common characteristics of later *ancien régime* military organization, let this section conclude with glances at the respective peculiarities of the major armed forces of pre-revolutionary Europe.

1. Prussia's army, about 194,000-strong in 1786 (it had been up to 260,000 in 1760),[16] became the most important one during the Seven Years' War. Its remarkable performance then compelled the leaders of military opinion everywhere else (especially in France, which felt humiliated) to inquire what their own countries might learn from the Prussian example. Prussian military writers now joined the French in the top league of recognized experts, and Frederick II turned into Frederick the Great, Europe's prime warlord until eclipsed by Napoleon Bonaparte on the crest of the wave of the French comeback. Most of what the French and others considered taking over from Prussia was in the way of discipline and tactics, Frederick's armies having obviously had more of the former than his foes and having used it on the battlefield to extraordinarily good effect; though opinion, as we shall see in chapter 4, was divided (even in Prussia itself) about the desirability of that sort of discipline, and the possibility of finding alternatives to those particular tactical methods. What no other country could possibly copy, however, was something else that was absolutely fundamental to Prussia's military prowess, but was in its nature inimitable: the social organization of the Prussian State, or, as it may just as well be put, Prussia's socio-political structure.

Prussia was unique, as a society hand-made for war. The makers were the ruling family, the Hohenzollerns. They had been at it since the mid-seventeenth-century years of the effective founder of Prussia's modern power, Frederick William 'the Great Elector' of Brandenburg. There is plenty of room for argument about some of the uses to which this military power was later applied, but none about its necessity in those early decades, when Prussia found mere respectable survival difficult enough with Europe's then military pacesetter, Sweden, to the north; a gigantic (though ailing) Poland to the east; the militarily powerful Habsburgs to the south; and other German States of not much smaller size (Saxony, Hesse, Hanover) around the rest of the perimeter. So Prussia – not at all a rich country, moreover – had to be ready to fight, and in the course of time, through the unceasing military dedication and professional ambition of its rulers, became uniquely geared to the fighting business; an army with a State, as was aptly remarked, rather than a State with an army, and its socio-political system designed with a view to maximum efficiency and economy.

Prussia's aristocracy was much more thoroughly and consistently militarized than any other. To serve as their king's army's officers had become their normal vocation; their many legal, political and fiscal privileges were designed to make it natural and easy, and the relative poverty of many of them forced them into it anyway. Prussia was not (yet) such a country as could reward its favourite sons with riches on the French or British scale. Officers commanding regiments and companies could make money out of them (as they could everywhere else), but the scale of social values was such that the prestige of this aristocratic officer corps acquired magnetic attractions of its own, and its members' sense of honourable distinction could be so exalted as to be worth any amount of material or financial reward. This class or even, one might almost say, caste, more or less dominated the Prussian State, just as it held the main strings of power in Prussian society. Most Prussian subjects of the lower orders were, in these years, peasants, serfs, tied to the land and responsible to their landlord. From these peasants the bulk of the nationally-raised proportion of the 'other ranks' of the army was conscripted. (The rest were national volunteers or, as will be remembered, foreigners; while workmen in Prussia's relatively few manufactories were deemed far too valuable economically to be conscriptable.)

The peasants' lords, especially throughout the eastern, the really Prussian, parts of the kingdom were usually the same aristocrats we have just been considering in their military aspect, and the *Landrat* who was head of the standard rural local authority, the *Canton*, was almost sure to be an ex-officer. *Canton* conscription supplied half or more of the troops on the national strength.[17] Each regiment recruited from 'its' *Canton*, and the average peasant's life was ordered at all points to suit the State's military requirements: schooling (perhaps) and religious instruction (certainly) in good Lutheran patriotic and authority-obeying principles; registration when old enough for military service unless – the grounds of exemption are significant – physically inadequate, economically so profitable as to be worth keeping alive at all costs or of a family so poor and wretched that it could not afford to give its soldier member(s) the degree of financial support actually expected. This latter circumstance was because the men chosen for service, after their full-time basic training period of about two years, normally went back (uniformed) to their *Canton* and family, and lived and worked part-time there except during the two months annually spent back with the army. The degree of support of the army demanded of the lower civilian population was more systematic and comprehensive than anywhere else: beyond heavy taxation, board and lodging, and transport or labour service when required, the provision of cheap forage in winter and cavalry grazing ground in summer. Military uniforms were everywhere and military persons were everywhere too. Policemen, tax officials and so on were mostly ex-soldiers. Provincial councils, the highest local authorities, were always chaired by generals. Disputes between civilian and military interests were adjudicated before mixed tribunals chaired by officers. As Corvisier sums it up, 'the military's precedence over the civilian had become a maxim of State'.[18] In such a society, the difference between 'civilian' and 'military' made little practical difference, and was not meant to.

2. Britain's big navy was the other armed service to command nearly universal fear and respect, but the admiration in which it was held was more qualified. It was feared and respected because the spectacularly successful Seven Years' War was only the last of a series of wars in which its near command of the seas enabled Britain to make mighty imperial advances. The imperially disastrous War of American Independence made but few dents in the British navy's reputation. Its ships were generally more successful at their wartime work, fighting or blockading, than anyone else's, and the reasons were not far to seek: discipline and practice. The degree of discipline observed and enforced on British 'men-of-war' (as her warships were familiarly known) was very

great and (another of the several parallels between the armed forces of Frederick the Great and Farmer George) British fleets and vessels were thereby enabled to do two things which tended to assist victory: fire more often and with better control; and manoeuvre more precisely, by using the winds more effectively. In the war of 1778-83 the French, who had been making tremendous efforts to do so, seemed to be catching up in these latter respects; but, as the next chapter will show, the Revolution set them back again. British crews were for a few years better protected than French against scurvy, typhus and other debilitating banes of ships' crews. About 1780, several notable British gunnery improvements came together to facilitate faster fire, oblique fire, and, through the wide-bored close-range gun known as a carronade, more deadly fire.[19] These advantages seem to have out-balanced the French tactical improvements just mentioned.

Otherwise the British navy had no obvious superiorities. British popular culture naturally embraced the notion that British sailors were more courageous than others, but there is no objective evidence that they really were so. The officer corps of both navies were recruited from similar sources; a predominance of aris-tocracy-gentry, but an influx of middle-class men, who experi-enced less prejudice against them on British than on French quarterdecks; well-matched in professional skill, science and dedication; together composing 'one of the most remarkable intellectual and political élites Europe had ever produced'.[20] (Never to be forgotten is the tremendous amount of skill and science it took to run those vast, complicated, wind-reliant fighting-machines, at once the most elaborate industrial products man had yet made and producers, in their broadsides, of the most concentrated man-made power.) British ships were better man-aged, not better designed. And the British navy was different from its main continental rival in one respect which made it, to many minds, morally inferior, and by universal judgment, invidiously different; the manner of its manning.

The general superiority of French naval administration inclu-ded its system for assembling crews for war service whenever they were required; the century-old *Inscription Maritime*, an efficiently maintained register of all seamen domiciled along the coasts and up the estuaries. It couldn't produce quite the total that was needed – there were many Italian volunteers in the Toulon fleet

– but on the eve of the Revolution it reckoned on mobilizing about 12,000 men at once, 40,000 within a month and its maximum, 70,000 in just over another month; most of them, of course, as their merchant and fishing ships came in.[21] It was an efficient, humane and equitable system, taken very much as a fact of life among the populations directly affected, and not notably unpopular.

The British system was none of these things. It was a mixture of carrots and sticks: financial inducements and a form of compulsory service, impressment, that was inefficient, inhumane and inequitable. The financial inducements were, simply, the bounties offered – by local authorities or patriotic associations as well as by government – to volunteers, and the prospect of prize-money; bounties becoming quite large at moments of national emergency, prize-money always seeming larger in lower-deck prospect than it ever turned out to be in practice (the proportions of its distribution ran from a proportionate share in one-quarter of the whole for each ordinary seaman of a 74-gun battleship to one-quarter for the captain(s) and one-eighth for the commander of the fleet).[22]

Some of the reluctant sailors came from the gaols and courts, serving in the navy in lieu of other punishment; but impressment was the main provider of manpower and Britain's unenviable speciality; loathed by the common people, a matter of regret and embarrassment to ordinarily decent people in any class of society, and by no means as unavoidable as apologists then and subsequently made out. Throughout our period, as already before it, schemes were canvassed for the raising of crews by less odious means. Their consistent failure was not because they were cranky or shallow but because they required, (1) more government intervention than propertied public opinion was ready to accept; (2) a de-brutalization of the regular military's habits of body and mind which they and their civilian supporters found inconceivable; and (3) a degree of practical patriotism among the lower orders which not all of them, clearly, were ready to provide. In other words, impressment-abolishing schemes presupposed social change to extents which the ruling class could call 'impractical' or 'utopian'. So the press gang continued to go about its work unmolested – except by the relations, neighbours and workmates of its victims, who repeatedly attempted to resist it.

Press gangs could be sent out by captains whenever they needed to make up their complements of men. This could happen at any time during the term of a ship's commission, on land or at sea; but most of all it happened when a warship was fitting-out and getting ready to sail. In proportion as the need of men was urgent, so would the press be 'hot' and ruthless, catching up helpless landsmen (as well as the seamen to whom it was supposed normally to be limited) and foreigners, and trapping them often with the aid of the local authorities and of the 'crimps' and contacts who were regularly to be found among the bars, taverns, dosshouses, marine stores, slop-shops and brothels in every port. Once caught, the wretched men's fate was sealed until the end of the commission, which could be for several years (unless obvious imbecility or physical feebleness caused the captain to reject them). Brought to the ship by force, they were held there by force and fear. Naval punishments were famously terrible; the lash was in increasing use as the century wore on; on every warship of any size was a detachment of marines whose main job it was to intimidate the crew and to protect the officers from mutiny. Pressed men might under these gruesome circumstances be made efficient enough at their work, and some intoxicating mixture of patriotism, camaraderie, *esprit de corps*, self-preservation and combat frenzy did its customary work, but pressed men could not be expected permanently to enthuse about it. The desertion rate was, despite all efforts made to check it (cordons of troops round major naval bases, and rewards for deserter-trackers etc.), enormous: for example, 42,000 out of the 176,000 men raised between 1774 and 1780.[23] Not all British warships were all the time or equally unpleasant to be on. Sadism, unreasonable severity and common brutality *could*, when it set the tone of all the commanding ranks of a vessel, make the atmosphere rather like that of an early Nazi concentration camp; but very few ships stayed that bad for long. That some lash was essential was hardly surprising, when one recalls the criminal and vagabond origins of some reluctant sailors, and the quantities of alcohol habitually consumed. Yet some officers managed with much less of the lash than others. It was perhaps as much a cultural habit as anything else – like corporal punishment of the young and the delinquent, obsession with which remains a British national peculiarity.

3. The British army, which passed the 100,000 mark during the

peak years of the Seven Years' and American Wars, like the British navy was always short of men, and had to get them by force or fraud – except for German mercenaries, 20,000 and more of whom could be got by finance. Not many voluntarily joined it who could safely stay in civilian life. Hence its riff-raff reputation – which was unfair at least to the perfectly respectable but old-fashioned, simple-spirited clansmen who filled most of the Scottish regiments. Fortescue's pages on recruitment problems are a litany of desperate expedients; the only practical one not to be tried (not before the 1790s, anyway) being the making of military life less forbidding and impoverishing. When war with Spain threatened in 1770, and Parliament had voted funds for recruitment of 12,000, 'such was the difficulty of raising even a fraction of them that, although it was undesirable [for political reasons] to enlist Protestants in Ireland and illegal to enlist Papists, recruiting parties were sent into Leinster, Munster and Connaught to gather in whatever material they might'. Of four regiments recruiting before sailing to India in 1787, two had to fill up with 'prisoners from Gloucester gaol, dismissed seamen and even out-pensioners from Chelsea Hospital', while the 60th Regiment, in the West Indies, had to 'buy recruits on the Continent of Europe at seven guineas a head'.[24] Impressment, just like the navy's, helped to fill the ranks until 1779. Conscription of a qualified and selective kind met the remainder of the army's needs in the form of the militia, which was thought adequate for national defence, and gave all but the very lowest classes of the community a sense of national military togetherness which had much to do, doubtless, with the way interest in, and enthusiasm for, military heroes and triumphs swelled from the 1760s onwards.

The other peculiarity of the British army which demands brief mention is the way its officer corps had become 'commercialized'. Money talked, in every army, more or less, but it talked loudest of all in the British where admission to *every* rank, from ensign up to colonel, had a cash label on it, and a quasi-official little branch of military bureaucracy established itself for the convenient negotiation of sales and purchases. None of this meant any lowering of aristocratic prestige. British peers and gentry were by now well accustomed to the cash nexus. It simply meant that aristocrats who wanted army careers had to be able to pay the going rate, and that anti-bourgeois prejudice was so much the less significant.

4. The French army seems to have been more largely an army of genuine volunteers than any other, which fits in with its appearance as a more nationally popular and acceptable force. There were foreign regiments but in nothing like Prussian proportions. The proportion of regular volunteers, *engagés*, was high, and extra numbers were made up, as and when needed, by recruitment from the local obligatory militias – a procedure often approximating to volunteering, as already described (p.31). The administration of the army was comfortably integrated with the rest of the administration of the realm – by far the most sophisticated bureaucracy in Europe – and, in stark contrast with Prussia and the other eastern military States, civilians were firmly in control of it; above all, the King and his Secretary of State. The French army was a large one, increasingly professional in ethos and with its own distinctively non-civilian, 'specialist' texture, so to speak, becoming steadily more marked. But that was strictly the fighting part of the army, its 'sharp end'. Its blunt backside, its merely material administration, was inextricable from the general civil administration which in fact existed largely on its account. Recruitment, formerly the (profitable) affair of the various regimental officers, was taken over by the King and the centre between 1763 and 1786. Feeding the troops was the affair of the *intendants d'armée* who, if not wholly civilian (they wore a sort of uniform) were not wholly military either. Many of the other affairs of the army were normally the responsibility of the heads of the provincial administrations, the *intendants de provinces*, who generally supervised recruitment, the work of the *commissaires des guerres*, military hospitals, the militia, and so on. Thus the French army was palpably part of the national administration, virtually one of the public services, and it had to march to the tune the government of the day set it. Since France was *not* a military State in the sense that the eastern monarchies were, and the government of France chopped and changed a good deal as it sought ways to deal with the mounting financial crisis of the country, the army suffered chops and changes too; its civil subordination and genuinely national character meant that it experienced in itself, in however

43

modified a form, the tensions and troubles which beset the country as a whole.

5. The Russian army was mysterious and peculiar; the full extent of its peculiarities – springing from its Asian edges and the profound distinctiveness of Russian culture – being somewhat concealed from 'western' eyes by the fact that Russia employed an unusually large number of foreign officers and technical experts. This was nothing new. In many respects of military affairs, Russia needed to catch up with 'the west' if it was not to be at a permanent disadvantage with regard to them. So, for instance, Russian warships were built according to the instructions of Samuel Bentham, and Russian fleets sailed under the orders of Admiral Greig. In the army, as in the general administration (itself of a hybrid civil-military character) and at court, German names were conspicuous. Not all had crossed a frontier to get there. The landowners of the Baltic provinces which Russia had ingested in the course of the eighteenth century were mostly of German origins with German interests, and such were natural importers of western or at any rate Prussian ideas. Really Russian Russians didn't much like them, but they were far too useful to be ignored.

On one side of its sprawling extent, then, the Russian army seemed as European and up-to-date as any, and in some respects – its excellent artillery, for one – really was so. On the other side, or simply viewed from a different angle, it was quite unlike anything in Europe except perhaps the army of the Habsburg Empire. Something between 400,000- and 500,000-strong in its regular parts, it could also summon nearly as many again of 'irregular' troops.[25] Its system of conscription was coarse and brutal. Nowhere else was an army more obviously used as a receptacle for men who were not wanted anywhere else; and, just as Russian landowners enjoyed more absolute powers over their serfs than most others, so were they able to pitch into the army their misfits and troublemakers. Military discipline was accordingly ferocious. Service was for twenty-five years. Until recently, it had been *for life*. But in effect it was still a life sentence, for a lad or man totally removed from his village and family, subjected to that sort of discipline, and brainwashed with the standard mixture of militaristic manliness and religious patriotism which Suvorov took to such a heady pitch, could not but become a wholly

44

militarized creature; as, of course, he was meant to do. But the proviso has to be entered: if he lasted so long. The Russian army was accustomed to an exceptionally high rate of loss from death or wounds in action and disease in general; perhaps from desertion too. If Andolenko's figures are right, the gross average wastage *from all causes* must have been at least 50 per cent every year.

The Cossacks were a characteristic and famous part of this massive military machine. Hereditary mounted fighting-men from tight-knit communities, along the southern frontiers, their lands and liberties were granted them on condition of military service when called. Of little use against trained regular troops in unbroken formation, they excelled in reconnaissance and communications, the pursuit of broken troops, the slaughter of stragglers and wounded (the western concept of a prisoner-of-war came hardly to them) and – most important – the suppression of domestic rebels and protesters. But it was not Cossacks alone or usually who maintained order in the Russian Empire. It was the army's normal business. So was it part of armies' business everywhere. But for the Tsars it was singularly vital. Only for the Habsburgs did it matter anything like as much.

6. The Habsburg army may, after all that has already been said, be quickly dealt with. In some respects it resembled the army just described. Its equivalent to the Cossacks were the mixed tribesmen from its long southern 'military frontier', similarly settled and privileged in return for military service, variously known as Croats, Pandours, *Grenzer*, etc. The rest of the army was got together in Russian-like ways. The principle of universal obligation was mitigated by so many exemptions that 'in practice only the peasants' sons, other than their heirs, and the rural and urban proletariats, ... were liable for conscription, and there were barely enough of these to make up the numbers. The quotas were largely made up by ... seizing certain unwanted persons, including rogues and vagabonds, persons without papers, and renegades from Catholicism, and delivering them to the barracks...; the remainder were selected by the lord of the manor or his agent.... The "volunteers" in Hungary [which was constitutionally privileged to escape conscription] were also largely produced by [in effect] Shanghaiing.'[26] Officers could be found from all over the Roman Catholic world; an empire which could

45

only hold its many nationalities together by cultivating a peculiarly intense loyalty to the family and person of its sovereign, found no difficulty in employing foreigners willing to share therein.

In other respects, however, the Habsburgs' military ambience was unlike the Russian. It had a long tradition of Italian and French influence. It had Balkan but no positively Asian aspects to its character. And the relations of its military with its civil administration were more like those in France. The army was large, larger indeed than the country could comfortably afford, but it was firmly under civilian control in a State where – as was not the case in Prussia – civilian officials were not soldiers underneath.

There is no space in a book of this size for systematic coverage of the lesser armed forces. It has been convenient to make a few references to them in passing but nothing has been said about, for example, Piedmont/Savoy or Sweden, which is the more unfortunate since they were full of military interest. But they were not in the main stream, wherein we must remain. Readers desirous to know more about them should turn first to Corvisier.

4

WINDS OF CHANGE

After that description of the armed forces of the *ancien régime*'s last quarter-century, there is no need to emphasize the extent to which they were symbiotically bound up with their 'national' societies. But the impression so far given may be too static. Change and the threat or promise of change were always in the air. Military opinion and that part of political opinion which attended to military matters were busy with ideas of improvement in every branch and aspect of them. The armed forces were immune neither from the general fever of revolutionary thought pandemic in the progressive parts of the more advanced countries, nor from the effects of the changes willy-nilly occurring in their economies. The French Revolution, in short, was on the way.

   It is no part of the business of a 'war and society' book to provide a general socio-economic history as well. This series has its work cut out, first to ascertain, and then to keep in focus, the military dimension of the social story, a dimension much less well known. The general history, therefore, must for most of the time be taken as read (with a reminder to the reader that the relevant volumes of the Fontana History of Europe, to look no further, stand ready to supply the lack). Of even giant themes like the making of the Revolution, we may write briskly. What, in short, was happening? An established order – in its politics mainly despotic, monarchical, hierarchical and centralizing, in its economic experience largely feudal and agrarian, in its economic thinking *dirigiste*, in its general social and psychological experience, repressive and cramping – was finding difficulty in handling two somewhat different movements of criticism and opposition. The first was an anti-centralizing, anti-authoritarian provincialism, to which freedom meant mainly an old-fashioned sort of freedom to enjoy traditional rights

47

and not to be badgered by reforming kings and smartly centralizing ministers. The second was a more forward-looking 'democratic' liberalism, whose ideas about representative government and constitutions were parliamentary (English-style) and who tended to have optimistic plans for political, economic and social improvement.

Common to both was the word 'liberty' (despite the different, even incompatible, meanings attached to it) and a conviction that a *more efficient ancien régime*, such as enlightened monarchs and their ministers were seeking to achieve, was no less unbearable than an inefficient, stagnant one. To a greater or lesser degree, according to the state of the country and the mix of their proportions, these men felt indignation at the denial of freedoms and powers which they believed desirable for their provinces or countries, even for mankind, as well as profitable and delightful for themselves: freedom under a rule of law to pursue knowledge wherever it might lead, freedom for the expansive powers of individual talents and economic self-interest, political freedom by such representative means – local, regional or parliamentary national – as were to be seen, through the hopeful eyes of many of them, in the United Kingdom of England and Scotland, to which, until the American colonists' complaints about George III's despotism made them think again, continental liberals hopefully looked as their great hope.

Historians continue to argue about the extent to which this was a class struggle. The French Revolution certainly *began* more as a conflict within a generally ruling class than as a class conflict clear and proper. But a 'bourgeois' revolutionary character became more apparent as it developed. It is true that some aristocrats sympathized with some of these revolutionary aspirations. So did many of the more educated craftsmen and artisans of urban Europe, while men and women of the lower orders, peasants, labourers, unemployed and so on, might of course feel revolutionary too. The histories of the American, French and other Revolutions of this epoch record their sometimes decisive interventions. In some countries the life of the peasant was never the same again. But neither the collaboration given by some of the aristocratic order, nor the violent support sometimes provided by many of the lower orders, significantly reduced the Revolution's character as, in the end, and insofar as it was a class matter, a 'middle class' one.

On the other hand the total revolution of these years – international phenomenon that it was – was more than a class matter. Along with the Enlightenment's wave of ideas and aspirations appealing particularly to the democratically and commercially minded were others of more universal appeal. You might have to be capitalistically minded to contemplate establishing a factory of the new textile-spinning machinery; you did not have to be so, to welcome the construction of canals, or improvements in the design of cannon and hand-guns. Few French craftsmen knew more about locks than Louis XVI. George III was quite an expert about scientific agriculture. Joseph II ardently patronized all sorts of inventors, before the Revolution taught him and conservatives the continent over that desirable innovation in one field might mean undesirable innovation in another. Pre-Revolutionary Europe was in an age of, so to speak, political innocence, when improvement was talked of in every sphere of life and labour, and the possible costs to the ruling class were as yet unimagined. The conservative beloved of liberal caricaturists, opposed on principle to change of *any* sort, was a post-1789 phenomenon. Ideas of innovation and improvement, so long as they were safe from religious and political censorship (which varied a good deal from country to country and time to time), circulated wherever they could be heard or read about. The humanitarianism and philanthropy of the later Enlightenment, for example, touched hearts at all levels above the brutish. The increasingly studied notions of the nation and the fatherland (the French *patrie*) could spur vibrations in any feeling breast. So could the steady march through those same years of the romantic idea of Man: 'naturally' virtuous and estimable, perhaps 'equal' too, and although in his contemporary condition corrupted by radically vicious social and political systems, capable of release and recovery, to his own and humankind's vast benefit.

Such was the spread of ideas about change and reform during the pre-Revolutionary generation; 'bourgeois' and 'liberal' at the political core, perhaps, but with a range and an appeal going well beyond those categories, and with no frightening political consequences, as yet, to block conservatives' minds against them. We shall therefore not be surprised to find discussion of the most searching kind going on among the political and military élites about how to improve military performance and how to make the armed forces serve most responsively the needs of – one's political inclinations were revealed in how one expressed it – empire, kingdom, state, nation, fatherland, or even, as 1789 drew nearer, people.

The net effect of these social and cultural changes was a series of technical developments and new ideas about recruitment, training, strategy and tactics which promised to broaden the base of armies and to loosen and enlarge their operational style. It parallelled and echoed the move in political style from enlightened despotism towards democratic constitutionalism. Frederick II's Prussian army, at the height of its powers and fame in the early sixties, was its starting point. As Paret well says, he 'had discerned the essential conditions imposed on war by contemporary society, economics, technology, and he had organized and trained his forces to make the most of them'.[27] But technology was not static (though our period was not one of big breakthroughs), economic forces were beckoning or bullying everywhere, including Prussia, and no other country resembled Prussia anyway. Frederick's achievement demanded study and provoked emulation, but in other countries there was always controversy as to how much of the Prussian model could be usefully imported, and whether one wanted all of it anyway. In Prussia itself, where the ageing monarch's mind became rather rigid, younger men thought about the need for change, and published what they thought. Regard for sheer combat efficiency had driven Frederick to accept some innovations offensive to his sense of order and propriety – for example, the regular recruitment of fusilier battalions of light infantry – but some Prussian experts thought he should be more welcoming to them. His inveterate prejudice against sub-aristocratic officers was not universally admired. Reform-minded Prussians, with an eye perhaps on the economic disadvantages of the neo-feudal agrarian system supposed to breed good peasants equally with good soldiers, were becoming increasingly aware that their national institutions' peculiar rigidity might not be an unmixed blessing.

All over Europe, then, in Prussia and even, slightly and secretly, in the eastern empires as well as in the more mobile west, there was lively discussion about the central military topics of the age:

how far the stiffness and limitations of Frederician operations might be transcended, and whether the nation's military dimension and performance could not be strengthened by involving 'the people' in some new way; a debate with technical tactics at one end, moral and political philosophy at the other.

Frederick's armies had done well by arriving at the battlefield in good order and by maintaining a high order of disciplined efficiency through the basic business of manoeuvring and firing. Volleys from the three-deep Prussian line came more often and more solidly than from the line of any other army, and that line could – thanks to its well-drilled preservation of parade-ground precision – be relied upon to move exactly as ordered into the most advantageous positions vis-à-vis the enemy. So long as the infantry line remained the centrepiece of battle success, so long would this Prussian model command admiration. But even in its heyday its limitations were acknowledged, and the more men studied it, the more did supplements and alternatives occur to them. Frederick's troops marched in exceptionally good order, but not very fast and for preference not through very rough country; their speed was limited largely by their attachment to an elaborate supply system, while wooded, hilly country offered too many opportunities to deserters. They were marvellous in line, but perhaps the line was not everything. 'Light infantry', nimble manoeuvrers in small detachments or even, as skirmishers (*tirailleurs, Jäger*) individually, could usefully erode the foe's strength and confidence in the early stages of battles, and could conduct useful operations of their own. But Frederick's ideal infantry could be neither trusted nor trained to do such things. He tolerated the use of light infantry and their cavalry counterparts, hussars, but with regret and distaste. Their kind of warfare worried him.

While military progressives in Prussia urged consideration of these novelties as boldly as they dared (Frederick didn't die till 1786), the same ideas caught on quicker in other countries, especially where freer or at any rate looser institutions made it easier to tolerate individual and detached activity, or to dispense with Frederician discipline. Not surprisingly it was in France that speculation and innovation flourished most. Already in the Seven Years' War the Duc de Broglie had shown how armies could travel more speedily and cheerfully *in divisions*, re-uniting *en masse* when they reached the battle-zone; divisions and brigades, ready for

51

combination but self-sufficient combat groups at the same time, were normal in France by 1789. Out of that war came also the crucial French and British introductions of light infantry companies, setting a trend in which Prussia, for a change, was the follower. Guibert and Mesnil-Durand led a lively controversy about how Prussian-type lines might be broken by what kind of attacking columns. Gribeauval's improved artillery of the seventies, besides having the advantage of standardization, was lighter and more mobile, and so was the admirable new musket of 1777, which could fire as many as eight thousand shots before needing major repairs.[28] De Bourcet and others took seriously 'irregular warfare' (i.e., operations of regular troops in rough country or behind enemy lines) and reduced to expository system the mass of scattered experience of it that had by then accumulated. Extensions of cartography and improvements in road-systems, quite marked in most countries in these very years, had an obvious share in making such progressives' dreams come true.

But even more important in unglueing the conduct of war (and the dress of the men thus drilled for the task) was the greater liberty which men could allow themselves in most countries to trust to something other than Prussian discipline for getting apt performance out of the troops, and to contemplate raising the troops themselves wholly from enthusiastic national sources, not from foreign, mercenary or criminal ones. Were soldiers not also *men*? And who should fight better for his regiment, king or country than a man and patriot who could feel loyalty and affection and who would fight from motives of love and belief, rather than from routine, roughness, and fear?

So we enter the later Enlightenment's circles of humanitarian, national and revolutionary ideas about Man and the Nation. These circles sometimes intersected. The early nineties will show how revolutionary a mixture such intersection brewed. But it was easy enough to have strong national feelings without seeking radical change, and easier still to pick up mere humanitarianism.

This turned up in the most impeccable pillars of the *ancien régime*. The training of the Russian army – whose uniform, moreover, by the end of the eighties was the most practical and comfortable in Europe (no pigtails, no buckles, short hair unpowdered, and so on) – was according to Roumiantzov's Manual which expressly recommended officers to win their men's trust and loyalty instead of bullying and terrifying them.[29] Fortescue says that some British generals (Wade, Wolfe, Monckton and Murray, for instance) 'looked upon their men not as marionettes to be dressed and undressed, used up and thrown away, but as human flesh and blood, with good feelings that could be played on, good under-standings that could be instructed, self-respect that needed only to be cultivated, and high instincts that waited only to be evoked'.[30] At least from Marshal Saxe's time, one stream of French military thought followed his belief in the soldier as potentially, and in his own lower-class fashion, a man of honour no less than his officers, and no articles of French army regulations were more hotly debated than those to do with punishments, for everyone knew that corporal punishment and honour went badly together. In Prussia too the new spirit was felt. 'The present generation of commanders', wrote Boyen optimistically in 1784, 'almost all detest the brutal old training system, and the accepted principle today is that recruits are to be taught their business without being beaten.'[31]

The softening of military discipline, then, and the humanization of relations between officers and men were in the air as the eighteenth century wore on, and made more or less of a mark in every army; more, certainly, in the French and probably less in the British than in most. (Against the fact of the humane school of thought has to be set the generally received impression that British flogging was in a crescendo until the early 1800s.) The more men could be trusted not to shirk or desert when allowed to fight on their own, the more might the new, looser tactics be undertaken; 'human tactics', instead of 'clockwork tactics', as one Prussian reformer put it. But this was, after all, only a negative inducement to fight with a will: the removal of deterrents. More important was the associated discovery of positive motives of patriotism and citizenship.

The debate about soldier-patriots and citizen-soldiers began before the American Revolution brought new excitement to it. Nationalism, of one sort or another, was at the bottom of it. Political and sociological thought, which during the earlier Enlightenment had been rather cosmopolitan in tone and scope, remained a good deal so till the end, but was increasingly infiltrated by grandiose ideas of the nation. Few of them at first were revolutionary, and some of them were never so, but all of them bore political implications in their identification of a nation, a people, with a legitimate interest in any war undertaken in their name or on the assumption that they would faithfully support whatever crowned sovereign undertook it. Not many outside England yet dared to say that the people themselves were sovereign, or that monarchs ought to rule constitutionally, like the British one, engaging only in wars of which the people, through a parliament, approved. But quite apart from radical suggestions of that sort, it was demonstrable fact in France and Britain at least, that 'the people' were interested in their countries' military prowess, and very ready to support popular wars. Could not then this mighty reservoir of patriotic fervour and yearning talent be encouraged and tapped, by monarchs confident of their subjects' devotion?

To that argument became added, as the century wore on, an obviously more revolutionary one in terms not of subjects but of *citizens*. From the sixties, this was associated above all with the prime revolutionary mover of the age, Rousseau. Other writers of the age had popularized the Graeco-Roman-based idea of the citizen-soldier, morally admirable because virtuous and self-sacrificing, and militarily admirable because, it was supposed, dedicated and indomitable. Now Rousseau popularized him as politically admirable too, because he did it all so freely, being himself an indissoluble part of the sovereign whose decisions he wholly obeyed.

All of these ideas about ways to involve subjects, citizens and the people generally in the country's war effort were circulating well before the French Revolution, in whose history they became of conspicuous importance. But ten years or so earlier they had already been on show in the American Revolution; and very instructive indeed, for that reason, had many European military men found it. Some had been there, serving on one side or the other, like Lafayette and Gneisenau; others mulled over excitedly what they read about it. It was to a great extent a war of detachments and outposts, using the new light infantry methods already mentioned and extending them further. Nothing surprising about that. Some parts of it became more rough, atrocious and lawless than had been usual in Europe, because of the employment of native auxiliaries and the ease with which local feuds, vendettas, animosities and brute backwoods lawlessness got into the act. Nothing surprising about that either, however much to regret. But what was novel and surprising, and quite intoxicating to younger European observers, was its character as a people's war. This was no war of the kind so familiar in the old world: war for traditional dynastic or expansionist aims, proclaimed by monarchs and acquiesced in (enthusiastically, if the monarchs were lucky) by their subjects. The Americans' war was proclaimed as a war of a people – a new, natural, nation, moving with the tide of progressive political thought to assert its independence of old despotism (as George III's régime was exaggeratedly described). It was presented as a war of one perhaps less attractive kind of military strength – that authoritarian, severely disciplined, highly pro-fessionalized but hardly 'national' kind typified by the Prussian and British armies – against a much more attractive new one: the strength of an independent-minded free people organizing itself militarily to fight for what it believed in – and succeeding.

I summarize the myth, not the facts. The facts offered a more mixed and complicated picture. The revolting colonials did not win the war on their own, or without the benefit of old-world military science. Direct French support, German methods of training, and the more or less open hostility to Britain of all the maritime States of Europe, were indispensable to victory; most of the crucial military operations that led to victory were orthodox ones; George Washington and his hard-pressed generals would have been delighted if there had in reality been anything like as much patriotic zeal as there was in the rhetoric of the rebel political leaders and in the gushings of their admirers. Nevertheless, some truths were self-evident. A people really had successfully con-ducted a war of national liberation against an imperial power perceived as alien and oppressive. It had made itself militarily formidable in a variety of ways, from guerrilla warfare of questionable legality to German-style disciplined drill and tactics. It had apparently shown what 'a people numerous and armed' could do, and the myth glowingly maintained that they could do it on their own.

Progressive-minded Europeans found this exciting because so much of their political and military speculation in these years was concerned with this very possibility. The greater involvement of the people in their country's affairs was commonplace in the nationalist and democratic movements of the age. What measure of involvement could be more convincing than willing and enthusiastic military service by respectable, independent men? But European armies and navies hardly invited that, and 'enlightened despots' like Frederick, Catherine and Joseph positively did not want them to do so. We have already noted how, even in Prussia, liberal reformers were beginning to suggest that a more national and actively patriotic army would probably fight better and certainly seem more fitting, more admirable, in an age which they believed irresistibly to demand the enlargement of government's social bases. But the idea of the patriot-soldier was the furthest to which their thought stretched: the loyal subject cheerfully serving his king because he had an emotional as well as a material stake in the country. It was in freer France that the more revolutionary idea of the citizen-soldier soldier really blossomed.

The citizen-soldier was a more revolutionary concept because he would be, ideally, a republican. He would therefore be fighting for his own country in a peculiarly real sense; his emotional and material stakes in it would be crowned by his personal share in its politics. Rousseau was the writer whose vision of the citizen in his republic enjoyed the widest circulation and influence, but his was – mainly because of its connection with his well-known other writings about equality, naturalness, ethics and education – only the best-known version of a familiar Enlightenment theme: the moral excellence as well as the political superiorities of the republican form of government, of which Greek and Roman models and precedents were plentifully available. Early republican Rome was a standard source of examples for moralists, for political and for military reformers well before the French Revolution seemed, for some of them, to recreate that age of gold; and George Washington, whom some admirers liked to present as a resurrection of the ancient Roman dictator, was more often represented as such than as the seventeenth-century English Whig constitutionalist he more closely resembled.

If Rousseau was the man who did most to popularize the citizen-soldier idea on the political and ethical side, its most striking application to the military world was made by Jacques de Guibert. Ambitious, confident and trendy son of a respected senior officer, he was responsive to all the progressive and exciting ideas of his generation – nationalism, 'democracy', Rousseau-an naturalness, Roman virtue and romanticism, besides all the new tactical developments – and poured a heady mixture of them into his *Essai General de Tactique*, 1772. The book was much read and discussed especially, it seems, among younger officers through the next twenty years. One of them was Lieutenant Bonaparte. He was still reading it, apparently, after he had become a general. But Guibert's importance should be properly understood. His celebrity was symptomatic rather than seminal. He was an imaginative, irresponsible and rather slap-dash compiler, not a deep or original thinker. His originality lay in putting together, regardless of inconsistencies and with much boldness and flourish, the new political and military ideas teeming around him.

Guibert was enthusiastically optimistic about the military potential of popular involvement in national wars. He expressed a conventional preference for peace but revealed a thorough relish for military glory and achievement. He was conventionally keen on the Roman-style citizen-soldier, but his admiration of popular national kings and princes – such, for example, as might lead subject peoples in wars of rebellion against imperial tyranny – forbids one to class him among the republicans. Again in conventional line with a strong stream of Enlightenment thought, he declaimed against the 'vice', 'luxury', 'corruption', 'artificiality' and so on of contemporary civilization, maintaining that societies of such a character deserved to succumb – and indeed *would* succumb – to the assault of more 'pure', 'virtuous' and 'hardy' societies, if such could be found or created. So far as strategy and tactics were concerned, his main interest was in the war of movement: promoting that mobility and flexibility of troop movements in which the Frederician system was, by common consent among the progressives, deficient.

Roman legions, he recalled, had no difficulty moving whenever they wanted to as fast as they could, because they travelled fairly light *and lived off the country as they went*. Thus, in the rather striking phrase he borrowed from Cato, war could be made to nourish war, and could even be self-supporting. In any case, he insisted, with a relishing claim to realism which was becoming more common, war is war, and non-combatants get hurt when they get in the way. Armies engaged in so serious a business cannot submit to march, as it were, in leg irons[32] and to observe all the niceties of the limited warfare upon which contemporary civilization prided itself;

neither, he asserted, should they want to. Real men – patriots, healthy, bold, fearless, and conscious of the virtue of their cause – could not be expected to fight in kid gloves and in fact would not do so.

Now came the passage which has most often been quoted, the passage usually supposed to prefigure the avenging armies of the revolutionary French Republic:

> Only suppose the appearance in Europe of a people who should join to austere virtues and a citizen army a fixed plan of aggression, who should stick to it, who – understanding how to conduct war economically and to live at enemy expense – should not be driven to give up by financial exhaustion. Such a people would subdue its neighbours and overthrow our feeble constitutions like the gale aquilon bends the reeds.

In the following pages he revealed his belief that the purified society of his imagination would try to be a good neighbour.

> But if, despite its moderation, its subjects, territory or honour are injured, it will fight.... Its style of war-making will be different from that practised by all States nowadays... Terrible in its anger, it will pursue its enemy with flame and steel. Its vengeance will astonish [épouvantera] all peoples who disturb its peace, [who draw down on themselves] these reprisals justified by the laws of nature.... It will fight to the last man, if need be. But it will obtain satisfaction....[33]

The most significant thing about such passages is their romanticism. It is a flattering fantasy of aggression and violence, excused by consciousness of virtue; a wild new look given to the increasingly familiar mixture of neo-classical, Rousseau-an and modern military themes by the dramatic exaggeration and moral egotism of the romantic movement, then just dawning. And its appeal accordingly was likely to be proportionate to the degree to which the reader was detachable from his pre-romantic roots. We know that the way Guibert put this was found by some to be appealing and exciting. We also know that others found it deplorable, for its apparently reckless jettisoning of Enlightenment restraint and the ideal of minimum bloodshed. One of the second rank of French military writers then was Le Michaud d'Arçon of the Engineers. His critical faculties were sharpened, indeed, by professional resentment of Guibert's contempt for the noble and ancient science of fortification and siege-work, but there was more to his dislike of Guibert than that. The warfare to which he and his like had been trained, he said, had as its ideal the infliction of minimum hurt and damage; 'the art of war is to win, to conquer and to conserve.... Everything beyond that, like setting fire to corn-fields, slaughtering defenceless men, ripping open pregnant women, bashing babies' heads against walls and so on [such were conventional excesses of unregulated warfare] – all that *cannot*, whatever Monsieur de Guibert says, serve the end for which wars are undertaken.'[34] Indeed it could not serve any end for which any normal monarch or statesman of the later Enlightenment might undertake a war, and their officers normally sought to stop such actions when their men, faithful to ancient habits, committed them. But visions such as Guibert's – which, to do him justice, were not as expressly horrific and abandoned as d'Arçon's extrapolation from them – were going to appeal to revolutionaries and romantics, and their style of war, in the early nineties, was going to have some uncanny correspondence with his projections. Through Guibert, the winds of change blew at their strongest.

Part II

*THE FRENCH
AND THE REST*

5
INTRODUCTORY

The story of these twenty-five years is a story of the challenge made by the French Revolution to the established monarchical, aristocratic order of Europe, and its response; the challenge made by the French nation turned imperialist to the other nations of Europe, and their responses. What made these challenges so formidable and demanded responses of comparable weight, was the extent to which the French, renewed by revolution, quickly became a military force of unprecedented magnitude and vitality: a nation in arms, such as had not been seen in Europe through many lifetimes, and indeed, strictly speaking, had never been seen before. A close observer from one of the responding States put it thus. In 1793, he said,

> a force appeared that beggared all imagination. Suddenly war again became the business of the people – a people of thirty millions, all of whom considered themselves to be citizens.... The people became a participant in war; instead of governments and armies as heretofore, the full weight of the nation was thrown into the balance. The resources and efforts now available for use surpassed all conventional limits: nothing now impeded the vigour with which war could be waged....[1]

War acquired a new – at any rate, what was felt by contemporaries to be a new – intensity, and this was possible only because society's involvement was more complete and hearty than anyone had thought possible.

To put it another way: the French Revolution began this process, and Napoleon as Emperor of the French completed it. It is a truth universally acknowledged by war history specialists that the revolutionary new style of warfare was 'perfected' by him. We shall have cause to inquire, at what social cost this perfection was achieved, and to note how un- or even anti-Revolutionary became the social sources of Napoleon's military might and reputation, once he was exclusively the man in charge. With the entry upon the stage of this Corsican professional soldier, and the remarkable extent to which he captivated or captured not only the people of France but also some of the people of other countries (continuing to do so for a hundred years and more after he ceased to rule the French) we encounter the one individual with whom in this volume we have to be much concerned. Napoleon Bonaparte, as Napoleone di Buonaparte called himself after he had decided to become thoroughly French, was the colossus of his age, and primarily on account of military prowess. He conducted campaigns, won battles, and cultivated the respect and affection of soldiers and subjects alike in ways that marked him, at least in that respect, as a genius. He took French power, briefly, to a pitch and a stretch unmatched before or since. His admirers praised him for achievements in other than military matters and it is true that during the years of his personal ascendancy great things were done, in France and in her allied, satellite and puppet countries alike, under his orders and with the benefit, more or less, of his personal interest. But the military power and presence was what mattered most, securing his greatness with chains as strong as they were brittle, and making all the other things stick; and the momentous question for the historian is, how far had the French people themselves (not to mention their country's allies, satellites, etc.) complicity with the great man in that basically military achievement, and how exactly was that potent conjuncture of forces brought about? Historians unsympathetic to Napoleon himself or to the 'great man' philosophy of history have always argued that fundamentally it was France which was flexing its muscles to the point of continental hegemony. But even historians ready to believe in great men's capacity to make history and to believe Napoleon to have been a very great man indeed never pretend that the great events tied to his name could have happened, had he not had a great military society willingly behind him.

From the point of view of the immediate victims of Napoleon's mainly French Empire – which, in the years of its furthest extent eastwards, ran from Hamburg through the Netherlands, down the

Rhine frontier, and after skirting Switzerland included Piedmont, Genoa, Tuscany and Rome; also, slightly detached, Dalmatia, otherwise the Illyrian Provinces – the precise definition of the ultimate source of their servitude mattered little compared to the costly, humiliating, and increasingly irksome fact of it; the immediate presence of French ministers, administrators and messengers, army officers and bodies of troops, who even if they were not numerous recalled the looming presence of the Napoleonic Army, from 1805 to 1812 apparently irresistible, betokening the will and the power to keep them under the French thumb.

That was what Napoleon meant outside his own country. The French Revolution had been different. Indeed it had taken on an expansive military form through the middle nineties, but its armies had not pressed aggressively into central and eastern Europe, or far into the Iberian Peninsula, as Napoleon's were to do; it had actively invited and encouraged emulation elsewhere, but its bayonets actually took the Revolution only to the Low Countries, the Rhineland, Savoy and Italy. It did not directly affront the independent sensibility of any other major powers except Great Britain and Austria, and certainly it did not purport to run the continent. From 1806 onwards, that was precisely what Napoleon did purport and seek to do; with the interesting consequence, from *our* point of view, that the other major powers thus affronted and sat upon discovered in themselves deep social reserves of national feeling and of patriotic military preparedness that they were able, in the end, to turn upon their intolerable imperial oppressor with a strength similar to his own, because similarly supplied.

So it was the 'nationalization' of the war and the militarization of national feeling and activity, swelling unevenly from country to country from 1806 until it burst out all over Europe in the winter of 1812-13, that enabled the last coalition against France to defeat Napoleon at last. The contemporary whom we quoted earlier, apropos of the military effect originally of the Revolution, commented with equal shrewdness on the significance of this anti-Napeolonic, newly nationalist, popular military surge. Let this introductory chapter end with another passage from Clausewitz's *On War*:

Since Bonaparte, then, war, first among the French and

subsequently among their enemies, again became the concern of the people as a whole, took on an entirely different character, or rather closely approached its true character, its absolute perfection. There seemed no end to the resources mobilized; all limits disappeared in the vigour and enthusiasm shown by governments and their subjects. Various factors powerfully increased that vigour: the vastness of available resources, the ample field of opportunity, and the depth of feeling generally aroused. The sole aim of war was to overthrow the opponent. Not until he was prostrate was it considered possible to pause and try to reconcile the opposing interests.

'War, untrammelled by any conventional restraints, had broken loose in all its elemental fury. This was due to the peoples' new share in these great affairs of state; and their participation, in turn, resulted partly from the impact that the Revolution had on the internal conditions of every state and partly from the danger that France posed to everyone.'[2]

6

THE COURSE OF FRENCH EVENTS BEFORE VALMY AND JEMAPPES

The French Revolution, which we will take to have 'begun' on Bastille Day, 14 July 1789, ran on its own French tracks for a clear two years before any of the other great powers of Europe began to wonder whether they might not have to do something military about it, and for nearly another year before French provocation finally compelled them to do so. The French declaration of war against Austria, the great power most closely adjacent and the one showing the most concern about Louis XVI and his Austrian-born Queen, was on 20 April 1792. So slow were their movements, and so complicated and distracted their decision-making processes, that it was not until late August that the combined Austrian and Prussian army of intervention crossed the French frontier. The momentous little battle of Valmy followed on 20 September. Just as the fall of the Bastille announced with signal clarity the popular will to destroy the *ancien régime*, so that régime's troops' withdrawal from the field at Valmy announced that the French people – contrary to general foreign expectation – were able as well as willing to defend the more open, free and equal society they had created in its place. From then on, France and its Revolution were at war with Europe, the further development of the Revolution was largely determined by military exigencies, and France had systematically to become a greater military power than it had ever been before. But for the first two years or so, revolutionary France was internationally quite passive, engrossed in its own passionate domestic concerns; among which, the establishment of a proper relationship between society and its armed force was not the least urgent.

The mutual relations of army, State, and society, always a question of interest to political theorists, excited increasing attention through the later eighteenth century, as the various military options and their respective political consequences or pre-conditions were assessed. Progressive military thinkers, as we partly saw near the end of the last chapter, warmly canvassed the idea of a more respectable and responsible soldiery – which would, they believed, derive valuable military results from its superior motivation. But what would be the political consequences of such reforms? Here came the more profound causes of disagreements. Social conservatives and enlightened despotism technocrats united in suspicion of such prospects; the former, from inability to imagine any viable society that did not rest on strict subordination, the latter because they shared the classic dynast's conviction that armies and autocrats sank or swam together, and that to deny a monarch total control of his army was to cut off his life-support system; and what would it avail an autocrat, if the means that won him a war should lose him his crown? On the other side, the advocates of a citizen-soldiery were not alone in liking these ideas not just because they were militarily attractive, but because they were socially and politically attractive too; they belonged with the schemes of liberalization which pointed towards 'revolution' (not expected to be a bloody event, we must remember) and which were in fact to guide the constructive work of the Revolution once it had got going. Liberal political thinkers came to the same conclusion from a different direction, a direction exactly the opposite of the monarchical conservatives. The monopolistic concentration of military power by the executive power (whether that meant an absolute monarch or not) was, so they argued, both dangerous for liberty – because it gave the perhaps despotic central power an ideal a-political instrument for suppressing opposition – and encouraging to the continuation of wars, which rulers could engage in irresponsibly so long as their soldiers automatically did what they were told, and a politically helpless people footed the bill willy-nilly. The 'publicists' of the later Enlightenment – i.e., experts on what we now call public international law – added the weight of their authority to the opinion already widely current among the philosophers and liberal political writers, that wars ought not to be conducted for frivolous, vicious, or simply personal causes. Some 'dynastic' wars certainly seemed to be like that. They were classified, according to the traditional juridical terminology, as 'unjust' wars. The fact that professionally-led 'standing armies' were the normal means of waging them did not endear those armies to progressives who thought that peace and liberty would go together, and believed that a State's defence needs – the only military needs of indisputable virtue – could be adequately met by something of a more popular, voluntary or part-time kind.

Standing navies, of course, were a different matter for the maritime commercial powers. But even over the strife-swept oceans the idea was beginning to dawn, that prosperity was not something that had to be jealously grabbed and snapped at, and that a state of peace might be more conducive to it than one of conflict all but unceasing. If wars would keep happening, better that they should be conducted lawfully by official units than by the guerrillas of the seas, privateers. The movement to ban privateering, which culminated in the 1856 Declaration of Paris, was just beginning. But navies were discussed in a political context quite different from that concerning armies. Royal navies were never felt to be the props of despotism that royal armies were; the extraordinarily oppressive way in which the British navy was supplied with manpower (see above, pp.40-1) was viewed by conscientious liberals more as a rather inexplicable blot on the admired British record than as an indication of anything radically amiss.

Theoretically inseparable from these loftier themes but more popularly discussed were the bread-and-butter, flesh-and-blood matters of pay, promotion, and discipline. To some officers, Prussian-style discipline seemed necessary if operational efficiency of the Prussian order was to be achieved. To others, a more humane and trusting regard for the soldier was thought capable of achieving results at least as good. Ordinary soldiers of course were strongly of this opinion, and so did the public at large, the *tiers état*, show itself to be, when the *cahiers des doléances* were compiled in the run-up to the meeting of the Estates-General. Compulsory service in the militia (see above, p.43) was a good deal complained of in the peoples' *cahiers*, preference being expressed for an army entirely of volunteers. As for recruitment and promotion of officers, the aristocracy's attempt to monopolize the corps of course continued to be the subject of bitter complaint by the commoners who could hardly get into it or, once in, could not hope ever to rise high.

Such were reformers' ideas about the armed forces and society during the months running up to the Revolution. But not ideas

69

alone were to determine the change in their relationship. That was already changing. The *ancien régime*'s loss of grip was nowhere more apparent than in the fact that some of its army, its ultimate security, sharing in the general political excitement and confusion of the time, took the revolutionary part.

What happened in the French armed forces reflected exactly what was happening in French society at large. The aristocrats and gentlemen of the officer corps, unaware of the doom impending over them collectively, were quarrelling among themselves in the way already noted. The lesser, poorer, nobility, who formed the great majority of the corps and for whom professional self-respect was a driving principle, looked forward to eliminating the elements of purchase and inheritance in appointments and promotions, so that merit and service could reap their just rewards. They also showed growing sympathy with the popular dislike of severe corporal punishment. That dislike, naturally, was most apparent in the schemes of reform promoted among the *tiers état*. For them – the people at large, other than the nobility and the clergy in the first and second estates respectively – the promise made in August 1788 that the Estates-General should meet next May was exhilarating. Punishments, compulsory militia service, quartering and requisitioning figured a good deal in their talk and writing and made much common ground with the aristocratic professionals. Of more revolutionary implication, however, was the demand now more strongly made than ever before for parity of esteem for the non-noble part of the naval officers corps (the *bleus*, snubbed and kept down by the *rouges*) and for the opening of both officer corps fairly to commoners; the abolition of aristocratic exclusiveness and the opening of the military career, along with careers in the other professions and public services, to *talent*, wherever (within the nation) it might come from. These demands, though pressed most persistently by men of the middle orders, did not envisage bourgeois domination of the officer corps. There seems to have been no objection to aristocratic officers provided they were properly qualified; there was positive approval of the practice of merited promotion to commissioned from the non-commissioned officers' level. But economic and social circumstances being what they were, the most probable consequence of reform in this matter was of course a substantial infusion of middle and lower-middle-class talent and ambition – an infusion which indeed soon happened, though not quite in the ways the reformers expected.

Such were the ideas of military reforms freely mooted among the military themselves, not to mention the general public, in those months of crisis which finished off the *ancien régime*. But the French armed forces were even more directly involved in that revolutionary ferment, partly by helping to stir it up, and partly by declining to cool it down. So far as that crisis and ferment were simply the conclusion of several decades of publicly voiced misgivings about France's form of government, brought now to a head by the government's inability to solve its financial crisis without revolutionary concessions, French soldiers and sailors, whose discipline was far freer than eastern European ones and who no doubt included a higher proportion of literates, could easily know what was going on and join in. But the ultimate crisis was precipitated by a more local and abrupt cause. The 1788 harvest was 'the worst in decades, and in a country where most of the inhabitants lived on a subsistence economy this was a major disaster'.[3] By early 1789 the lower orders were responding to the consequent pain and hardship in their conventional way – by rioting. This had often happened before, but not often as badly and never before in this atmosphere of radical talk about popular rights and of plausible utopian predictions. The army was called upon to aid the civil power; in 1788 by helping it to enforce royal orders against provincial *parlement* opposition and obstructionism, and from early 1789 by putting down the food riots. It proved to be unreliable. Again and again the men of some regiments showed sympathy with revolutionary and popular demonstrators by reluctance to obey orders or even by refusal to obey them at all. By the early summer of 1789, when the Estates-General at last met (5 May) and the tense trial of strength between Court and *tiers état* began, enough of the army was affected for many officers to feel inhibited from ordering their troops to act firmly, while some regiments had been permeated by revolutionary sentiment and propaganda.

Thus the government's ultimate security system crumbled in its grasp. It had relied on the army to see it safely past the confrontation with the *tiers* and by early July more than 20,000 troops were in Paris or on their way. But from many of their officers came reports that some at least of them were not to be relied on. Scott gives a good sketch of the process at its most extreme among

71

the French Guards, an 'élite unit' quartered in Paris (where its men 'worked at various trades during off-duty hours'). Its men were 'fraternizing with the crowds and agitators at the Palais Royal' by mid-June; refusing to perform police duties from the 23rd; beginning to desert from the 27th. On the 30th, ten of them who had been locked up for insubordination were liberated by a large and cheering crowd. By 6 July they were picking patriotic quarrels with German-speaking hussars, on the 12th taking demonstrators' sides against still loyal cavalry (again, Germano-phones) – and on the famous 14th, by which time most had defected, French Guardsmen were conspicuous among the regulars, well over a hundred of them, who took leading parts in the attack on the Bastille. Scott doubts whether as many of the men in other regiments were as radicalized as their officers certainly feared, but the fact was that their fears were taken for real, and the great military force assembled to suppress the Revolution was never called to that service. And the events of Bastille Day were crucial, because of the message the provinces and the troops in them got from it. The army remained active against public disorder through 1790 but, 'after 14 July any chance of halting or controlling the [political] revolutionary movement by use of the Royal Army was lost'.[4]

That was important – crucial, indeed – for the progress of the Revolution. More important for the army and the navy was the fact that the revolutionary movement continued within them, adding to the complications of the revolutionaries' task of transforming what had been the main props of the old régime into the main props of the new one. It cannot be too much insisted on, that the men who made the French Revolution neither desired nor expected to have to do much with their country's armed forces. Their intentions and hopes were peaceable. Those who had associated old-style absolutists with bad, 'unjust', sorts of wars, wars for mere glory and vanity or for greedy annexation, expected that the foreign policy of a freed people would be more creditable. It was also supposed that international peace would be among the by-products of freedom's spread to other countries and that domestic calm and contentment would spread at home as the rest of the people's grievances against the *ancien régime* followed the Bastille to the grave. Of course an army and navy for defensive purposes could never be dispensed with; exactly how such forces should be recruited and organized was an interesting, even delicate, question, to which we shall come presently. Had the question been dealt with in calm and peaceful circumstances, it might have been difficult enough. But circumstances turned out to be anything but calm and peaceful.

In the first place, both army and navy had, during the months before Bastille Day, acquired unmilitary habits of insubordination and political activity which were not easily got rid of. They persisted, in fact, into 1793, when they were not so much overcome by a reassertion of the old style of discipline as absorbed by the introduction of a new revolutionary one. Their persistence was part and parcel of the other continuing aggravation of the military situation: the increasing political disaffection of the old officer corps, and the emigration, by 1793, of the greater part of it. Soldiers and sailors had begun to disobey their officers' orders before the Revolution largely because they disapproved of the military system the officers were running. Once the Revolution had begun and that system had begun to be changed for (from their point of view) the better, they had the more political ground for disobedience, that they suspected their officers of liking neither the changes nor the Revolution which produced them. Which indeed was the case.

There was no problem to begin with. The king to whom the officers had sworn allegiance was still king. Few who mattered yet muttered about republicanism. France was to become a constitutional monarchy like Britain, that was all – and no one who knew about Britain could doubt aristocracy's ability to co-exist with constitutionalism. Along with aristocratic fears and misgivings went, in those early months, much persistent patriotism and hoping for the best. As for the king, Louis was known not much to like it; but time and again he dodged opportunities to make a firm stand, and until he did so, his more resolute relations and courtiers were stuck. With Marie Antoinette at their head, they very much disliked their caste's loss of dignity and authority, the cracking of the ancient code of hierarchy, and their estimates of the course of political events was not hopeful. Already by early October 1789 this group had cause to conclude that their estimates were the more realistic. They vented their feelings at a regimental banquet at Versailles on the first of the month: acclamation of the royal family, loyal cries, songs and toasts, and insults to the

73

tricolour. The tale of this counter-revolutionary demonstration was not spoilt in the telling to the common people of the metropolis, just then irritable and resentful on account of high prices and unemployment. In one of the more extraordinary of the Paris crowd's forceful interventions into politics in these years, many women from the central working-class quarters organized (or were organized into) a march to Versailles on the 5th, which after much confusion and indecency, and the killing of a few royal bodyguards, carted the king and his family back to Paris next afternoon. No European monarch had ever been so treated before. The impact of these events upon the aristocracy was terrific. Their king had been taken captive by an amorphous, plebeian revolutionary movement which seemed to be getting out of respectable control. From this early time the aristocratically-led counter-revolutionary movement steadily gained strength, and the emigration began, encouraged by the indiscipline which continued among the soldiers and sailors and was freely egged on by radical revolutionaries who had such new forms of army and navy in view that they wanted to destroy the old forms altogether. Some aristocrats could stand it, were ready to take the mounting personal risk, and to take also the new oath prescribed for them on 11 June 1791; loyalty to nation and law as well as king. But most decided to get out, especially after the failure at Varennes of Louis' flight to join his *émigrés* loyalists in the Rhineland in late June. That put an end to the fiction that he wanted them to go along with the Revolution. From then on he really was a prisoner, submitted to popular indignities and personal dangers whose natural culmination was his execution in January 1793. By then the war which the *émigrés* leaders had encouraged Austria and Prussia to conduct against France had been on for many months.

Desertion and insubordination in the ranks – resignation or emigration of the majority of officers – were the main systemic weakenings of the old royal army (the 'line army' as it was often and in some books still is referred to), as it marched into the new era. Desertion was the least of them, if only because it was nothing new. For the time being its incidence had been raised by the novel political distractions to which the soldier was subjected. With their subsidence, desertion reverted to the status of a problem taken for granted in all armies fed by compulsory service. The armies of the Revolution in this respect – *a fortiori*, the armies of Napoleon – were no exceptions to the general rule. The insubordination and mutineering which became rife throughout army and navy alike in 1790 were more peculiarly a French phenomenon, directly provoked by revolutionary circumstances, encouraged and exploited by revolutionary activists, who liked thus to confront conservative officers and to cripple counter-revolutionary ones. The militarily fatal idea got abroad, that orders given by officers and (supposed) gentlemen could properly be questioned and if necessary flouted by free and equal French men happening to be soldiers at the time. Revolutionary politicians in charge of defence and security had no difficulty in seeing that this would not do. By 1793 the remedy was being elaborated: 'revolutionary discipline', urged by revolution-minded officers (no longer necessarily gentlemen) on ideological as well as patriotic grounds, and supported among the men themselves by the revolutionary ethos. As the early fervours of the Revolution subsided, so did this zealotry turn into something less exceptional. But the discipline and demeanour of the French armies of this period retained to the end the stamp of their revolutionary reconstruction. Orders were less forbiddingly given, they were more informally carried out to the accompaniment of an amount of chat and comment that surprised most foreign observers; while the French, becoming increasingly conscious of this creditable distinction, made propaganda out of it by jeering at the 'miserable slaves of Pitt and George' who were flogged into service as 'mechanical soldiers' by York and later, the cold, stiff and haughty Wellington.[5]

Part-cause of the same revolutionary development was the way in which the command gaps made by the resignation or emigration of anti-revolutionary officers were filled by men of middle- and lower-class origins. The Revolution's readiness to open the way to such proved otiose; the way opened by itself, and government had no choice but to take such talent and ambition as were available. It is a famous fact, and did much to further France's military success in these years, that the supply of ambitious talent was abundant. It was less so, admittedly, at sea than on land. Some of the old 'Grand Corps' of naval officers, the aristocratic élite, were still there in 1793, but not many survived the purge of that autumn, when the Brest fleet's mutiny and the treasonous goings-on at Toulon determined the Committee of Public Safety at all costs to prefer political reliability to professional aptitude, whenever the two could not be combined. Hampson remarks that the professional interest suffered from this. Even with the merchant marine to draw on, there simply were not enough experienced sea officers to go round. The superior levels were well enough served, but the lower ones took in, just because they were politically respectable, a lot of incompetents, windbags, and (for such will take advantage of openings even in virtuous republics) plain humbugs.[6] Efficient officers could complain bitterly about them, and doubtless they took their toll. Yet the consensus of a-patriotic naval historians seems to be that the French navy's operational shortcomings much more resulted from sheer lack of practice than from failures of human quality.

Politically safe men for a few years got on quicker in the army too than their talents might justify. But they could do less damage than at sea, they lost less public money (warships being so expensive), and zeal for the Revolution in fact often accompanied military skill and ambition and endowed operational performance with distinctive dash and fury. Numerous successful officers, generals and marshals included, had before the Revolution been only rankers or NCOs. Talent was quickly spotted and richly rewarded. Nothing was more unlike the old armies' predominant gerontocracy than the speed with which youth now got to the top. General Bonaparte, the most notable example, was only twenty-seven when he took command of the army of Italy in 1796; but he had begun as an officer. At that date he was not nearly so well known as, for instance, General Lazare Hoche, who had been a sergeant in the French Guards and was the same age when he quelled the Vendée insurrection.

In the ways just described, the French armed forces' character changed during and along with the Revolution, conforming them to its spirit and requirements. But conscious design was at work as well. Army and navy matters occupied a good deal of legislative time – humanizing discipline, improving pay and soldiers' families' welfare, opening the way to non-aristocratic talent, and so on; and above and through all of these particular questions continued for about four years discussion of the most fundamental question of all: how should the army of the new France be constituted? How different should or need it be from the old one? For the moment, we may more or less forget about the navy; for one thing there was only one sensible way to constitute a worthwhile navy, and for another, the navy was irrelevant to the discussion of constitutional principle. But the army was very relevant indeed, 'standing armies' having long been identified as potentially inimical to liberty, and the Revolution perhaps being unsafe while anything like an *ancien régime* army remained in being.

What it boiled down to was the extent to which the national army should, in its manning and management, be nationalized. The army before 1789, we recall, had been less than perfectly national. A substantial proportion of its men at all levels were pure professionals, internationally transferable, and some actually were foreigners. But now that the French nation had, to the revolutionary mind, found itself, foreigners were not wanted anymore. The *émigrés* might consort with them but loyal Frenchmen would not want to. And pure professionals likewise became very suspect. The new ideology looked down on men who served for money, calling them hirelings and mercenaries. Soldiering was only respectable when it was done voluntarily by citizens from love of their country; under which circumstances it became morally admirable – and politically safe. Hireling standing armies might endanger the liberties of peoples, but how could armies of citizen volunteers do that?

Armed bodies of citizen volunteers were in fact on the scene already – a fact which for the first few years complicated the search for a new military constitution. The National Guard was in effect functioning and flourishing all over the country well before its national standardization was completed in the summer of 1790. Its shadowy origins lie in the spring of 1789, as hopeful solid citizens here and there began to prepare for trouble. By the summer its nuclei (by far the biggest, of course, in Paris, making its first big mark in the attack on the Bastille) were operating everywhere.

The rapidity of its formation was remarkable, but its explanation was simple enough: it enabled the bourgeoisie to overawe opponents of its revolution, to maintain order and protect property by its own means and in entirely its own way, and it corresponded to a stirring theme of revolutionary rhetoric: men of public spirit in arms to promote the good cause and protect it. As the months went by, these protagonists of the Revolution became more and more prominent as its representatives and agents, rallying public opinion behind the movement and demonstrating revolutionary

77

solidarity by 'federating' with units in neighbouring places. The quality of their armament improved with time, and their standardization included a common, familiar uniform of the national tricolour: blue coat, white waistcoat, and red trimmings. So the National Guard soon and naturally became a national institution, embodying *all* 'active citizens' (i.e., independent householders and taxpayers over twenty-five) and proclaiming this para-military service as a primary right *and duty* of the full, first-rate citizen.

But if this National Guard in its first couple of years was in such a sense the nation in arms, those arms were not expected to be used against foreigners. It was an inward-looking body, a civic and bourgeois militia merely, neither trained nor equipped for serious international occasions. Producing a politically safe army of quality to deal with such was a different matter. Of increasing seriousness as the willingness of some officers and regiments of the old 'line' army to accept the Revolution became suspect, it imperatively demanded settlement after the events surrounding Louis' failed flight to Varennes spotlighted the danger in which France internationally now stood: a counter-revolutionary invasion force gathering just across the eastern frontier, no military defence against it but an army considerably disorganized, in part untrustworthy, and not an ally in sight.

France's response to this challenge was staggering. The nation that was already in arms for internal, domestic purposes, turned its bayonets outwards. One day after Louis' bungled flight, the constituent assembly set about raising from the National Guard companies of one-year Volunteers: nine companies to a battalion, the men to elect their officers and NCOs, the pay twice that of the regular infantry, the uniform to be that of the National Guard. By mid-August over 100,000 such Volunteers were in process of recruitment; a real citizen army, drawn direct from the bourgeois and artisan classes (only about 15 per cent were peasants, so far as we know); locally recruited, democratically organized, voluntarily submitting to the discipline of an elected leadership, and preparing to defend the frontiers alongside the regular 'line' army. These 'Volunteers of '91' at once achieved celebrity. In most parts of France, especially the towns and cities, volunteers came forward in gratifying quantity, and the occasions of their enlistment and departure were made the most of by revolutionary patriotic enthusiasts. The local church was the usual venue for a ceremony presided over by the priest (unless he was a non-juror) and an army officer, culminating in the blessing and acclamation of the flag. Their tricolour flag, lovingly made by their womenfolk and expressive equally of their locality and their nation, mattered as much to them as ever did the regimental flag to old-style soldiers; as one of them described it: 'an earnest of their devotion and friendship for their fellow-citizens', to defend which these 'heroes of Equality' swore they would fight to the death.[7]

The Volunteers of '91 got going at the start of a war scare which lasted many months. Louis' crowned cousins huffed and puffed about the indignities forced upon him and their royal order, but they took a very long time to come to terms with each other and with the *émigrés* now based, a counter-revolutionary government in embryo, at Coblenz. The effect, meanwhile, of their huffing and puffing, which came to a climax in their commander-in-chief the Duke of Brunswick's fierce-sounding proclamation of late July 1792, was to feed the fires of French patriotism and to invite the French government to rally support (for month by month, now, resistance was growing to further revolutionary change) to itself and the national cause. In the end, the formal declaration of war and the first aggressive operations were undertaken by the French. The latter, for which Rouget de Lisle specially wrote the splendid 'War Song for the Rhine Army' misleadingly known ever since as *La Marseillaise*, went embarrassingly badly, and lack of revolutionary enthusiasm and unity among the military and political élites was one of the causes. Suspicion about this and about the real intentions of the king and queen, still virtually prisoners in Paris though still putting on a front of national leadership, contributed to bring about, that summer, what many historians call the Second French Revolution, the bloodier, more ideological and plebeian one which turned to terror and toughness to achieve its ends; a national government justifying its increasingly totalitarian measures by reference to one exclusive end – the 'public safety', *securité publique*.

In this hectic and sanguinary atmosphere, further appeals for one-year Volunteers were successfully made; but the Volunteers of '92 were not quite as impressive as those of '91. The supply of 'active citizens' was drying up. Now lower-class citizens were persuaded or pressed to enlist (local authorities could at a pinch compel suitable men to fill their quotas) and some of them were as reluctant (and therefore prone to shirking and desertion) as others were primitive and fiery. The men of '91 felt superior to these worse-behaved followers who besides being generally shorter could be as young as sixteen. By the end of the year over 110,000 of them had been summoned.

Ready in the summer of 1792 to deal with the Prusso-Austrian invasion, then, and to raise the spirits of the Belgian and Rhineland co-revolutionaries, were two organizationally distinct bodies of troops: these Volunteers of '91 and '92, raised from and through the National Guard (not forgetting that many of them insisted on returning home when their twelve months were up), and the regular army still well over 100,000 strong and with most of its professional sense and standards still intact. The Legislative Assembly correctly judged that line army recruitment could proceed *pari passu* with volunteering, and made tentative first steps towards conscription by requiring departments to furnish quotas of men, whose recruiting costs it quite generously reimbursed. Over 70,000 were so raised in 1792. The two streams of recruitment thus stayed separate, and there was as yet little talk of assimilating them. Yet we can see that the two were in fact already drifting towards that amalgamation which would be made official policy early in the next year. The same patriotic spirit suffused both streams, the regular recruits of '92 would tend strongly to embody it, and incorrigible conservatives had by now resigned in despair or disgust. The new officers on the regular side, promoted from the other ranks, were at least as efficient as the aristos had been, probably more so, and there were more than enough of them to affect the tone of the whole corps.

The Volunteers, for their part, included many who had served under the *ancien régime*, and the men they elected as officers had often been NCOs. Incidents of rivalry and expressions of disapproval were only to be expected and much was made of them in these early operations when things often went wrong and blame had to be pinned. More significant to the modern historian however are the amalgamations in practice which some generals went ahead with as a matter of common sense, and the evidences of fellow-feeling and successful co-operation, which led to, among other things, the revolutionary victories of Valmy and Jemappes.

Valmy, 20 September 1792, was not much of a battle. Forty-four regular infantry battalions and thirty-one Volunteer ones, together with a group of regular artillery men, confronted a considerably smaller army of Prussians and compelled them to retreat. General Kellermann was not keen to fight there, the Prussians were in a bad way from dysentery and exposure and withdrew from the field more through depression of spirits than a sense of defeat. Only about five hundred men were killed or injured. And although the French infantry stood its ground stoutly and did some firing, it was the French artillery, of purest *ancien régime* construction and training, whose 'cannonade' did most to win the day. Jemappes, 6 November, was more like the real thing, but the overwhelming of 14,000 Austrians surprised in their winter quarters near Mons by General Dumouriez's 40,000 Frenchmen was again, militarily, nothing to be exceptionally proud of. But in the circumstances of that autumn those victories were of enormous political, propaganda, and symbolic value; and since Valmy, the first of them, was actually experienced by one of the very greatest men of the age, it is right and proper to close by repeating his famous comment. Goethe ended the day sitting with some Prussian soldiers round what would in better weather have been a camp fire. They were unusually silent, reflective. 'At last, someone asked me what I thought about it all.... I said: From this place and from this day begins a new era in the history of the world, and you will be able to say, I was there.'[8]

7

THE 'BOURGEOIS REPUBLIC' AT WAR, 1793-7

These were the real republican years. The monarchy was clearly done for after the rabbling of the Tuileries on 10 August 1792; 'Year I of the Republic' was proclaimed directly after Valmy, four months before Louis lost his head. Republican years went on being calculated into the beginning of the Empire, but the Republic had turned into a military régime well before then. The Jacobins firmly retained control both of their generals and the nation's war effort, and the Directory which followed them began by doing the same. By 1797/8 however it was clear that they were not succeeding. The grinding administrative pressures of war unceasing, the necessarily growing importance of the permanent professional military establishment and the steady strength of French popular response to militaristic nationalism moved power in the generals' direction; power which one of them was exceedingly ready to grasp and enlarge.

This was also the time when war became the main determinant of events in France. The constitutional monarchy of 1791/2 had got into war with Prussia and Austria; a limited war, which by the time winter set its annual term to operations was as good as won. But the boldness brought by victory combined with revolutionary nationalist enthusiasm and sheer force of political circumstances to raise the stakes. On 16 November some mixture of geopolitical, romantic and natural law notions induced the Executive Council to proclaim, *de facto* and *de jure*, the opening of the Scheldt. Three days later the Convention was moved to offer 'fraternity and assistance to all peoples who seek to recover their liberty'. That did it. Revolutionary and by now republican France was just what alarmist conservatives had predicted. It was actively exporting revolution and breaking the established international order. Radicals and revolutionaries throughout the continent applauded, while kings and cabinets found their minds wonderfully concen-trated. One by one, the countries which had so far maintained diplomatic relations with France broke them; among those countries – a development which made sure that the war would be carried on to higher planes of intensity and drama – was Britain. Rather suddenly, it was France against the rest.

The consequence for the French people was to be a rapid stepping-up of the degree of participation and sacrifice required of them, a phase lasting from early 1793 through 1794. It was without modern European precedent, and so far as I can judge Europe knew nothing like it for at least a century and a quarter afterwards. That is not to say that 1794 was followed by a general falling-off of effort from the Jacobins' peaks. We shall see how national involvement remained in some respects just as intense. Compulsion to military service, for example, was only perfected in 1798. The French nation was brought to its completest complicity in military enterprise and imperialism by Napoleon. Nevertheless it remains this author's impression that the partici-patory effort demanded of French society in this phase of their revolutionary history, and the extent to which people's conscious-ness was militarized, was exceptional. Never, surely, was this nation more in arms.

The nation's situation in early 1793 was rather desperate. France had challenged Europe, without the military means of doing anything about it. Among the challengers were some visionaries who imagined (just as Bolsheviks would similarly imagine at the turn of 1918) that the walls of the wicked old order would crumble into ruins and revolutionaries elsewhere rise irresistibly at the blast of the French trumpet. The plan which Cambon put to the Convention on 15 December made ingenious use of circumstances. France's armies, he pointed out, had entered neighbouring countries (the Austrian Netherlands and the middle Rhineland) in a generous and helpful spirit. They were taking with them the Revolution's message of freedom and equality. But they were not being welcomed and supported as they had a right, surely, to expect. Why should the French foot the bill for others' liberation? It was only fair that the beneficiaries should pay. Revolutionary governments should at once be established in the liberated territories; funds to pay French military costs should in the first instance be seized from the aristocracy, the church, and the better-off; what more the French had to spend on their work of brotherliness could be reimbursed when the fighting was over. The debate became tremendously excited. Representatives who sought to point out the inequity of despoiling, in Belgium, the very classes which had made their revolution, were shouted down. More popular was the speaker who said, in effect, that the Belgians were too slow and stupid to know what was good for them, and that they and the rest had to be compelled to be free. Cambon's proposal was enthusiastically adopted. But, as Robespierre and others remarked, this was to risk sacrificing long-term objectives to short-term gains. Within a few months it was clear, to those with eyes to see, that though the immediate difficulties of supplying the French armies and of promoting French administrative solvency had been relieved, enthusiasm for the revolution in the liberated lands had sharply cooled, and France's military capability, far from being fundamentally improved in the face of a continent becoming every week more hostile, was actually weakening as Volunteers of '91, having done their twelve-month stint, insisted on returning home.

And not only were the continental neighbours becoming more hostile. Britain had by now settled for hostility too, and France, itself in critical turmoil, was unmistakeably going to have to fight a war at sea as well as on every front on land. The French navy, that winter, was in as bad a state as could be; stores run down, discipline decaying, royalist officers getting out, and politics pervading everything. But when the Convention turned to consider what war with Britain would mean, revolutionary exaltation and ideological absolutism again coloured its view of things. The keynotes were struck by Kersaint in a debate on 1 January 1793. He drew a distinction dear to revolutionaries, between the good English people (not to mention the oppressed Scotch and Irish people) and the bad British political establishment headed by the thick-headed George and the malevolent Pitt. The people, he believed, felt little or no attachment to their ruling oligarchy, and benefited not much from the riches which that oligarchy derived from its overseas trade and empire. Stop that trade, disrupt that empire, and Britain, the modern Carthage, would find its strength sinking as its credit failed. Like the ancient Carthage, it must be broken utterly. (Fancying themselves as the modern Romans, the French revolutionaries were just the people to undertake this world-improving task.) A series of well-aimed blows at sensitive imperial spots would prepare the way for the invasion which would finish the job: 'it is over the ruins of the Tower of London that France will conclude with the liberated English people the Treaty which will guide the future development of the nations and establish the liberty of the world.'[9]

War with Britain officially began on 1 February. During the next few months the 'first coalition' against France got going, some countries not so far at war with France now determining to become so. It was not in fact as effective a coalition as the French expected, the larger members being out for themselves as well as for monarchical principle, and two of them being out for Poland in particular. But from the French viewpoint the prospect was terrific. Even given the coalition's rickety character, it could hardly have failed to achieve its object had not the French response to it been terrific too.

Scott tells us that by February '93 French army strength was down to about 228,000, only about 50,000 of them being Volunteers.[10] The Convention's plan for raising the army's spirit and strength to meet the demand soon to be made upon it had two wings. On the one hand it was necessary to homogenize the two main branches of the army into a single force. Administrative convenience required this but there were also political consider- ations. National Guardsmen and the Volunteers drawn mainly from them must get over thinking of themselves as morally superior to, and politically more reliable than, the 'regulars'; regulars of the 'line' army must stop sneering at the others' military inexperience and learn to live with the fact that a republican army must have a different atmosphere and tone to it from the old royal and aristocratically-led one. On the basis of a shared patriotism they were to be amalgamated (as some units actually had, without positive encouragement from the centre, been already); the characteristic strengths of each element would, it was hoped, become common property; and posts of authority were to be filled by (various permutations of) election, technical qualification, and seniority. From this revolutionary innovation came in the course of the next year or so the final and definitive form of the nation in arms: the principle of amalgamation spread from the infantry to the other branches, and so a single army united national and patriotic, even some democratic principle, with regular professional standards. It was an amalgam of what was militarily most effective in old and new alike.

The other wing of the Convention's army development programme in February 1793 was, simply, to get into this new-modelled army a great many more men. On the 24th of the month a levy of 300,000 was authorized: unmarried men between eighteen and forty, quota-fixed quantities of them to be found by local authorities by voluntary enlistments if possible, by ballot or by popular vote if not. The national emergency was unmistakeable, the patriotic spirit of most revolutionaries undamped, but now troubles were encountered, the like of which were to continue into Napoleon's time. Compulsory military service tended to be unpopular. In the form of militia service before the Revolution, it always had been. Seeing the army take one's sons was only less odious than seeing it take one's horses. Departments and districts varied, of course. Some had more of a military tradition than others, a few by now were rebelliously anti-revolutionary (the Vendée insurgency was sparked off by these demands), and much depended on the heat of patriotic fervour which local administrators and organizations (clubs etc.) could work up. So some departments returned something like their quotas quite quickly, while others returned none at all, ever; only about half of the 300,000 looked for ever entered the service.

The fruits of that February levy having been relatively so mouldy, and France's military situation thereafter deteriorating so much, another levy was desperately necessary in the summer. It came as part of the *levée en masse* decreed on 23 August and is often presented as the whole of it, but we shall miss the degree to which French society was so to speak electrified into revolutionary consciousness and activity at this critical juncture (invaders all round, the Toulon fleet lost, civil war in the west and south) if we fail to note that the *levée en masse* and the extravagant rhetoric by which it was accompanied were an attempt to mobilize not just a mass army in a hurry but, behind it, a whole politicized population – the whole people united in patriotic, revolutionary and belligerent zeal as the *Sans-culottes*, originators of this measure, liked to imagine them. This idea of a *levée en masse* went far beyond the age-old feudal practice from which the term derived. That had called to the king's aid, for a short while, all men capable of bearing arms. This called in the first instance all single men from eighteen to twenty-five, but looked way beyond them.

> Until the enemies of France shall have been chased off the territory of the Republic, every French person must stand ready to serve and support our armed forces. Young men will go to fight, husbands will forge weapons and manage the transport services; wives and daughters will make tents and uniforms and will serve in the hospitals; old men taking their stand in public places will inflame the bravery of our soldiers and preach the hatefulness of kings, the unity of the Republic....[11]

The rhetoric was splendid and, for once, reality was not embarrassingly far behind it. Under the quasi-dictatorship of the Committee of Public Safety, with the high-pressure organization of patriotic opinion on one side and the threat of the guillotine on the other, the bulk of French society leapt or scrambled into mass military participation, keeping it up for long enough to overcome the desperate shortages of weapons, equipment and men to use them, and to keep France (despite its continuing insurrections) going until its war economy and massive military organization could be put on a more stable and permanent footing.

The *levée en masse* found for France, in the years of its great danger, 1793-4, an army at least large enough to protect it; over a million men in all, of whom about 750,000 were actively serviceable in the campaigns of 1794. Wherever an army was needed, the French government managed to provide one. In the end there were eleven in the field (one of them fighting the Vendéens in the west). Such an enormous number of armed men so hastily raised and so sketchily trained, serving a government in such straits and a society under such strains, was not to be expected to conform to any of the old rules of conduct whether in battle or out of it. Despite the government's extraordinary measures and Lazare Carnot's resourcefulness in their direction, the administration and supply of these masses of men remained haphazard and faulty. They probably lived better on foreign soil than on French, for they were instructed to subsist at the expense of their involuntary hosts and became skilful at doing so. Occupied populations suffered a great deal from them, and local famines sometimes resulted. But French populations of the regions where

87

they most congregated, or marched through, behind the eastern fronts, suffered nearly as much, for their demands for victuals, equipment and transport far exceeded what the local inhabitants could provide and what local authorities and army administration could control or bring in from less heavily soldiered parts.

Indiscipline, desertion, marauding and brigandage abounded. These were unkempt, disorderly, in many respects primitive armies, with more than the normal amount of ruffianism in them and much more than the normal amount of politics. 'Revolutionary discipline' by now worked well enough for training or fighting but it certainly did not aim to prevent citizens in arms from keeping up their proper political interests and, so far as circumstances permitted, activities; from December 1793 soldiers were forbidden to present group petitions, but political talk continued to fill the hours in billets and around camp fires, and if they wanted to go 'out of hours' to political meetings, only collective disapproval by their comrades-in-arms could stop them. The revolutionaries who during these critical months took such firm grip of the country positively encouraged correct politics in the armed forces. 'In Year II,' notes Soboul, 'patriotic papers were regularly sent to the armies by the War Ministry, especially those run by Marat and Hébert. The clubs and popular societies, for their part, ... counted military affairs among the most important that ever came before them. They helped to raise recruits and to equip them ... they listened to their complaints, constituted themselves their advisers and protectors.'[12] The Committee of Public Safety (CPS) and the Convention emphasized the political nature and ultimate responsibility of the army by sending *représentants en mission* (something like the Soviet Union's political commissars) to the armies, to maintain the proper political atmosphere and, above all, to keep a close eye on the generals, many of whose loyalty and zeal had become suspect. General Houchard, for example, who was adjudged culpable for having missed a victory at Courtrai in mid-September 1793, was one of seventeen generals to be executed that year. No less than sixty-seven went the same way in 1794.[13]

In the campaigns of 1793-4 these messy, massive armies achieved all that was expected of them and even more. The counter-revolutionary coalition's armies, which had been quite threatening to begin with in the earlier summer of 1793, were by the end of the year back where they began, and did even worse in

1794 when the French armies 'liberated' the whole of Belgium, pressed on into Holland, got back to the line of the Rhine, and discouraged the Prussians and Spaniards to the point of contemplating peace. These remarkable French successes on land (the record was more mixed at sea) were due partly to their high spirits and sense of purpose, partly to the excellence of the leadership at all levels which quickly discovered how best to use such novel raw military material. By the end of 1794 a distinctive new style of warfare had taken shape. The nation in arms had found an apt way to fight. A style just stumbled upon at Jemappes had become systematic by the time of Tourcoing and Fleurus (May and June 1794). Instead of trying to match the coalition's regulars by fighting them in their way, the old way, the French bothered and overwhelmed them by mass and by movement. Living, as they did, off the land; bivouacking where they chose; marching light, and freely dispersing to make enterprising use of the terrain, they moved quickly and attacked, when the time came, with a mixture of intense preparatory skirmishing and massive columns somewhat raggedly charging as fast as musket-and-bayonet-carrying men could go, to the accompaniment of revolutionary drums, songs, slogans and yells. Such tactics cost them heavy losses, but what of that? Nations in arms under dictatorial régimes are psychologically braced to bear big losses, and none was allowed to doubt the religious rightness of the ancient Roman axiom: *dulce et decorum est pro patria mori*.

The armies of the Republic, made so large by the unprecedented levies of 1793, did not stay that size for long. The three-quarters-of-a-million Frenchmen in arms by the spring of 1794 had shrunk by 1797 to less than 400,000. To some extent this shrinkage was 'accidental'; the desertion rate was high, understandably so inasmuch as the class of young men called up in August 1793 were supposed to stay in arms while the next four classes of eighteen-year-olds were left uncalled; but it was also intended by the successive governments of these years, compulsion to service being so unpopular as to require a great deal of propaganda to counteract it, and France's enemies on land posing a diminishing threat. Until 1797, when Austria, the most dogged of them, was driven to make the peace treaty of Campo Formio, it looked for a while as if the army could be allowed to revert to voluntarism, and the war with Britain be left to the navy. In 1797-8, however, a great new national military effort was found to be necessary. The restless pressures of French expansionism (ideological, imperialist, economic-exploitative) on the monarchies beyond Rhine and Alps and on their spheres of influence suggested a second coalition; a coalition which the British people and government, brought patriotically together by the threat of invasion in 1797, were very ready to organize and finance. France, moreover, had by now become very much of a militarized State, organically committed to military activity and perhaps unable to do without it. (See below, pp. 97-8, for more on this.) In 1798, therefore, following the lead of General Jourdan (now a deputy), France took a giant further step towards the systematic funnelling of manpower into the army: the completion, really, of what had been begun at the time of the 1793 *levée en masse*. Here at last was unmistakeable conscription: compulsory military service of twenty- to twenty-five-year-olds to serve for five years (or for the duration of a war), beginning with the youngest. At first it was ordained that no exemptions or replacements should be allowed. In 1799 however that attempt at egalitarian democratic principle was abandoned and those who could afford it were allowed to buy replacements.

Thus was established in outline and principle the system of conscription, year in year out, peace or war, with which French society was going to have to live for many decades. The allowance of replacements, which they came to call 'the blood tax', would provoke class-conscious radicals to denounce it as systematically biased on the bourgeois behalf. But it is evident that such bias was not needed to make conscription unpopular with the lower classes, upon whom in any case must have fallen the greater part of the annual demand. We find ourselves faced by the paradox or mere inconsistency, that the French people, clearly in some sense enthusiastic about their armies' achievements and their collective military standing, which an absolute government did everything in its power to encourage, showed much resistance to conscription, and became resourceful in means to dodge it. In some places now, especially west and south, resistance was so strong as to turn into rebellion, naturally egged on by semi-underground royalists. In most rural areas extraordinary difficulties were encountered in finding the young men at the right time and from 1799 we read of countermeasures being taken, the like of which were to go on until 1814; night raids on houses, the gendarmerie and even soldiers closing escape routes and combing forests, and – what became government's most effective device – the seizure of hostages from uncooperative families or the billetting of troops on them until they produced their boy. It was in the year of Napoleon's greatest glory that Clausewitz, prisoner-of-war for a short while, was astounded to see thirty or forty fresh conscripts roped together, two by two, being led by gendarmes to the prefecture.[14] So determined were so many French people that they or their young male relations should escape the call-up, and so many were the loop-holes through which influence, corruption and benevolent blind-eye-turning could work, that the *loi Jourdan* and its successors never brought in more than about half the military manpower annually expected. In 1799, indeed, when the national danger became acute and all five classes of conscripts were called, not more than 400,000 of the potential million in the end joined the ranks. But even so small a proportion of *la grande nation* sufficed.

Conscription and the resistance to it lead us back from the Republic's armies and their normal activities – the most normal being, it must again be said, living on allied or enemy soil as well as they could, at allied or enemy expense – to the society from whence they were drawn. What was new about the amount and the manner of its participation in the dramatic military achievements done in its name?

With limited space and a precise brief, we must discriminate. French public finances quickly got into a terrible mess, but war did that to most States in the eighteenth century (Britain's contrary experience was singular), and if the degree of inflation and the destruction of public credit were exceptional by 1794, what else was to be expected when a revolution went into a skid and at the same time took on the world? France recovered from that skid, kept the world at bay, and then went on to dominate as much of it as it could for as long as possible. The other nations of Europe had to exist as best they could under this shadow and their political histories, their economies, their public finances, their class relationships and so on were all more or less affected by the same all-mastering phenomenon: a twenty-year war, at some stages and in some respects as total a war as could be, between the two greatest powers of the age; each willing to make whatever demands on the others, to take whatever advantages of them, might suit its insatiable imperial purposes. When such were the circumstances, of course every country's history was more or less conditioned by war's impacts and demands, a natural fact to which every good general history book duly bears witness. The history of Europe in these years is the history of its wars, perhaps a little more, but surely not much less.

What, then, specifically of war and society in these same years? We must be particularly interested in the participation of society at large, in episodes when popular participation in the wars was especially intense, direct and significant. This significance was twofold. We are considering episodes which became of singular importance to national history through the next hundred years; and because they were in a general sense military episodes, their subsequent effect was militarizing. What each society achieved in its great moments of that great fighting time – a time when most nations and nationalities were, for all sorts of reasons, rapidly growing in self-consciousness – acquired special significance in its evolving national self-image. All peoples pick up an accumulation of national myths and legends, folk stories, pantheon figures and historical landmarks as they go through the centuries. What is so interesting about these years 1793-1815 is that they provided an unusually rich harvest of the same – and that all were war-connected. The marks made on nineteenth-century European society (to come on no further) by national experience in these wars were peculiarly deep and lingering. They made sure that it would be war-minded.

Returning now smartly to France, we note that it became for nearly twenty years what, previously, had been Prussia's speciality: a society organized through and through for war, and dependent on war, moreover, even more than Prussia had been. This war-addiction had its petty origins as early as 1792 and 1793, when the young Republic's armies first discovered that it was prudent, and then were instructed as a matter of government policy, to stay on enemy soil as long as they could simply in order to improve their chances of adequate food and clothing. 'Our expedition [across] the Rhine', wrote one participant, was due 'entirely to pecuniary considerations .... Our incursion into a rich and defenceless country was to procure us the money of which we were in such dire need.'[15] What began purely from necessity continued largely for profit. What Custine and Cambon had begun, the Jacobins, the Directory, the Consulate and the Empire successively continued and improved upon; war was not merely to nourish war in the crude immediate sense of covering its costs but to enrich *la grande nation* by systematic planned economic and financial exploitation – let alone mere looting, of which there was, of course, an enormous amount. Almost every French soldier going abroad had hopes of enrichment by theft and plunder. Each did it in a style suitable to his rank and station. Bonaparte, whose mind rose above commonplace looting for personal enrichment, went in especially for works of high art. Italy was for years an inexhaustible fount of riches. Generals Augereau and Masséna in the later nineties filled their carriages with church plate and tribute money. The common footslogger might not often get much more than the clock or tablecloth from where he was billetted, and whatever he could detach from the wounded and the dead. Of course the French were not singular in this pursuit, but their naturally freer discipline combined with force of habit to make them the most notorious. Some of that loot got back to France, enriching individuals and families. Of the 'contributions' levied and the taxes imposed upon invaded, conquered and allied territories, a greater proportion went to Paris, its collection and conveyance being made part of the work of the bureaucracy attached to the army. We shall return to this subject in connection with Napoleon under whom it reached perfection.

Thus was the cost of France's vast armies largely borne by France's neighbours, friends and foes alike, and thus was France's own budget part-balanced by tribute wrung from them. By the time of the Empire, this amounted to a great deal, and French society and economy were not conscious of any particular strain. In the early years, however, the war effort had to be mounted and paid for entirely from French resources; which meant to begin with the overcoming of tremendous difficulties. At no stage of these wars was any country's whole society more wholly involved in the preparation and delivery of its collective military capability than France in 1793-4, when so huge an armed force was suddenly found necessary, and its equipment and support had to be undertaken almost from scratch. In the history of no other European country is there any comparable feat of total mobilization for war purposes before the twentieth century. The way the

CPS managed it has remained a model of emergency dictatorship.

Merely to produce enough guns and bayonets was a giant problem. Of the *ancien régime*'s seven State weapons manufactories, five (Douai and Strasbourg, for cannon; Klingenthal in Alsace, bayonets and swords; Charleville and Maubeuge, muskets) were dangerously close to eastern frontiers. Between July 1792 and July 1793 the government had prudently established three others at Moulins, Autun and Clermont-Ferrand; but the needs of the *levée en masse* would far outstrip their capacity. The CSP man in charge, Prieur de la Côte-d'Or, quickly got going twelve new gun factories, twenty sword-and-bayonet ones. Biggest by far was that in Paris, where about five thousand workers (many of them drafted in from Charleville, Maubeuge and elsewhere) were so organized as ultimately to produce, by domestic piece-work and from the 258 forges set up in public places, nearly 700 muskets daily. (Adam Smith would have admired the way their sixty-eight parts were made separately by specialists before being assembled.) They worked up to fourteen hours a day and the rate of wages was determined by an arbitration tribunal of sixty members, most of them elected by the workers in the trade. Between November 1793 and January 1795, this enterprise provided nearly 150,000 muskets and pistols.[16]

Even more remarkable, perhaps, and certainly more costly, was the business of hurriedly bringing the French navy up to parity with the British one. In numbers and strength it was not so much inferior: about 62 ships of the line (counting as such those with 74 or more guns) against about 85; which meant, since the French ships tended to be more heavily armed, a fleet broadside of 61,000 pounds against 71,000. But the French fleet by early 1793 was in a bad way, its morale, discipline and leadership decayed and its stocks of materials – the huge quantities of timber, copper, iron, rope etc. needed for construction and repairs – gravely depleted. Steadily through that year the situation was saved, with a splendid crescendo once the CSP's man on naval affairs, Jeanbon Saint-André, took charge of them, on the spot in Brest itself. By the spring of 1794 he had the shipyards at Brest, Lorient and Rochefort humming with activity; workers and materials requisitioned from throughout the coastal departments (and from inland too, when urgent need arose), 'private' forests surveyed for suitable timber, the forests of the Pyrenees hopefully searched for what might be made into masts, and a general atmosphere of patriotic and revolutionary enthusiasm apparently successful in keeping the relentless toil going and the requisitioned workers more or less happy though far from home. The effort was prodigious – but so was the cost. Hampson (from whom most of this is taken) reckons that the 1794 naval building programme was costing (at 1789 prices) 30 million livres, while the mere maintenance of such expensive war machinery as the fleet already existing in the spring of that year cost 39 million. Navies, he repeatedly points out, were much more expensive than armies that got foreigners to pay for them, and this vast expenditure was only possible when total economic controls were imposed by a revolutionary government, and could only seem to be paid for under such circumstances. 'The revolutionary navy was only the reflection on the waters of the political and economic dictatorship exercised by the Montagnards between the fall of the Girondins and the death of Robespierre.'[17] With the fall of that dictatorship fell its great fleet plan, only half accomplished.

Space does not permit description in further detail of the total mobilization of French society attempted by the Committee of Public Safety. In every branch of basic military effort it was the same, from the heroic endeavour to persuade the troops that to go barefoot in good weather and to wear *sabots* (clogs) in bad was actually good for them, and the melting down of iron-railings, church-bells, and kitchen utensils (particularly those left behind by *émigrés*), to that celebrated mobilization of scientists to give instruction, for example, in how to handle that metallic melt-down and to discover new means of making war materials in short supply, like saltpetre and gunpowder. Early in 1794 the CSP organized four intensive courses in Paris, about eight days' long, on the manufacture of saltpetre, gunpowder and cannon. Over a thousand men came from all over France. 'At the end of the third course the students, led by their professors [Fourcroy was among them] marched through Paris in a great procession, bearing banners and slogans such as '*Mort aux Tyrans*' and presented samples of their products to the grateful Convention.[18] The semaphore which soon joined the War Office to the north-eastern army HQ, and the reconnaissance balloon flying over the battlefield of Fleurus, signalized what they had to offer.

Beneath and behind this concentration of specifically military effort lay many dimensions of social and cultural support. Patriotic poets, playwrights and painters had early been glad to acclaim the Revolution and cheer it on its way. Now Jacques-Louis David harnessed the arts to serve the revolutionary State every bit as much as they had ever served the Sun King, arranging the great festivals of State to maximum aesthetic impact and secular religious splendour. The multi-media experiences thus given to Paris were emulated right down the provincial scale, and certain regular public rituals became part of social life, with music, singing, soldiers and public officials, speeches galore, and the new national emblems of trees and caps of liberty and the tricolour bright above all. Floods of oratory were unleashed upon the people, and social solidarity was cemented by the warmth, excitement and moral exaltation of the republican *Weltanschauung*; the benefits of their form of government, the virtues of the true republican character, the generosity of their sentiments regarding others, the invincible spirit and courage of their soldiers and sailors, the certainty of Light's victory over Darkness.

Let us sample a rich specimen of it: Barère's speech to the Convention on 9 July 1794 about the crew of the *Vengeur du Peuple*, lost in the battle of the First of June. Of the French sailors picked up from the sea and taken prisoner, he said:

The English have seized their bodies and their ships, but the virtues of the Republican – that lofty patriotic courage; that love of one's country, the idol of every French warrior; that proud and high-minded republican spirit – these could never crouch to France's ancient enemy; despite adversity, the free man towers over the tyrant, even when in chains.

Barère went on to describe the battle, how the *Vengeur* was shot to pieces and began to sink. But would the crew surrender? No! [Actually, yes.]

Calm resolution succeeded to the heat of combat. Imagine that ship, the *Vengeur*, riddled by cannon-balls and cracking at every seam, surrounded by the English tigers and leopards, a crew now composed of the dead and dying, struggling against waves and cannons both; suddenly the tumult of combat, the cries of the suffering wounded cease; they all go or are carried to the deck. Every flag and pennant flies out; on every side rise cries of *Vive la République! Vivent la liberté et la France!*; all the animation and feeling of a civic festival, in the terrible last moments of a shipwreck.

Such men, he told the Convention, should not be pitied but envied and revered; and a new three-decker would be christened with the same great name. 'So shall we conserve for ever the memory of this ship which has been a theatre of glory and of republican virtue.'[19]

Such was the cultural froth on the mental surface of this society taken totally to war, with, for a while, price-controls and the requisitioning of labour, products and property, to a degree unprecedented and unmatched until the Second World War. It did not go on at that intensity for long, and perhaps could not have done so. The political and human costs of maintaining such a régime over a country wracked by civil war and counter-revolutionary disaffection were enormous. It rested ultimately on compulsion and terror in the regions which it did control, armed force and terrible retribution against the regions it didn't. Self-sacrificing enthusiasm in the service of a one-party State could not be kept red-hot for ever, and when the Robespierre-St Just CSP came to an end, in Thermidor (27 July 1794), its controls and compulsions began to relax or to disappear. At no subsequent phase of these wars were the French people subjected to anything like the same forcing-house heat and pressure. This experience left its mark. France at war remained politically an unfree country with a State-directed economy (within which, to be sure, entrepreneurs could do very well), a controlled press, a ubiquitous secret police, but also with a symbiotic *penchant* for its military heroes and their glorious exploits which inclined it to keep them going to the bitter end. It is difficult not to conclude that military glory was addictive.

France in fact became more and more of a military State through the later nineties; to such an extent that its turning into a military dictatorship marked the end of a logical road. The CSP, as we have seen, kept a tight civilian hold of its war-effort, its generals and its armies. The Directory set out to do the same but as the years went by and so much of France's interests increasingly depended upon the success of its arms, the military establishment's roots fanned out in government and society and the more successful and glamorous generals were able to play independent of it to a degree which would have been literally fatal to them three or four years before. The public loved them and some of them knew how to cultivate this popularity and to make political capital from it. Of these ambitious and confident generals, the one who forged furthest forward in the later nineties was Bonaparte.

8

INTERLUDE: THE WARS FROM BENEATH

Most 'military history' and a great deal of the history of wars is about what it was like to be among the fighting men. It is their experience of war and of battle which primarily interests the historian and his sometimes avid reader. This section sketches what must be on the other side of the medal: what it was like to be a civilian when the soldier was around. I have sampled more than enough of the literature to know that, at least through the whole of the last century, its tendency so glamorized and sentimentalized military experience that it obscured the facts about its effect on civilians. Yet what was society at large but 'civilians'? Some of war's impacts on them are dealt with elsewhere – the effects of economic warfare, for example, of propaganda and of the manipulation of mass opinion. But what deserves more comment than it usually gets is the sharp end of civilians' experience in wartime. How did military activity directly affect them? This is where society actually experienced war. Let us run through the likeliest occasions.

Civilians did not get much mixed up in battles. The bigger the battle, the likelier it was to be on relatively open ground. Only there could big battalions get at each other on tolerably equal terms. Such places, by definition, were rural, and since the rural population on the continent tended to cluster in villages and little towns (the British rural scatter of cottages was exceptional), only a few such populations might be in the firing line. Their homes, barns and churches would of course be used as defensive positions if that made tactical sense – for example, preventing the crossing of a bridge. Buildings would then be damaged or destroyed by gunfire and flames. But their inhabitants would have had the prudence to get out of them, unless the war going on was a people's war, as in Spain and, normally, the Balkans, where they would join

99

in the fighting and get killed. But inhabitants of the villages nearby would probably be safe at any rate from that. They would decide to stay in residence, as the lesser of two evils; we will soon see why.

Sieges and their violent endings, assaults, were very different. This is where civilian lives were most directly at risk from military action (except – our constant proviso – in the case of people's warfare). There were a great many sieges in these wars, some of them of great strategic significance: e.g., Mantua in 1796-7, Genoa in 1800, Copenhagen in 1807, Dantzig in 1812-13 and Hamburg in 1813-14. Except when they ended in assaults and sackings, they seem to lack the drama and excitement of marches and battlefields, and probably for that reason have not been so much noticed. But the inquirer into civilian experience must notice them, for civilians not merely suffered the same rigours and dangers of the siege as the soldiers defending the place, they also suffered very much more when it was over.

Let us follow the civilians' story through a typical siege. It is a fortified city, perhaps existing more for that national defence purpose than for any other (like so many frontier fortresses). It has been besieged before, so local tradition warns people what it may be like. There are at least a few days' warning, time for the military governor to clear away such vegetation or buildings around the perimeter as may block lines of fire or give attackers cover, and to lay in some last stores. People from the suburbs will try to move in; the richer and better connected may succeed in doing so. The enemy's troops begin to appear. Summoned to open the gates, the governor refuses in a few well-chosen words about honour, duty, loyalty, the certainties of relief and of his country's ultimate victory. Now the siege-works are begun; opening of an old-established tactical routine with, as has often been observed, much formal theatre in it, much style and polish. 'Parallels' are dug, trenches and protections for the assault troops are steadily pushed closer to that part of the walls which has been selected as likeliest to break under bombardment, and bombardment begins. So far as it is straight battering and shelling of fortifications, civilians suffer only accidentally. But it may be the sort of bombardment expressly meant to terrify them into panic and despair, the attacker's hope being that their plight and pleadings might influence the governor to surrender. (It could do so if he were soft enough, or they, the people, politically 'unsound'.) Not many civilian deaths or injuries would be caused but much damage might be done by the ensuing fires.

Now, let us suppose, bombardment of the fortifications has done its work. Old hands note with satisfaction that they have made or are about to make a 'practicable breach'; enough of the wall knocked down for assaulters to have a good chance of getting through. This is a great moment, for by the traditional law of war the governor of the fortress and the commander of the attackers respectively may now honourably decide to call it a day. As Marshal Suchet put it after his besiegers had softened up Valencia for twenty-four hours: 'General! The laws of war do not allow people's sufferings to go on for ever. The time has come to end them.'[20] The governor, perceiving that he is sure to lose, if not at the first assault, then surely at the next, may therefore capitulate on good and honourable terms. The attacking commander, if his summons to capitulate is met with a refusal, may threaten to put survivors to the sword if his men are put to the pains and dangers of a formal assault. If the governor capitulates, civilians who have not yet starved to death (as many did in the longest-drawn-out sieges – e.g., about 15,000 in Genoa, the most dreadful of all) have not much more physically to fear, though their new ruler may mulct them even worse than their old. But the civilians are really in trouble if there has to be an assault, and it succeeds.

The assault of a defended fortified city was the most hair-raising incident in an infantryman's life; at once terrifying and fascinating. Terrifying, because the risks were so great and the glowering forms of death or mutilation so many; mines to go off in the broken masonry beneath you, teetering ladders to climb, spikes and rotating blades to get over, and at the top, unless something had gone strangely wrong, the bayonets, swords and guns of the defenders. Losses among assault troops were correspondingly high, and often their conventional courage was compounded by the Dutch kind. Some men simply could not tackle the job sober. Yet assaults always succeeded in the end; if not at the first attempt, then at the second or third; and men could always be found to undertake them, in part because of the competitiveness in bravery and bravado which any good army must cultivate, but also because riches beyond the dreams of avarice awaited the survivor; riches, and indulgence unlimited. For what the soldier looked forward to beyond survival and glory was loot. 'My fortune is in that there town,' said a private of the British 40th Regiment to a bystander as they looked at San Sebastian not long before the assault in 1813.[21] This was the one occasion in his ordinary life when he was allowed to loot. His officers might nominally forbid it, they would probably try to set limits to it when it happened, but custom permitted it, rationalizing it as a reward for courage beyond the call of duty, and circumstances assisted it. In the noise, smoke, confusion and danger of a city successfully assaulted and partly on fire, how could officers control their hectic, high-wrought, infuriated soldiery, some already drunk and all lusting for loot and, unless they were rather unusual, drink and sex as well? They couldn't; and some didn't try much anyway. So what *always* happened after a successful assault was more or less of mayhem. Looting the place came first. What was missed by the first and therefore most deserving wave of assaulters would be snapped up by those just behind. But drink was a close second, and what came after that.... It sometimes took days to restore order and discipline, and officers took their lives in their hands who tried to do too much too soon. More damage might be done by conflagrations started after the assault than by bombardments preceding it. But most damage was done, undoubtedly, to the wretched civilian inhabitants. They would suffer worst, of course, where traditional popular animosities were sharpest and not much balanced by the influences of polite culture. Not many Turks of any age or sex were left alive in Ochakov and Ismail after the Russians took them in, respectively '88 and '90; most of the fifteen thousand Spaniards reckoned to have perished when the French took Tarragona in 1811 were civilians.[22] But so it was, *mutatis mutandis*, in all such cases. Soldiers got off more lightly. In central and western Europe, threats to 'put them to the sword' were rarely carried out. Fellow-professionals had respect for each other. In fact, as events showed again and again, they tended to respect each other much more than they respected civilians. Soldiers after an assault would usually be taken prisoner; but civilians would be taken advantage of. A civilian family in an assaulted city was unlikely to come out of it without some experience of house-breaking, vandalism, robbery, rape, maiming or murder.

All of those nasty things could happen (though they would be less likely to happen all together and suddenly) to civilians while soldiers were stationed in their neighbourhood or passing through it. This, no doubt, was civilians' commonest encounter by far with men of war at war, and fairly disagreeable did it usually turn out to be. Let us be reminded that requisitioning was from the start of these wars the French armies' standard method of feeding and transporting themselves, and sometimes of clothing themselves too. It helped them to achieve the superiorities which even unfriendly observers could hardly fail to see in them, and so their opponents found it difficult not to follow suit, though for most of the time there was this big difference between the two sides, that the French were on foreign, subject soil, while the others were on their own or their allies' and thus had to tread more softly.

Clausewitz reviewed the matter (Book 5, chapter 14) with characteristic *sang-froid* and a significant neglect of the possibility that an invading or occupying army might find it good policy to pay for its victuals, reminding his readers early on that for every three or four men in a modern army to be fed, there was a horse, which ate ten times as much. Armies' means of subsisting nowadays, he wrote, were fourfold, and most armies used combinations of them. They could 'live off local households or the community'; the troops could be left to requisition on the spot what they needed; local authorities could be induced to co-operate with the military authorities in an organized requisition – 'the simplest and most efficient way'; or they could 'subsist by means of depots' – but only if they wanted to be thoroughly old-fashioned and beatable. The chapter is richly thoughtful and discriminating, but the historian with an interest in humanity will notice above all one thing; Clausewitz takes it for granted that armies will exhaust the towns and countrysides they settle in or go through. His constructive comments are aimed to help achieve that exhaustion with minimum time and fuss. Requisitioning with local government 'help' was best because it was the most systematic. 'Every day will ease the shortages. If only 100 square miles can be drawn upon the first day, there will be 400 the second, and 900 the third.... This method knows no limits other than the complete exhaustion, impoverishment and devastation of the country.' Troops' requisitioning on their own was a poor, haphazard system: 'What, after all, can be expected where 30,000 men are extorting food within a range of 5 miles, or 15 to 20 square miles?' 'Living off households' was fine so long as it didn't go on for too long. 'A farmer's stock of bread is usually enough to feed his family for a week or two. Meat can be come by every day, and there is generally a big enough stock of vegetables to last till the next harvest. As a result, in billets that have not been previously occupied, one can generally find food for three or four times the number of inhabitants for several days, which again works out extremely well.'[23]

Extremely well for the troops, perhaps! But by now the thoughtful reader will have realized what all this meant for the civilians. 'War is a terrible evil, particularly to those who reside in those parts of the country which are the seat of the operations of hostile armies', reflected Wellington in 1810.[24] At the very least – when the troops did not stay to the bitter end, when the requisitioning was orderly and equitably spread, when good discipline was maintained, no bad spirit bred between occupier and occupied, and the seed-corn and seed-potatoes left un-devoured – it meant personal hardship and temporary economic ruin. But we know that things didn't often work out as smoothly as that – and so also, presumably, did Clausewitz, famous identifier of the ubiquity of 'friction' in war. Not even the hardiest French footsloggers would go without a little shelter at night if they could manipulate some bits of tree, fence or chicken-coop to provide it. No soldier who could grab a chicken or a piglet would pass up the chance. Next to food, fire was the campaigning soldier's most urgent craving; the laxer the discipline, the quicker the conversion into heat of furniture, shutters, window-frames, floorboards.... The great determinants every time were (1) the strength of the officers' will to enforce discipline; (2) the presence or otherwise of the inhabitants; (3) soldiers' perceptions of the inhabitants; (4) soldiers' pay: whether it was in arrears or not; (5) simply, circumstances. Officers really determined to keep their men in order despite hostile circumstances *could* do it, and occasionally one finds them doing so – e.g., during the rapid Prussian retreat after Jena, or the British, Russian and Austrian invasions and occupations of France from 1814. But if the officers – who would normally take their cue from the general command-ing – did not insist on good behaviour, inevitably would it worsen. It would be at its worst, of course, if the troops felt popular hostility around them, or if, cherishing grievances from some previous experience, they felt they had old scores to settle. Under any circumstances behaviour would be worse in proportion as the inhabitants were resident or not. All sources unite to testify that the worst thing a home-owner desirous of preserving his house and its contents could do was to lock it up and leave it. It would be broken open, troops would be lodged in it just the same. A resident owner could often establish a *modus vivendi* with his unsolicited guests and in many circumstances the officers would attend to his complaints. But when circumstances were hostile, the officers' will to prevent depredations might diminish along with their power to do so, and official-sounding requisitions became mere marauding. It could be the only way to keep alive. The shivering, hungry officer who yielded to the temptation of a piece of stolen chicken by a bivouac fire became implicated in the crime. That story, which I have encountered in several versions, is affecting and exemplary. But it had been some civilian's chicken.... Private Wheeler and some chums, scouring out a wood near Vitoria in mid-summer 1813, 'relieved' an old shepherd 'of all he had, viz. a four-pound loaf, some cheese and about a quart of wine. The poor old fellow cried. It was no use, we had not seen a bit of bread these eleven days. The old man was not far from home and could get more.'[25]

Some localities at some epochs, we know, got on with their occupiers well enough and even made money out of them. Wellington's men in Spain – a 'friendly country' from the British point of view – were tremendous pilferers and looters, not to say drunkards, but peasants and shopkeepers who managed not to be damaged by those anti-social attributes were pleased to sell food, drink, footwear, blankets and so on either to the commissaries buying supplies with government money (for Wellington was usually able to manage without requisitioning) or to soldiers and officers' servants buying with their own. Civilians were most likely to prosper and sleep sound at nights along the regular main military routes, where there had long been a disciplined military presence and people knew from experience how to handle it. A Black Forest clergyman whose parish, Hinterzarten, was on a high road recently built from Freiburg-im-Breisgau to Neustadt, recorded about 1810 his impressions of what it had been like under the successive waves of Austrians, French, and their dependents (respectively, Pandours from the *Militärgrenze*, who behaved badly, and in 1809 some Portuguese, memorable 'for their taciturn

character, their orderly demeanour, and their extreme temper-
ance'). He personally preferred the French, who were sometimes
quite cultivated and genial; the Austrians were coarser, ate more,
and were freer with blows. On the whole it had not been too bad;
uncomfortable, of course, but the harvests had been pretty good
and a lot of money had been made by supplying food, forage and
services to the military authorities; discipline had been good and
complaints had been attended to when the regular military were
there in force; trouble came mostly from stragglers and deserters,
who became indistinguishable from brigands.[26]

The longer the wars went on, the larger became the numbers
of deserters living as best they could (it might be very well) and
of semi-military riff-raff exploiting war's attendant confusions and
disorders. In France, the country about which we know most,
bands of deserters and draft-dodgers were a real menace to public
order and private security by the last years of the Empire. In
Spain, Italy, the Balkans, much of Poland, things were only
different inasmuch as such bands might functionally overlap with
partisan national resistance groups. It is clear that these pro-
tracted and demanding wars spawned a lot of human flotsam and
jetsam which surged about with the waves and tides of military
activity, adding significantly (for a time) to the ordinary hazards,
losses and dangers of life. But mankind's relations with war are full
of paradoxes and surprises. While the net impact of this flotsam
and jetsam in bulk was generally impoverishing and depressing,
individual members of it, wounded or sick, sometimes encountered
much generosity and sympathy from the inhabitants of the
countries where they were marooned, the residents along the roads
which saw them hobbling or trudging towards home. Only in the
Peninsula, south Italy and the Balkans was it really unsafe for an
army to leave a hospital-full of sick and wounded for the
inhabitants and the next military arrivals to care for; the
defenestration of hundreds of such at Vilna in mid December 1812
was unusual. And just as civilians, in some countries anyway,
sometimes showed compassion on suffering enemies, so sometimes
did soldiers on suffering or helpless civilians. Right in the middle
of some very nasty counterinsurgency operations, the French
officer, Fantin des Odoards, in Spain in 1808, took under his
protection the nineteen-year-old widow of the local landowner.
She had been raped by marauders, her husband killed for resisting.

The troops of course thought he just wanted her for sex, but 'no matter; when one's trying to do good, one has to put up with whatever interpretations people put on appearances'. He handed Maria over safely to her mother a few days later. Meanwhile his men brought back a six-year-old girl they found sharing a cave with two corpses. He looked after her too, and after a few days she found her voice again.[27]

Thus could instincts and principles of humanity alleviate, very slightly, the otherwise terrible impact of these wars and the armed hordes waging them on the continent's civilians.

9

NAPOLEON AND THE FRENCH

He was born in 1759. In 1785 he passed out of the *Ecole Militaire* and was posted lieutenant in a crack artillery regiment. His first experience of action was in a bungled attack on a small island off Sardinia early in 1793. He first impressed the men at the top in the autumn of that year; his management of the artillery at the reduction of Toulon earned him promotion to Brigadier-General. Sedulous cultivation of political connections, and usefulness to them, once, in dispersing a mob, kept his career on sound tracks. He knew the right people and he was clearly a very bright, ambitious young officer. (And what a time it was for the ambitious and talented young!) He was appointed to the command of the Army of Italy early in 1796. By the end of the following year his victories, his political presumption and his calculating pursuit of celebrity had made him one of the best-known generals. What would be his next command? (He was determined it should be something breathtaking.) For a few months it looked like the invasion of England, but in the spring of 1798 he persuaded the Directory to put him instead in charge of a secretly-prepared expedition to Egypt. The British reasserted naval supremacy in the Mediterranean and destroyed the fleet that took him there at Aboukir, but on land he was almost consistently victorious. It is characteristic that he got the French to forget the defeats and remember only the victories. He returned to France determined, apparently, to get back to the centre of affairs and to master them, or to die in the attempt. From the day of his return (13 October 1799) he was a popular hero, 'the conqueror', a standing which helped him through the messy politickings of *Brûmaire* which by the end of the year made him First Consul. That constitutional position and his own ambition and abilities administrative at home as well as military abroad, made him virtually a dictator.

The French constitution respectfully followed the course of events. In 1802 he became Consul for life, in May 1804 he was proclaimed Emperor of the French, and on 4 December of that year a most extraordinary ceremony in Notre Dame sealed his secular fame; the Pope, who had gone to Paris specially for the occasion, anointed him Emperor, after which *Napoleon crowned himself* – a gesture of imperial pretension practised only by one other ruler in Europe, the Tsar. His imperial sway soon covered most of Europe. The Treaty of Tilsit, July 1807, marked its apogee. The United Kingdom and its swelling overseas empire stood intact, but France owned, managed or dominated continental Europe from the Pyrenees to the Russian frontier, from Denmark down to Naples; while Russia, Spain and Sweden seemed ready to be strung along. The Corsican squire's son had come a long way, and battles were the staging-posts.

Not even Napoleon believed that it was all his own work. To be sure he was a proud, arrogant and rather selfish man, never doubting that his triumphs were well-earned, and not above taking to himself credit more fairly due to colleagues. But it was part of the image he liked to project, to insist that the French people were behind him (as a few plebiscites indeed could be pressed to show) and that he was in any case dependent on the invincible courage etc. of French soldiers. So by his own evidence we are led to consider the question which any reflective reader would discover for himself anyway: how much of this colossal success story was inseparable from the great man himself, and how much due to the great nation, people or society – call it what you will – behind him?

The question is fascinating and ultimately unanswerable. It is, of course, only the particular form of a famous general question – what influence after all do great men have upon the course of history? – and as such it is a matter upon which writers who believe they really understand the historical process tend to have strong views. Marxists and very social scientific historians, for instance, affirm that the apparently great man cannot matter much, greatness of his sort being thrust upon him by force of mighty circumstances. In the case of Napoleon, such historians argue that the appearance of someone like him was entirely predictable. The bourgeois revolution bursting upon so populous, resourceful and politically united a nation as France must, they say, have produced

109

military power and leadership proportionate to its capabilities and its needs. France was already a great warrior nation, oozing with military talent. If it had not been Napoleon, it would have been another. So far, many non-Marxists and sub-*Annales* types might agree, so good. The Revolution was in the nature of things likely to get into conflict with surviving *anciens régimes*, and the longer the struggle went on, the greater was the probability (we suppose) that the most popular general would become a military dictator.... But already quite large assumptions are being made, and they have to become larger still if that military dictator, whomsoever he was – a Moreau, a Jourdan, a Bernadotte – is further supposed to have been very likely to enter the same course of behaviour which marked Napoleon's: arrogance, susceptibility to flattery, megalomania, and a compulsion to play God on earth.

To suppose so much is to stretch things too far for this historian. And surely also the titanic Tolstoy stretches them too far in his grappling with these same philosophico-historical problems? The writing of *War and Peace* drove him to offer an explanation of Napoleon within a theory about great men. Being somewhat inclined to play God himself and very critical of others' doing so, he argued ingeniously that the more powerful a man seems in politics, the less independent innovative power can he actually possess. 'Kings are history's slaves.' Napoleon was only a sort of puppet, projected by some ultimately mysterious mass movement of the French people to advance from western to eastern Europe, until met and beaten back by a popular mass equally potent.

It is ingenious, there is a lot of truth and an immense amount of cleverness and depth in what Tolstoy writes, but no more than doctrinaire Marxism will it do. What Napoleon did as a despot was surely not what *any* French general, similarly placed, would have done! We may agree that absolute power corrupts absolutely, and that his putative replacement would not have emerged from the absolute experience morally unscathed. But to suppose that he must have handled (or mishandled) relations with Britain, Spain and Russia more or less as Napoleon did (picking out just foreign policy follies) is, again, too much. *Pace* Tolstoy and Marx's principal expositor in this matter, Plekhanov, there is no escape from acknowledgment that part – we will not dare to measure how large a part – of what France did under Napoleon was due to the man Napoleon's own fundamental character traits; though we have to double back at once in Tolstoy's direction by adding, out of fairness, that part of what Napoleon managed to do with France was due to the national character traits which allowed him to do it. But in any case it was the symbiosis of Napoleon and the French people, or (to borrow the terminology of infatuation and love) the intensity of his long affair with them, that made such ineffaceable impressions on history.

Beside the personal Napoleonic aspect of this affair, there is the question of the support he got from French society; how much of it there was and how far it was freely given, how far gained by force or fraud. Napoleonic France calls to mind, as does no other State in our period, the description of Prussia as not so much a State with an army as an army with a State. The Republic had not been like this. State, society and army had then for a few years been harmonized in a national defence effort of unusual intensity. The army had been enormous but it was close in every respect to the people from which it came, the people among whom (when not abroad) it lived. The army of 1792-5 really was 'the people's army' by all criteria applicable in such matters, worked up to combat zeal not so much by the soldier's usual closest allegiances (regiment, officers, general, national leader) but by conscious devotion to the *patrie* and the Revolution.

Napoleon's army, evolved from this, retained many of its characteristics while adopting a different ethos. It was still popular enough. Its victories, its achievements, its sufferings and as time went by its defeats evoked appropriate responses of admiration and condolence (with some help in the orchestration by the Emperor and his opinion-managers). It was still democratic, so far as effective armies can internally be so. Many ways continued to be open from the bottom to the top, discipline remained relatively free and easy, officers and men did not live worlds apart (egalitarian aspects of army life which '*le petit caporal*' sedulously cultivated). There is said to have survived in it, especially among its veterans from the early days, more frank and earnest republicanism than could be found anywhere else in the Emperor's France; indication at least of the Emperor's success in portraying himself to them as the man of France's destiny.

But in some essential respects it was increasingly a sort of State within the State, less responsibly rooted in French society than it used to be. Apart from the fact that a large proportion of its costs continued to come from abroad (nothing new in that), a large proportion of its men came from abroad too, and when in his ultimate crisis Napoleon sought an increased contribution from his own people, he was met by extraordinary resistance. The National Guard, which had in early days been such an important vehicle of citizen-soldiering, Napoleon downgraded and, so far as he could, neglected; otherwise it could have become the same sort of threat to his security as originally it had been to Louis XVI, and as the other rulers of Europe feared similar bodies might be to them. His own army became more and more professional and self-sufficient. Every encouragement was given to soldiers to bring their sons up to be soldiers too, and in 1811 he institutionalized what was already, indeed, a common enough practice, by requiring foundling hospitals and homes to decant their lads into the army when they reached the age of twelve.[28] At the top end, he was in his later years planning to turn the Imperial Guard, notoriously over-funded and privileged, into an army within the army – indeed a super-army, 'a self-contained force of all arms' including artillery, 80,000-strong.[29] The personal loyalty of the Guard to their Emperor was famous, but except in rare private moments of cynical realism he liked to maintain that the whole army was equally faithful and loyal. At the collapse of his régime it became clear that the loyalty of some senior officers in particular was not as sublime and universal as he usually professed to believe, but there certainly was enough of it, then and thereafter, to catch the historian's eye. He had the supreme leader's talent of inspiring devotion among his followers and of making others imagine they would have liked to follow too. Above all a soldier himself, he was above all a soldiers' man. But it was not only to soldiers that he successfully appealed. The French people evidently did not now much wish to be soldiers themselves, but Napoleon's army, so long as it fought in other countries and there gained glory and victories, remained highly interesting to them. Meantime, whatever tendencies towards popular militarism were already there from before the years of his despotism (and obviously there were plenty), he only strengthened and consolidated. Everything he did to French government and society was cut after the military pattern. There is no evidence that the French people found it uncongenial.

Such in outline was the relationship between the people of

France and their protean warlord. We conclude by examining the main points in more detail.

1. *The financial cost* was met largely by contributions and extortions from allied and conquered countries. The less formal side of this – the requisitions in kind always made by French military commanders in foreign territory, and kept on at least to the point of local exhaustion – we have already covered. What all that amounted to is beyond calculation. More calculable are the sums of money regularly demanded from occupied cities and rulers, usually on top of requisitions. So Masséna, after the battle of Zurich in September 1799, after requisitioning from that city and St Gall 800,000 rations of bread, 20,000 bottles of wine, 10,000 bottles of brandy, and 100 oxen, squeezed 800,000 *livres* out of them too. The Austrian Archduke Charles, their last occupier, having already taken 5 million florins, they had every ground for squealing.[30] This sort of thing was absolutely normal. Napoleon himself did it on the grandest scale, announcing an astronomical contributions figure to begin with and lowering it in proportion as the vanquished saw sense. The Austrians in 1809 saw sense quickly, so the 200 million francs initially demanded was reduced at the peace treaty to a mere 85.[31] But Napoleon actually got as much again out of them in kind.[32] Prussia gave a lot more trouble, haggling and foot-dragging for two years from the start of the business in November 1806. Napoleon felt no great urgency to conclude it, since his 150,000 troops were living on Prussian soil entirely at Prussian expense. In the end the Prussians had to agree to pay 140 of the 154 million originally asked, and while continuing to support big French garrisons at Glogau, Stettin and Küstrin they managed to spin that payment out long enough to have some of it still owing when they took up arms against France again early in 1813. But that was by no means all the profit gained in the two years following Jena. Daru, Napoleon's most trusted military administrator, presented to his master in January 1809 a 'General Report on the Administration of the Grand Army and the conquered territories during the campaigns in Prussia and Poland', summing up the financial results *apart from that indemnity*. (The profits included what was wrung out of Prussia's German allies and goods, ships, and bank deposits seized from British nationals.) Receipts in silver and kind came to 604 millions;

'campaign expenses' had been 234 millions; in hand at military depots were provisions to the value of 11 millions; net profit therefore, 'handed over to the treasury', 359 millions.[33] That was about half the French State's total income for 1807.[34] 'About half the Italian tax revenue went to the French in 1805-12.'[35] War managed on such terms was good business for Napoleon and for France too insofar as French merchants and manufacturers could make money out of the subject territories and French soldiers and bureaucrats would overawe and manage them. But the wars that began in Spain in 1808, in Russia in 1812, were anything but profitable. It is no accident that French enthusiasm for war thereafter steadily declined.

2. *The cost in men* to the French people was considerable. This was not surprising, given that their ruler was so ready to spill their blood. But the cost to the French would have been greater, had Napoleon not brought hosts of foreigners to their aid. Only vague figures are available. Godechot's conclusion is that about 750,000 French soldiers died between 1800 and 1815; not enough to do anything to the steady long-term population growth except to increase its female proportion.[36] Lefebvre summarizes the latest learning by saying that 'less than a million Frenchmen were lost', i.e., about 40 per cent of the total in arms; adding at once a reminder that 'a third of them had simply disappeared, and surely were not all dead'.[37] We may also remind ourselves that death in battle accounted for only a small proportion of the total. Sickness, hardships and hospitals did for the majority. How many others died on the French behalf? Including as 'others' for this purpose residents of annexed territories (Belgium, Savoy, the Moselle-Rhine country etc.) as well as vassals and satellites (e.g., Holland and Italy under many forms) and allies (often compulsory), it seems that the figure may be something like 400,000.[38]

Here was a striking reversion to *ancien régime* practice. The Revolution, we have seen, got rid of foreigners from its army. Only Frenchmen were wanted. 'Foreigners' who wanted to continue in French service (e.g., some Swiss and 'Germans' – the latter however from disputed Rhinelands) were wise to wax warm for France. Only as the numbers of Frenchmen under arms shrank through the mid-nineties did policy begin to change. Bonaparte was in on this from the outset. A 'Polish legion' of political refugees

114

was formed to help him fight Austria in north Italy. Polish troops, especially lancers, were prominent in French service through the remainder of the wars. Disliking the ardent republicanism of the first lot, Bonaparte dispatched them after the Treaty of Lunéville (which disappointed them) to San Domingo, where most succumbed. A much larger force, of 40,000, was aimed at when Napoleon's imperial *Drang nach Osten* reached Poland. Enough Poles continued to fall for his sweet-talk to enable the Grand Duchy of Warsaw to be established at Tilsit as a military satellite, two-thirds of its budget being earmarked for the French army-in-residence and its own proportionately immense army.[39] Together with a Lithuanian contingent, the fruit of a similar liberating process, there were about 90,000 of them in the Grand Army of 1812.[40] Italians began to be enlisted at the same time as Poles. From as early as the autumn of 1797 it was clear that Bonaparte's first thought in contemplating a prospective satellite or ally was its military capability. When the formation of the north Italian Cisalpine Republic was under discussion, he confided to the French Minister for Foreign Affairs his belief that something might yet be made out of the Italians. 'Little by little the people of this republic will come to care for liberty, ... and perhaps in four years it may have a passable army of 30,000.' By the time it became the Italian Republic it was well on the way to that, and Italian contingents were quite active and successful in the campaigns of 1805-8. By then Italian cannon-fodder was available also from the vassal kingdom of Naples. Some thousands went to Spain, a few miserably to Russia. There were also Swiss, Dutch, Illyrians, even a few Spaniards and Portuguese.

But the greatest levy by far was of those solidly reliable fighting folk, the Germans. Napoleon's drastic refashioning of the German world was accompanied by its attachment to the French chariot. Each treaty with each new or revised State specified a military contribution (apart from maintenance of French garrison and communications forces, etc.). The new States of Berg and Westphalia suffered terribly. Berg's contribution 'was fixed in 1806 at 5000 men or one-tenth of the population'. By June 1811 it had risen to 8180. In October 1811 'Napoleon demanded an additional 1200 men and after the Russian disaster could still exact from Berg over 3000 men in addition to the contingent already sent to the *Grande Armée* and wiped out'. Of Westphalia's population of 2 million (proprietor: Napoleon's brother Jerome), '600,000 had been conscripted between 1807 and 1813'. Baden, Würtenberg, Hesse Darmstadt and Bavaria were bled nearly as badly. The Bavaria which had managed with Britain's help to put 12,000 in the field in 1799 was (after slight territorial expansion) forced by France to field 40,000 by 1809.[41] Prussia and Austria also after their defeats were compelled to contribute troops; Austria sent 30,000 in 1812, Prussia 20,000. None went on the Moscow road and the Prussians changed sides after the debacle, so they turned out to be counterproductive. It is an interesting comment on the nature of war in these years that troops under compulsion or merely half-hearted were nevertheless found useful or believed to be so. The Grand Army of 1812, in which Napoleon's reliance on non-Frenchmen was at its most conspicuous, was 'rather less than half' French: about 302,000 out of the '614,000 troops of the first and second lines'.[42]

By the last years of the Empire, Frenchmen were showing great dislike for conscription, and as for volunteering, that was negligible – only 52,000 since the beginning of the Consulate.[43] Government propaganda exerted itself to put a brighter appearance on things but the fact was that Napoleon's French-recruited armies corresponded hardly at all to the Revolution's ideal of 'the nation in arms'. Several categories of young men, notably those who had got married, were exempt. Bourgeois who could afford to buy replacements did so; peasants and others who could not dodged conscription by all the means already mentioned, and often took it tragically. Extreme examples of common behaviour came from Brittany, where conscripts from some villages wore mourning on the eve of departure, and in Finistère, 1813, it was reported that on the dreadful day itself, 'their families go some of the way with them, embrace them and bid them farewell for ever, then return home saying prayers, sometimes the De Profundis'.[44] The price of replacements, which varied from region to region, went up all the time; by 1812-13 it was usually around 4000 francs. Not more than five per cent at most of the called came from families able to afford that sort of money. The proportion of the rest which somehow or other got out of going varied greatly from department to department and from year to year. From 1806 to 1812 the prefects and gendarmerie felt they were on top of things but even so the average evasion rate topped ten per cent, and in 1810

116

evaders were offered the third of three amnesties. Evasion and resistance rocketed in 1813-14, in some places topping 40 per cent.[45] In the Nord, at last, with covert British and Dutch encouragement, draft-dodgers and deserters joined to create a veritable *chouannerie*.[46] The actual approach of foreign invaders in 1814 and 1815 – an inconvenience of belligerency unknown to Frenchmen for twenty years – did something to restore honourable purpose to military service, but to rally to the defence of France by then was not necessarily to continue in admiration of Napoleon. So far as we can judge, the French people were on the whole relieved when his latterly insatiable demands for cannon-fodder ceased and the other pressures of his police State likewise eased.

3. To what extent, then, was *French society militarized?* The argument here is (unoriginally enough) that the net effect of these Napoleonic years was to strengthen the militarist tendencies already implanted from the early nineties and to give them a sinister twist – imperialist, dictatorial, military for militarism's own sake; and that although there was some resistance to it, some dislike of it while it was going on, more obvious and longer-lasting was the relish which French people had for it, the willingness of the response they made to him while he was there and to his legend after he had gone. Whether they solicited it or not, what Napoleon gave the French people was a more military-minded and generally more war-accustomed State, officialdom and climate of public opinion than they had had before he took them over.

Beneath the superficial tolerance and generosity resulting from his lack of ordinary political and religious principle was one constant cardinal principle which governed all his inclinations and decisions: the compleat officer's *idée fixe* about order, hierarchy and subordination. In religion he was a sort of rationalist deist, completely of the Enlightenment. He played the Muslim during his Egyptian adventure; he favoured Freemasons, he emancipated Jews and (where they needed it) Protestants; he went through Roman Catholic ceremonies with aplomb. Men had to have religion, he was pleased to let them have it, with as much of himself in the mixture as they pleased to put; but its only real importance so far as he was concerned was its indispensability as an encouragement to citizens to be moral and to soldiers not to fear death. In politics he could take anything and anyone so long as his cardinal principle was respected. Returned aristocratic *émigrés*, unrepentant men of 1789, reconstructed Jacobins could all be fitted in provided they accepted the new order he had given their country (with himself at the apex of it) and left their political preferences in the closet; only monarchists, constitutionalists and republicans who really cared about their preference were at risk. But most welcome and safest of all were men who like him thought not in political terms at all but in administrative ones. For politics, in Napoleon's view of life, read administration; administration, ideally on military lines, with clear chains of command coming down from a single well-oiled centre. To extend or introduce administration of that kind was, indeed, not difficult in France, of all countries, where a tradition of centralized bureaucracy already existed. Napoleon rejoiced to extend it, to strengthen it, and to further the process already dimly beginning before the Revolution, by which military administration became more self-sufficient and independent of civilian control.

Where institutions could, to his mind, usefully be militarized, they were so. This occurred most strikingly in the educational field. In this as in so many other respects he was not introducing novelties but putting his characteristic military-authoritarian stamp on what had either been long established or recently instituted by the revolutionaries in the nineties. Part of the Jacobins' plan of national regeneration had been an *Ecole centrale des travaux publics*, with a wonderfully high-powered faculty (e.g., Lagrange, Laplace and Monge) and no more military purpose than its title implied. In 1799 Bonaparte turned it into the *Ecole polytechnique* to serve the scientific branches of the armed services, engineers and artillery, as well as the State's civil engineering needs. 'Militarization became total after the law of 16 July 1804 which placed the Ecole under the authority of the War Minister and the direction of a general.'[47] When in the following year the Emperor ordered the students to be wholly resident, in order to check their radicalism, they aptly called it their *casernement*. Of the 'Imperial University' idea and system, which was no less than an attempt to assert absolute State control over the whole of French national education at all levels, it need only be remarked that its perfectly hierarchical organization was in essence military, with the First Consul Emperor as commander-in-chief. To anyone who objects that a man does not have to be a soldier to appreciate the economy and efficiency of a pyramidal command structure, and that despotic and dictatorial governments have sought to establish such both before Napoleon and since, the answer is simply that the military model came first; such governments' existence depended on military force, and it was from the armies which gave it them that appropriate management methods were to be learnt. Napoleon's State system stood in relation to, say, Louis Quatorze's just as did their respective armies. Napoleon's was so much the more tight-knit, closely inspected, managed and disciplined. Both rulers wanted to control what their subjects read and thought. The means at Napoleon's disposal – means for devising which he had larger personal responsibility than for most of the 'innovations' of his reign – promised to be more perfect than any available to Louis could have been, and his national educational system was necessarily at the roots of it, with censorship, propaganda, and the suppression of independent political activity filling the mental interstices, together with what Hinsley has judged to be 'perhaps the earliest [example] of a modern Ministry of Information'.[48]

Censorship and prevention of independent politics had impeccable lineages from the deep past. The propaganda was more original. Before 1789, States had normally relied on their established churches to help them with whatever propaganda they needed to inject into their social system. It was understood to be part of their job, and they provided a ready-made machinery for doing it. From the early nineties the French had to devise new machinery for their suddenly inflated propaganda needs. (I am using the word largely and loosely to include the whole attempt to form and inflame public opinion.) Napoleon's régime did little more on this side of national affairs than continue an already going concern in its own inimitable, heavy, martial way. No political or foreign news could be published which was not taken from the *de facto* official *Moniteur*. The Emperor's bulletins about military operations (always glorious, of course; 'to lie like a bulletin' gradually became a common idiom) might, with not too much imagination, be seen as the start of the practice which in course of time, as media development made it possible, produced President Roosevelt's fireside chats and the dictators' radio speeches. And national festivals and public patriotic ceremonies continued to abound. The military element had been strong in them early but now it became predominant, as was only natural, considering the martial fixations of the man at the top and his régime's acute need to keep the French martially alert and eager.

A nice example of the style comes from the dying months of the Directory, when the war was going badly for France and Bonaparte not yet back from Egypt. A suitable incident provided an opportunity to whip up enthusiasm and discourage draft-dodgers. The French delegates to the congress of Rastatt were dramatically assassinated on 28 April 1799. The Ministry of Information decreed a *fête funéraire* for 21 May, with the theme of: Vengeance! It offered local authorities some ideas. 'Miss no opportunity to give the ceremonies a solemn, inspirational character. On urns, mausoleums, pyramids and funerary columns [these were the stock neo-classical effects of official art] let artists place broken olive trees stained with blood, Nature veiled, Humanity in tears .... Show Despotism gathering their blood in a goblet. Depict all the evils which come in its train: famine, fire, war and death; depict Republicans rushing to arms to withstand the monster.... Let funeral music of desolating sadness be followed by a period of silence, and then – suddenly – let it be broken by the cry: Vengeance!' And so on. The circular concluded with a request for reports to be sent in on the popular reaction.[49] Occasions as big as that were not so common but the attempt to manipulate public feeling and opinion went on all the time. Here is a thoroughly Napoleonic example to conclude with. Its occasion was his second marriage in 1810, to the Austrian princess Marie-Louise. A national *fête* was announced for 24 April, with Marriage and Fruitfulness as its central themes. Then, amidst the usual outpourings of poetry and declamation, marriage ceremonies were held in provincial centres for 6000 ex-soldiers and the girls lucky enough to be picked by local councils as deserving the Emperor's dowry (1200 livres in Paris, 600 elsewhere in the Empire). Napoleon liked to arrange what he considered to be suitable marriages at all levels of society; this batch at once rewarded worthy veterans and promised a harvest of youngsters, the male ones being almost certain to join the army in due course. Some of them were already available passively to participate in the follow-up *fête* held on 9 June 1811 to celebrate the birth of the King of Rome. But the celebrations did not, it seems, go off with the fizz and fun of the 1810 ones, partly because of creeping war-weariness and partly because of the upper bourgeoisie's growing dislike of Napoleon's irresistible pressure upon them to send their school-leaving sons (for whom they would expect to buy replacements) into the army *as volunteers*.[50]

To sum up – the French people's response to Napoleon was mixed. The desire to have one's cake and at the same time to eat it being so natural among mankind, we need not be surprised to find equally strong evidences of respect, enthusiasm, reverence, even love for the great man on one side, of coolness, fear and loathing on the other; sometimes, with no more than common human inconsistency, of both sides in the same persons. The proportions of such responses defy measurement. All we can say is that this pre-eminent soldier stamped himself upon French consciousness as no other Frenchman ever has done, and the question to which we shall never have the perfect answer is – since his régime, like the revolutionary one it succeeded, did all it could to control men's hearts, minds and expressions – how far was the vogue for him spontaneous, how far forced? This historian has come to the conclusion that it was more spontaneous and willing than not; further evidence of which is the vogue for him outside France, in countries more or less beyond his control – a curious matter to which we shall turn later in this book (see below, pp.200-3).

10

THE NOT-SO-UNITED KINGDOM

This section began with Clausewitz's observation that revolutionary France became a nation in arms, the like of which had not been seen before; and went on to quote his conclusion, that France's neighbours had to become something similar, if they were to withstand the French onslaught. There is more than enough truth in his remarks for them to serve as texts for this chapter, but also enough that is questionable for it to be worthwhile to wonder why. Napoleon's imperialism was in the end thwarted and thrust back on the continent by great waves of national resistance which in very different ways gave military embodiment to something like 'the national will', insofar as so wobbly a concept can be identified. But not every nation's army was correspondingly revolutionized. The Prussian and other German armies, which Clausewitz knew best, were for a while the most nearly so; but the Austrian changed less, and as for the Russian and Spanish armies (the armies proper, as distinct from the auxiliary, partisan and irregular activities which gave the people military expression around them), it seems impossible to find any respect in which their organization or ethos were much different in 1812 from what they had been in 1792.

The British army and navy did not change very much in such respects either. We now come to Clausewitz's oddest omission. That he was not much interested in the British army may perhaps be forgiven him; by continental standards it was a small one, and its expeditionary forces to the continent did nothing to demand favourable notice until near the end of the wars. But his absolute neglect of British naval power is rather astounding, to be explained only in terms of an insularity of mind every bit as great as that from which the British themselves undoubtedly suffered. In Clausewitz's case, it was of course the reversed insularity of a Prussian preoccupied with his country's own exclusively continental problems; a land-war man, who assumed – if he thought about it at all – that anyone to whom sea war mattered would find war at sea must be conducted by the same principles as on land. Whether that was or is actually the case is a question we may leave to others. Its use to us is simply as an introduction to facts which must now be explored: that, of all external factors, it was British invincibility and persistence that ultimately drove Napoleon to the frustration and desperation of his last, self-destructive, over-reaching moves; that Napoleon's intermittent continental foes could have done little of what they did without British subsidies and supplies; and that the United Kingdom must therefore be considered to have accumulated will and strength to fight France in the striking equivalent measure Clausewitz indicated. But how this was done, he was beyond inquiring. We shall discover that it was, in common with most other aspects and episodes of British history, quite unlike anything anywhere else.

The United Kingdom (of England, Wales and Scotland only, let us recall, until the incorporation of Ireland in 1801) was the last of the greater western European powers to become persuaded of the necessity to engage in war. Only in the last months of 1792 did the government, with a sufficient degree of parliamentary support, decide that there was no alternative. Until then, the British armed forces were in fact considerably run-down, and war was about the last thing Pitt wanted. The French Revolution to begin with had seemed a good thing to most British people. In some respects it appeared to be no more than a catching-up on the example set by the British 'constitutional revolution' of the previous century: the reduction of the king's status from divine right to contract, the extinction of 'feudal' rights and privileges, legal and political equality for commoners, and so on. Britons who applauded these things did so in almost perfect safety through 1788-91. As the months went by the news of 'excesses' began to cross the Channel, increasingly by the agency of *émigrés* aristocrats and priests (not that the priests counted for much in Protestantism's sceptred isle), definite anti-Revolutionary opinion crystallized. Sympathizers with the Revolution correspondingly adopted a harder line, and by 1792 conservatives were forced to recognize that French example and rhetoric was giving an unwelcome fillip to the well-established native radical movement. British politics hotted up.

Yet still Pitt's cabinet had little thought of war until well into the second half of the year. What made it think of war was the Convention's Belgian policy, what made its mind up were the decrees in rapid succession declaring open the Scheldt and offering 'fraternity' and armed aid to peoples seeking freedom (see above, pp.82-7). Pitt had so far sensibly weighed conservative alarmism and common revulsion at the spectacle of mob violence and terror against a perception of national interests which told him that the collapse of French civilization would rather weaken France than otherwise as an imperial and commercial competitor. The November decrees, not surprisingly, destabilized him. This new France after all seemed just as determined to contest British oceanic supremacy as the old one; and perhaps the French really would support British and Irish revolutionary fellow-travellers with more than words. The Home Office began to listen to what magistrates and self-styled loyalists and its own spies told it about the radical political societies, their leaders began to be prosecuted, and their public doings, from the autumn of 1793 onwards, were viewed by the conservative establishment with hostile resentment until legislation stopped them altogether at the end of 1795. Unprecedented laws controlling aliens and 'traitorous correspondence' with France were quickly passed, the export of grain to France was prohibited, and the armed services were put on to what was expected (or, in the case of the army, so much less well-organized than the navy, hoped) to be an adequate war footing. 'Within a matter of weeks ... the navy had fifty-four battleships in commission and another thirty-nine ready.'[51] More remarkably, a continental commitment was accepted too. Ten thousand Hanoverian troops were promptly hired, and already before the end of February '93 a small but select British expeditionary force was on its way to join them in the Low Countries.

All this, brisk and business-like though it was, did not signify expectation of a long and difficult war. Pitt was not foolish in the winter and spring of 1792-3 to judge that France was tearing itself to pieces. We have seen how the Committee of Public Safety saved France from doing so and established French power on an altogether new social, political and ideological basis. Now we shall survey the curious contrast of the United Kingdom rising to the full height of the challenge thus made to it, without changing its social, political or ideological basis in the slightest. For the fact is that, although the wars were immensely expensive in money (about £1500,000,000, which Hobsbawm reckons to have been 'between three and four times' what they cost the French)[52] and in men (about 315,000, which by one statistical method can be presented as a higher proportion of servicemen than that lost in 1914-18),[53] the UK accomplished this effort without yielding at all to the pressures and temptations to change in the liberal direction, let alone the radical or revolutionary ones. Indeed, exactly the opposite! The wars actually gave British conservatism a new lease of life, and delayed liberalizing change by about thirty years.

What we are looking at, then, is a very big war effort, *prima facie* at least as big as France's, made by a non-revolutionary country and interestingly different from France in almost every respect. The most obvious difference, so crucial, and familiar as to need no labouring here, was the geographical one: France the dominant land-power, Britain the dominant sea-power, each supreme in its own element and neither able to get on top of the other until and unless enemy blunders made an opening for it. British grand strategy through the first fourteen years, moreover, was not well suited to the major task in hand. Picking off the colonies of France and France's allies, into which the bulk of military effort and expense was put, and in course of which the greater part of British losses were suffered through disease, brought some benefits to British trade, but did not greatly bother either the Republicans, who did not care so much about colonies, or Napoleon, who, though he fancied overseas colonies and empire and delighted to divert British energies into remote fields, fancied continental empire more. Subsidizing continental coalitions to fight France on land was of course accepted from the outset *de rigueur*, but how could they bring the war near victory while they kept being defeated? Generally ill-planned, numerically insubstantial, short-lived interventions in the Low Countries and along France's Mediterranean underbelly were no more than costly pin-pricks. Only when the British government committed itself to maintaining a decent-sized army in the Iberian peninsula – which its maritime supremacy alone enabled it to do – while becoming readier than ever to pour subsidies into the military coffers of Napoleon's eastern neighbours, did British grand strategy attain the level of vision called for by such a contest with such a giant.

125

At sea and, ultimately, on land as well, then, Britain managed to maintain large and (on land after 1808) thoroughly effective armed forces, at the same time as Britain found the money not only to support them but also to subsidize her coalition allies. How this was done, the remainder of this chapter will explain. But before we proceed, let us examine a little further the national context of these considerable achievements. Though not revolutionary, it was far from untroubled and Britain's peculiar military set-up, so very unlike France's, perhaps made those achievements all the more surprising.

Though war-enriched and war-accustomed, the UK was not at all 'war-organized', in the sense that were the great continental military powers. For one thing, by comparison with them, it lacked government and administration; the ordinary business of government being devolved and decentralized to an exceptional degree, a peculiarity possible only for a nation to whom external danger came only slowly and from afar. The navy, upon which it could therefore confidently rely for protection, at its maximum extent was large, expert and unbeatable, but as an organization it contrasted curiously with the French one, its nearest rival. While the French navy relied for the bulk of its construction timber upon the yield of great national forests, British domestic supply was so chancey that we find Admiral Collingwood in 1804 carrying pocketfuls of acorns about with him to pop into hedgerows ('let them take their chance'), reflecting that if other country gentlemen did the same, Britain's naval needs might be better met.[54] Its ships were not particularly well designed and, lacking the uniform measurements and standards which French organization-consciousness had recently introduced, they were troublesome to repair and re-fit. And reliance upon impressment in moments of crisis, though in the end it always produced enough men for the job in hand, did so in a slapdash, abrasive way that had a permanent air of the makeshift about it. (See above, pp.40-1.) It worked, but the continual controversy and unpleasantness about it showed that no one thought it worked well. In 1792, after several years of reforming administration by Sir Charles Middleton, the machinery was, in fact, in better order than ever before, and a formidable fleet was quickly in being, but it was a messy, creaking sort of machinery all the same, which the British were only not more aware of because of their congenital lack of concern about continental comparisons.

Yet the British navy at the start of the wars was a marvel of 'white-hot technology' and managerial skill by the side of the British army, whose administration at some points – as parliamentary inquirers found out to their cost – was so confused and peculiar as absolutely to defy understanding. Readers must not misunderstand this. We are considering the army, the standing army, as a national instrument, ready to serve the nation's war purposes and open to appraisal by the same utilitarian criteria as any other such. For most of its purposes in ordinary times this British army was not bad, as armies went. It was just big enough (something over 40,000) to provide garrisons for the many places around the empire which needed them (especially in India), a backbone for the maintenance of law and order at home (meaning above all Ireland) and a cadre for expansion in time of war. Some of its officers were extraordinarily bad but others were very good. A tradition which included Wolfe, Marlborough, Cromwell and Prince Rupert, after all, commanded respect and prompted emulation. There were would-be reformers in the British army as in all the others, and when the demands of desperate war began to melt the ice floes, they got to work to quite good effect. Courage and, among the line troops at least, discipline were almost always exemplary. It was in intelligence, adaptability, ability to work together, and efficiency in the planning and support of operations that it was lacking, and in practice so often went wrong. 'Once the organization of the high command of the British army is understood, what is surprising is not that the British fought so ineffectively during most of this [first] period [of the war] but that they were able to fight at all.'[55]

We have been considering 'the army' in our common British sense of the word: an army of professional, full-time soldiers; the line or the standing army, in the eighteenth century's expressive terms; what would soon be known in Britain as the regular army. But we now enter the rich realm of British oddities, noting side by side with it other bodies of officially armed men. In Ireland there were nearly 20,000 'Volunteers'; in Scotland, the regiments of fencibles raised without much difficulty from the clansmen of the Highlands. Above all there was, in England and Wales, apparently another and almost as big an army, the militia; a simpler,

127

less professional army for home defence and security, run on the cheap. It was organized on a territorial basis, county by county, with their Lords-Lieutenants in charge of most appointments and recruitment. Each county's quota was supplied by a ballot among eligible men (there were many exemptions) from 18- to 45-years-old. It was characteristic of British war organization that the quotas fixed in 1757 had not been up-dated to follow the nation's rapid demographic change, so that the chances, for example, of being picked in Dorset and Lancashire were, respectively, 1:8 and 1:43.[56] Substitutes were allowed, and exemption could be bought for £10. But the duties awaiting the militiamen were not normally arduous; one month's training annually for five years. Only when a state of national danger caused them to be 'embodied' was their service made, temporarily, full-time.

This extraordinary semi-professional armed force was not up to much in military terms, but British public opinion set great store on it, and an understanding of the reason why is an essential preliminary to understanding the peculiar British approach to the whole question of national military organization. For the fact was, that standing armies were viewed with extreme suspicion and fear. It was from Britain that continental liberals and peace-people had learnt thus to look at them. The two Charleses and the second James really had posed a threat to parliamentary government and the rule of law and their armies – really *their* armies, outside parliament's control – were the trumps in their hands. From 'the glorious revolution' of 1688, it was axiomatic with the freedom-conscious that the standing army should be kept as small as was consistent with national security, that parliament should retain control of its vital parts (i.e., its finance and its independent judiciary secured by the annual 'Mutiny Acts'), and that it should be complemented for every domestic purpose by a more 'popular' or national force, raised through the ordinary local government of the land and led by its ordinary leaders. This militia existed and remained so central in Britons' thinking about war precisely because they experienced constitutional difficulty in getting good at war on land. (It must also be admitted that geographical circumstances had saved them from having to do so.) War at sea was a different matter. No monarch had ever threatened Englishmen's liberties from that direction, and in any case the navy was symbiotically linked with foreign trade. Warships and seamen, to put it bluntly, were a good investment. But although soldiers – who after all were mostly occupied in imperial security – could equally be seen as such, it could only be after clearing away dense clouds of constitutional suspicion and prejudice, and not many Englishmen (Scotsmen, habitually more martial, perhaps were different) were perspicacious enough to penetrate them.

So there were at the outbreak of the wars, the militia and the line or standing army; the militia 'not in any true [continental] sense a militia' but a semi-professional army, its quasi-conscripts' services, 'instead of being bought by the State, having been bought by private individuals chosen at haphazard, and the cost therefore not appearing in the budget';[57] and the army proper, 'not an efficient, a national, or a particularly happy force',[58] grudgingly accepted as a rather disagreeable necessity. But although men worried about even this army's capacity for turning on its creators and rending them, they really need not have done so, for it was conditioned to only less a degree than the militia by the characteristics of the ruling classes which in the end ran them both; ruling classes distinguished by their social breadth and by the extent to which blood had learnt to mate with money.

Army, militia and navy alike were of course cast in the image of the class for whose benefit they primarily existed; but in terms of efficiency and aptness to its task the navy suffered less, because amateurism and inefficiency at sea spelt death. The navy's officers, as has already been remarked, composed a highly skilled corps, and the hard discipline by which they stood had at any rate this understandable rationale to it, that unless the orders of the experts in charge were carried out, everyone was wrecked, and extremely expensive pieces of equipment were lost. No country – not even the affluent UK – could afford an inefficient or merely ornamental naval officer corps. But war on land knew not the natural discipline of storms and rocks. Moreover, land armies had a much wider range of tasks to perform, many of them – ceremonial parades, for instance, and routine garrison duties – without a trace of danger, some merely ornamental, and a few – cavalry life especially – pure fun. All over Europe a very natural tendency turned cavalry officer corps into preserves of the richer and faster aristocracy. The horse and its capabilities engrossed them in peace and war alike, and transition from the one to the other made little existential difference. British cavalry officers shared these characteristics to the full and were, of all the branches of the British army, the most indisciplined. Even Wellington was to find them difficult to manage. But it was not only they who thus offended him. The freedom of comment on their commanders' plans which British officers allowed themselves and their lack of scrupulous attention to orders seems to have been exceptional. 'If discipline means ... obedience to orders as well as military instruction, we have but little in the army. Nobody ever thinks of obeying an order. All the regulations, etc., are so much waste paper,' he complained early in 1814.[59] The British ruling classes carried their prejudice against bureaucracy from the civil to the military sphere, and with it they carried the proud individualism and 'gentlemanly pretensions' which were another element of their ideology. 'It was difficult to persuade anyone to serve under Wellington, because he was so junior in rank. It was even more difficult to persuade generals or admirals to serve under one another. British combined operations frequently failed solely because the British would not – or could not – appoint supreme commanders.'[60] To quote the master again: 'Nobody ... ever reads a regulation or an order as if it were to be a guide for his conduct, or in any other manner than as an amusing novel; and the consequence is, that when complicated arrangements are to be carried into execution, ... every *gentleman* proceeds according to his fancy....'[61] It was not thus that things were ordered within range of Clausewitz's and Jomini's notebooks. Land army professionalism of the Franco-Prussian style did not acclimatize easily in the offshore islands.

That British army officers up to the rank of colonel purchased their commissions was a further insular oddity. Radical reformers and Potsdamophiles used to join to condemn the practice. The best recent writers tend to confirm its contemporary advocates' judgment, that it was not on its own an obstruction to professional improvement, any more than was the system of patronage which riddled the navy. But from our point of view the significance of purchase and its militia equivalent, the strict scaling of rank to match income, was simply its ensuring that the hierarchy of military rank would correspond to the social hierarchy from which the officer corps was drawn. To that extent the officer corps at least seemed thoroughly national.

But in another sense they were not, and things were not so simple. The very word 'nation' in this context reminds us that

Britain was a very different sort of nation from France, if indeed it was a nation in that sense at all. We are actually speaking of a self-styled United Kingdom which was not nearly as united as its rulers would have liked it to be, and was much more fissiparous than France. French governments had to cope with Frenchmen who didn't like the Revolution; British governments had to cope not only with men who didn't like Britain and didn't wish to fight France but who, if they were Irish, might not want to be linked with Britain either. And we may further recall that, quite apart from these problems of nationalities and ideologies, the society we are now considering was, during these very years of war, unwittingly serving as mankind's guinea-pig in going through the manifold strains and shocks of the first industrial revolution – a process which, by accelerating the growth of the non-agricultural sectors of economy and society, imperilled the perfection of the old mainly landed ruling class's control of them, and perhaps (it was too early to say for sure) would endanger its existence altogether.

Ireland gave the British government even more trouble than the Vendée gave the French. The age-old volcanic violence – now just simmering, now in bloody eruption – of its agrarian system was the lesser part of the problem. More serious now was the up-to-date revolutionary nationalism which had gripped some of the middling and even a few of the upper classes, Protestants and Catholics alike. If ever it allied with that semi-subterranean Catholic peasant discontent, it could become very dangerous indeed. France, long familiar with Britain's Irish difficulties, looked again in the nineties for an Irish back door to go in by, and a certain sort of Irish nationalists, the United Irishmen, welcomed this, concluding that only with French military aid could they ever achieve their revolution and gain their independence. General Hoche got within sight of Bantry Bay in December 1796, but 'Protestant winds' beat him back. General Humbert did land, at Killala in the north-west, in August 1798, but 'too little and too late'; premature insurgencies in Ulster and the south had already been put down, Humbert and his thousand Frenchmen surrendered on 8 September, and the Irishmen who had risen to march with him were dealt with in the many ruthless ways familiar to the local landowner yeomanry and the professional military. Ireland gave little further serious trouble after 'the year of the French';[62]

but a large force of troops remained stationed there, all the same, and the War Office generally made sure that it did not include Irish regiments.

No less serious than the danger of insurrection in Ireland, was thought to be the danger of insurrection in Britain. The Gordon riots in 1780, which had required considerable military effort to suppress them, were a very recent reminder of what a metropolitan mob could do when suitably inflamed. The fear of a recurrence of that sort and size of mob violence remained a nightmare with respectable people for well over half a century. French happenings added to it the possibility that such horrendous force might be harnessed to hard political purposes. Radical politics were already freely available, and highly encouraged by news from Paris. (See above, p.124.) The question for the government and 'the establishment' was, would radicalism become revolutionary? There were certainly hints that it might do so. The probability of its turning to violence of course increased in proportion with the severity of its repression; but so did the possibility that repression would work and prevent the violence from achieving anything. We cannot be sure what happened between 1796, when the repression really began to bite, and 1810-11, when a radically new variant of political violence, bred by experience of industrialization, caused a larger force of troops to be stationed in northern England and Scotland than was serving in the Peninsula. There was no mistaking the dangerous potential of 'Luddism', and part of its leadership was in the old radical-cum-revolutionary tradition. We shall turn to Luddism presently. But what had the men of that tradition been up to in the meantime? So effective in general was the repression of the late nineties and so well-camouflaged in the opaque, not to say muddy, waters of lower-class life were the revolutionaries, that we know of them nothing more certain than that, despite continual French encouragement and the natural alliance of the United Irishmen, they achieved nothing. The war and its executives indeed were intermittently unpopular on account of the personal and material hardships they brought with them, and there was normally little love lost between the working classes and the rich, their masters. But it does not look as if those 'gut reactions' and standing class antipathies were turned into deliberate political channels until the wars were three-quarters over, and when that happened, sympathy for the French or admiration of them formed no part of Luddite thinking. Lower-class Britons, after all, had had many decades in which to acquire a common contempt for stereotyped Frenchmen, and it took a hard political head to stick to respect for revolutionary principles in the face of so much revolutionary, and almost all post-revolutionary, practice. A few Whig aristocrats and intellectuals managed to do so and were socially secure enough to get away with it; anyone of *really* radical mind was like to see the good aspects of Jacobinism and even Napoleon rather than the bad ones; but it does not look as if it was safe to come out with pro-French sentiments in public at any social level. Clive Emsley comes back to this point again and again in his fine study of *British Society and the French Wars*. Comb the evidence as he may, he cannot find much evidence of popular pro-Frenchness or revolutionary activity, while mere acceptance of the war and conventional patriotism – mindless, instinctive and shallow, perhaps, but patriotism all the same – shows again and again. George III's carriage window was broken by a missile in late October 1795 but most of the great quantity of British glass deliberately broken during the wars was in the windows of radicals who refused, or absent-minded persons who neglected, to illuminate their windows with candles in ritual celebration of naval victories and other such opportunities for national rejoicing.

The behaviour of the soldiers and sailors, themselves drawn from the common people, interestingly corroborates this judgment. All governments and governing classes are hypersensitive to the question of their armed men's loyalty in revolutionary epochs, and the British in the early nineties had everything to fear. The French Revolution's first couple of years had been marked by mutinies, insubordination, and some murders of officers. Might not British soldiers and sailors, by no means overpaid or attractively housed and fed, find those examples attractive? The British Jacobins with their French and United Irish connections were observed to make some attempts to exploit the opportunity.

Come, little Drummer Boy, lay down your knapsack here:
....
Here's half-a-crown for you – here are some handbills too –
Go to the Barracks, and give all the soldiers some.

133

Tell them the sailors are all in a Mutiny....[63]

The naval mutinies of the later nineties brought the danger very close. They added up to a far graver danger of military collapse than anything France ever faced. Occasional mutinies by individual crews had long been a normal feature of naval life (all too natural, considering the atrocious conditions which could result from inefficient or corrupt administration, bureaucratic dilatoriness and insensitivity, gross disparities between the different ranks' pay and conditions of service, and the brutality and sadism of particular commanders) and the separate mutinies on the *Culloden* and *Windsor Castle* in late 1794, for example, gave no particular cause for concern. But the mutinies which ran through the Channel, North Sea, South Atlantic and Mediterranean fleets in 1797-8 were something new. The fleet at Spithead (Portsmouth) was out of action from mid-April to mid-May and that at The Nore (Thames estuary) from mid-May to mid-June 1797; the fleet off Cadiz was on the verge of mutiny from May '97 to the final crisis twelve months later; sporadic mutinies were commoner than usual through the next few years, and at least two ships were carried by their crews into enemy ports. But on the whole it was not revolutionary principles or even native British radicalism which prompted these desperate risings. It was simply the sailors' long-accumulated irritation and sense of profound injustice at the conditions and rewards of their service. The Spithead mutineers, who as the first in the field had the easiest run and who, besides, seem to have been better led and organized, revealed no lack of patriotism whatever. Some radicalism there must have been but it was kept prudently concealed and it was not at all revolutionary, the leaders repeatedly insisting that their comrades wanted nothing more than to get back to fighting the French. It was more like a strike than a mutiny. There was hardly any bloodshed. Officers of sense and humanity (notably 'Black Dick', the great Admiral Lord Howe, a gouty septuagenarian brought out of retirement at the men's request) dominated the negotiating, the sailors got most of what they wanted, and it ended in an orgy of patriotic reconciliation which expressed the prevailing popular sentiments of the early and middle war years – the years when there really was a prospect of French invasion.

This was so significant and amazing (containing as it does

elements of the Eatonswill election, a Durham Miners' Gala, victory celebrations, and that invaluable common touch which has so often been the British ruling classes' ultimate salvation) that Temple Patterson's admirable description of it must be cited. After three days' hard negotiating, ship by ship, Howe and the men's leader, quartermaster's-mate Valentine Joyce, met at the Governor's House to arrange the details, Joyce 'asking Lady Howe to honour the occasion with her company, assuring her that she need have no fear. She replied that she was not in the least afraid and would be delighted to come, after which her husband invited Joyce to come in and have a glass of wine with him. This the ex-mutineer leader accepted "with a manly freedom, unaccompanied by the least particle of familiarity or rudeness".' To round off this truly English finish, news now came by the telegraph (ten minutes from London on a clear day) that the pardon was on its way, and in fact it arrived in the early evening, brought by a rider who (with relays of horses) had made the journey from London in the record time of four-and-a-half hours.

At dawn on Monday the procession of boats reappeared, with the leading one flying the Union Jack, and the delegates landed at the Sally Port.... Despite his fatigue, Howe had roused himself betimes, and he now invited them all into the house to drink wine with him and then took them on to the balcony to receive the thunderous applause of the crowd. He and Lady Howe then walked back with them to the Sally Port with the bands (for the marine band and various ships' bands had now arrived and joined in with gusto) blaring away in front. Here it seemed as if every boat in the Solent was waiting to take part in the triumphal procession.... Howe went first to the Royal George, on whose quarterdeck he read out the pardon, showing it afterwards to the few seamen who could read. Then he went from ship to ship.... At six o'clock the boats returned once more to the Sally Port, with Howe so exhausted that he had to be lifted from the barge. The seamen who did so carried him on their shoulders back to the Governor's house with the Union Jack held over his head, through crowds such as Portsmouth had never seen before.... Then, rallying his last energies, he invited them in to supper, before they rowed back to St Helen's in the moonlight and reported for duty to the officers old and new who were now aboard their ships.[64]

The Nore mutiny began the same way but ended much less happily, with twenty-nine hangings, nine floggings and many lesser punishments. It was – or its leaders were – somewhat more political than at Spithead, but even so the men were fundamentally patriotic, and it turned sour mainly because in place of Joyce there was the more aggressive and possibly seditious 'President' (as he was called) Richard Parker, in place of Howe the dour and intractable Rear-Admiral Lord Keith. Off Cadiz, Admiral the Earl of Saint-Vincent was even tougher, overruling softer-hearted captains under his command just as firmly as he refused to show any sign of yielding to lower-deck pressure.

> The capital sentence was repeatedly inflicted: . . . the crews were invariably [made to be] the executioners of their own rebels. . . . To a plea for mercy on the grounds of good character ... St Vincent turned a deaf ear. 'Those who have suffered hitherto,' he replied, 'have for the most part been worthless fellows; I shall now convince the seamen that no character, however good, shall save a man who is guilty of mutiny.'[65]

But the grim old man, who understood well enough the material causes of the men's unrest, through all those anxious months was striving to improve the men's condition in every way *he* could control it; and the government, once it had duly taken the measure of the events of Spithead, saw the wisdom of raising not only sailors' pay but that of soldiers too. The need to do that, the danger of not doing it, had been evident for years to those who cared. It needed a reluctant mutiny by patriotic (and largely conscripted) seamen to get it done.

So much for disunities within the armed forces which threatened to break the national ability to fight. Now for disunities within the governing classes which threatened to break the national will to fight. We need not linger on the Foxite Whigs of the nineties, or get involved in the argument as to whether they broke away from the rest of the party or were abandoned by them. The fact is that by the summer of 1794 the greater part of the Whig party, the historic champions of liberty, was allied to a sort of national government coalition, determined to fight it out with France, leaving Charles James Fox and a rump of the party in opposition, explaining to any part of the public which would listen that, so far as France itself was concerned, you couldn't make omelettes without breaking eggs (which British radicals have said about foreign revolutions ever since), and that France's effect on her neighbours was largely advantageous to liberty, enlightenment and progress. They were accused of being soft-headed as well as soft-hearted, at best neglecting vital strategic and economic interests and at worst of talking treason. Governments at war of course always react thus to critics – if there are any. It is a measure of the relative liberality of British principles, as well as of the all-importance of birth and connections, that these high-class Whig critics were never shut up. But for a while they shut up themselves, feeling the impossibility of achieving anything. This was especially so during the great patriotic upsurges of 1798-9 and 1803-5. At other times during the early and middle war years, when there was no invasion scare, they could get more of a hearing by representing the hardships which war made or seemed to make for the lower orders, taxpayers, and certain industries; but still it is impossible to see them as indicating anything like a serious rift within the governing classes. During the last long haul, however, from 1806 onwards, something like that began to appear, and from 1811 to the end it was unmistakeable. By then many prosperous Britons publicly wanted peace, and wanted it badly.

The roots of this rift, like the roots of those men, lay in the industrial revolution, which British society had been experiencing, by the common judgment and criteria of economic historians, since about 1780. It 'began' or, in W.W. Rostow's once celebrated phrase, 'took off' before the wars, and being intrinsically a turbulent, exploratory, rough process, would have had its ups and downs in any case. It is an open question, whether its coinciding so soon with twenty years of war as total as Britain could wage it, made those ups and downs worse than they would otherwise have been. Harvests were still by far the greatest annual facts of social life and the ultimate determinants of the state of the economy. Overseas trade, upon which so much of the country's wealth and employment depended, was always at risk from the chops and changes of international relations. It is impossible to calculate which markets British manufactures might under other circum-

137

stances have found in place of those which under the given circumstances they actually did find. It is clear that war was kind to some sectors of the economy. The whole of the metallurgical side was bound to do well. Every warship had to be copper-bottomed. Cannon, muskets and bullets were in all but inexhaustible demand when the government was supplying not only its own army and navy but most of its allies' too (e.g., £2,000,000's worth in 1813 alone).[66] The trades making naval and military equipment did equally well, and best of all, of course, did the contractors who supplied the stuff. Rapid population growth and the intermittent cessation of foreign supplies meant a twenty-year boom in farming, carefully cultivated by a government equally interested in avoiding bread-riots and taxing landowners. But overseas trade and manufactures dependent on it fared much more variably. Overall figures for foreign trade continued to leap up through the nineties, but the costs were high (French privateers and premiums of insurance against them, sailors' wages much increased by scarcity) and markets disordered, new ones opened across the oceans being matched by sporadic continental closures, as Paris pulled what strings it could to bar the British trader.

Only after the 1803 resumption of war, however, did it really threaten to cripple the British economy and drive the British commercial community to revolt against its continuation. This was because it now became economic warfare with a vengeance, and the more capitalistic and modern-industrialized of the two mighty antagonists suffered the more acutely. In principle, of course, economic warfare was nothing new. Britain's wars successively with Spain, Holland and France over the past two hundred years had been about trade and empire, and each belligerent party had been wont to put as much economic screw on the other as it could and as it felt advisable. In practice, however, this often meant a good deal of give and take and laxity, not least because of the trouble neutrals made if it did not. Neutral opinion impinged hardly at all on the conduct of war on land but it mattered a lot to maritime belligerents, who might not wish to press their 'rights' (a matter of controversy unceasing) of blockade, stoppage of enemy trade and seizure of enemy goods or goods *en route* to the enemy beyond the point that would drive neutrals to become enemies. Britain, as befitted the strongest single naval power, had the highest idea of a belligerent's rights, and regularly ran into trouble with neutral opinion by trying to enforce them. In the Seven Years' War she got away with it, but not in the War of American Independence, when in 1780 'The Armed Neutrality' ganged up against her, and not entirely in the French wars either. Resentments among southern neutrals didn't matter much but Holland, Denmark, Sweden, Prussia and Russia were another matter, covering as they did so much of Britain's essential naval supplies and a sizeable proportion of Britain's foreign trade (whether in home-manufactured stuff or re-exports from elsewhere). And the new voice in the neutral choir, the United States, proved to be a more insistent one than Britain had expected. Britain's intermittent disputes with the northern States (which produced another, shorter-lived, Russian-led ganging-up in 1800) proved nothing like so vexatious in the long run as the all-but-continuous dispute with the United States, which turned into the lamentable, unwanted war of 1812. Britain's ruthlessness in enforcing her idea of a maritime belligerent's rights, together of course with the obviousness of her pursuit under all circumstances of commercial advantage, did much to prevent her claims to be fighting for small States' rights from being taken seriously on the continent, and gave a good handle to French propagandists. They turned it merrily, from 1793 to the end. From the continental point of view, it was not difficult to believe that France, not Britain, stood for that splendid-sounding concept, 'the freedom of the seas'.

Napoleon, when he became master of the French Empire, made much of this, but – the parallel is striking – *his* claims to represent the interests of continental and smaller States were belied by their experience of his hegemony on land. And it was when his assertion of that hegemony reached its highest pitch that economic warfare became for a few years total. From the resumption of hostilities in 1803, he worked towards it. After the successive smashings of Austria, Prussia and Russia in 1805-7, he had nearly achieved it. There were scarcely any neutrals left in Europe, and the 'Continental System' outlined in his Berlin and Milan Decrees envisaged the total exclusion of British, British-carried, and even British-touched (i.e., neutral shipping which had called at a UK port *en route*) goods. The UK responded with its 'Orders in Council', declaring the continent closed to neutral trade unless it went via Britain, expensively and subject to British conditions.

So each party staked all on a desperate effort to break its enemy's economy. Napoleon refused to allow into the Europe he controlled anything from or via the UK; Britain refused to allow into it anything *not* from or via the UK. Each drove with equal ruthlessness over neutral interests. Which would crack first?

In the event, it was Napoleon; but it was a near run thing. Each side ran into trouble with the remaining neutrals, and Napoleon's troubles were the more damaging: Spain and Russia. But by the time Napoleon was marshalling the *grande armée* for his Russian venture, the British government was in dire straits, not far from considering a negotiated peace. And it was in such straits for economic, not military, reasons. In military terms, Britain was doing quite well. Her control of the seas was absolute. Thanks to it, small but muscular British expeditionary forces could operate where they pleased; Wellington's was proving an enormous nuisance to the French in the Peninsula, while a smaller nuisance forever hovered off Italy. Britain's overseas trade was booming brashly in the newly-opened South American market, and met no competition in the tropics. Such was the credit side of the account. The debit side, however, had become critical. Relations with the United States had been broken. Maddened by British maritime presumption, the US had decided that, if their trade with continental Europe should be stopped, so in retaliation should British trade with the US. This hit American interests badly, but they reckoned that British interests would be hit worse. Accompanying that was the near collapse of the north and east European markets. The revolutionizing sectors of the British economy had not the tensile flexibility to stand such strains. Hectically expanding according to the laws of the process which was gripping them, they now found supplies of raw materials irregular, stocks piling up unsaleable, and their credit, together with that of the banks facilitating their operations, over-extended. 1808 was a bad year, almost disastrous. 1811, after the temporary recovery year 1810, was entirely so.

In a country enormously taxed, with dear food, subject to common harvests hazards, undergoing a population explosion and all the jumps and jolts of the first industrial revolution at the same time, the results were awful and dramatic. For the work force of the textile industries above all, but not for them alone, it meant unemployment, privation, humiliation, and a prospect of starvation. They did not suffer dumbly. Something like a mass insurrection spread through the northern textile counties. Called 'the Luddites' because of their mythical leader, 'General Ned Ludd', their principal mode of venting their rage and desperation, apart from traditional food riots, was by breaking the new machinery and sometimes breaking into manufacturers' premises to do so. Nocturnally, and in as much secret as circumstances and informers allowed, there were mass meetings and 'drillings', not without arms. The many murders of the time included that of Prime Minister Spencer Perceval, not by one of the Luddites – though they thought he deserved it. Soon 12,000 troops were deployed in those counties, the homes and factories of threatened owners were under military protection, and Luddite leaders were being ferreted out, prosecuted and punished. How far Luddism had revolutionary politics in it as well as hunger, desperation and economic traditionalism, we do not know. It was entirely a working-class movement, and so 'opaque' (to use again E.P. Thompson's apt word) did that class make itself to authority's intruding eye that neither then nor since have its secrets been unveiled.

The exclusively lower-class character which made it so intangible made it also, as it happened, less dangerous to the government than it might have been if higher-class characters had been involved in it. 'The Luddite disorders', concludes Emsley, 'probably [actually] served to unite the government and the propertied classes.'[67] The government kept its head and controlled the insurgency. More dangerous to its war effort was the other, associated reaction of industrializing society in crisis which the astute Emperor had anticipated: a bourgeoisie utterly disenchanted with the war, and openly demanding peace. While workmen went hungry and lost hope, manufacturers, merchants and bankers went bankrupt and lost confidence. These were the new men of the new industrial society. Not yet were they very numerous. But year by year their number and class-consciousness was increasing. Their relations with the land-based aristocracy and gentry, the traditional ruling class, had always been ambiguous – they had common interests as property owners, but culturally and politically were often inassimilable – and now they were numerous, prosperous and influential enough to challenge that ruling class directly. The war was ruining them and the prospects of the British economy, and it was time to stop it. Nor was their peace movement in 1811-12 as exclusively a class affair as Luddism. Some of the petitions to parliament supporting it were signed by employers and workmen both.

This unabashed expression of war-weariness, coming on top of such violent manifestations of discontent at what the war was doing to the new society, were not the government's only cause for concern. Britain's ability to go on paying for the war depended on its prosperity. If prosperity evaporated, so must the war effort. So great were these compounded dangers by the summer of 1812 that the government began to yield. Policy vis-à-vis the United States was moderated (too late, however, for news of it to stop their declaration of war), and there is no knowing how much further this bourgeois-industrial revolt might have gone, had not a completely new appearance been put on affairs by the collapse of French power in eastern Europe and the consequently brighter prospects for war and economy alike. Had Napoleon not thus overreached himself, and had he continued to play his other economic cards right – e.g., had he not, in doctrinaire pursuance of his grand design to drain Britain of its bullion, continued to issue licences for the exportation of grain to Britain, just when Britain was *in* economic *extremis* – Britain might well have been compelled to negotiate. France and *a fortiori* its vassal-allies suffered badly from this titanic economic struggle, but Britain suffered worse.

The industrial revolution, then, with its accompanying social convulsions, brought a new kind of vulnerability to a nation at war, which in the final account has to be balanced against its benefits. Of those, by far the largest was, simply, wealth. Wealthy from agricultural production and commerce before the industrial revolution took off, Britain now became wealthier still and, except at bad moments, at more rapid a rate. The vast cost of the war could therefore be carried without unbearable strain except on the poorer people, of whose resentments and rages the government, as we have seen, refused to be afraid. Money to pay the necessarily heavy taxation (the novel income tax not the least part of it) and to make the necessary loans (most of the cost being carried by an enormously swollen National Debt) never ran out. It was this financial capability and solidity which repeatedly misled French grand strategists. They kept looking for a collapse which never

142

came, not even in 1811-12. British industrial growth continued through the war and 'the accessible evidence taken as a whole does not support the view that the war ... exerted a serious brake' on it. 'Whether the overall pace of industrial growth would have been appreciably faster had there been no war it is impossible to say.'[68] Some industries no doubt developed faster in the wartime hot-house – the metal ones, most obviously – while some (brick-making, and coal-mining, for instance) were probably retarded. Economic historians, a cautious lot, quite properly refuse to guess what would have happened to the British economy had there not been such a war, but all agree that its net effect was to increase Britain's industrial lead over its nearest European rivals, and to transform its industrial structure in ways that would help that lead become even greater. Apart from wealth and industrial progress, however, our awareness of the extent to which war was in due course going to be transformed by modern industrial capacity and methods makes us inquire whether this war gave any intimation of the shape of things to come.

The answer is no; hardly at all. It came in between two waves of technological progress. Whatever else was new or revolutionary about the style of warfare of Napoleon, Scharnhorst *et al.*, it was not weaponry. There were inventions, but none achieved much and the warlords were not much interested in them. Napoleon closed down the French army's aeronautical department, Congreve's rockets frightened Wellington more than they frightened the enemy, young Lord Cochrane's passion for chemical warfare won him more enemies than friends, the possible naval uses of steam power (certainly clear by about 1810) were wholly ignored, and when the American Fulton produced his idea of using his pioneer submarine to blow up the British ships blockading Brest, 'Villaret-Joyeuse, the admiral, and Caffarelli, the [maritime] prefect, discountenanced the proposal, on grounds of humanity', the latter adding that it was such a 'disgraceful way of making war ... that those engaged in it deserved to be hanged'.[69] Like their enemies, Nelson and his band of brothers were hard men, but they knew ungentlemanly ways of fighting when they saw them. So scientific progress and industrialization at this stage were adding very little to the armoury, except to its size. The quantities of weapons used in these wars far outpassed any previous experience, and their production had the usual results on manufacturers and governments. French feats of mass musket, pistol and side-arms production were mentioned above (p.94). The British Board of Ordnance had to pull its socks up. Its gunpowder works at Waltham early went on to Sunday working. Its arsenal at Woolwich in 1809 cast 385 cannon. After the 1803 resumption it not only set up a Birmingham office to deal briskly with the (private) suppliers and test their products but it actually began to manufacture muskets itself.[70] Portsmouth Dockyard meanwhile became the scene of 'the first instance of machine tools being employed for mass production': the French immigrant Marc Brunel's famous steam-powered machinery for replacing manual skills in the making of pulley blocks, needed by the navy to the tune of 100,000 a year. Less famous but no less significant in its implications for the future were 'the beginnings of the modern assembly line' making 'ship's biscuit', the staff of sailors' life, at the Victualling Office at Deptford.[71] Major Shrapnell's invention depended on two feats of extraordinary technical sophistication: the mass production of an absolutely consistent quality of powder and the production (top secret) of hyperprecise fuses.[72] But those seem to be the only notable examples of directly war-induced technical advances in the first industrial nation, and of scientific advances proper, like those made in France to beat the shortages, there were none.

The navy was of course the more important of the two armed services. It was large and expensive. By 1813 there were nearly 140,000 men serving on board His Majesty's Ships; ships of all sizes and uses, from the great 'men of war' with seventy-four or more guns through the smaller, older battleships, the frigates with between thirty and forty guns, the bomb-ketches (for short-range bombardment work) and sloops, down to the brigs and cutters which alone could operate in shallow and complicated waters. Although there were no great naval battles after 21 October 1805 (except the small but crucial one on Lake Erie in 1813), the British navy's heaviest work continued to the end to be what it had been from the start: the blockading of the enemy's naval ports, the prevention of commercial traffic to or from enemy and enemy-controlled coasts, and the protection of British vessels from attack by enemy frigates and privateers. Not much of this was spectacular.

Frigate duels, Anglo-American after they had ceased to be Anglo-French, were undoubtedly so, and provided matter for many of the best sea-war stories and songs. French privateers, knowing the Channel and the North Sea just as well as British seamen, kept up a dashing maritime guerrilla war, capturing many sailors, ships and cargos; pestilential and 'insolent' from the haughty British viewpoint, they provided the French with most of their maritime folk-heroes, besides an optimistic illusion that privateering was a tolerable substitute for real naval power. Commerce protection, convoying and blockade were of necessity less eventful (except when close-blockading in stormy weather, which required superlative seamanship) and incapable of catching the public eye. Yet they were what really mattered, and it was in doing them that the British navy spent by far the greater and most profitable part of its time. For every day Nelson spent in battle, he spent a year cruising and blockading. When he went on his last leave in the summer of 1805, he had not set foot on shore for two years. The years-long blockade of Brest, at its most intense and efficient from 1800 to 1805, was by universal consent a unique masterpiece of naval skill. Successful in all its aims, it much advanced the winning of the war. But besides being intermittently very dangerous, it was generally uncomfortable, and very boring. No wonder, perhaps, that British sailors approached battles with enthusiasm. At least, and at last, they were *fighting*!

They fought very well and were usually victorious (except against Americans in the war of 1812). Discipline and experience had much to do with it. The French, who whatever their shortcomings seem always to have been more efficient than the Spanish, had nearly caught up with British standards by the 1780s (see above, p.39), but once the blockades were biting their big ships rarely got the practice they needed for effective fleet operations, and their gun crews never, or hardly ever, attained the normal British rate of a shot at least every ninety seconds; which British crews managed in part because of the clockwork discipline to which they were accustomed. (But that cannot have been the whole of the explanation, since the Yankees, not thus regulated, did just as well or better.) A set battle once joined was usually ferocious and desperate, ending only when one party surrendered. Then hostile feelings as well as hostilities abruptly ceased, giving way to the promptings of humanity, the principles of a civilized

145

code of war-conduct, and the fellow-feeling which seamen often have for each other. Victors would at once take risks to rescue vanquished from wreck and water. But so long as the enemy flag flew, the object was simply to smash the enemy into submission. Ship would lay itself close to ship and go to work in its own national way – the French setting more store on the destruction of masts and rigging, the shooting of Britons visible on deck (thus Nelson died), and the virtues of boarding; the British preferring to put the bulk of their efforts into the hull- and gun-crew-smashing at which they excelled. Most bloody of all actions were those like Aboukir Bay (1 August 1798) and Copenhagen (2 April 1801) when one of the lines was at anchor and nothing could happen but a slogging-match. As the *Edgar* at the head of the British line sailed slowly past the first Danish ship on the latter occasion, she received a full broadside: 'keeled over as if she had been struck by a heavy sea ... the blood of the killed and wounded pouring out of her scupper holes and making the sea red....' So observed a young sailor on the *Agamemnon*. He recalled what it was like on his own ship as it got into action – the officers crying, '"King and country – fighting for king and country" ... our men at work with their guns, crying out amidst the roar of cannon, "Hold on", "get ready", "England for ever", "cheer up", "if we are wounded we shall get down to the doctor", "good bye, shipmates", "my turn next", "fight for king and country", "a good drop of grog when we are done", with all such idle nonsense.'[73]

The crews thus compounded into highly effective fighting units continued to come, the greater number of them unwillingly, from the same variety of sources as before (see above, pp.40-1). By 1812, says Michael Lewis, volunteers formed only about 15 per cent of the average crew; 'foreigners', who may really have been volunteers but could also be serving in lieu of internment, 15 per cent; 'boys', also volunteers of a sort, 8 per cent; 60+ per cent pressed and more-or-less pressed men, including the debtors, vagabonds and so on sent to sea instead of gaol.[74] The press gangs continued to work in much the same old way, becoming however more regular and systematic, and in some peculiarly touchy areas like Tyneside achieving a *modus vivendi* with what we would now call the seamen's union. Organized worker resistance, illegal but too strong to be crushed and in any case involving, as on the Tyne, skilled men doing work of national importance, was only one of the many modes of resistance to impressment. Riots and rescue attempts were commonplace. The British people may have been patriotic – in some sense they clearly were more so than not – but they did not wish to serve their country in that way. Naval victories were matters for national rejoicings and victorious commanders became popular celebrities, but life on naval shipboard positively attracted few below the officer-minded classes. Desertion remained a tremendous problem. Yet conditions were very slowly ameliorating. About 90,000 sailors died during the wars.[75] Only about 7 per cent of this mortality was due to enemy action, and the other causes of it (disease, about 50 per cent; 'accidents', mostly due to drink, about 30 per cent; about 13 per cent 'the perils of the sea')[76] would yield gradually to the force of improvements in health, navigation, and moral climate. And the disciplinary style was slowly changing too. Increasing numbers of commanders found it was possible to do with less lash. Collingwood, indeed, dispensed with it almost completely (the presence of impressed criminals required retention of a minimum) and advised his subordinates to address their men with civility. The navy was on the way to its Victorian popularity. But all improvement and humanizing could not but be superficial, so long as impressment remained the navy's ultimate means of completing its crews.

Compulsion was not unknown in the land forces, but was exercised in more complicated ways. The line army, the part of the army which had to be ready to go anywhere around the globe, was always composed entirely of volunteers or mercenaries. The volunteers of course could include foreigners, either by the complete unit – like The King's German Legion, one of the best regiments under Wellington's command – or by recruiting into depleted British ranks: e.g., the 60th Regiment 'at Plymouth, procuring volunteers from the remains of the [French] garrison of St Sebastian's. A number of very fine fellows, Germans, Dutch and Italians, have entered....'[77] Men volunteered mainly for traditional reasons (see above, p.42), salted no doubt by patriotic or ideological urges in those whom counter-revolutionary propaganda had caused to hate Frenchmen and the half-dangerous, half-contemptible Boney, and tempted by a variety of monetary inducements. Especially in the first, improvising years of the war did these flourish. Patriotic committees subscribed to offer bounties, the government for a while offered individuals officer ranks on a scale proportionate with the number of men they brought with them, and in December 1794, says Fortescue, was even desperate enough to contract with an individual, bearing the rank of Captain, for 2000 Irishmen at 20 guineas per head.[78] Although the men thus brought into military service were by no means all as bad as Wellington later alleged ('the scum of the earth enlisted for drink', etc.) they were clearly likely to be less than ideal. Army authorities faced the same problem as navy ones, of making effective fighting units out of initially unpromising material.

But that army material was, we repeat, voluntary. Compulsion was only used to fill the ranks of the militia, the greater part of the national defence force. The obligation to serve in the militia being ancient and respected, it need never have brought inadequate results or aroused resentment, had not government's lack of consistent policy wrought so much confusion. Eager to swell the defensive ranks and to rally reliable patriots to the national and counter-revolutionary cause, it encouraged several varieties of volunteers (simply so called, or yeomanry, or fencibles – *not*, as some Irishmen at first wanted, national guards!) which could be little more than property-owners' vigilante corps and which sometimes carried with them immunity from militia service, which was thus somewhat undermined. There is no point in describing this 'shambles of a system' in any detail.[79] As the years went by, it shed its early extravagances, and by 1803-5, the years of greatest invasion danger, there were, reckons Emsley, about 450,000 volunteers in the UK over and above the militia and the home-based regulars, by now increasingly lodged in the barracks newly-built all over the British Isles but thickest in the districts nearest France. In no other aspect did Britain look more like a nation in arms than in this posture around 1805, with troops in camps and quarters all over the southern and south-eastern counties, military training going on everywhere, the vulnerable coastline itself newly fortified (Martello Towers and the Military Canal), military matters on everybody's lips and a prevailing mood of confident defiance. Once Boney's Boulogne camp had disbanded and national danger become difficult to believe in, enthusiasm for volunteering waned, difficulties were increasingly made about militia service, and riotous or even mutinous conduct among the militia was increasingly common. By the time of the Luddites, that appearance of national unity had given way to the spectacle of military repression by regulars, militia, and yeomanry together, making England for a while, in that respect, like Ireland usually was.

11

PRUSSIA'S TRAUMA

To no society did Napoleonic France give more severe a shock than Prussia. It was all the more severe for happening so suddenly – all over between 1806 and 1813 – and for including the sudden release of social and political pressures built up over many decades. Getting rid of the French was only part of the problem that occupied, squeezed and bullied Prussia had to solve as quickly as it could. There was also the problem of getting Prussia into a shape which would better its prospects of preventing the recurrence of such disasters. Sensible Prussians might disagree about the direction which radical change should take; only very blinkered Prussians denied that the need for radical change existed. (There were, however, many such – a fact significant for the future.)

Prussia was a peculiar State. We have already noticed how it made – Prussian apologists would say, how it had to make – more of its army than any other and how that very large army (by *ancien régime* standards) was wedded to a particular social order. (See above, pp.36-8.) A writer without prejudice against compound adjectives might describe it as a socio-politico-economic order, for that is precisely how the Hohenzollerns, whose construction it was, thought of it. It was a comprehensively regulated machine for producing revenue and soldiers. A modest and protected commercial and industrial sector produced the army's equipment, much of the taxable wealth, and most of the consumer goods needed by rather unusually plain-living and thrifty middle and upper classes. Peasant serfs (by 1800, many of them recently incorporated Poles) did the work in the agricultural sector (which produced a surplus for export) and supplied the bulk of the domestically raised military manpower. Unchallenged social élite and all-but-monopolists of the officer corps were the landed aristocracy, the *Junkers*, to whom in effect their warlord kings had given economic security

150

and large powers of self-government on and around their estates in return for dedicated military specialization. Military purposes and manners governed the administration, and politics in the British, French and Dutch senses did not exist. The civilian, such as he was, was meant to observe the laws and regulations and to accept unquestioningly the existing order of things with quasi-military obedience – and most, apparently, did so. Professor Kant's mind may have moved across strange seas of thought alone, but his body took its daily walk through the streets of Königsberg with clockwork regularity, and he never, never spoke of his State with disrespect.

Such a State may have been – indeed, for a while in the eighteenth century clearly was – well adapted to a fixed military purpose. It was not well adapted to social and economic change. Being a deliberate construct, it had itself originally marked a change from what had gone before, and successive monarchs had modified its arrangements from time to time. But by the time of the French Revolution fundamental change was more and more difficult to envisage. Prussian society was petrifying. This mattered politically as well as socially and economically. It is true that, of the many Germans excited by revolutionary ideas and examples, most were in non-Prussian parts of Germany (it must be remembered that at this date Prussia owned only a few insignificant enclaves west of the Elbe). Frederick William II at first responded to revolution in the Netherlands and France as any self-respecting absolute monarch was bound to do, but he did not feel so threatened by its lusty survival that he dared not withdraw from the first coalition in the spring of 1795. Thereafter he and his successor kept out of trouble for years, until Napoleon peremptorily brought it to Frederick William III in 1806. Through those years the kings of Prussia and the bulk – *not all* – of their councillors remained complacently blind to the growing possibility that such an eventuality would crack their system to pieces.

Prussians and non-Prussian Germans in Prussian service who recognized this possibility – not many, it seems, and hardly at all in public – did so for these reasons. France, they perceived – Clausewitz was the one of them who would in due course do historical justice to this perception – had produced in its nation in arms at once an example and a menace which other States ignored at their peril. If they knew what was good for them, they had to try to match it; and to match it required such structural changes as would give Prussians at least something of the sense of national membership and active involvement which so obviously now possessed the French. French-style political changes did not appeal to them. Very few of these reformers could conceive of democratization, and to have done so would have been wholly impractical. But there were other ways of making men feel that they had a stake in the country, of liberating their energies as members of it, and of making their country all the stronger in consequence. Prussia's petrifying structures, its bureaucratized feudalism, needed to be changed. France had got rid of its remnants of feudalism in a way that made France a more formidable nation and was calculated to assist its economic development; Prussia, which had much further to go, should smartly begin to move in the same direction. Men should no longer be serfs. The status of serf was unsuitable in an age of national consciousness, patriotic pride, and the cult of economic growth. Serfs could not feel they were free and therefore enthusiastic members of a national body. Nor was serfdom and all its accompanying restrictions on movement of labour, land and capital good for growth. Progressive landowners believed they could get on better without it. The men of the towns wanted, as in fact for the most part they had, nothing to do with it. But they did want something which the Frederician system denied them. In their own way and at their own middling level they wanted to be taken seriously as men and as fellow-subjects.

They were useful – nay, indispensable – to the State as managers, bureaucrats, wealth-makers and learned professionals; why should the profession of arms be so different? The nobility's near-monopoly of it could annoy the bourgeois, partly perhaps for relatively base reasons of social standing and economic self-advancement, but partly also because they too felt capable of noble-mindedness; they wanted to have such an interest in their country that to die for it would be really worthwhile. Sub-noble Prussians capable of national reformist reflections like these could not for the life of them understand why noble foreigners should have precedence over themselves in the Prussian officer corps, or why their desire to do military service on equal terms with the rest of the king's subjects should be snubbed.

In the slow steady accumulation of such reflections became clear an idea of society different from the traditional one lodged in the minds of most Junkers and built into their agrarian-military way of life. The traditional idea, we must at once admit, proved in the long run to be the stronger. It prevailed, keeping the body of reforming ideas just summarized very much in the background, until 1806; it only half-yielded during the time of trauma; it would make a comeback through the Restoration decades, as we shall see in due course. The abolition of serfdom was not a topic safely to be talked about in public – nor generally in private, for that matter – before the year of catastrophe. The idea of interfering with the grand structure of military organization and civil subordination was felt by most aristocrats to be personally offensive and structurally dangerous. Like most well-entrenched ruling classes, they had difficulty in imagining a social order founded on different premises; being more of a caste than a class, they were unaccustomed to adaptation and assimilation anyway; and possessing more than a fair share of aristocratic pride, sense of honour, etc., they felt threatened in their vitals when the national usefulness of those cherished attributes was called into question. No structural change actually happened in Prussia, therefore, during Napoleon's rising years. Its military aristocracy remained locked in complacent senescence, shying off reforms that suggested social as well as professional change. The idea of a nationwide *levée en masse* was much discussed after the French one of '93 and the several attempted south-west German ones which followed, but the dominant conservatives could only conceive of it in chillingly non-popular terms. Discipline continued to become less brutal, conditions of service (and pension arrangements) were bettered, schools were provided for soldiers and their children, and freer, looser infantry tactics were to some extent adopted. The Prussian army certainly did not stand still while the French one revolution-ized itself. But it did not move nearly as much or as fast as the radical reformers – Boyen, Berenhorst, Bülow, Scharnhorst, Stein, Clausewitz and so on – believed it ought to move, or as some of the west German armies moved; that of Hesse most conspicuously. For every reformer who thought that soldiers should be imbued with national spirit and trusted to do things on their own, there were many conservatives who thought that it was enough for soldiers to love their profession and be proud of it, absolutely to trust their officers, and to honour not their country but their king.

153

Foreigners still filled over one-third of the ranks in 1800, about a third of the infantry officers from lieutenant-colonel upwards were not Prussian, and some of the most senior engineer officers weren't even German.[80] Nationality may not on its own have mattered – Scharnhorst, Stein and others after all were not Prussians – but age was bound to matter, and perhaps the most fatal consequence of the nobility's monopoly of the higher offices in this highly professionalized army was the antiquity of so many of their holders. These figures, from Demeter, tell their own story:[81]

Age:–	80+	70+	60+	50+	Under 50
Generals	4	13	62	—— 63 ——	
Field-Officers:					
Infantry	0	7	110	187	236
Cavalry	0	0	25	129	73
Artillery	0	4	22	—— 13 ——	
Captains:					
Infantry	0	2	18	119	806
Cavalry	0	0	0	18	223
Artillery	0	0	6	26	31

An army thus arthritically commanded, and bureaucratically constipated to boot, was, we may think, unlikely to be a match for the youthful and flexible French. So arrogant and complacent were Prussia's rulers however that their colossal collapse in 1806 seems really to have surprised them. The readiness with which many of them now became willing for a while, at least, to contemplate big changes is a measure of the shock they had received, the humiliation at the way they had received it. For the fact is that after the twin defeats of Jena and Auerstädt (14 October 1806) there followed 'one of the least glorious chapters in Prussian military annals',[82] the all-but-complete collapse of the army's morale, the almost unresisting surrenders of its fortresses and remaining field forces, and of course the total lack of any kind of popular resistance from a people so perfectly subjected and indoctrinated. Even worse followed. The king and a remnant of his army got away to east Prussia and kept up the struggle in alliance with Russia. But it was all over by the summer of 1807. After carving up the continent with Alexander, Napoleon at Tilsit dictated to Frederick William III exceptionally harsh terms of peace, including the loss of about half of his territory and subjects. 'The Prussia which had been created and made a major power by the exertions of its army had now been swept away by the failures of that army to adjust itself to changing methods of warfare and by the unwillingness of its rulers to exploit the undeveloped energies of the Prussian people.'[83]

The Prussian story through the next six years is of such considerable reforms in State and society as were to enable it to make a creditable comeback against Napoleon and to launch itself with new vigour into the era which followed. The background to this was a ground-swell of German national feeling more or less everywhere German was spoken. Nationalism was to Germany what industrialization was to Britain – mainspring of the means of war. Indeed Napoleon's German enemies (it must not be forgotten that through the year 1812 *all* Germans were nominally Napoleon's allies, and some remained so in 1813) had to rely on Britain for most of their war material, but that was not their special strength. It lay rather in the fire and exhilaration of national self-discovery, suddenly brought to the boil after decades of sporadic simmering. What brought it to the boil all over Germany (as everywhere else) was simply close-up experience of the French. Prussia's experience of the French was peculiarly painful but every part of Germany experienced something like it sooner or later, and no nationalist indoctrinator could have devised a better practical course for achieving his object. The German nation, it is scarcely too much to say, discovered itself by contrast with the French and through loathing of them. Distance alone lent enchantment to the German view of the French. Early enthusiasts later turned haters; a transformation facilitated, of course, by the Revolution's simultaneous turning into the Empire. West and south-west German simmerings before 1806, Napoleon managed to suppress. It was beyond his power to stop the spread and the boiling once his troops and collectors had got to Vienna and Berlin. All he could do was to intimidate the Germans from thoughts of armed insurgency, and to compel the suppression of sentiments too overtly anti-French. But the nationalist writers, orators, scholars and potential organizers who now found themselves enjoying a bonanza did not need to be too explicit about whom they were against. That was understood. Whether the Hohenzollerns or the Habsburgs would make the pace for the rest was as yet of little import. All that mattered was to be sufficiently pro-*German*; which in those heady early days mainly meant defining what made Germans marvellously unique and suggesting how they could benefit themselves and mankind at large by making themselves even more so. Among the earliest of these, as it has remained one of the most enduring, was Fichte's series of public lectures given in Berlin through the winter of 1807-8 and immediately published under the title *Addresses to the German Nation*. There was nothing in them explicitly about military revival. They were about the national revival which – it could be understood – must precede it. Searching almost frantically for explanations of their upset, Prussia's rulers were ready to listen to voices they had hitherto on the whole ignored. The reformers seized their opportunity. Nothing less than total structural change would suffice. Army and society had to move together. Only a people feeling themselves to be free men could fight hard enough to sustain a free State.

In Prussian army, State and society alike, reform for a few years made giant strides. Conservatism never yielded wholly. It retained more than enough foothold for its later comeback. But for a few years the liberal reformers seemed to be winning more than they lost. In October 1807 serfdom was abolished. True, the terms of the abolition did more good to the landowners than the peasants, now mostly landless; but at least they were now personally free and legally equal subjects of the crown, their latent patriotism and national zeal no longer clogged by the sense of servitude which all but the dullest-spirited must (to the mind of the reformers) have felt. Freed also now was the land. The nobility's near-monopoly of it was ended. It became a commodity like anything else from which capital and labour might wring a profit. Together with other liberalizing measures, this put the economy back on the royal road to adaptation and growth. Within two years the social and economic basis of the Prussian State was revolutionized.

Army reforms began simultaneously. The reformers' vision was of a new-style Prussia sprouting a new-style army; the best of its historic qualities – professionalism, honour, courage, discipline and so on – grafted into institutions befitting a constitutional State.

For the most progressive of them, class mattered less than national spirit. They cannot have expected lower-class Prussians to wear the sword; they certainly wanted middle-class ones to be able to qualify to do so. Conversely, their modern revolutionary idea of the nation inclined them towards a system of universal military service, obligatory upon all fit adult males and honourable equally for all; a service and duty which middle-class Prussians could gladly accept alongside the rest. This offered a unique crossing of French revolutionary aspiration with Prussian earnestness. Upon no matter were the reformers more convinced than the necessity of so to speak nationalizing the army. The Frederician army had well served Prussia half a century before, and its feats of arms had been celebrated both in high and low culture. But the world had moved on. The national idea was abroad, nationally-enthused subjects would be ready to take turns in military service, and ruling classes – so further believed the reformers, who did not recognize the conservatives' portrait of them as destructive of their own class – only needed to swing sensibly with the tide to retain their natural leadership. In place of the sort of army which had come to pieces amidst an indifferent people in 1806, they planned one drawn directly from the people at large, a people themselves made militarily as well as nationally conscious. Within the framework and flexibility of liberal institutions, class differences, they never doubted, would remain, but national feeling would surmount all others. 'The annulment of bondage, the awakening of a feeling for the worth of the individual in every subject, the abolition of the old brutal discipline in the army, the encouragement of the military spirit of the people by means of all the resources of national education – these were the prerequisites for the creation of a people's army, the excellence of which would be based on a sense of honour and a love of country rather than on slavish obedience.'[84]

From 1808 the reformers pressed for the establishment of armed forces founded on these principles. Many plans were canvassed. Usually they were in terms of a *Landwehr*, a provincial militia for men of full military fitness, backed by a *Landsturm*, best rendered for a British readership as 'home guard'. None came to anything before the next national crisis in the winter of 1812-13. One obvious obstacle was Napoleon's imposition of a 42,000 men limit on the Prussian army; to some extent that could be circumvented

157

(as later was to be the Versailles limitation on the Weimar Republic's army), but not possibly as much as the reformers demanded. It did not help that the reformers were not able to speak with one voice, some of them (Stein and Gneisenau, for example) being more ready than others to arm the lower classes. But the main obstacle was the conservatives' distrust of all such schemes. None of them could conceive of a Prussia with its social priorities so dramatically changed. It would no longer, they felt, be *their* Prussia. They wondered whether nationalism would be compatible with royalism. The admission of sub-nobles to the officer corps (which the king early agreed to) was distasteful. The transformation of the army into a genuinely national body would be downright dangerous, and the use of such a force, hastily improvised, for a popular national insurrection against the French, as Gneisenau and Stein particularly urged, seemed to them lunatic. They encouraged the king to refuse to countenance such changes and, being constitutionally well able to do so, he did.

Prussian society in these years of great distress was thus, in its own characteristic way, much divided; no rebellions, no working-class unrest, not much independent middle-class agitation, but deep divisions within its ruling class, some prescribed ways of salvation radically differing from those preferred by the rest (divisions rather similar to those which split the French military and political élites in 1940-2). Some reformers, happier with half a loaf than none, hung on hopefully. Scharnhorst, their anchor man on the military side, despite his enforced retirement from directing the War Office (*Allgemeine Kriegsdepartement*), kept his head and his influence in the general staff. But the combination of Napoleon's menaces and Frederick William's collaborationism – 'cowardly' or 'realistic' according to taste – was too much for many. Stein, their chief political hope, had to take refuge in Bohemia in early 1809. A steady trickle of resignations (sometimes prefatory to foreign, anti-French service) showed what was in their minds. The trickle became a torrent early in 1812 when over three hundred officers resigned upon their monarch's agreement to provide 20,000 troops in support of Napoleon against Russia. Scharnhorst's bright protégé, Clausewitz, was one of those who went so far as to sign on with the Tsar. Their loyalty to their idea

of their nation thus cut dramatically across the loyalty conventionally owed to their king.

Clearly the Prussian aristocracy was profoundly disturbed,
when such a thing could happen. But this had been brewing for
five years. To enter the service of a monarch about to be nominally
at war with your own was not much of a step beyond taking up
arms in your monarch's name against one with whom he was
nominally at peace, and without his authority. Some Germans had
been doing that since the winter of 1807-8, when small-scale
partisan resistance sporadically began, becoming for a while quite
formidable under Graf von Goetzen in the Silesian uplands. News
from Spain encouraged thoughts of popular insurgency, and
Gneisenau, Grolmann, Yorck and others laid plans, against the
day when the king might assent to it. Hotter heads however would
not wait. All over Germany the Napoleonic presence was working
like a hot-house on national sentiment. The Habsburgs placed
some reliance on it when they went to war with Napoleon in
February 1809 (though their counsels were similarly divided, and
nationalism even more suspect). The spring and summer saw a
succession of armed risings in the new kingdom of Westphalia
where French imperialism was offensively concentrated in Napoleon's brother Jerome: Lieutenant von Katte, a young Prussian
officer; Freiherr von Dörnberg, a Hessian who had served under
Blücher; Professor Sternberg of Marburg and a Hessian veteran
colonel, Emmerich; the dashing Prussian Major von Schill, one of
the few heroes of 1806 and so popular now for his patriotic bravado
that the king had to let him get away with it; and the Frederick
William dispossessed of the duchy of Brunswick. Disappointed of
both Prussian and Austrian support, none lasted long. The only
rising which achieved more than national propaganda value was
that of Austrian Tyrolese under a resourceful partisan leader,
Andreas Hofer. Napoleon's map-changing had given those
Tyrolese to Bavaria. During the spring they cleared their valleys
of Bavarians and Frenchmen both, and they stayed in action after
Austria made peace in October. Hofer, taken and executed early
in 1810, joined Schill, Brunswick and the others in the new
nationalist pantheon. Closely observing these signs of the times,
Gneisenau and the other reformist Prussians who were particularly fascinated by the idea of a national rising had to possess their
souls in patience. While the young fire-eaters let off steam by

159

ostentatiously sharpening their swords on the stonework outside the French embassy, their seniors contented themselves with being rude to such Frenchmen as they met, and waited until Frederick William or fate should give them the lead they wanted.

It came in the extraordinary circumstances of mid-winter 1812-13. Scraps of news about the retreat from Moscow began to arrive via Denmark quite early in December. At first it was almost beyond belief. But on the 12th Napoleon and Caulaincourt were reported at Glogau, heading for Dresden and home; within a week the *Moniteur* had sown the seed of the legend that exceptionally severe weather was the main cause of the admitted disaster; and soon the Prussians had ocular evidence of it as broken fragments of the Grand Army began to straggle along their roadways. Had not the long-awaited moment come at last? Frederick William received much advice to the effect that it had, but, mindful of the presence on or near his territories of several French armies as yet unblooded, and with high diplomatic cares heavy upon him, hesitated to give a lead. It was given instead by Yorck, the general commanding Prussia's contingent with the Grand Army. Subject to intense pressure from his officers, from compatriot 'political refugees', and from certain leaders of the east Prussian community, when a Russian force (which happened, helpfully, to be commanded by the Prussian-born Diebitsch) interposed between his retreating column and the French one ahead of him, he took the opportunity to withdraw from the French connection. The Convention of Taurrogen (30 December) followed a familiar model for the honourable cessation of hostilities, but its political purpose and follow-up were unique: to move on from that quasi-neutrality to positive belligerence on the other side. 'Now or never', was how he put it to the still hesitating king. Very soon Stein, Clausewitz, and other notable patriots arrived. With the tide of nationalist fervour ever rising, they promoted in early February the summoning of the provincial assembly (*Landtag*), which in turn summoned the sort of *Landwehr* the reformers had long desiderated.

At last Frederick William III was ready to assume the mantle prepared for him in so extraordinary – one may surely dare to say, revolutionary, considering the absolutist principles normally professed by the actors in this patriotic drama – a way. In the early spring of 1813 the conservatives were, for a season, *hors concours*.

Now was set going the machinery of national liberation long prepared in the notebooks and imaginations of the reformers. They sought to mobilize Prussian society for war as totally as they thought the French had been twenty years before. The reader will recall the terms of the Jacobins' *levée en masse* and the war-effort that followed (above, pp.86-9). German national historiography and its associated arts through the century following were to celebrate this anti-French upheaval as one of the German people's most heroic moments ever, when everyone and all classes were united in a common endeavour; simply Prussians and (for the spirit was much more than Prussian, even if the organization was not) Germans, cleansed of thoughts of self. A great national adventure story was born, rich in materials for poets and painters, politicians and (for the pious Prussians were peculiarly explicit about God being on their side) preachers. Myth and fantasy naturally got into it. The reality was never as complete as the reformers hoped. But even after the myths have been sifted out, what is left is still remarkable. All classes were consumed with righteous fierceness against the French, readiness to fight them was found at every level, and it was commonly urged that the German people should show themselves the equal in this respect of the Spanish, whose example was hugely admired. Old men and women took over the work laid down by the men called to the colours. Wives and daughters made bandages, warm clothing and comforts for the troops. People contributed jewellery, plate, etc., to the war fund. Patriotic poets and preachers, who were plentiful enough, poured out encouragement. And men of almost any age from sixteen to sixty could find some means of, to put it minimally, cutting a military figure – especially if they were of the middling and upper classes. There is no reason to believe that the Prussian lower classes were anything but anti-French; but they were *not* encouraged to rise spontaneously against the French in Spanish style, and in fact seem not much to have done so. East German historians, dedicated of course to the discovery of edifying mass movements in history, have ransacked the records for evidence of mass patriotic militancy, and have found a certain amount of it but it does not amount to much compared with the militancy of the propertied.[85] Prussia, after all, was not much like Spain – and Prussia's ruling class had no intention that it should become more so.

The nearest they got to their Spanish inspiration was in the *Landsturm*, summoned on 21 April 1813. This was five weeks after Frederick William's declaration of war and his unprecedented 'Call to his People' (*Aufruf an mein Volk*) to prepare for sacrifices *in their common cause*. Evidently modelled in part on the proclamation issued in 1809 by the Junta of Seville, it was introduced as completing the process of national arming already well begun in the regular army, the *Jäger*, the Volunteers and the *Landwehr* (see below, pp.165-7). Men who were not already in the regular army or the *Landwehr* were instructed what they were to do. The tone was set, first, by several references to the popular resistance movements which had recently done so well in every kind of environment: 'the bogs of the Germans of older times, the ditches and canals of Holland, the hedges and thickets of the Vendée, the deserts of Arabia, the mountains of Switzerland, the varied landscapes of Spain and Portugal...' (Preamble). Second, there was revolutionary exhortation to, apparently, unlimited warfare. *Citizens* (*Staatsbürger*, as Prussian subjects now found themselves unfamiliarly addressed) were told it was their duty to tackle the enemy 'with every kind of weapon', not to obey his orders as *soi-disant* occupier, and to damage him 'by all means possible' (Article 1). In Article 7 the same grim note was sounded. The sanction of international law was invoked to persuade them that in self-defence, *Notwehr*, 'all means are hallowed. The most severe are in fact to be preferred, since they get it over most triumphantly and quickly.' That was peculiarly the German idea of the law in this respect – already explicitly tougher than jurists in other cultural traditions liked to admit. It showed itself again in Article 39 which justified the absence of uniforms or distinctive clothing on the ground that they would only make the Landsturmers recognizable, and hamper their operations. (This was flatly contrary to the professional military ethic of the age, and cannot have been liked by any but fiercest fire-breathers. German jurists specializing in the law of war had a lot of difficulty explaining it away, later in the century. It was particularly inconsistent with Article 29, insisting that *Landsturm* men were to be recognized as lawful combatants by the enemy in case of being taken prisoner, and threatening instant reprisals if they were not.)

In such respects, the *Landsturm* ordinance had a rousing, rather ruthless tone to it, expressive of the Prussian government's will to work its people up to a high pitch of patriotic fury. But in other and more numerous respects, the ordinance was more circumspect. None of these all-out measures was to be taken unless and until the *Landsturm* had been officially mobilized by the proper authorities. 'Mobilization without orders will be punished as mutiny' (Article 6). Any attempt to use the emergency as an excuse for looting, rowdiness, evasion of taxes or escape from labour services would be punished by death (Article 25). For the first three months the officers, etc., were to be appointed by the district military commanders. Thereafter, the men might elect their officers; but only 'landowners and other men of property, central or local government officers, mayors, stewards and bailiffs, inn-keepers, foresters and schoolteachers'. And so on. By the time one has read the whole document, it is clear that the wild peninsular example has been transmuted into proper Prussian form. The *Landsturm* – when and where it was mobilized, which was as little and for as short a while as possible – was not meant to unloose a Spanish-style people's war, and was less important from a military point of view than as an exercise in patriotic propaganda and public relations. Kitchen cites Friedrich Köppen's sketch of the *Landsturm* units composed of the Berlin intellectual and artistic élites; Schleiermacher, Savigny, Niebuhr, Fichte and so on more or less ineptly going through parade-ground exercises, decked out with theatre props, broadswords, cudgels, breastplates, shields and lances.[86] It was magnificent for the new national tradition, but it was not really war.

There were other, more direct ways for men really of military age and urge to take part in the war. They might join a corps of officially-authorized Volunteers, *Freikorps*, adapting to contemporary purposes an old German tradition. Some of the 1809 ventures had been after this style. Once Taurrogen had given them the cue, ardent patriots took it up in the early weeks of 1813, and the Russians encouraged them. Mixed Prussian-Russian *Freikorps* were hastily formed, to race into the German countries occupied (actually or nominally) by the French and to rouse them to resistance. It was not normal for one monarch unsolicitedly to foment insurrection among a neighbouring monarch's subjects (which is what it amounted to, while Frederick William was still making up his mind), but as the Tsar put it, 'the time has come for going beyond the normal conventions of warfare'.[87] So

Czernichev and Tettenborn with their breathless *Freikorps* rushed to Berlin, which didn't rise, and Tettenborn went on to Hamburg, which did. Soon after, Dörnberg with the first wholly Prussian one got to Hanover, and Lützow with another was seeking to raise the smaller States southwards. Such deeds were dashing, but since no States took Prussia's side and no general insurrection happened, these first *Freikorps* of the war of liberation achieved little beyond minor, temporary nuisance to the French, and a lot of pain and grief to the inhabitants of the cities where the French had to restore their rule. *Freikorps* continued in colourful and (because like all such bodies, their membership included roughnecks and buc-caneers, and their discipline was shaky) intermittently trouble-some action through the remainder of the war, increasing their usefulness in proportion as they more and more became assimi-lated to regular practice and assisted in regular warfare. Lützow's and de Colomb's corps in particular had quite distinguished records by the end. But, as with the *Landsturm*, one is driven to conclude that their main significance was psychological and myth-making, and their subsequent fame owed a lot to the presence with Lützow, until he was killed at Gadebusch in August 1813, of the young poet Karl Theodor Körner. His rather bombastic patriotic verse, in what was by then an established national tradition, partly owed its enormous subsequent popular-ity to the romantic circumstance of his finishing 'The Song of the Sword' only on the morning of the battle:[88]

> So let my beloved sword sing at its task,
> And send the bright sparks flying!
> The dawn of our wedding-day is here –
> Hurrah, my iron bride!
> Hurrah!

The volunteer *Jäger* from 3 February, when they were instituted, offered another mode of entry into the army for middle-class patriots. To bring the middle classes into honourable service had long been on the reformers' agenda. The universalization of military service, which was ordained a few days later, would have done this. But, anxious to temper the military wind to the middle-class lamb, Scharnhorst introduced the *Jäger* scheme first, to make the terms of service as attractive as they could be, and to rid it of that prospect of rubbing shoulders with men of the lower classes which was so distressing to the rightly-constituted Prussian bourgeois mind. Men who could afford (or at any rate find family or community money for) their own uniforms and equipment were invited to volunteer ahead of the conscripted rest and to form a corps of uncommon education and respectability, which could be allowed a good deal of self-government in respect of discipline and the appointment of officers. Men of this class, not (yet) compelled by law to serve, would, reckoned Scharnhorst, feel moral obligation to do so. The example would be nationally inspiriting, and the corps itself would turn out a model of its kind. For a while, it seemed to be so. Twelve thousand *Jäger* were enlisted, and their campaign performance was good. After Scharnhorst's death in June, however, the lines he had laid down for their development became blurred. Increasingly they suffered from the transfer of their officers into the regular infantry regiments, and by the end of the war Scharnhorst's idea of them had ceased to be. The social sensibilities of middle-class youth would have to be accommodated by other means.

The *Landwehr* was the other great innovation, on 9 February. Scharnhorst, Boyen and the more liberal reformers had been seeking this for five years. The king and the conservatives had shied off it – the king, indeed, seems to have been positively glad that Napoleon, who feared such an innovation for different reasons, made it virtually impossible for him. A proper militia of this sort, a citizen army, was thought to be potentially revolutionary – and perhaps it really was. In the national crisis of early 1813 however the case for it was momentarily unanswerable. East Prussia's model was applied nationwide. All men between seventeen and forty, not in the regular army or the *Jäger*, were invited to volunteer for the *Landwehr*. The required number, 120,000, would be made up by ballot. Its officers were picked, subject to government approval, by local committees consisting of two noblemen and two men representing respectively the middle and lower classes. So many fit young men of the propertied classes being engaged in *Jäger* or even *Freikorps*, and a few professions being exempt, the rank-and-file was even more lower-class than it would anyway have been. 'The typical *Landwehr* man was a Silesian weaver, wretchedly clothed, often barefoot, with obsolete equipment, poorly fed, and with no protection against rain and snow.' It is therefore hardly surprising that morale was not particularly high, and it was certainly not improved by harsh discipline. 'What is truly remarkable is the great contribution which the *Landwehr* made to the liberation in spite of all these difficulties, and the degree to which it was held in popular esteem. It was the affection shown towards the *Landwehr* by the people which convinced conservatives that it was indeed a revolutionary force.'[89] In due course, as we shall see (below, p.209), the conservatives would emasculate it. But for the present it held its form as a secondary army, not a reservoir for the regular one but a sort of citizens' army in its own right, with its own distinctive leadership and territorial organization; its badges suitably proclaiming 'With God for King and Fatherland'; the nearest Prussian thing to 'the nation in arms', and the principal means by which, in 1813, no less than six per cent of the population was got into the field.[90]

Finally, the regular army itself; too easy to forget when *Landwehr* and *Landsturm*, *Jäger* and *Freikorps* fill the limelight. The regular army was there all the time, recruited in the old way from foreign 'mercenaries' and canton (mainly peasant) conscripts, missing all the many men in exempt occupations and districts (which meant most of Silesia). Restricted by Napoleon's treaty terms, it was only about 65,000-strong when war resumed. But it was a much better army than the 1806 one in several important respects. The crusted hand of inadaptable aristocracy no longer lay so heavy on it. Scharnhorst's party, by no means non-aristocratic but open to bourgeois influence and keen on bourgeois incorporation, had been at work. It had managed to speed up that sticky process of de-brutalizing discipline and restoring some human dignity to the soldier, inseparable from the increased use of French-style open formations and the tactical advantages accruing thereto. By 1813-14, says Paret, over half of the Prussian infantry consisted of troops that were expected to know how to fight in open order as a matter of course.[91] At the same time most of the old dead wood had been removed from the officer corps. The new wood sprang from a wider social sector and was better educated, and Scharnhorst's and Gneisenau's organizational innovations gave the army the first effective general staff; not the sort of matter which a book of this kind need dwell on, but significant for the future, since it was this more than anything else which within the next half-century helped the Prussian model to outclass the French as Europe's and the world's military cynosure. Together with the *Landwehr* and such support as *Jäger* and *Freikorps* might provide, this Prussian army now undertook with the Russians and, later, the Austrians the cheering work of clearing the French out of Germany. It was not as uniformly glorious and enthusiastic as subsequent nationalist legend made out. For each brave bourgeois who joined the *Jäger* there was at least another who did not; although the *Landwehr* who fought at Leipzig in mid-October fought well, about a quarter of the whole force deserted.[92] But it was, all things considered, an extraordinary national effort, and a successful one. By the time winter set in, the work was done. Of all the troops who took the war on to French soil early in 1814, the Prussians had the greatest relish for their task, keyed up as they were to the conviction that through them their nation was avenging the insults and oppressions of many years (their historical writers liked to take the story back ever so far) and that they were doing God's work in the world. The French had begun the turning of these wars into a war of nations; it was the Prussians who in a sense perfected the conversion by making the French people in their own persons feel the consequences of what they had done. As invaders and occupiers, the Prussian armies were on such a high horse of aggrieved nationalism that they punished the French people much more than did their allies, and would have been even more punitive had not those allies and their own monarch, seeking to restore the proprieties of European civilization, with difficulty restrained them. Frederick William had cause at times to wonder whether the mutino-patriotic examples of Schill in 1809 and Yorck in 1812-13 were going to prove contagious.[93] Wellington posted a British sentry on the *Pont de Jéna* to make sure Blücher did not blow it up.

So began the Franco-German national obsession with military tit-for-tat which would persist, at much cost of blood, for the next hundred years.

12

PEOPLE'S WAR; CHIEFLY SPANISH

Most peoples whom the French dominated or sought to dominate during these wars sooner or later offered armed resistance in one mode or another. Prussia's resistance happened later rather than sooner, but when it did happen it was exceptionally thorough. That was largely because Prussian society experienced little ambiguity of feelings about the French. The original Revolution had not been as much admired in Prussian as in other parts of Germany; its ruling class was intellectually more self-sufficient than most; however impressed other Germans might be with revolutionary or Napoleonic models, hardly any Prussians were interested in them before 1806, and none, of course, thereafter. And when Prussia did at last summon its energies to expel the foreign body, it did so, as we have just seen, in an exceptionally statist way. The energies and passions of the Prussian people, such as they were, allowed themselves to be guided by the public authorities; society's collective will and muscle was channelled into military force entirely according to the principles and plans of the king, his ministers and his generals. Whether any significant proportion of the Prussian people willed and wanted otherwise, we can only guess. In such a society, there was scant space for the voicing of independent opinions. Evidently some Prussians (those *Landwehr* deserters, for instance) felt negatively about what their rulers told them to do; but none of them ever acted positively in any other direction. Prussia was not that kind of a country.

Spain however was. Spain offers the most complete example of a people which resisted the French itself, directly, in the way that came naturally to it: by popular national resistance and guerrilla warfare. The State had some involvement with it but not much. It happened more or less spontaneously, and the State's participation in it had the appearance chiefly of an attempt to catch up with,

168

and to control if it could, a movement with a life of its own. As an institution, moreover, the State was relatively feeble. Again we are at the antipodes from Prussia, where two centuries of consistent absolutist family management had produced in a small flat country a homogenized society run by an omnicompetent bureaucracy. Mainland Spain, however, was the underdeveloped, mountainous, fissiparous, sluggish heart of a decaying empire, which the enlightened despotism of Charles III (1759-88) nobly struggled to revive. Its governments had sought for centuries to solidify and centralize it. Geography and history combined to thwart them. The centre hardly held. The many parts from which 'united' Spain had been compounded retained strongly separate and independent characteristics, and much went on in them beyond the knowledge and even the liking of Madrid. There was little explicit separatism only because there was little to feel separatist about. The State did not matter that much to the mass of the people. They knew it mainly through its conscription to army and navy service and its collection of taxes, which inclined them to dislike it. Their religion and monarchy mattered enormously, in connection with some apprehension of Spain's (passing) greatness in the world and a common culture which included, among other things, a great deal of national pride. But with a Spaniard's proud national consciousness would normally be linked the equal, perhaps even greater, pride of the Basque, the Catalan, the Galician and so on; and beyond that perhaps his greatest pride of all in being a man of Valencia, Oviedo or Jaén. Spaniards naturally thought and behaved in the ways appropriate to their own regions and towns, as they still do, and of all conceivable calls from Madrid the least likely to succeed would be one which offered centralization, higher taxes and heavier military obligations in support of a less-than-convincingly Catholic usurper installed by French imperialism.

This, however, is what happened in 1808. Napoleon now impatiently sought to secure Spain for his new continental order. Spain had never been an enthusiastic or an efficient ally. He believed that better management would greatly boost its military capability as well as its economy. Only through Spain could he get at Britain's docile ally Portugal. His 'continental system' had a hole in it so long as the peninsula remained unplugged. A certain set of mainly middling-class Spaniards, the *Afrancesados* (i.e., the

Frenchified), were ready to help him. Intellectuals, administrators and continentally-minded business-men, they had long hankered after a firm French connection; founding a new phase of greatness and prosperity by marching into the future alongside their confident neighbours. Modernizers and progressives, they had little respect for their country's traditional Catholicism, and none for the religious susceptibilities of their simpler-minded compatriots. Spain, they felt, needed a Napoleon. Since there was no hope of a native one, the original was better than nothing. The *Afrancesados* were not numerous but they were quite influential – especially, it goes without saying, in Madrid and the larger cities. Relying on their political support and taking smart advantage of certain court intrigues and royal family quarrels which are none of our business, Napoleon by the end of April 1808 had placed one army (Junot's) in Lisbon, and another (Murat's) in Madrid; French troops were conveniently parked here and there along the northern, central and eastern highways; the king of Portugal had fled to Brazil; Charles IV of Spain had abdicated and gone to Bayonne where Napoleon, writing off his admittedly awful son Ferdinand as a nincompoop, was hawking the Spanish throne round his brothers. (After Louis and Jerome had declined it, it went to Joseph, who exchanged it for the kingdom of Naples.)

It was at the start of May that the Spanish people began their war of independence. On the morning of the 2nd, the *Dos de Mayo* destined for fame in national folklore ever thereafter, the people of Madrid (some large number of them, anyway, and mostly of the lower classes, joined by only a few soldiers), rose against Murat's occupying troops and slaughtered some of them. Retribution at once followed. Goya later immortalized the patriotic martyrdom side of it in his internationally famous rendering of what happened on the *Tres de Mayo*. Murat and the municipal authorities had little difficulty in restoring order. In some countries that might have been the end of it. In Spain, it was only the beginning. As news of the *Dos de Mayo* rippled around a country already perturbed by patriotic objections to what Napoleon was doing to Ferdinand and religious fears of what Napoleon might do to Spain, a national will to resist almost everywhere materialized in patriotic riots and lynchings and the formation of local and provincial committees of resistance, the Juntas. Names of noblemen and other local worthies appeared on them, but the pressure to form them was predominantly popular, and common to all were the clergy, who in Spain, as not in the same way anywhere else in Europe, were popular in recruitment, manner, and standing. Not for nothing did the national language use the same term for being Spanish and for being Catholic. Some Juntas were chaired by bishops or priests. Priests, monks and friars were prominent everywhere. Thus 'the people' in an unusually literal sense began it. Wherever French military might was not already present, they refused to regard as lawful orders coming from branches of government working with the French. If Madrid had gone French, they would dispense with Madrid until better times and their true king returned. The situation being so confused, it is difficult to say exactly when war began against the invader but the national historical tradition relishes the fact that the first apparent declaration of it came not from any Junta or general but on the evening of 2 May from Andrés Torrejón, mayor of the insignificant township of Móstoles twelve miles or so south-west of Madrid. Very different from Taurrogen! But the same thought, apparently, was occurring to individuals and Juntas all over. In the name of Ferdinand VII (who was to enjoy a comfortable captivity in France until early 1814) and referring often to their 'rights' (which could and did mean very different things to different people) they declared the Spanish people's resistance to the French and to their (as we would now put it) collaborators, and began to organize armed resistance.

The reader must now try to imagine a Spain governed, so far as it was governed through the next five-and-a-half years, by alternative, parallel and fluctuating authorities. In Madrid for most of the time was 'King' Joseph and his central core of French and *Afrancesado* administrators, governing or sharing with military governors the government of the regions of Spain where the French occupation held firm, as it did for much of the time in e.g., Aragon, Castile, Catalonia, and some strips of the Basque lands. Elsewhere ran or was supposed to run the writ of the independent Spanish government, either directly or through the provincial Juntas. At the time of its lowest ebb, that Spanish government (to begin with, the 'central Junta', then a Regency on Ferdinand's behalf, finally the Regency with a *Cortes* and the constitution of 1812) directly controlled little more than the city of Cadiz, where British command of the seas assured its survival. It shared power – such limited and wavering power as it had – with the provincial Juntas.

It managed what was left of the empire and the higher levels of foreign relations, above all with Britain, almost its only source of income. It attempted to control its generals and to prevent them quarrelling with each other, the British, and the Juntas. The Juntas' powers waxed and waned in proportion with the French. If the French had been able to be everywhere at once, in force, the Juntas would have been fugitive underground bodies all the time; since, however, the French certainly could not find the men for such a vast operation and had to be content in much of Spain with maintaining garrisons along highways (except when they were actually campaigning), the Juntas sometimes held a good deal of independent authority. A further touch of confusion is added to this picture when we remark that the Juntas' areas of authority (e.g., to levy taxes and to make requisitions) often overlapped with the fringes of the French ones, so that the wretched inhabitants thereof would be under two heels at once; under three or more, perhaps, if there should also be gangs of French marauders or native bandits in the vicinity....

We may now return to the war of independence and the way it was conducted in these extraordinarily confused circumstances. The most original part of it, the most significant for the future, and in some respects the most successful, was the guerrilla part, and the steady, obstinate popular resistance which buttressed it. The Spanish government's more regular military forces however must not be forgotten – even if only because their almost complete uselessness placed the guerrillas' performance in a better light, and because it was from their broken ranks that a good many guerrillas came. The government's persistence with regular operations in the face of repeated disasters illustrates also, in rather an extreme form, the profound preference of all governments, given the choice, for regular and aristocratically-directed over irregular and popularly-based armed forces. There were in 1808 well over 100,000 Spanish regulars on the rolls and although only about half of them were effective and equipment was defective – e.g., only 9000 horses for the 16,000 nominal cavalry, only 400 animals to move the 216 cannon etc., etc. – the government did not hesitate to use them.[94] In the first weeks the armies made up from these and some additional militia did no better than was to be expected. But in mid-July, General Castaños met with an extraordinary success. General Dupont, on his way back towards Madrid from Cordova

172

with 18,000 men, ran into difficulties at Bailén and capitulated. Nothing like this had happened to any of Napoleon's armies before. The news infuriated Napoleon, astounded France, and raised spirits in every occupied territory where people longed for liberation. If the Spaniards could do it, who could not? In Prussia above all the effect of Bailén and the (temporary) French evacuation of Madrid which followed it was electrifying. In fact Bailén was hardly worth it. Distance lent enchantment to the news. Dupont was not much of a general, his army was raw and inexperienced, and the way the Spaniards subsequently treated the surrendered French was so atrocious as to make the affair as much a matter of shame to them as glory. But all that Spain knew was that a Napoleonic army had surrendered, and the government was encouraged to press on with conventional military operations. The pitched battles which resulted were almost uniformly disastrous; so much so, that the historian is tempted to wonder why they persisted. Pride no doubt had much to do with it. Self-respect and habit too; the 'central Junta', first of Seville, then of Cádiz, had to be as much of a normal government as it could, and what sort of government would it be without an army? More or less regular Spanish armies, losing exceptional quantities of men by desertion and simple disappearance, therefore marched hopefully from one unsuccessful battle to another all over the less occupied parts of the peninsula through the remainder of the war. After unhappy early experiences Wellington, allied commander-in-chief from 1812, did not feel able to do much with them. They helped maintain national self-respect, they defended besieged towns stoutly enough, and they performed the usual law-enforcing functions in government-controlled territories; but it is difficult to see that they did much towards liberating Spain, and he declined to take them with him into France.

That the other branch of the Spanish war of independence, its guerrilla warfare and general national resistance, did more to help liberate Spain is beyond dispute; yet its evaluation presents problems too. The first great fact about it is that it started and existed before the Juntas authorized it and set about the tricky task of trying to control it. 'Resistance', active or passive, was fairly ubiquitous; guerrilla operations were a particular barbed form of resistance which many Spaniards took to naturally (smuggling, after all, was endemic and popularly admired) and which proved to be the most damaging to French power. No more in Spain than anywhere else, ever, could guerrillas remain in being without the support of populations of the towns and villages and the almost uninhabited countrysides in which they operated. That support might be willing or constrained. But if it was to be constrained, it was in every patriot's interest that the constraint should have law and government behind it. The bandit brand of guerrilla very soon wore out his welcome with the people and became a dangerous nuisance to the Juntas. The Juntas and (once it was established) the Regency, for their part, had something to offer the guerrillas besides seeking some control of them. Beyond a small prospect of supplies of (British) equipment and money, they offered patriotic dignity and constitutional status. The rougher, more 'primitive', perhaps aggressively plebeian guerrilla leaders would not care much about this, but the more 'liberal' of them, with Juan Martín Díaz ('El Empecinado') and Francisco Espoz y Mina at their head, did. By the end of the war these two held general's rank in the Spanish army and were leading semi-uniformed forces respectively about 5000 and 13,500 strong.[95] Mina's force actually counted as part of the Spanish 7th Army, and occasionally joined it to put down bandits. Whether they were still 'guerrillas' or not may well be questioned. The government of their country had succeeded in their cases in doing what all governments must wish to do, and all professional military men wished to do. It had brought society's violence-potential under its own control.

A vast and awful amount of violence was released in the peninsula through these six years. In the context of people's war, Spain and Portugal may be treated together, for most of its aspects appeared in both lands. Portugal indeed had no equivalent to the *Afrancesados*, and did not produce guerrilla bands in the same way. The will to do so was there, but so were the British, who proved able to turn Spanish guerrillas to advantage but were incapable of promoting guerrillas themselves. The Portuguese people seem to have resisted the invader in much the same way as the Spanish, and the French made no material distinction between them. Neither country was known for gentleness and passivity before the French arrived. Violence therefore erupted as soon as the French provoked it. Almost at once began the dreadful cycles of oppression and outrage, atrocity and counter-atrocity; pillage, marauding, starvation, maiming, torture and murder. As usual the number and the nastiness of atrocities became much magnified in popular narration, and it was the alleged rather than the proven ones which prompted reaction. But the proven ones were numerous and nasty enough. The peninsula from 1808 through 1813 became for subsequent military historians (non-Spanish) and international jurists a cautionary example of what war should *not* be like, of what sort of things must at all costs be avoided. Professional soldiers loathed it, humanitarians deplored it, economists and liberal progressives counted the cost, and had no difficulty in reckoning through the next hundred years and more that this was when Spanish society acquired or emphasized certain bad habits – 'caesarism', for instance, easy tolerance of social bloodshed, and that straight recourse to regional arming which fuelled civil war – which proved lastingly self-damaging. Only the simpler sorts of Spanish patriot and nationalist (which however meant the great majority of the Spanish people) could without strain swallow the stirring story and myth as admirable, exemplary. The generation of 1936-9 in due course paid a heavy price for this war of all wars having become a magazine of models.

The objective horror of it all can scarcely be exaggerated. The essential truthfulness of Goya's terrifying series of etchings, *The Disasters of War*, has never been doubted. The French and their 'allies', though probably the largest category of sufferers, were not the only one. *Afrancesados* were fair game – one of Goya's most horrible scenes, 'Populacho', is of peasants torturing one – and in the ultra-confused early stages of the war patriotic middle-class liberals were sometimes victimized by furious friars and demagogues who could not see the patriotism for the liberalism. Then of course there was the criminal, habitually lawless element. Bandits and smugglers were common in Spain as in all south European mountainous countries, and the sort of man who took to the one means of livelihood was likely to take to the other. But he was equally likely to become a nuisance to government. Smugglers were the more adaptable. In most Spaniards' eyes, anyway, they were useful citizens. Bandits were more of a problem. Bandit mentality was not compatible with the style of government-authorized guerrilla leadership which gradually developed, and Spain in fact was not rich in the 'Robin Hood' type social bandits who became national resistance leaders in the Balkans and southern

Italy. It is significant that of the enduringly famous leaders, none had begun as a bandit; Mina began as an independent peasant, El Empecinado and Sánchez similarly (the former with early military inclinations), Merino as a priest, El Médico as a doctor, etc. But the bandit and merely criminal fringe of this guerrilla warfare was there, as it always is, making rougher still what was bound to be rough anyway. Guerrillas lived off the land like the French, and farmers and merchants who would not willingly supply their needs had to be made to. Their security and operational success depended on the complicity of the inhabitants. When patriotism and persuasion failed, terror had to be used to force compliance – as it was, indeed, in the urban branches of the war too; it was as risky to be lukewarm about the national cause inside besieged Zarogoza and Gerona, for instance, as to tell tales to the French in the mountains. No more than in other people's wars may we assume that terror and compulsion made no contribution to the appearance of a popular front, though the evidence of popularity has never been stronger.

Whatever the Spanish people suffered from their own side, however, it was nothing like what they suffered from the French – i.e., the mixture of French, Belgian, Polish, Italian, Swiss and German troops and hangers-on the French brought with them. French methods of subsisting would have brought suffering anyway. It is impossible to judge to what extent the roughness used towards Spaniards and Portuguese along the French armies' lines of march was the fruit not merely of material circumstances – the difficulty of finding food and warmth in an inhospitable, mainly empty peninsula – but also of the stories they had heard of indigenous atrocities, or their actual experience of them. Only professional soldiers or educated liberals knew about the laws and customs of warfare between civilized States. The French military certainly valued them greatly, usually observed them pretty well (except – admittedly an enormous and crucial exception – when circumstances made it impossible), and began its campaigns in expectation that its enemy would observe them too. In Spain this was a mistake. The Spanish peasant knew nothing of 'civilized warfare'. One could debate forever the question whether Spain would have been better off in the long run if it had been otherwise. Enthusiasts for people's wars rarely count the cost. In Spain, the cost in lives, sufferings and mental poisoning was colossal, and

176

precisely because the resistance movement was so popular, spontaneous and diffused, with so largely demotic leadership, it included no vision of the values of restraint in warfare. Least restraint-minded of all seem to have been the lower clergy. In many countries such men might have been expected to moderate and humanize violence. In Spain they did rather the opposite. French messengers, commissary men, stragglers because sick or wounded, were picked off and more or less nastily put to death from the very beginning. The first big anti-French atrocity of which Dupont's troops would have heard on their march from Toledo to Cordoba was the priest-inspired massacre of the several hundred French internees at Valencia. General Vedel's small force on its way south to join them found at Manzanares the mutilated bodies of the sick men whom Dupont, following the inevitable procedure of that age, had left in a hospital there. On their way back to meet Vedel, Dupont's men saw along the highway 'the awfully mutilated bodies of their comrades, often hanging from trees. At Montoro they found the remains of more than 200 men, some of whom had been torn to pieces, others crucified on trees or sawed between boards....'[96] No wonder that thoughts of 'Vengeance!' filled the French mind. But the Spaniards too had cause for complaint. Apart from taking what it needed and protecting its security in the usual way, Dupont's army had looted a good deal in Cordoba, and while it was being enmeshed at Bailén, Marshal Bessières' army in Old Castile was following up its victory at Medina del Rio Seco over General Blake's army with comprehensive savagery against the civilians in the town, who had in fact *not* offered the mass resistance that many towns did. Thus early began the spiral escalation of savageries which added dreadful distinction to this peninsula war. It is impossible to unravel the tangle of arguments as to 'who started it'. All we can do is to recognize that the bringing together of Napoleonic imperialism, French campaign methods, and the national peculiarities of the Spanish people was sure to produce such a result, whoever started it. Once the cycle of retaliations starts, it is next to impossible to stop even when political and cultural circumstances (e.g., normal diplomatic channels, the good offices of third parties, and a common idea of religion) are working with you. In Spain they all worked against.

What this war did to Spain and Spanish society is one thing;

what it did to France and Napoleon is another. The description of it as Napoleon's Spanish ulcer is apt. He had anticipated no trouble: a show of force, a puppet government, and French-modelled armed forces abundant enough to contribute largely to his imperial needs as well as policing the peninsula. What he got instead was a permanent commitment of large numbers of soldiers, with no end in sight and the merely defensive purpose of securing France against a second front. The guerrillas on their own were not responsible for so great a damage. If they had constituted Napoleon's only armed enemy in the peninsula, his armies could have wiped them out. The French generals knew how to do it: mobile columns to harry the guerrillas through their hiding-areas while plentiful garrisons held the inhabited places until the guerrillas had been starved to surrender or extinction. But to make such a plan work required many more troops than could be devoted to it while there were regular armies to be confronted. Of those armies, the British were by far the most important. The Spanish ones were never much of a menace to the French. The Portuguese one only became a bit of a menace after General Beresford smartened it up. But Wellington's expeditionary army and the smaller British one(s) that worked their way up the southern coast had to be faced with equal force. So long as large French armies had to remain in being for that purpose, effective counter-guerrilla operations were not on. Thus were the French swung from one position off-balance to another. It only needed a concentration of their superior numbers to send the prudent Wellington scuttling back to his Portuguese redoubt – but such very concentrations weakened their hold over Joseph's parts of Spain and emphasized especially the fragility of their lines of communication. Partly because there was never much collaboration between Wellington and the guerrillas (whom on the whole, as we shall soon see, he didn't like), and largely because most of them have written for national readerships, British and Spanish historians have tended to take mutually exclusive positions about their compatriots' relative shares in achieving the jointly-desired result. Each is blind to what lies on the other side of the hill. To a historian aspiring to view the whole (however distantly) from a transnational summit, the conclusion seems inescapable, that each indispensably complemented the other, and that neither could have won the Peninsular War on its own.

Wellington didn't like guerrillas for the same reason as every other professional officer and aristocrat disliked them; and the dislike was mutual. The war in the peninsula was a laboratory of military attitudes as well as of types of warfare. The international professionalism developing uninterruptedly from the eighteenth century never revealed its character more clearly than in the way the British and French, 'enemies', liked and respected each other more than either liked or respected the Spanish. The French could not have been expected to like them. The British, however, could. They were supposedly fighting in Spain for a common cause. Yet all levels of the British army showed a strain of dislike and contempt for their allies which had something in common with the French, and was certainly not what could have been expected of an 'ally'. 'No wild horde of Tartars ever fell with more licence upon rich neighbours, than did the English troops upon the Spanish towns taken by storm.'[97] In less abnormal circumstances the British troops were still notorious for pilfering and plundering, sometimes with their officers' connivance. Wellington's orders to stop it never had much effect. Clearly the men felt they were among an inferior people ('superstitious', 'dirty', etc.) and in some ways an unpleasant people; although their individual dealings with Spanish people, especially Spanish people in trouble, could be generous and kindly, collectively they tended to sympathize with the French in their sufferings at Spanish hands, and often did their best to rescue French sick and wounded from what awaited them at Spanish hands. This fellow-feeling with the official enemy showed itself more strongly at officer level. Enormous offence was given to the Spaniards by the way British and French officers would hob-nob with each other after battles; the British victors even, as in Vitoria, walking arm-in-arm through the streets with their surrendered French equivalents, and together snubbing their supposed Spanish equivalents. Despising the ineptitudes of the Spanish army, they enjoyed the fellow-feeling of superior professionalism and, probably, 'gentlemanliness'. But their professionalism went further, to give them a shared dislike of the ferocity injected into the war by the natives' participation in it, and the guerrillas' departures from 'regular' practice. The professionals' code included those laws and conventions of war which few guerrillas knew or cared about, and only the most nearly 'regular' of them could observe; e.g., the taking of prisoners, which

179

non-regular fighters tended to be bad at, so that Wellington was driven to offer cash to his Portuguese semi-regulars, the *Ordenanza*, for prisoners brought in live and undamaged.[98] (Strictly speaking the *Ordenanza* were militia, not guerrillas, and wore enough uniform to entitle Wellington to demand of Masséna that he so regard them. But their instincts and behaviour were similar to guerrillas.) Those laws and conventions included the exclusion of civilian population from participation in hostilities. The distinction between the civilian and the combatant was already central to the law of war, and was to become positively crucial to it in the coming time. What happened in Spain between 1808 and 1813 gave the professional military, the swelling band of military historical writers and the just-appearing profession of international jurists, a glimpse into what seemed to them an appalling abyss.

Most of this chapter's space has been given to the Spanish people's war because it was the most original, the most sustained, and the most effective of its kind. In many respects it stands as the classic example; testimony to which is the fact that the Spanish word for it, *guerrilla*, has been warped into common use as the universal word for the person who fights it (he was actually a *guerrillero*). But the people actively participated in war, and guerrilla bands conducted their sorts of campaigns, in many other countries. Nowhere else did they get as near to having decisive effect as in Spain. The main stream of military historical writing has understandably neglected them, both for that reason and probably also because they are in fact difficult to categorize and assess. Nothing approaching an adequate typology of them yet exists. We will make shift by examining the linked problems of their identification and their direction.

The direction of them mattered enormously to governments, first because they had revolutionary potential and, second, because they embodied those disorderly tendencies of society which it was the acknowledged interest and duty of governments to master. That the common people (a relative concept; bourgeois liberals would seem such to caste-conscious nobility) should possess arms or the means to make them was in any case worrying, though ruling classes had to accept it in a world where the scythe, the pitchfork and the home-made pike had their military uses, however limited, and ancient notions of the national turn-out to resist invasion still had some life in them. But that they should be positively provided with arms and encouraged to use them was to go against the first principle of modern statecraft, which was that the State should monopolize the means of violence, partly to protect itself from rebellion and revolution, partly to ensure that it could keep control of whatever violence was done in its name. Every other régime and ruling class of Europe was quick to notice what had happened in France when the people acquired arms in 1789 and the early nineties; the Directory and Napoleon, having noticed it too, got the arms back under official control as fast as they safely could. From the French Revolution on, revolutionaries and radicals longed to get hold of arms, and established governments normally strove to prevent them. We have seen how the Prussian government, when national crisis led it to 'arm the people' in the late spring of 1813, did so with many prudent precautions (above, p.161). The Habsburgs went even more prudently at their moment of crisis in 1809, never going beyond cautiously selective *Landwehr* and Volunteers to *Landsturm* extremes, and later declining to raise the peoples of the Alpine countries to hasten the French withdrawal in 1813. The British government, which not so long ago had disarmed the Scottish Highlanders and more recently learnt in Ireland how arms authorized for use against invaders from abroad could be turned against governments at home, made sure that the militia stayed under proper military discipline. The Tsar could afford to leave to their own devices the relatively few Russian peasants within reach of the French lines of march in later 1812; once Napoleon had made it clear he was not about to emancipate the serfs, he and his horde simply seemed an odious foreign body which all Russians could cheerfully combine to expel. When in 1814 and 1815 the coalition armies threatened France, Napoleon ordered something like a general rising to stop them and the formation of partisan units to harass them. (Napoleon, one may add, was not above egging on the Polish people to rise against the Russians in 1812, the Hungarians against the Habsburgs in 1809.) In only one of these cases of strong administrations well in command of their political situation, did popular intervention in war and the irregular sort of warfare that went with it much affect the outcome, and that was in Russia where the associated harassments of an enraged peasantry and partisan cavalry attacks aggravated the pains and losses of the French retreat. But it was Russia's armies, and what the Russian climate did to men already nearly starving, that really saw the French off.

Guerrillas and popular action were able to make more of a mark in countries where national governments were either not well-established or were actually non-existent. In particular was this true of three peoples becoming preoccupied during these years with recovery or assertion of their independence: the peoples of Poland, Serbia and Greece. From 1794 until 1863, when a quieter fifty years began, independent-minded Poles pursued the goal of national liberation from, above all, alien Russian rule. Their intermittent insurgencies included a certain amount of popular and partisan action as well as regular-style formations and operations, the concept of which came naturally to men with so grand a military tradition behind them and so much continuing professional military activity in their present. From Serbia and Greece no such regular operations could be expected. There, popular warfare against Ottoman rule was at its most rugged and 'bandit-like'. 'National' leadership came naturally from men distinguished by resistance to the alien régime, and the mode in which that resistance expressed itself appeared to the régime (and to the unsympathetic outsider) as rebellion and often as banditry besides. In such circumstances the chieftain who looked a bandit from one point of view looked a popular hero from another, and became a leader of national liberation in the age of modern nationalism. Nowhere had guerrillas and bandits more functional overlap, and nowhere was guerrilla warfare more nearly the norm, than in these difficult Balkan countries where official government was alien, unpopular, and, at the invisible other end of its chain of devolution, remote. The insurgents wanted no part of it and brought their own idea of government with them.

With Spain as an intermediate case – half-way, so to speak, between Serbia and Prussia – may be linked Italy, where régimes, intrinsically weak anyway, were repeatedly interfered with by the French and where the French were popular with only a tiny progressive élite – an élite which moreover found its dawning sense of national identity increasingly at odds with its sense of indebtedness to the pioneer crackers of the *ancien régime*. The varieties of popular resistance the French met in Italy after 1796 amounted to a small-scale, piece-meal pre-run of what Spain had in store for them: urban *émeutes* and assassinations, rural sullenness and sniping, a lot of leadership from the lower clergy and traditionalist religion ('Viva Maria!', etc.) among their followers, and some bandit-like guerrilla warfare. Its most celebrated chieftain indeed, Michele Pezza, had been a bandit pure and simple before the due processes of Neapolitan law in 1798 drafted him into the army to expiate a double homicide. His lawlessness as a soldier was matched by conspicuous enough a military talent for King Ferdinand to make him a colonel. After the defeat of the royal army in 1806, Pezza reverted to type and became the guerrilla leader, Fra Diavolo, whom it took Victor Hugo's father, the general, several months of predictably savage operations in the Abruzzi to exterminate. That such a man should become a sort of popular hero, and that a would-be absolute monarch should actually have recourse to him for State purposes, speaks volumes about the natures of the Neapolitan régime and the society beneath it. Fra Diavolo was to Naples what El Empecinado was to Spain, Major von Schill to Prussia. But then, only the Kingdom of the Two Sicilies sheltered the Camorra and the Mafia.

13

THE MILITARY EMPIRES OF THE EAST

I have left these till last because there is not much to be said about them in this part of the book, and some of what has to be said has been said already. Their régimes survived the challenges of the French Revolution and Napoleonic imperialism without having to change their practices to any significant extent; their armed forces continued to be recruited in much the same ways as before the storm; the societies over which they held sway were not yet sufficiently touched by liberal and revolutionary ideas to make inevitable some modification of the inherited relationship between armed forces and society.

Geographically immense, economically backward, with governments at once extravagant and needy, terrified of peasant and minority rebellion, and inclined to expand at Ottoman expense as and when they got the chance, Austria and Russia maintained armies that were large and expensive; expensive to an extent that political arithmeticians and economists further west would have judged crippling, and that would have been felt so in Austria and Russia too, could any member of their ruling classes or administrations have been able to imagine doing without armies of such size and structure. (And Russia maintained a navy of sorts too.) The kind of debates about army reform initiated by the French in the 1760s and taken up in Britain and Germany were but palely followed. That is not to say that no fashionable change happened. The proportion of light infantry was increased, training manuals followed the new tactical models of skirmishing and mobility, and in artillery the Russian army was so completely re-equipped after 1805 that by the end of the war it shared pride of place with the British as the best in Europe. Voices recommending milder discipline continued to be heard and in the Austrian army at any rate they made some difference.

In both armies, however, would-be reformers met tough obstacles, characteristic of their respective régimes. In the Habsburg Empire, for instance, there was its multinational character, which caused it to be considered unsafe to recruit Polish Galicians for the *Landwehr*, and impossible to order the Hungarians to do anything; the feebleness of its finances, which meant that it could never muster and equip as many troops as appeared on paper, and made it peculiarly dependent on British subsidies; and the profound – though on the Viennese side at any rate highly cultivated – conservatism of its ruling circles, which Peter Paret has beautifully expressed in his remark about the Archduke Charles, the Habsburgs' most enterprising and (for after all he did defeat Napoleon at Aspern-Essling in May 1809) successful soldier: 'A service whose most influential reformer was a conservative contending against soundly entrenched reactionaries could never become fully reconciled to the techniques and to the energy and activity demanded of modern war.'[99]

What happened in the Russian empire was of course *sui generis*. Its version of conservatism came from deep religious and cultural sources quite different from the new counter-revolutionary conservatisms of 'the west'. Well-accustomed by now to importing from more advanced countries practical innovations and technical experts to improve performance on sides of its life which had to meet 'the west', the thick core of Russian society remained impervious to 'westernization' and deeply suspicious of it. Challenges from the west – Napoleon in 1812 being the most striking thereof – Russia met in its own impenetrable traditional way. A society in which serfdom was so fundamental, fear of rebellion so lively, and anything like the 'western' middling classes so nearly invisible, could not contemplate reforming its methods of recruitment in anything like the French or post-1808 Prussian styles. The Archduke Charles with great difficulty persuaded his colleagues at the top to shorten the term of infantry service to ten years. In Russia all that happened was a nominal reduction in 1793 from life to twenty-five years – the same life sentence under a slightly sweeter name. The prevailing conservatism of almost everybody, the absence of those middling social ranks from which France, Britain and Prussia derived NCOs and regimental officers of some education and independent spirit, and the docile simplicity of the rankers made sure that good new ideas introduced at the top were likely to peter out or petrify before they reached the bottom. And movement away from classic *ancien régime* absolutist models was hampered by their persisting attractions for the Russian ruling mind. Here again Russia was in a different league from Austria. The Habsburg emperors aspired with imperfect success to be absolute rulers. The Tsars were more than absolute; they were autocrats. The army had for them vital interest as not merely the actual agency of their unaccountable authority, but also the symbolic representation of it, whose impressive show and machine-like drills and rituals were more important than economy or efficiency; living toy soldiers to express the despotic will, and to convey to the rest the driving spirit of the whole. Old German models not surprisingly therefore continued to fascinate Tsars and some advisers long after rulers and generals elsewhere had learnt to distinguish substance from show. While the eccentric Suvorov was setting a very different (though still extremely Russian) example, the future Paul I was out-Potsdamming Potsdam in the drill, discipline and dress of the troops under his control – an interest taken up enthusiastically by his successor after 1815.

In some ways therefore the Russian army was the most singular and old-fashioned appearing on European battlefields, for all its innovations retaining a character all its own. Its discipline remained untouched by the humanizing swell of the period. Its troops, famed for dogged pluck and fortitude, were accustomed to a higher rate of loss than any others; the medical services were terrible, typhus and dysentery could kill just as many in northern climes as yellow fever etc. in the tropics, and Russian commanders felt no objection to sacrificing unusually high proportions of men in action. Yet through them and through the society encompassing them ran an exalted spirit of patriotic fellow-feeling which enabled the Tsar to feel, in 1812 at any rate, that he too was leading a nation in arms – serfs not excepted. Alexander's official pro-French foreign policy after Tilsit never became popular. The French invasion (Napoleon crossed the Niemen on 23 June) released a Russian passion which had been long preparing. The nobility of Moscow contributed three million roubles to the war-chest and 80,000 serfs to the militia; Moscow's merchants gave ten million. The Orthodox clergy lent themselves zealously to the presentation of the war – which was, indeed, as an entirely defensive one, the most 'just' that religion and ethics could identify – as a holy one. Napoleon had expected his capture of Smolensk, a 'holy city', to lower Russian spirits, but the tables were turned on him when its thaumaturgic Black Virgin was removed in safety and committed, with other scarcely less efficacious ikons, to the army's care and protection. The Tsar reminded the people of 'God-protected Russia' not only of 'the well-being which [they] alone in the whole world enjoyed' under his 'mild sceptre', but also that 'the furious enemy' and 'false Messiah' who had attacked them was notoriously a friend to Moslems and Jews.[100] Kutuzov, saluting his troops as 'Brothers!' on the eve of Borodino, reminded them not only that the Virgin of Smolensk and God were with them but that 'this tyrant who disturbs the universe' had caused the destruction of their cities and the sufferings of their children. Such destruction and suffering had already by then been great. Russian policy, now as later, was one of 'scorched earth' in the path of the invader. The Russian peasantry stubbornly co-operated, if not always by destroying its crops and cottages before the invading foragers and marauders got there, at least by putting up a resistance when they did. For a few months Napoleon's men encountered something like Spanish conditions. Moscow, where they might have passed a relatively cosy winter, was too scorched to permit it. On their way back they were hemmed in and hustled by all levels of Russian society in arms: regular line army, national-emergency militia, Cossacks, partisans, and peasants doing what came naturally.

It was a rough and bloody business. The Russian army's losses by the end of the year were proportionately not a lot less than the French, and a credible estimate of the total population loss in the year of 1812 is one-and-a-half million.[101] But Russian national spokesmen dwelt not on the losses but on the achievement. Tolstoy, whose account of it in *War and Peace* remains the best place for anyone to begin, observed that when the common people got into a war, the normal rules and conventions went by the board. 'Let us imagine two men who have come out to fight a duel with rapiers according to all the rules of the art of fencing. The fencing has gone on for some time: suddenly one of the combatants, feeling himself wounded and understanding that the matter is no joke but concerns his life, throws down his rapier, and seizing the first cudgel that comes to hand begins to brandish it.' Napoleon 'did not cease to complain to Kutuzov and to the Emperor Alexander that the war was being carried on contrary to all the rules – as if there were any rules for killing people. In spite of the complaints of the French as to the non-observance of the rules, in spite of the fact that to some highly placed Russians it seemed rather disgraceful to fight with a cudgel and they wanted to assume a pose *en quarte* or *en tierce* according to all the rules and to make an adroit thrust *en prime*, and so on – the cudgel of the people's war was lifted with all its menacing and majestic strength, and without consulting anyone's tastes or rules, and regardless of anything else, it rose and fell with stupid simplicity, but consistently, and belaboured the French till the whole invasion had perished.'[102]

It was no accident that the Russian and Soviet historian Tarle's excellent book on *Napoleon's Invasion of Russia, 1812*, when it came out in 1938, should have concluded with a recommendation to Germans that they study it carefully.

Part III

AFTER NAPOLEON

14

THE INHERITANCE

Using the word generation loosely, one may obviously say that the generation of 1790-1815 became accustomed to war. War present, war threatened, war in prospect, war not long past, war in every known shape and form, war happening to someone else even if not just then to you yourself, and talk of war as the ultimate conditioner of your existence – this was the common European experience of that epoch. With Waterloo, the second Treaty of Paris, and St Helena, it came to an end. Europe and its people had to get used to something different. It turned out to be very different indeed. The next generation experienced no international war at all. It experienced a great deal of internal war – civil war, insurgency, rebellion – which in some respects, and to the minds of many of the combatants, was no more than the conclusion or continuation of business not yet finished in 1815. But the contrast between the two generations was none the less enormous. Before 1815, almost all war; after 1815, until the later fifties and with exception made for the endemic rebelliousness which will fill most of this part of the book, hardly any war at all. It was, comparatively speaking, an age of peace; and is often characterized as such by historians who survey it.

Such characterization is reasonable enough, provided we forget not its inheritance. Post-1815 Europe carried the burden of the aftermath of the war. If it was peace, it was also picking up the pieces, and putting them back in place. For statesmen and rulers, this was above all their 'restoration'. The old royal families, the *legitimate* rulers of Europe, returned to their palaces. The peoples of Europe, many of whom had known other forms of government and other *soi-disant* kings, returned, if not to exactly what they had known before, at any rate to something like it in principle. Many of them quickly made clear the fact that they didn't like it. The intervening years had raised liberal hopes and national aspirations of which the peacemakers at Vienna took little notice. It was their purpose to put the revolutionary djin back into the bottle, but he was too big to be squeezed in. Hence to some extent (for it was also a time of awkward readjustment and natural hazard for the economies of Europe) the rebellions, insurgencies and civil strife which followed.

To the vast majority of the people of Europe, preoccupied as they had to be with the day-to-day problems of living or partly living, and with clearing up the mess the wars had left behind them, 'peace' meant no more than a change in the rulers and circumstances governing how they did it. That change came to most of them as a change for the worse. The European economy went into convulsions. Napoleon had aimed to gear all of it that he could control to French needs and advantages. The absolute loss of their extra-European commerce and the confining of their European commerce to what would suit the French in one sense damaged non-French manufacturers and traders but suited some well for a while. The market at their disposal might not be affluent or free, but they were (while Napoleon's writ ran) sure of it, and there was little or no British competition. While some industries and industrial regions had been ruined, others had in the end done rather well out of the 'continental system'. The region later to be known as Belgium, for example, had actually begun the second industrial revolution, based on coal, metals and cotton. The cotton textile business had boomed in Austria, Saxony, Switzerland and Catalonia too.

All people and places connected with the making and sale of armaments and military equipment became rich, and so did most army contractors who were not bankrupted *en route* by governments' slowness to pay their bills. (Napoleon had an extraordinary prejudice against contractors and liked to make them sweat.) Refining sugar from beet – one of the war's most notable scientific innovations – became big business in the Low Countries. But now, with the collapse of that protected trading system, the reappearance of colonial goods and the in-rush of cheap goods from a Britain by now well ahead in the industrialization race, continental business-men found themselves quickly in difficulties. Nor could those who had formerly been wont to export grain and timber to Britain easily resume so doing. Its own agricultural

192

resources much expanded by wartime exigencies, Britain protected its farmers with the 1815 Corn Law tariff, and continued to search across the Atlantic for what had previously come all from the Baltic. Britain was held by many continentals to be responsible for the war's uncomfortable economic aftermath, but its causes were more universal; the aftermath was, *relatively*, just as uncomfortable for the British, though such was the difference by now between the British and the other European economies that Britain did not go into a classic 'subsistence crisis' in 1816-17, while most of them did.

Along with these major jolts in the course of commerce came a variety of other troubles, some normal enough at such a juncture, others, like the very bad harvests of 1815 and 1816, 'accidental'. Demobilization poured hundreds of thousands of troops back into a civilian world which had nothing like enough jobs for them. Un- or underemployment in the peasant society from which most of them came was not too conspicuous. There, they simply suffered the ordinary hardships of the rural poor, which would turn the minds of many towards migration. In industrial villages and towns their plight was more apparent, for they came back just when employers were more likely to be paying men off than taking them on. They went 'on welfare' where there was any, contributed to the grisly statistics of unhealthy urban overcrowding and early mortality, and to an extent which we are unlikely ever to be able to measure, helped to build up their better-off contemporaries' probably unfair impression that there were too many beggars, vagabonds and criminals about.

Accompanying these more immediate economic consequences of restored peace was the usual post-war problem of repairing war's material and human damage. Uninvaded Britain was of course in this respect unscathed, and so in fact was most of France, though the invasion of 1814 did a little damage, the four years' military occupation which followed had to be paid for, and the Allies collected well over a thousand million francs of reparations and debts, which were quickly paid off. But some parts of Europe and the people in them had suffered very badly; whether entirely because of the war, or because the war had coincided with other troubles, we shall not pause to inquire. Spain was a major victim. Its agriculture, going so well through the late eighteenth century, was ruined. By 1811-13, classic famines were hitting most regions.

One person in five died in many villages; 'many towns took until 1820 or '30 to regain the population they had had in 1790-3'.[1] Italy was in equally bad shape. The north especially had suffered from French exploitation of its material and human resources over nearly twenty years, besides being a good deal fought over. Stuart Woolf cites a French official reporting in 1810 that the past fifteen years had seen no popular insurrections in his department, Marengo, only because of 'the state of almost continuous illness in which these people languish'; he himself concludes that 'famine and extreme hardship' largely explain Italy's failure to produce a Spanish-style popular revolt to speed the French homewards in 1813-14.[2] Poland was another country which had a very bad time. Not rich or populous, it was much fought over, armies often passed through or attempted to stay there, and it was itself compelled to provide Napoleon after 1807 with a large contingent. Parts of Austria and Germany produced terrible sights. One authority recalled that Saxony in 1812 had reminded him of what he had read about the Thirty Years' War.[3] A young officer writing home from Frankfort-am-Main late in 1813 told his family that war now was just 'stupidly barbaric...; the road from Leipzig to this place is hideous because there are at least 15,000 corpses and 10,000 horses left on the highways so that one can neither ride nor travel without stamping on dead people. There is no village in the whole region which has not been burned down or pillaged.'[4] And so on. It is true that despite these ridings of the apocalypse horsemen there was no overall check to Europe's long-term demographic upward trend. But that is a statistical summary. As Clapham remarked, 'The average wage-earner ... is not a man of flesh and blood. He is a most important figure, but not human.'[5] Nor is 'the average European' c. 1815 human. Behind him stand tragic crowds of cripples, derelicts, widows and orphans – the 'hundreds' of the latter, for instance, whom Stein happened to notice falling into public care in 1807 because their parents were dead or disappeared, the scores whom Pestalozzi set out to salvage in 1798.[6] The actual losses and damages caused by the wars to some particular parts and people must have taken years to remedy. (San Sebastian, close to the French border, and all but wholly destroyed in 1813, had to be rebuilt by its brisk Basque bourgeoisie. The work was not finished until 1836.) If little of this normally appears in the general or military history books, it is only because historians have allowed themselves to be over-fascinated by the high drama of what came before, the magnitude of the political problems which immediately followed.

Equally part of those wars' legacy, though in the nature of things beyond even the most dedicated quantification, is their effect upon what we may vaguely call the European mind: its values, ideals and ways of thinking in the context of the literature and visual arts, the oral traditions and folklore, the general culture in fact which expressed them and carried them down the years. Thus would Europe's twenty years' war experience, once it had been ground into the cultural soil, become part of the mental inheritance of subsequent generations, and perhaps do more to condition *their* thinking than it had done at the time to some of its more stolid or sheltered contemporaries. All we can do with this mental and cultural inheritance here is to summarize the aspects of the wars which in recollection were on the whole judged bad and repulsive, those which on the other hand were judged good and admirable. It may certainly be said that ideas about war in the nineteenth century worked out less to the promotion of peace than war.[7]

First, then, some of the ways in which the wars were among the century's bad memories. They concentrated the minds and consolidated the energies of people predisposed to consider war lamentable, wasteful, and avoidable: e.g., all Quakers and many Unitarians (élite denominations on both sides of the Atlantic, entering the age of their largest intellectual influence); certain prominent Protestants with particular sympathy for radical Protestantism's pacifistic tradition or particular distaste for established churches' all-too-ready equation of patriotism with piety; unromanticized survivors from the Enlightenment like Saint-Simonians and Utilitarians, for whom the wars had simply marked a gigantic breakdown of mankind's proper scientific and rational paths of progress; and other liberal trumpeters of the new economic order, coming to believe that the wealth and happiness of nations must be better promoted by international organization and collaboration. From the coming together of people thus-minded under, usually, Quaker leadership, very soon after the wars were over, crystallized the Peace Movement which, by the forties, was big and brash enough to be attracting much attention in Britain, the Low Countries and France (not to mention the USA), some attention in Germany, Austria and Italy. Connected with it was a larger, vaguer movement of internationalism, not necessarily pacifist but generally committed to the belief that peace was better for mankind than war, and that the proper business of States was to relate peacefully to each other, not to get into fights; 'I don't want my country to become the Tom Cribb of Europe,' as J. S. Mill once remarked. (Tom Cribb was the British heavyweight boxing champion of the day.) Both movements' propaganda made selective use of wartime evidence to press their case, and recalled the wars as an episode when continental Europe's natural development had been retarded.

This internationalism derived cautious encouragement from certain aspects of the 1815 peace settlement and its immediate development. 'The Concert of Europe' (the great powers' collective security system) held the good of the whole continent deliberately in view and explicitly aimed to preserve its peace. 'The Congress System' which came out of the Concert really was a conflict-minimizing way of settling international disputes, however much political radicals might dislike the consequences. The internationalization of the Danube navigation was a novelty with colossal implications for the future. The 1817 Rush-Bagot Convention between the UK and the USA for the demilitarization of the Great Lakes was another. In these aspects, at any rate, it seemed that peaceful lessons might have been learnt.

Goya's *Disasters of War*, which he did not etch until the international conflict had ended, represented a third vein of regretful recollection. Such was their originality and force, they became, for such cultivated people who knew of them, the arts' supreme condemnation of the Napoleonic war in particular, perhaps of war in general. War's disasters and horrors were often enough recognized in painting and writing: combatants collapse or lie dead, blood flows, shells explode, buildings collapse, villages are destroyed, retreaters and fugitives trudge along muddy roads, wreck-survivors struggle in the water, and so on; but much more often than not, these are but the realistic stage-settings for dramas whose drift is overall positive. A Stendhal in *The Charterhouse of Parma*, 1839, a Tolstoy in *War and Peace*, 1863-9, made no bones about the cruelties, the absurdities, the corruptions and hypocrisies incidental to the wars, but that clarity of vision did not turn their books into anti-war books. At the popular level, recognitions of the savage side of war seem to have been subsumed into that general acquiescence in the ways of an often malevolent fate characteristic of poor peasants and pre-political proletarians, or frankly rejoiced in as exciting and exalting. Whatever may have been the poignancy and persistence of collective and local recollections of disasters and horrors, they never, apparently, got into wide enough circulation to correct the dominant national myths. Whatever may have been the sharpness of private grief, it died with the persons who felt it, while over it rolled the tide of national and military glorification, to which we now turn.

Commemoration of war and celebration of warrior heroes is at least as old as ancient history. Historians curious about this natural phenomenon might indeed discover, upon close inquiry, that 'recollections' of wars varied from class to class, even that certain wars recalled as glorious by one class were recalled as infamous by another, and that one country's experience in this respect might differ greatly from another's. What such study would show about the development of national military myths before the wars of 1792-1815, can only be guessed at. But I am in good company in finding it impossible to doubt that those wars solidified and energized them. The sheer quantity of varied war experience, the 'totality', the popular character and the evident popularity of much of it, contributed to militarize the European mind; it spread familiarity with fighting far further than ever before, and presented all this war experience and fantasy in attractive and admirable lights.

On the political plane, this was intelligible enough. For many peoples, their war years could be telescoped into a cheering tale of national self-defence or liberation. This required some glossing over the awkward passages: for Spain, Holland, Austria, Switzerland, Russia, Prussia and nearly every smaller German State, for example, the years of alliance with France, or servitude to it, demanded explanation. But those unhappy chapters were outshone by the ones which told the story of their operations against France, with common happy endings in national liberation and in some cases, revenge. No matter how the pandemic nationalism of the age took them, each continental State and national grouping from 1815 was able to build into its national story a stirring batch of military adventures and the exemplification in battle of qualities the nation-builder especially valued: heroism, dedication, discipline, sacrifice, and love of country; a concentrated contemporary topping-up of the received version of the people's history, with exploits and heroes to match the greatest of the past. For the Italians and Belgians, who had been of all continental peoples the longest under the French thumb, it was a bit different. Both could dwell on a certain amount of popular insurgency, but until 1815 their regular soldiers never had any choice but to fight on the French side, and some of them did it pretty well. No matter! Such was the force of the prevailing disposition to admire the military and to share their professional approach to war, that national historians were able to derive consolation from the fact that their soldiers had nevertheless always 'done their duty' (by obeying their rulers) and 'fought bravely', even though it was on the side of the French. If you hadn't fought on the right side, at least you had fought well. If you weren't directly defending or freeing your country, at least you had 'covered yourself with glory'.

With those extrapolations we come to the most remarkable and, for the future, significant aspect of the 1815 inheritance: its popularization of professional military activity for its own sake, its savouring of war as such – war and all the seemingly splendid things that went with it, with the events of 1792-1815 providing a common culture. It is true that old-fashioned and unromantic people for some years yet would continue to talk of war in the civilized Enlightenment way, as a regrettable necessity in which a few redeeming features could be found. Armies and soldiers in fact for a while sank into relative unpopularity and neglect. But what had been done could not be undone. The spirits of revolutionary liberation and nationalism were abroad, providing a wide new range of 'objective' justifications for war. Romanticism could only have the effect of enlarging the range of 'subjective' reasons for enjoying it. (It might be added, that those strands of the professional military tradition coming from chivalry and cherishing honour etc. had a sort of natural romanticism in them anyway.) Actual soldiering in the Restoration present was generally a dull enough business, but now it had a glamorous past and potentiality which kept the idea of it bright and shining in readiness for the return of, from the soldier's point of view, better days.

It showed itself, first, in a cult of the Revolutionary and Napoleonic soldier, which would conveniently lend itself to contemporary application as soon as the time grew ripe. The soldier had not generally been popular under the *ancien régime*, though by the end of it, in some countries, he was becoming better known and trusted than before. About the sailor's popularity there had been less difficulty. He was not around for much of the time and he could not credibly be seen in any of the countries where he existed as a tool of despotism. Now the soldier moved forward to join him as a possible object of public esteem. It was in France and, by the end, Prussia that he most became so. Old habits of thought died hard in Britain, and the campaigning, fighting part of the British army included no mass of conscripts gone from hearth and plough to fight in foreign lands, etc. But even in Britain and despite the Duke of Wellington, the common soldier and his trade were a bit better respected, not to mention better publicized, after the war than before it. As for France, where the rise in his reputation took off from a higher threshold, already by the mid-nineties he was clearly launched, not without much aid from revolutionary propaganda, into a new era of popular affection and respect. Its very reasonable roots lay in the fact that the volunteers and conscripts of 1791-4 really were drawn straight from the community at large, and could credibly be represented as fighting the nation's battles for it, not because they were professional fighters but – much more admirable – because they had driven their normally peaceable civilian selves to become good at fighting. The professionals however were battling in the same good cause, and once there were no longer any doubts about their loyalty to the new régime, all French soldiers commanded equal admiration. So effectively did Napoleon promote and enlarge this cult of the soldier that no part of his army was more revered by the end of his reign than the ultra-professional Imperial Guard, focus of legends and stories innumerable, all heroic and exemplary. But Napoleon's careful cultivation of the image of soldiering as man's finest calling (which was of a piece with his cultivation of a special quasi-paternal, pseudo-divine relationship with his own men) did no less for them all.

This went well beyond the mere conveying to the common soldier (and to the country under whose flag he fought) the sense that he too mattered, which had of course been among the goals of the pre-revolutionary army reformers. Not all countries took it on to the same extent as the French, and no other commanders went in for it as much as Napoleon. Wellington could never bring himself to do it. But Nelson could: 'England expects that every man will do his duty.' What could be more flattering? It was not that Nelson was any more liberal or democratic than Wellington. He was simply more romantic: fervent, dramatic and showy. He was also, like Napoleon, more wholly devoted to war. Wellington did not actually enjoy war as they did and as became the fashion among their followers; and I am not aware that he ever used the Franco-Napoleonic language about *Gloire*/Glory. In this as in so much else he was trailing behind the times. Glorious feats of arms became for modish military men their great ambition, and for the non-military a matter of uncritical admiration. This cult of *Gloire* spread rapidly throughout Europe during the wars, and the Emperor himself hailed Glory the whole time, in his appeals to the warlike spirit among other nations besides his own, urging Italians, Bavarians, Poles and so on to show what they were made of by fighting so as to 'cover themselves with glory'. Nothing better illustrates or exemplifies the way this self-sustaining militaristic impulse acquired continent-wide currency than the hold its supreme exponent acquired over the imaginations of his enemies. Napoleon, after receiving their surrender, was wont gravely to congratulate enemy commanders 'for having put up such a good fight', and so on; and they used, it seems, to lap it up. Tolstoy gives a hilarious description of his awarding a medal to the bravest soldier in the Russian army after Tilsit, about the time when the two armies, so recently at one another's throat, had turned to feasting each other.[8] The Russian officers taken prisoner after the battle of Zürich, after expressing gratitude for their good treatment, addressed Napoleon thus: 'It now lies within your power, General, to mitigate their fate and to attach the banners of humanity to the chariot of your glory,' etc. What they were after was to be allowed to wear their swords again. Napoleon, for his part, benignly assented, and congratulated them on having displayed such courage and loyalty; qualities he loved (he said) to see practised by the French.[9] Crowds turned out at Plymouth in July 1815 to look at Napoleon on the quarterdeck of the *Bellerophon*, *and cheered him*. One is driven to wonder whether the late nineteenth-century connection often detected between sport and war ought not to be moved back in time and reversed, for these Napoleonic incidents recall nothing more than the ethics of the sports field: good show, bad luck, sporting spirit, and so on. Not indeed all, but certainly very many of the military grandees shared this exemplary ethic, as if Europe was their stage and posterity their audience. Chivalrous admiration of opponents' good qualities of course was long-established among the nobility and the professional military taking their tone from them, but the widespread vogue for it was new. Soult raised a monument to Moore's memory at La Coruña. Gravina, dying soon after Trafalgar, said, 'I go to join the brave Nelson, the greatest hero of all time.' As for Nelson, he could adopt the Napoleonic style better than any other British warlord; addressing a note to the Danish Prince Regent in the middle of the battle of Copenhagen, 'To the Brothers of Englishmen, the Danes', and regretting that unless they ceased firing, he would be 'obliged to set on fire all the Floating-Batteries he has taken, without having the power of saving the brave Danes who have defended them'. At a court banquet during the armistice, he distinguished a young Danish lieutenant by telling the Prince that he had fought so stoutly, he ought to be made an admiral. And when Nelson went back to his ship, the crowd on the quay shouted applause.[10]

This style and that popular appreciation were not universal. Some warlords couldn't or wouldn't adopt it; some national antipathies were too profound to support it. No Prussian crowd could have cheered Napoleon. Gneisenau and Kutuzov would not have erected monuments to Davoût or Murat. Perhaps class affected cheering habits; town-dwellers probably behaved differently from country ones. National and social cross-currents during these wars invite study. But it remains true to say that, by the time the war ended, the sort of appreciation of military prowess and glory which I have been sketching was widespread across a continent which had been fed so richly on it. With all its mixed virtues and vices, benefits and costs, it was ripe for lodgement in the European mind. Such lodgement was at once made surer by the way the writers and artists of the next decades exploited the dramatic and emotive materials thus made ready to their hands. Some of those writers were ex-servicemen. The flood of war memoirs published in every country of Europe was absolutely unprecedented; fruit of the fecund marriage between armed forces for the first time containing at all levels some significant proportion of the educated and articulate, and a fast-growing reading public avid for war books. Very little of this output tended to chill the public's enthusiasm. Disasters and horrors, normally attributed in any case to the other side or simply, old-soldier-style, to fate, were seen from the bright side. 'Glory' could be extracted from even the most unpromising situations, and what appeared in one belligerent's books as victories (e.g., Busaco in British books, or Borodino in French) could well appear the other way round in the other's. The professionals' sturdy confidence in the naturalness and virtue of almost everything they had been engaged in was readily adopted by 'civilian' society. The war's heroes became the heroes for nations and continent alike through the succeeding century, yielding place only to the equally magnificent reputations sent into orbit. The cult of the common soldier was launched. Warm-hearted officers like Benedek were now joined by warm-hearted civilians like, for instance, the French jurist and mandarin, Count Joseph-Marie Portalis. 'They understand human dignity,' he wrote of the soldiery in mid-century. 'Whether they come from the country or the town, it has become a particular matter of honour with them not to humiliate or oppress those who don't carry arms. Though far from being models of virtue, they no longer indulge in licentious orgies.... You can see them, like Homeric heroes, sadly standing by their arms the day after a bloody battle.... A new chivalry will date from our century,' he concluded, 'a chivalry with nothing gothic or fantastic about it. The military spirit has been re-born.'[11]

Respect for the respectable military character proved perfectly compatible with an actual desire to evade military service among all who could do so, and an actual continuing wariness about standing armies among liberals and radicals. The point is not that soldiers and sailors could not be so sympathetic, but that this sort of reverent sentimentality led largely by past glories wishfully exaggerated the extent to which they were so. The stereotype serviceman of nineteenth-century literature was much more attractive than repulsive, and for each Goya, Daumier (faithful expressor of the ideas of the internationalist and peace movements) and Verestchagin (a kind of Russian Courbet, who really knew what war was about) there were dozens like Gros, Charlet, Vernet and Détaille, Haydon, Bleibtreu, von Werner and Elizabeth Butler, for whom battles, charges, marches, camps, parades and military paraphernalia and goings-on were inspiring theatre and ritual sacrifice. They were in their way immortalizing and displaying the beauty of what war-lovers really thought to merit such treatment; e.g., Marmont's references in his famous 1845 book to the 'immortal' campaigns of 1796 and 1800, the 'beautiful' march from the Channel through Germany in 1805.[12]

The cult of the soldier and of the stars of the war world culminated, unsurprisingly, in the cult of the superstar most responsible for it. Latently strongest in France (where for obvious reasons it had to go under wraps for a while) some form or other of it was to be found everywhere else, and in Britain it seems to have waxed ever warmer as the century wore on. The fascination of 'the man of destiny' was inexhaustible, and although little research has been done into Napoleon's after-life outside France, it is clear at any rate that its influence worked mainly to promote (in the loose sense) militarism and to numb critical faculties in the face of it. A man had to be a very clear-headed critic to withstand such a tide.[13] All good modern Napoleon books devote some proportion of space to it. In France, where the phenomenon has been thoroughly studied, there was a persistent strain of criticism.[14] But it was very difficult for patriotic Frenchmen, even if they were convinced monarchists or republicans, to resist Napoleon's tunes of glory or to forget how much of their France had actually been built by him. Most put up no resistance. The incidents (some, apocryphal) which had made him beloved and revered in his own lifetime were worked over again and again in every artistic medium and at every social and intellectual level. Some worshipped him too. One of the ways in which artists loved to represent him was among the gods, close to God like a sort of archangel, or as a god himself. Four years after the *Arc de Triomphe* (begun, 1806) was completed in a Paris later to be indexed with the names of his generals and his victories, a long crescendo of Napoleon revivalism climaxed in the religious ceremonies of 'the return of the ashes' and their deposition in the Invalides shrine. Napoleon dead won a victory denied to Napoleon living, when Queen Victoria, on a state visit fifteen years later, bade the future King Edward VII 'kneel down before the tomb of the great Napoleon'.[15]

'It is possible to lead astray an entire generation, to strike it blind, to drive it insane, to direct it towards a false goal,' wrote Herzen about that same time. 'Napoleon proved this.'[16]

15

ORDER RESTORED AND MAINTAINED, 1815-55

Neither the great powers' statesmen whose deliberations at Vienna de-Napoleonized the States of Europe, nor the kings and princes who through 1814-15 moved back to govern them, expected an easy time. The longer a storm has gone on, the longer the sea takes to calm down. The order they were determined to restore was 'external' and 'internal' alike: stability of the European States-system, security of the régimes ruling the States. The first meant a balance of interests acceptable to the great powers (among whom France's place was sensibly not questioned), the second a common will to repress revolutionism. The first would be relatively easy, so long as the great powers acted in concert. Whether France, under restored Bourbon management, would co-operate, and for how long, was open to doubt; territorial rearrangements and the construction or refurbishing of stout fortresses along her eastern frontiers were designed to deter the recurrence of French imperialism. But the repression of revolutionism was an altogether more difficult business. The world had moved on since 1789. Many of the changes that had happened since then were either unalterable or actually even acceptable (e.g., 'internally', French-style administrative and legal systems; 'externally', the rationalization of Germany's political structure), 'revolutionary' ideas had got into wide circulation (constitutionalism, democracy, nationalism and the propriety of armed action to achieve them), and it was a question which only time could answer, whether the men who had taken these ideas to heart could be compelled to forget, sublimate or suppress them. If they could, and if the next generation could be properly indoctrinated with anti-revolutionary principles, then all that was needed was a holding operation until society in due course calmed down. The more optimistic sort of conservatives – and none but conservatives mattered in 1815 – believed this was within the range of possibility. The rest reconciled themselves to repression for ever. However different their visions of the long-term, they saw no alternative to a strict enforcement of discipline and order, moral as well as material, for the time being, and the maintenance of armies large enough to guarantee it.

Armies therefore easily slid from their recent exhilarating role as operators mainly against a foreign enemy to the more police-like one of preventing unrest and insurgency, and the at least potentially political role of, in the last resort, holding the country together; something which they alone might be able to do, when all else failed. Not every country, of course, got into so extreme a situation as to invite such military salvation. Britain never neared such a precipice, and much more surprisingly France, where something of the sort might have been expected, never went over it. But Prussia and Austria both did, in 1848, while Spain was in such a peculiar and disordered state that its army actually became the principal permanent public institution, and its generals, ordinary political operators, with highly polished claims to 'represent the interests of the nation'. Such language of course implied the presence of rival claimants. Two distinct ideas of what sort of army best represented the interests of nations continued in competition with each other, and the national liberation movements of Poland and Italy, Belgium, Serbia and Greece, will remind us that the armed forces of established anti-revolutionary régimes were not the only ones in the field. The ways in which armies related to societies and governments suddenly became remarkably varied, complicated and politically significant. The common feature in almost every case however was their prominence in the internal affairs of States; a prominence which was proportionate to the strength of the local likelihood of disorder, and which unprecedentedly made 'policing' seem for many their *raison d'être* through the next forty years.

Of primary concern to the governments of the Restoration was their armies' political reliability. (Navies in Europe gave no such cause for concern.) Conservatives could not believe that the Revolution would have got going in France if the army had been perfectly loyal to the throne, and were obsessed with the necessity of keeping armies loyal now. Liberals on the other hand, besides noting the reactionary capability of loyal and obedient armed automata in a counter-revolutionary climate, tended to believe that armies could actually be better as such when closer in outlook and composition to 'the people'. Extreme liberals and real revolutionaries went further, advocating the direct arming of the people as a necessary condition of political progress, and promising to do it when and as they got the chance. 'To be armed is to be free', etc. These extreme spirits will be dealt with in the next chapter. They merit a chapter to themselves, and are in any case irrelevant to our present theme of Restoration-period Order – except insofar as they were what the men of order were most worried about. But the ordinary bourgeois liberal, with his higher and lower-class fellow-travellers, could be just as interested in order (i.e., just as anxious to keep the mob in its place and to protect property) as the conservative or simple reactionary. The National Guard had secured his interests in the French Revolution: direct involvement of the respectable citizenry in protection of order and property against the plebs and in pressing the establishment for liberalizing change. Often between 1815 and the 1850s shall we find National Guards appearing in one form or another to play these roles. But the respectable liberal, demanding his proper place in the scheme of things, looked beyond armed police work to national defence. His ambition was gratified by the composition of the revolutionary armies and the congenial place made for him in the Prussian and even to a lesser extent the Austrian armies when hope and desperation together drove their governments, in 1813 and 1809 respectively, to 'go national'. How much of these wartime gains could liberalism preserve in the colder post-war climate?

16

PRUSSIA: AN ARMY DE-LIBERALIZED

By far the most important contest between liberalism and conservatism occurred in Prussia. It was important because Europe's destiny hung (we can see it clearly enough now, though it wasn't at all clear then) on which way Prussia swung. The other great powers – all of them, by the criteria of 1815, actually greater than Prussia – were politically fairly fixed. Britain, so long borne on a liberalizing tide, was undergoing what could not be more than a temporary conservative reaction. France's more recent, smarter, experience of liberalism was more mixed but there too the general direction for the future seemed fixed. Austria and Russia seemed fixed too, in the other direction; liberalism had hardly a toe-hold in Russia, and Metternich was bent on denying it even that, though the Habsburgs were clearly more exposed to infection than the Romanovs. But Prussia, uneasy new boy at the top table, was not, in 1815, clearly in one camp or the other. Liberalization had advanced with sizeable strides since 1808, in the military field not least. In chapter 11 we observed the several ways in which the people were made part of Prussia's national defence programme and how the door to the officers' mess was opened to the bourgeoisie. The Army Law of September 1814 confirmed at least the former gains. Universal military service was (with one exception, allowing men prosperous enough to pay for their own weapons and uniforms to serve as 'one year volunteers') to remain the rule during the peacetime which seemed to have dawned; the *Landwehr*, the people's militia which signified so much to the liberal mind, was to remain in being. After three years' full-time service with the colours, the Prussian male would do part-time service successively in the active reserve (two years), the front-line *Landwehr* (seven years) and the home-defence *Landwehr* (another seven). A year later the *Landwehr*'s distinctive character and purpose were clarified as a national militia territorially-organized and recruited, with middle- or upper-class officers elected by their own sort after nomination by local government authorities, separately inspected, and uniting with the standing army only in time of war. In the minds of the more liberal statesmen and generals (above all Boyen, Gneisenau, Grolmann, Clausewitz and even old Blücher) the *Landwehr* was not a rival to the regulars but a complement, whose political advantages outweighed its possible military defects. They thought of it in the broadest State-and-society context. 'If the standing army was designed to awaken the martial spirit in the people as a whole, the *Landwehr*, in Boyen's mind, was designed to provide a bond of intimacy between military and civilian society, preventing mutual antipathy and assuring the continuation of the concept of a civilian army'; signifying also, to the minds of those who loved it, 'that the duty of military service should be balanced by the right to some share in the politics of the state', and that the *Landwehr* could become 'a school for teaching the people how to bear civic responsibility'.[17]

For a few years only, army and society seemed to have met and mated on this ideal plateau as they were doing nowhere else in Europe. Then the idyll ended. The majority of Prussian aristocrats were dyed-in-the-wool conservatives and snobs, who had never much believed in citizen armies (considering them militarily feeble as well as politically distasteful) and who had never felt able to take the bourgeois to their bosom, on the ground simply that his mental background and social milieu made him incapable of understanding what honour and loyalty were all about. The arch-Junker Marwitz had attributed much of the blame for 1806 to the presence in the officer corps of men who, 'contaminated by associating with the educated middle classes, had become useless and unwarlike'.[18] The bourgeois officer was a long-term problem and not a pressing one either. But the *Landwehr* was a pressing problem, because each year that passed offered to conservatives new reminders that they had only scotched the liberal snake, not killed it. Even the most restricted sort of constitutionalism shocked and alarmed them. The *Landwehr*, to bourgeois minds the more attractive half of the armed forces, was perceived by the conservatives as giving the middle (*a fortiori*, the lower) classes ideas above their station, and all too probably instruction in, and access to, the weapons with which they might try to implement them. In 1819 political circumstances played into their lap. There were tensions within the administration because Boyen and the few other relatively liberal ministers objected to Chancellor Hardenberg's ready accession to the repressive Austria-originated 'Carlsbad Decrees'. But the king was with Hardenberg and the conservatives pressed their attack home. Already suspecting the *Landwehr* of political unreliability (i.e., democratic leanings and fidgety nationalism), they insisted that its military shortcomings (which indeed were obvious enough, since it had been stinted of funds) were so severe that it would never be any good unless it came under regular army control. The king was persuaded. He ordered appropriate changes. Boyen and Grolmann resigned. They would not be parties to the undoing of their plans for a liberal-minded 'citizen army' alongside the standing one and thus, with luck, a gradual *rapprochement* between the civilian and the military dimensions of society.

From this setback, which was only one of a series suffered by liberalism all along the line (not to mention the internal disorders produced by the passion of its nationalism) the *Landwehr* never recovered. In the sixties, while retaining its name, at last it became fused with the regular army. To the liberal mind, it remained attractive; in the liberals' version of 1813, it glowed heroic; liberal constitutionalists, when they got the chance in the *Landtag* from 1849, continued to hark back to it as the model of what a free people's armed force should be. But the remorseless tenacity of Prussian aristocratic power within the State made sure that the *Junker* idea of the army would prevail; an army separated from politics (they liked to think it was 'a-political'), devoted directly and entirely to the service of the king ('All-Highest Warlord'), officered for the greater part and in all the commanding branches by men of their own kind, men with the finest qualities and sensibilities of the officer and gentleman in their bones and blood and with the right amount of pride to keep it from contamination. 'In the Rhineland,' mused an intelligent and humane Prussian prince in 1860, 'things of course are not easy for the officers. Life there is not at all like it is in Prussia. All classes without exception consort together, and in the wine- and beer-shops officers have to mix with tradesmen, etc., who are richer than they are.'[19] *Landwehr* officers being for the most part bourgeois had normally been looked down on by aristocratic regulars with their peculiarly exclusive code of attitudes and conduct. The kind of bourgeois they most suspected was the man of commerce. The more numerous, wealthy and (at least potentially) influential men of commerce became in Europe, the further away from them did hereditary aristocrats try to stand. Junkers stood as far as any and further than most. But sheer shortage of aristocrats compelled them to accept a certain proportion of non-noble intake. This was bearable so long as it came mainly from the 'official' and professional classes, who at least understood the principles of obedience to authority and sacrificial service to high ideals. Young men from these social regions were supposed to be more susceptible than commercial ones to picking up the aristocratic style in the military academy, the cadet corps, and at last the officers' mess. But this required total immersion in the regular milieu – something the *Landwehr* by definition could not provide. Its absorption in the sixties took one weight off the *Junker* mind, leaving it so much the freer to protect its army from liberal dilution and parliamentary prying on the other fronts where it felt itself threatened.

Thus did the regular Prussian army ward off such liberals, democrats and in course of time – most abhorrent of all from its point of view! – socialists as would have dismantled the walls traditionally separating it from the rest of society and rescued their country from the reproach of still being to some unique extent more like an army with a State than a State with an army. It was more ubiquitous and universally demanding than any other of Europe's armies. This was not because it had in peacetime a larger proportion of men with the colours than any of them, but because it could in emergency call on a larger proportion of more or less trained men, all fit Prussian males having gone through it in their early twenties, and all remaining theoretically liable to recall until they reached sixty – though the *Landsturm* in which they were supposed at last to serve existed by 1855 only on paper, and Engels wrote in his famous survey of 'The Armies of Europe' that year that 'it would not be found fit for anything but police duty at home, and for a tremendous consumption of strong drink'.[20] The *Landsturm* however remained stirringly symbolic of the collective military capability of a people systematically geared to war and accustomed, therefore, to give precedence to the men of war and their alleged necessities. Prussian officers got away with a haughtiness and insolence of manner towards non-aristocratic civilians that was not to be encountered anywhere else, though something like it could be encountered in most continental countries, and civilians in most countries might be called out or beaten up for aspersing the honour of monarch, army or nation. No scientific comparative study of the numbers of ex-service men in government posts has come to my attention, but throughout Germany it was certainly very large. The military ethos continued to dominate public administration, partly because much of it was in effect military administration managed by military men, partly because higher civil servants mostly came from the same social circles as the soldiers. The physical presence of the military was especially prominent in fortified towns (under permanent army control) and garrison towns (in which over half the Prussian urban population lived). One soldier to five or six civilians was normal in fortresses; garrison towns ranged from 1:11 (Posen) and 1:14 (Magdeburg and Dantzig) to 1:22 (Köln) and 1:25 (Breslau and Berlin).[21] Soldiers were integrally involved in the social, commercial and administrative existences of these places, and continually interfering in them. Until Prussia at last equipped itself with an efficient police-force in the fifties, the military were relied on for all but the pettiest of police duties, from guarding post offices and prisons to suppressing riots – riots sometimes caused, in fact, by military abrasiveness itself. Even when there was a police force adequate for ordinary peace-keeping purposes, troops continued to be used whenever riots or strikes got serious. In sharp contrast with Britain, the military in Germany launched into repressive police action with ruthless readiness, immune at civil law for whatever hurt they might do to civilians who got in their way. The commanders of the military districts into which Prussia was divided (headquarters respectively Berlin, Königsberg, Stettin, Magdeburg, Posen, Breslau, Munster and Coblentz) enjoyed precedence over the civil authorities whenever circumstances seemed to them to demand it. Evaluation of the circumstances was up to them, not civilians, and they were perfectly protected from civil or political check and censure by the independence of military law and administration right up to the only sovereign authority the *Junkers* would acknowledge – their king. Forming in some respects a state within the State, and embodying values which gave them something to live and die for which was ultimately separable from it, their army nevertheless remained integral to the ordinary life of the people and from its privileged position influenced them (or attempted to influence them; civilian resistance to it never wholly ceased) in its direction – exactly the opposite of what the liberal reformers and defensive *Landwehr* enthusiasts of 1808-19 had hoped for.

German liberals however did not easily abandon hope. They continued to fight this battle and to retain some appearance of being able to win it until the mid-sixties. After 1848, the battleground was in the *Landtag* and shifted from the question of army composition and character to that (ultimately the crucial one) of constitutional control. While every other army in every European country that had any sort of parliament moved, if it moved at all, in the direction of parliamentary control, the Prussian monarch and officer corps found enough support from conservative and nationalist groups to take on democratic liberalism in a prolonged constitutional confrontation and in the end to beat it. (See below, p.283.) The officers claimed, as was becoming their wont in States with representative governments, to be non-political, but of course they were (as officer corps always are when they say that) acting with counter-revolutionary intent. 'Out of the mud-bath of a new revolution,' wrote General von Roon, the Minister of War, to his king in June 1861, 'Prussia can emerge with new strength; in the sewer of doctrinaire liberalism she will rot without redemption....'[22] *Junkers* like Roon *hated* liberalism (let alone democracy, socialism, etc., or even Roman Catholicism) and with the king at the prow and Bismarck at the helm they thwarted it, even though 'large sections of the population' supported it. The army remained *their* army, and in their minds equivalent with their country. As General von Roon put it at the end of his career:

> an efficient army ... is the only feasible protection against the red as well as against the black spectre. If they ruin the army the end has arrived; then farewell to Prussian military glory and to German splendour![23]

Something must be said about the non-Prussian parts of Germany, other than Austria which demands separate treatment. By Germany we mean the Congress of Vienna's German Confederation set up in 1815, a league or diplomatic alliance of thirty-five 'sovereign princes' and four 'free cities', and with a federal diet, under Austrian presidency, a sort of negotiating body, to meet in its 'capital' in Frankfurt. This was a simpler and more 'rational' arrangement for the German-speaking nations, collectively conceived by pan-German nationalists as their *Volk*. It offered a structure within which combinations for mutual advantage and even mergers might be organized. Some things along those lines were indeed to be achieved in the years to come. But 'sovereignty!' is well known to be a cry that no one gives up readily; and besides that, every German political question had to be considered in the light of the greatest German political question of all: were the German-speaking peoples – the nations within the *Volk* – to be brought together under Hohenzollern or Habsburg headship?

A resolution (for the time being) of that question, into whose complicated history we have no call to go, was not found till the sixties; the first phase of it, after the failure of rational discourse, being the appeal to 'blood and iron' in the war of 1866: Prussia and some minor north German States against Austria and all the rest – Bavaria, Saxony, Hanover, Baden, Württemberg, the two Hesses, Nassau, etc. The nature and purpose of that short sharp war were strikingly like those of the war just concluded in North America: a war between 'brothers' to settle whether their family was to stay united or not. Austria's defeat meant the dissolution of the Confederation and the Habsburgs' withdrawal from it, leaving the Hohenzollerns as top dogs of what became a few years later, in phase two, the German Empire: an empire comprising all the non-Habsburg German countries, sealed in the blood-brotherhood of the war of 1870-1, governed from Berlin, and provocatively proclaimed in, of all places, the palace of Versailles, then under German military occupation.

With Prussia thus taking undisputed lead of the ancient *Volk* and mythically restored *Reich*, it was only to be expected that Prussian ways of doing things would decisively oust the Austrian and even French ones with which they had so far been in competition. This did not mean militarization *ab novo*, except insofar as Prussian ways were more sharply militaristic than the easier-going ways they now sought to correct. The other German States had been markedly military all along. Their traditions were unbroken, and their international vocation remained fixed. The 1815 Confeder-

213

ation expected each member State to contribute an appropriate force to the common army whose most likely use, men supposed, would be to resist French imperial resurgence: 35,000 troops from Bavaria, 13,054 from Hanover, etc., down to the 2000 due from Hamburg, Bremen and Lübeck together.[24] Prussia willingly took the lead in planning for this eventuality; *Die Wacht am Rhein* was a popular Prussian song of 1840. Animosity against France was not so keen in the other German States, nor was Prussia particularly popular with them; but their armies mattered to them hardly less than the Prussian one mattered in Prussia's spreading lands. Uniforms were as familiar in the streets, bands in the squares and public parks; local economies turned as largely on supplying and servicing garrisons in their barracks and billets and were as much affected by the requisitioning of labour and vehicles during manoeuvres; officers were probably less exclusive and arrogant and military manners less abrasive, but the same military air suffused civil administration and police-work; the principal difference from Prussia was simply the method of recruitment, which was generally more like the French one – general conscription, with exemptions for protected categories and permission of substitutes for those who could afford them.[25] The other German armies had not got their roots as wide and deep down among the people as the Prussian one, and they did not spend as much on them. On the surface, however, they made much the same impression.

17

FRANCE : AN ARMY
DE-POLITICIZED

France faced peculiar problems in achieving its version of the common goal, the establishment of a post-war armed force suited to a counter-revolutionary role. It was in France, after all, that the twenty-years' troubles had begun, and France had gone through a variety of political character-changes since then. How many attributes from those years remained? How much of the experience and achievement of those years were Frenchmen willing, even able, to forget?

The culture and politics of France in fact were to carry the stamp of these extraordinary years through all the years to come. Divisions in French society were to be drawn largely in terms of them, with pride in at least some of the military achievements of the French people between 1792 and 1814-15 as a constant element in their historico-political thinking. Hardly any ordinarily patriotic Frenchman, one must suppose, could bring himself positively to detest and deplore events like Ulm, Austerlitz, Jena and Tilsit. Whatever the man at the top was like, it was France's grandeur that was proclaimed; good Restoration monarchists who conscientiously abhorred Napoleon were not obliged to regret everything that had been done in his time – nor even, perhaps, everything earlier done by the Revolution he collared.

This natural ambivalence of attitudes helped to ease and overcome the very problems it created. 'Veterans' alive and still more or less serviceable at the début of Louis XVIII's France may individually have liked to give a political or ideological description to what they had been fighting for – 'La Révolution', 'Liberté, Egalité, Fraternité', 'Humanité', the Code Napoléon and all the benefits going with it, etc. – but they had been fighting also for France, many of them under more than one of its successive varieties of government. Only if their political principles or emotional attachments were unusually powerful or obsessive would patriotism not be enough to ease their transfers of allegiance. When the Bourbons came back, some ardent Bonapartists did in fact find the transfer beyond them, and became a disgruntled sect of retired or half-pay soldiers (the *demi-soldes*) notable for big talk and military nostalgia. Some of them preferring to be republican than royalist would merge with the Republicans proper, men whose devotion to the Jacobin creed of 1793-4 made the restored Bourbon as distasteful to them as the military dictator he replaced; from the king's government's point of view a more dangerous set of men than the Bonapartists, because politically more adept, not so military in make-up, and rather given to believing that they were participating in an international revolutionary movement with 'history' on its side. They were to make big trouble for the men of order; we shall meet them and their foreign friends more extensively in the next chapter. But in 1815 for the time being they had to sing small, while the men of order, with sometimes very disorderly counter-revolutionary 'throne and altar' mob support, imposed the new régime and purged its civil and military branches of persons unlikely to back it.

The purge of 1815-16 overlapping with an urgent economy campaign – the new French government being as anxious as any in Europe to cut its armed forces down to a size it could afford – it will be understood that not all of the 15,000 officers dismissed were got rid of because they were considered politically unreliable, though many certainly were. Some Napoleonic veterans who did stay on, or who were re-admitted to the service after the first furies of Restoration were over, remained suspect and, within their regiments, unpopular. But more significant for the future and more representative of what was happening in French society at large was the large number of ex-Napoleonic soldiers who accepted the constitutional monarchy without much difficulty, even if without much enthusiasm. At their head were several of Napoleon's Marshals, whose sense of obligation to their country (not unmixed with a sense of obligation to themselves, their families and their fortunes) had detached them from him before it was too late, or who, even after abetting Napoleon's 'hundred days', as did Soult, Suchet and Grouchy, were allowed to work their way back into public esteem and trust until at last, with all the other Marshals who survived past 1815 (twenty-two in all), they died in their beds full of years and honours; prime proof, until outclassed by Napoleon's grandson at the end of the forties, of the success with which France digested and throve on its Napoleonic inheritance.

One of those Marshals, Gouvion-Saint-Cyr, War Minister in 1817-19, gave his name to the law of 1818 which ingeniously re-established a national army in a style designed to satisfy a variety of expectations: of the conservative royalist Ultras, that it would be immune to Republicanism and Bonapartism; of Ultras and the bourgeoisie together, that it would reliably stand by government against the mob; of military professionals, that it would be up to its job in case of war; of French national sentiment generally, that it would be 'worthy of its great past', etc.; and of mere political prudence, that it might keep in the army, under military discipline, troublesome characters liable to be more dangerous outside. To the common preoccupations of Restoration governments throughout Europe were thus added peculiar problems in respect of loyalty and obedience; potentially disruptive ideas and elements, which the other crowned heads of Europe could perceive as external to their armed forces, could not be so simply seen by a king of France. Prudence in the French context dictated accommodation of those ideas and elements rather than their wholesale suppression. Some Ultras of course were willing to go in for suppression, by means of a Bourbon army separate from society as the pre-Revolutionary army more or less had been. But where would such an army come from? Frenchmen showed only less readiness to volunteer as time went by. Conscription, then, seemed virtually indispensable, besides in any case being popular with liberals and democrats, to whom it spoke of equality and civic virtue. But total conscription, after the 1814 Prussian model, would be far too democratic for conservatives and bourgeoisie to bear, besides being needlessly costly; while professional opinion on the whole preferred a smaller army of long-service soldiers to a larger army of short-service ones. Saint-Cyr's scheme therefore angled to have it every way at once. 'The army relies entirely on volunteers', it began, but if they fell short it would rely on conscription. Service was to be for six years – just long enough to 'make a man a soldier' and, with luck, sufficiently to unfit him for

217

other occupations to the point where he would wish to re-enlist and so contribute to a professional core. But service was not universally compulsory. Bourgeois prejudices had to be respected. In the first place, only a small proportion of the annual class (40,000 out of about 300,000) would be needed, and they would be picked by ballot. Secondly, anyone thus selected (it was called 'drawing a bad number') could do as he had been able to do through most of the preceding quarter-century, and buy a replacement (who might well be an ex-soldier; another tributary stream of professionalism). Six years with the colours was to be followed by six years with the reserve, which would also provide useful occupation, in time of national danger, for that awkward class of frustrated Frenchman, the *demi-soldes* veterans of Napoleonic wars for whom no full-time military employment had been found. Saint-Cyr was above all anxious to incorporate those veterans and their tradition in France's continuing army. 'The question of the army,' he said in debate, 'is a national question. We must ask whether we have two armies and two nations, one of which is cursed and considered unworthy to serve king and country. And . . . we must ask if we will again call on those soldiers who made France great, or if we will condemn them as a threat to our security.'[26] Another pre-1815 principle he was successful in retaining in face of aristocratic presumption and administrative interference was that of officers' admission and promotion by merit. In France alone this principle prevailed. The 1818 law opened two doors to 'the epaulette': either through one of the two great military schools (Saint-Cyr for the infantry, Metz for the artillery and engineers) or through the ranks. At least one-third of promotions to sub-lieutenant were to be of non-commissioned officers. The French officer corps, thus recruited, was unique in Europe.

The outline of Gouvion-Saint-Cyr's structure remained intact for nearly fifty years. The classes whose opinions mattered most to government were satisfied with it; the classes who were not satisfied with it did not matter so much. Of course it underwent changes, following the stormy course of French politics (revolutions in 1730 and 1748; kings from two mutually antipathetic families followed, after a short-lived Second Republic, by a plebiscitary dictator who proclaimed himself Emperor). The demands of the international situation after the Crimean War brought external force to bear too, and at last prompted big changes in the later sixties. It was appropriate that those changes came too late to save the Emperor's armies from the König-Kaiser's, for domestic considerations all along were the prime determinants of change in military organization. Until 1866 no one seems to have had any idea that the French army might not be well able to look after itself in any international conflict that might occur. Therefore it could be shaped according to domestic needs and opportunities. These continued to centre on the two standing arguments already mentioned: the 'loyalty' of the army and the propriety of the conscription system as actually operated.

The Revolution of 1830 showed that the reliability of the army was still a big problem. The Revolution could not have happened unless the army had let it happen; some of it was actually achieved by soldiers themselves. Republicans and fellow-travellers had been working on the troops ever since the Restoration – all the easier to do, since relatively few were secluded in self-contained barracks – and found response especially among NCOs, who could share with the men general criticisms of army management and conditions while having their own keen interest in the making of changes that might expedite promotion. A trickle of mutinous and seditious incidents preceded (as it was also for a few years to follow) the mass incidents of 1830; some of them were undoubtedly revolutionary, and some NCOs and officers were subsequently found to have used their positions for political purposes. But, as Douglas Porch has shown us, much of the steam in the army's revolutionary-looking activities came, not directly from the republican ideology with which it tended to colour its speech, but simply from 'job-dissatisfaction' and the very real difficulty of knowing whom to obey, in revolutionary situations such as France seemed likely to go on producing.

The July Monarchy produced in the end a fairly satisfactory solution to these linked problems. Casimir Perier's government, with Soult at the War Ministry (another Napoleonic Marshal still going strong!), began it early in 1831 when the army was still riddled with insubordination and republican politicking. A resolute mixture of purges, punishments, amnesties and real reforms in service conditions steadily prevailed against the disorders, which reached their peak in the Lyon garrison's evaporation in the face of insurrection at the end of 1831 – a collapse of order promptly remedied by the arrival of Soult and the

Duke of Orleans at the head of 20,000 men. Soult's army law, passed early the following year, amended the 1818 system in ways calculated to make the army more professional; principally by upping the term of service to seven years, and letting slip still further than it had already slipped, Saint-Cyr's provision of a reserve (which had worked badly when the line army marched into Spain in 1823, and which, involving now again the 1830-revived National Guard, was politically contentious). This distancing of the army from society, materially effected by the more copious provision of barrack accommodation so as to minimize billetting, was viewed with misgivings by radical and liberal ideologues who sought through the forties to shorten the term of service and to universalize conscription. In vain! The bourgeoisie did not like the prospect because it would compel their sons to serve, besides calling up more urban workers, politically the most alarming. 'Expert' military opinion still on the whole much preferred a long-term army fed partly by replacements.

The revolutions of 1848-51 seemed to prove both, from their own points of view, right. In striking contrast with 1830-1, the troops remained generally obedient to their officers and their officers generally accepted the *de facto* replacements of Louis Philippe successively by the Provisional Government, the Second Republic, and at last the third Napoleon. Some part of this easy sliding from one allegiance to another was due to military preference. His sons' cheerful bellicosity in fact did nothing to toughen the image of the peace-loving 'bourgeois monarch', and since moreover he put up no fight for his throne, the army was ready to think the best of the men who were ousting him. It protected them unhesitatingly against the Paris insurrection in June. But there was nothing about the style or ideas of the Second Republic to make the army love it. Louis Napoleon on the other hand, his star steadily rising from the presidential elections of December 1848, offered the army a great deal: all the magic of the family name, unconcealed appreciation of military worth, an active and interventionist foreign policy, and so on. And he was President, head of the executive side of government, to whom the officers had earlier that year sworn allegiance. It was therefore not too difficult for them to rationalize acceptance of a *coup d'état* which appealed to most of them anyway, and of which General Saint-Arnaud and others were primary makers. Only strongly-principled Republican officers were likely not to go along with it. The most obvious and politically active of them – Cavaignac, Changarnier, Leflô, Lamoricière, Charras *et al.* – were among the arrestees on the night of the coup. With them out of the way, the army accepted the coup without a squeak. The third Napoleon was much more congenial than the Second Republic to this by now very professional, de-civilianized army. But personal preference was not the only factor at work. The French army by now had become thoroughly de-politicized too. The active Republicanism which had continued to fascinate so many soldiers in the early thirties had been ironed out; Algeria had opened up a new field for military enterprise, glory and promotion, and the army was fast acquiring a stolidly non-political stance at least to the extent that serving soldiers were expected to keep out of politics, were kept out to the extent that the franchise was withheld from them, and concentrated their minds on serving *France*, not this or that ideological representation of it. They acquired a tradition of obedience to whatever authority represented France and of passive acquiescence in it, though with a natural predilection for parties of national pride and order.

Napoleon III's army, which made such a mark in the fifties, had increasingly the character of a long-service professional one, very unlike the Prussian army which was soon to thrash it, and a lot further from the ordinary run of civilian life. Embarrassed by the difficulties of training all the raw recruits suddenly enlisted during the Crimean War, the government in 1855 modified the recruitment system in a way meant to raise professional quality without upsetting the bourgeoisie. Instead of finding and paying for substitutes (*remplacements*) they would pay to be exonerated from military service, and the government would use the money to induce NCOs and good soldiers whose time had run out to re-enlist. Two thousand francs plus proved insufficient as a lure for such. Not much happened except that the commercial companies which had done well out of providing replacements (price in the Bordeaux region swinging between 1250 and 2000 francs, 1821-53)[27] gave way to companies doing well out of insuring the prosperous against the risk of having to pay for exoneration; companies with pleasant names like the *Caisse militaire des enfants*, *L'Avenir*, *Caisse de Libération*, and the *Aigle Impérial Libérateur*. About 20 per cent of the 'bad numbers' men called to military service thus continued to get out of it – a figure which had been pretty constant from the start. But it was not long before Napoleon III's government, awed by Prussia's success in the 1866 war against Austria and by the prospect consequently of a vast Prussian-style North German Confederation army to deal with, decided that their people must at last take conscription seriously. Nothing was achieved until after nearly two years' acrimonious public debate, and the 1868 army law was a messy compromise achieving very little of the reformers' purpose: five years' line service followed by four in the reserve *or* five months' line and nine years' reserve, for those called-up and unable to escape; escape still possible by both exonerations and replacement, on condition simply of two weeks' training every year in a new citizen reserve, practically segregated from the proper army, the *Garde Mobile*. Whether or not this might in time have turned into anything worthwhile, time never allowed to appear. Within two years the north German armies were in France and Napoleon III's, numerically much smaller and ineptly managed, were laid low at Sedan and Metz. The question of inept management apart, it became clear to even the most hidebound blimps that a nation not prepared to call the whole of its manhood into military service could not hope to stand up in war to one which was.

18

THE GENDARME OF EUROPE

It was Nicholas I (1825-55) who earned that description, but his predecessor Alexander was already rehearsing for the role in 1815. Russia appeared at the end of the wars as rather a superpower, ready to play as dominating a part in continental affairs as the other great powers would permit, and resembling the other superpower, the UK, in several suggestive respects. Russia and Britain were the only actively expansionist imperial powers (Russia's expansion being of course all landward in Asia) and Russia was for nearly two decades the only other naval power of any consequence in Europe. Superficially it might appear that the Tsar of All the Russias was as ready to lay down law for the continent as was His Britannic Majesty to lay it down on the oceans.

There, however, the resemblance ended. The Russian ability to throw its weight about internationally was not matched by material ability to do so. Unlike Britain, which soon detached itself from the repressive interventionism favoured by the Tsars, Russia proved to be something of a paper bear. Its power, though immense in the aggregate, was for territorial and systemic reasons incapable of concentration. The British navy was able to concentrate the armed strength of its empire more economically and even more quickly than could the Russian army; again and again through the first half of the century military analysts were to find it necessary to explain how it was that, with an army on paper of more than a million, the Tsar could never put into the field more than about 300,000, and even those with painful slowness. The quality of the armies and navies when at last they materialized left much to be desired too. A curious mixture of modern and antiquated, more like the Habsburg land forces than any others but not really like any other land forces at all, they were

– how could it have been otherwise? – a natural military representation of what was generally the most 'backward' and repressive society in Europe.

The more 'modern' part of the army, without which it could not have figured in the big league at all, was of course to be found within the officer corps. Foreign observers repeatedly remarked upon its contrasts, sharper and starker by far than anywhere else: lethargy, ignorance, corruption and incapacity in depressingly large quantity at one end, intelligence, energy and polished cosmopolitan professionalism at the other. The top military colleges were good, not unfit to match the best further west, and when their products came west to visit they made a good impression; but not many officers passed through them, the educational level of the whole was low, and what there was of intelligence and perceptiveness among the bright minority (many of them not 'Russian' Russians at all but Baltic German or Polish Russians, and even complete foreigners) had no power to leaven such a lump. The specialized arms were capable, and the engineer in charge of Sebastopol, Todleben (a Baltic German), became in the fifties the most famous of his kind; but in Russia even more than elsewhere, the standing and influence of the 'mere technicians' was low. Another vein of contrasts which astonished the foreign observer was in officer behaviour. The messes of the smart aristocratic regiments were gorgeous, officers had comfortable lives with lots of servants and material perks and rake-offs, but here was an army in which it was known for senior officers to strike or publicly menace officers junior to them. In a sense, such behaviour was nothing to be surprised at, physical roughness in personal relations being a national characteristic and flogging and beating being standard sanctions of social subordination; each level being accustomed to bully and beat the one below it. Yet western officers *were* surprised when they saw a Russian general chasing a colonel off a parade-ground with curses and blows.

About five-sixths of the Russian officer corps were 'noble' by one definition or another.[28] Service to the Emperor on either the military or the civil side was virtually obligatory for noble families (they forfeited their privileges if they missed out for three generations) and even though the army had a smaller ratio of officers to men than any other, the number needed was still immense. Most young noblemen therefore, without any professional preparation, served their minimal terms of five or ten years with line regiments and withdrew when they could to merely nominal service on the rolls of the *depôt*. Hardly any, it seems, went into the navy. Nicholas sought to overcome aristocratic disdain for it by making his second son Constantine admiral-in-chief, but like most navies it remained the province of the sea-faring professional or professional careerist, and like the navy of the Ottoman Empire continued to rely considerably on foreign talent. Commissioned service in either armed force brought noble status of a sort with it: each degree of status being exactly stipulated and matched against its civil equivalent in the celebrated Table of Ranks, the official backbone of the most formally, though not the most efficiently, subordinated society we are dealing with.

These armed forces were mostly composed of very long service and, initially at any rate, reluctant conscripts. Every two years or so came the levy of so many per thousand, allocated to the several classes of the population by the district governors and actually picked by local authorities among whom the nobility inevitably predominated. No one wanted to go, not least because it was – given the terms, conditions and risks of service – not so much a life as a death sentence; twenty-five years was the stipulated term, and although men of unblemished characters might be furloughed after ten or fifteen years, they might not survive long enough to enjoy it. Bourgeois families and urban artisans escaped by paying for substitutes. Recruiting occasions were tragic ones for families, and strong drink – the recruiter's elixir all over Europe – was regularly used to raise the victim's spirits above those of his relations. Some sizeable proportion of men picked (they might be of any age from eighteen to forty) continued to be the criminals, troublemakers, misfits and disobedient sons who were tradition-ally got rid of in this way; for such, the army was literally a form of punishment and incarceration. To escape finding themselves among the rest, the proportion picked simply because by no other way could the demand be met, young men sometimes mutilated themselves or had their families do it for them. Cutting off toes or fingers, and pulling out front teeth, indispensable for cartridge opening, were the usual procedures; but even grislier things happened in Jewish communities, whose general exemption (on condition of substitution) Nicholas terminated in 1827 and among

225

whom a figure known as 'the crippler' is heard of covertly getting to work on the newborn.

A pre-conscription source of recruits which Russia uniquely developed was boys. In every country some attempt was made to secure a regular supply of malleable youths from army or navy schools, orphanages, etc., but only in Russia did much come of it. Only in Russia, moreover, were soldiers positively encouraged to get married – presumably because law required *all* soldiers' sons to follow their fathers' boot-steps; 'this principle [being] carried so far that children borne by soldiers' wives are claimed by the State, though the husband may have been serving at the other end of the empire for five or ten years.'[29] Most of these boys, with others scooped up elsewhere, were brought up from quite a tender age (perhaps as young as six) in military schools and therefore known as 'cantonists'. Inured to hardship and knowing nothing of any other form of life, these became the principal source of supply of NCOs, who mattered all the more in the Russian army in proportion as it was not the practice for officers to see much of or take any interest in the troops. Much less seems to be known about naval recruiting but an apparently sensible British writer about the condition of Jews in Russian Poland (where they were most numerous) said: 'Boys from ten to twelve years of age are usually carried off and sent to naval establishments to be trained for sailors', and about one in three Russian navy sailors were, he reckoned, Jewish.[30] He also said that about two-thirds of those wretched lads 'die prematurely from the hardships they undergo'. Two-thirds seems dreadfully many but unfortunately is not incredible. The Russian dissident exile Herzen could never forget the pathetic 'chain-gang' of juvenile conscripts he once saw. The Russian armed forces like the Russian people at large were accustomed to severities from all quarters, and their military mortality continued extraordinarily high. Bungling, tactical inflexibility and their own blindly courageous ethic combined to make their losses in action higher than was thought bearable elsewhere, while bungling and corruption combined with low standards in the army medical service to boost losses not in action. Most of their huge mortality in the Turkish war of 1828-9 was due to scurvy.[31] Thirty-eight out of every 1000 died from sickness annually through the forties – about twice the 'western' military rate.[32] The British people might not have thought so badly of pre-Nightingalean Scutari if they had known what things were like inside Sebastopol.

The Cossacks and the Military Colonies demand notice. Little need be added to what has been said already about the Cossacks, except that new varieties of them were constantly being planted and raised as the empire spread south – and eastwards. By far the largest single body of them remained the Cossacks of the Don – at the turn of the fifties about 35,000 men, most of them cavalry of their irregular kind. But the rest of the more-than-100,000 Cossack irregulars nominally available were by then spread from Bessarabia and the Black Sea (Tshornamor) on the one side, through the Sea of Azov (naval Cossacks) and the Kuban and Terek across the northern edge of the Caucasus through Astrakhan to the lands of the Bashkirs and Kalmuks, the Tungusians, Buriates and other Siberians, and the people around Lake Baikal.[33] Of only limited use in regular European-style warfare, they contributed much to the régime's internal security capability and their regions of settlement or, to put it simply, colonies, constituted a military frontier rather like the Habsburgs' Balkan one.

The same principle of planting troops in strategically vital territories partly explained the most remarkable institution of all, the Military Colonies developed rapidly after 1815. Fancied especially, and actually pioneered on his own estates, by Alexander's most ruthless adviser, Arakcheev, they represented the biggest and bluntest bid made by any European government through the whole of our period to militarize totally a segment of peasant society. Near St Petersburg and in the Ukraine, facing respectively the strategic threats posed by Sweden and Turkey (feared not so much on their own account but because of the backing they were expected to receive from Britain and Austria), were established these novel military administrations whose combined objects were to maintain soldiers directly upon land they helped to cultivate and to turn the whole male peasant population therein into soldiers. The most rigorous of them made Frederick II's Prussia by comparison look more like Rhode Island. Everything was done in military style, including discipline. Peasants had to turn out for drill, classes, 'fatigues', etc. when they were not in the fields supposedly teaching the soldiers billetted on them how to farm. In such circumstances the only things that had made peasant life worth living, the semi-autonomous village community and what little family life it allowed, completely disappeared. The infantry ones of the north-west were the most rigorous and uncomfortable, being mostly planted by military martinets on land often agriculturally difficult and filled by Crown peasants forcibly drafted in from their aboriginal villages. Whether and in what sense these military collectives can ever have seemed successful to any but a martinet mind is difficult to say, for foreign visitors were hardly ever allowed near them, even well-placed Russians could not easily visit them, and when the Tsar and his entourage did so they were of course shown only what would favourably impress them. Unremitting peasant resistance culminating in mass rebellion in mid-1831 (fearfully punished) helped to explain changes and softenings in their arrangements in the early thirties. They continued to be established in the Ukraine and the Caucasus into the fifties. Cavalry regiments fitted less uncomfortably into Ukrainian village life than infantry, the colonies were implanted into the peasants' own villages, variations seen to have been made to suit local needs and conditions, and by 1847 when the Austrian Pidoll wrote his comparison of them with the institutions of his own country's military frontier, only an 'ordinary passport' was needed to visit them. Thus the original arch-militarist, quasi-penal-colony design slightly faded, but what remained was still pretty fearful, with absurd regimentation and 'inspections' of farm operations, and a peasantry actually glad to get out of it into the army proper.[34]

Military Colonies were thus experimented with as an attempt towards resolving Russia's main military dilemma: how to ensure internal security at the same time as providing enough force for all external contingencies. Concentrating a strong force for a particular campaign along any point of that giant perimeter took months not only because of the distances to be travelled, but also because it could not be done at the expense of the forces planted all around the realm for security reasons. The British government, whose resources were overstretched in a similar way, would have been strategically hamstrung if Britain had not been an island, and if internal security remained as big a worry. But once the new police forces were functioning effectively on both sides of the Irish Channel, the UK could be nearly denuded of troops without internal risk. (Risk of continental commitment was of course another matter.) Russia however had to maintain a respectable level of forces all round its frontiers all the time besides a substantial military presence throughout the more populous parts of the empire, to keep down the peasants and the minority peoples. An estimate of the Russian army's disposition at the time of the Turkish war of 1828-9 reckoned that only 181,000 men had been available for the campaign because 472,000 were tied down thus:[35]

Caucasus	80,000	Revenue collection	6,000
Siberia etc.	21,000	Cossacks at home	40,000
Finland	25,000	Garrisons of capital and fortified cities	80,000
Lithuania and Poland	40,000		
Military Colonies	60,000	Interior Guard (i.e., in effect, *police*)	120,000

The Polish national insurrection of 1830 was only able to survive as long as it did because Russia took so long to bring sufficient force against it. When the crisis of what western Europeans too simply call 'the Crimean War' prompted Russia to extraordinary measures, including the raising of archaic militia in the western provinces, some of the troops from Siberia had been marching for more than twelve months before they arrived at St Petersburg or Poland, and all had to march for weeks or months from homes to depôts, from depôts to corps concentration points, from there to the front, with all the losses from sickness and desertion that can be imagined, before they were of any practical strategic use.

These acknowledged and notorious military incapacities, culminating at last in the traumatic shocks of 1854-5, helped to produce in Russia effects of the same gigantic order as were later produced by the equally unexpected defeats of 1904 and 1917. If that was the best a serf-supported autocracy could do, then the autocracy must find a better support than serfdom. That the autocracy should radically reform itself was scarcely to be expected. Serfdom, however, had for long been a standing topic of concern within government as well as, subject to the usual Russian hazards of censorship, Siberia etc., outside it. The endemic rebelliousness of a semi-slave peasant populace and the 'backwardness' of mind and methods to which such a populace tended were weighty factors in persuading Alexander at last to do something; there seems to be little doubt but that the post-mortem on the military humiliation was the catalyst which persuaded him to do it at once.

19

BRITANNIA,
AT HOME AND ABROAD

The United Kingdom, like all the other European countries, cut down its army and navy at the end of the wars, retaining the minimum necessary (i.e., what governments considered to be necessary) for tasks as onerous as any and more onerous than most: order and security within the realm, defence against potential (French) aggression, and support of imperial needs overseas. In fact this amounted to a great deal, and was most closely parallelled by Russia, the only other imperially-expanding great power of the age until France began its north African annexations in the thirties. Misled by the absence of the greater part of the armed forces from UK lands and waters, the British people themselves and militarily-uninterested domestic historians have got the impression that the army after Waterloo turned into a prototype of that 'contemptible little army' about which the Kaiser was so mistaken nearly a century later. And what on earth can the navy have been doing when notoriously it never fought another proper battle until 1914?

It is true that the navy quickly shed half its ships. By 1820, of the 1000 or so on its lists at the end of the war, 374 had been sold and 178 broken up.[36] It is true that the army within the same quinquennium more than halved its effective strength: from 234,000 in 1815 to 115,000 in the 1820s.[37] It is true also that there was a taxpayers' revolt immediately peace was concluded, and that army and navy expenditure continued through most of the century (with a few panicky splurges when danger seemed near) to be kept at a cheese-paring minimum, partly because of the perennial sniping of a certain sort of anti-military radical politician, partly because cheese-paring in public expenditure had for many Victorians – Peel and Gladstone not least – a positively religious value. But nevertheless the navy remained the largest and

231

most formidable in the world, and the army, once past the immediate post-war cuts and mood of imperial satiation, maintained until the Crimean War a strength of between about 100,000 and 130,000 which, although unbacked by the reserves that continental powers could also call on, was in itself not negligible beside the armies they normally kept in being. Bismarck's goal in the sixties was to keep the Prussian army size pegged at 1 per cent or a bit more of the total population. The British regular army hung around half that proportion until the mid-fifties, and cost much more per soldier.[38]

The problem for Britain was not how to recruit its armed forces – no debate about that! – but how to bring in enough men from the open labour market to which it was committed. The arguments more or less familiar in every continental country relative to conscription, exemptions etc., and duration of service had no parallel in the UK. There was never any question of compulsion once the wars were over. Impressment for the navy had been loathed by the population at large and evaluated as at best an unfortunate necessity by the patriots and naval officers who had been wont to defend it. No one had maintained that it was desirable in itself. An obligation to serve in the home defence militia remained on the statute book and was in a dilapidated manner sporadically enforced, but until real danger of invasion was perceived (as it was not until 1847) nothing serious would be done about it, and in any case the nation's main line of defence was still its navy. The country's military needs were therefore to be supplied by a mixture of paid professionals, upon whom must fall all the overseas work, and unpaid volunteers, to share some of the burden of work at home.

The Royal Navy had continual difficulty in manning its ships. The difficulty was twofold. First, the recruitment system reverted in 1815 to the haphazard one it had been in peacetime before 1793. 'When a ship was brought into commission, the newly appointed captain and officers had to find their crew. The complement of boys, it is true, came from the flagship, and marines were marched on board from barracks; but the vital part of the crew, the seamen, had to be recruited. Handbills were distributed and placards displayed in the seaport.... Volunteers began to trickle into the local rendezvous, and some might be sent down from the rendezvous at Liverpool or Bristol, or the Tower of London....

232

Eventually the ship sailed....'[39] Completing a crew took many weeks – much depended on the reputation of the captain and the destination – and it can well be imagined that it was many months before a crew thus assembled worked well together. But, impressment apart, this was the way things had always been done. Seamen liked it (because it guaranteed them periods of leave, whose length they could even determine for themselves, in between commissions). To every more efficient alternative scheme could be opposed the objection, so cogent in early-nineteenth-century Britain, that it could cost money. The second major difficulty was simply that naval pay and conditions were unattractive. The glamour of patriotism, the fascination of guns, and the prospect of a pension after twenty-one years' service without more than a five-years' intermission kept some sailors faithful to the navy, but the ever-growing merchant marine offered competition that was hard for Admiralty and parliamentary minds to beat. Naval discipline, though somewhat less savage, remained rigid and rebarbative – life on ship, though somewhat healthier and less drunken, remained lean and hungry – and worst of all, perhaps, in a society which increasingly respected women and marriage, the coarse and callous old naval ways of handling wives, women and sex offended any man with an ordinary sense of family responsibility or a hankering after 'respectability'. Many who signed on soon regretted it. The desertion rate was still about one in thirteen as late as 1846,[40] and apart from that about one in twenty-seven were quitting after only a short period of service.[41] The French, from whom naval challenge was increasingly expected, were supposed to be able to do things much better by their *Inscription Maritime* (though in 1854 they actually didn't).[42] By the turn of the fifties the case for change had become irresistible, and in 1853 it took the form of, first, a rather startling improvement in wages and conditions (e.g., paid leave, sick pay, and a career structure with incentives in it) and second, a resolute attempt to attract more boys into naval schools and so by natural force of circumstances into the service at the right age. Before the efficacy of these reforms could be fully assessed, the Crimean War occurred, exposing most painfully the inadequacy of the old system. The fleet for the Baltic set out late with only handfuls of trained sailors (and those often elderly ones or coastguardsmen from the tiny reserve) leavening the lump of 'cabmen, navvies, butcher boys and riff-raff who piled into the navy'.[43] Admiral Napier scouted for Scandinavian volunteers when he got to the Baltic and lived in terror lest his ill-sailing ships should collide with each other. It was good for Britain that the Russian Baltic fleet was even worse.

That embarrassing experience once past, the 1853 reforms had a chance to work, and on the whole did so, though characteristically the Admiralty, with the unregenerate Treasury on its back, nearly spoilt its new 'model-employer' image by over-precipitateness in economies once the war was over. But it was more clear than ever before that what was needed now was a proper reserve of men adequate to the needs of a navy whose move towards steam power and revolutionized gunnery (rifled steel cannon in turrets, etc.) demanded men of some technical accomplishment. Attempts to form such a reserve from coastguardsmen, pensioners and dockyard workers having failed, a satisfactory one was at last found among the merchant marine, organized in 1859 as the Royal Naval Reserve. Merchant mariners' understandable suspicions of what might be old Admiralty and impressment wolves in new sheep's clothing were gradually overcome; the Admiralty learnt at last the necessity of respecting the susceptibilities of free-born Britons; and patriotism came to the scheme's rescue early in the American Civil War, when popular indignation over the '*Trent*' incident – 'insult to the flag', etc. – bumped the numbers up within a year from 3000 to 12,000. Its average through the remainder of the sixties was about 15,000. At last the Royal Navy looked as if it could rely on getting the men it needed, without making itself a force which Britons hated as much as they loved.

The British army experienced equal difficulty with the navy in filling its ranks and for similar reasons. The difficulty was not so much to get enough men (though there hardly ever were enough) as to get the right sort of men. What the colonels would have liked to fill their regiments with was healthy well-built men from rural regions, of modest intelligence, good morals and conventional patriotism, who would stay in the army for life. Never in our period (nor, as a matter of fact, for several decades subsequently) could the army offer either pay or conditions sure to attract such. Instead of country chaps, they had increasingly to put up with townees, who were smaller and unhealthier and whom colonels suspected of being too 'smart' and politically-minded to be reliable material. Instead of men who signed on with positive motives of eagerness, ambition and patriotism, they got instead men more negatively motivated by desire to get out of civilian life, because they couldn't get on in it. The only respectable families which encouraged sons to enlist seem to have been those with established army traditions; NCOs often came from such. Otherwise, not many joined the army who could keep any sort of a civilian job.

The real basic pay (i.e., what was left after all the deductions, cunningly concealed from the gullible applicant) came out at far less than the least they would get so long as they were in work. Incidental attractions and benefits other than security from civil process, satisfaction of the thirst for adventure, glamour of uniform and weapons and so on only multiplied from the post-Crimean reforms. Already before those flood-loosing events of the early fifties, the death of Wellington and the Crimean scandals, some conscientious and progressive regimental officers had been making small-scale local improvements in the conditions and atmosphere of service at the same time as early Victorian philanthropy was offering uplift and aid from without. Life in many camps and barracks (their number was increasing, as in every other country) was less unhealthy and drink-sodden in 1850 than in 1830, about when those piecemeal 'private-enterprise' improvements seem to have begun. Discipline, too, was perceptibly softening. Whereas 'during the last half of the 1820s, the army was [only] flogging about 1 in 50 soldiers every year', and in 1829 a maximum of 300 lashes was generally imposed, the maximum was down to 50 by mid-century and only 45 rankers were flogged in 1852.[44] So 'the Horse Guards', as the War Office was called after its location, gradually yielded to public opinion, which increasingly held this hateful army habit in abhorrence. Yet officers who argued that it could not be dispensed with were not necessarily brutes or fools. It was not easy to get out of their vicious circle: respectable men not joining the army because, *inter alia*, of flogging; flogging indispensable because so many non-respectable men joining the army. Only slowly and reluctantly did the generals discover that it was possible to maintain discipline without it. It was not absolutely abolished (except of course in military prisons) until 1881.

Soldiers enlisted more or less for life. Wellington and the rest of the army élite had no doubt that long service was best. In practice life meant twenty-one years for infantrymen, twenty-four for the rest. Enlistment for ten years (or twelve) was invited by what was supposed to be a popularizing reform in 1847, but pensions only went to men who re-enlisted for another eleven (or twelve). Given the continuation of the Wellington tradition, the standard practice of alternating periods of service at home and abroad, and the fact that service abroad (India and Africa particularly) often meant fighting, it was not surprising that many British regulars had a battle-hardened air and that the infantry at any rate enjoyed the respect of military experts throughout the continent; the best in the world, probably. But there were not many of them, their death-rate in some parts of the empire was terrifyingly high (12 per cent yearly in Jamaica, 1816-36, and 75 per cent in the 'condemned battalions' or penal corps sent to West Africa, according to Fortescue), and there was no reserve. This latter was the ultimately fateful circumstance. British imperial and commercial interests and expansiveness being as brisk as they were, the British army and navy were all the time stretched to the limits of their capacities. Already by the 1830s shrewd observers were saying what could go on being said with equal justice up to the Second World War; 'our military arrangements are utterly at variance with our foreign relations'.[45] When war with Russia was announced, in the spring of 1854, the UK was nearly denuded of regular troops for the 27,000-strong expeditionary force. Since it was neither prudent nor materially possible similarly to denude the empire of troops to back them, and following its failure to squeeze enough volunteers out of the militia,[46] the government was reduced to the humiliating expedient of advertising in the international underworld of political refugees (mainly Germans and Italians) for mercenaries. Army and navy alike laboured under the same difficulties.

The reactions of British society to what it heard of the events in the Crimean peninsula are too well known to demand space here. Opportunity was now given for a wide-angled review of the whole state of the army, salt being rubbed into the wound of British pride by the scarcely blinkable fact that the French army had managed things better. (Which was very damning evidence of British mismanagement, in as much as the French in fact were not particularly good on the staff and administrative sides; as events would soon show.) Along with pride in the courage of the British soldier, signalized by the invention of the Victoria Cross as an award 'for valour' ('for the merit of conspicuous bravery'), went irritation at the apparent incompetence of the British officer who had, it seemed, let the soldier down. Criticisms of the prevailing system long made by progressive and discontented members of the corps as well as noisier liberal and radical civilian reformers were now consolidated and pressed home in an unprecedented series of parliamentary debates and official inquiries. Were not the manifest shortcomings of British army management – thick-headedness, inflexibility, snobbishness, gerontocracy and so on – attributable above all to 'the purchase system'?

Purchase, as it was commonly known, was an extraordinary peculiarity of the British army – *not* the navy – in the early nineteenth century. Military commissions were still purchased in the Habsburg Empire but even there it had nothing like the centrality it enjoyed in Britain and the consequent social significance. We see in it as signal an instance as may be found of that recurrent phenomenon in the history of armed forces – the primacy, sometimes, of sectional social interests over military efficiency. Yet in some respects it was natural enough. Where else should officers' commissions have been bought and sold from near the top to the very bottom of the corps if not in the country longest familiar with 'market forces' and with, in fact, the most money too? The purchase system had rooted itself through the preceding century and become integral to upper-class control of the army, achieving for the aristocracy and gentry of the UK what law, royal direction, and tradition did for the *Junkers*. Admission to the officer corps of the infantry and cavalry and promotion within them depended almost entirely on the payment of large sums of money according to an official scale, exception made only for the approvals required of the monarch and the colonels of regiments who had certain powers of veto. There was also, it is true, a trickle of appointments and promotions without payment. Artillery and engineer officers did not buy commissions; they earned them as professional qualifications at the Royal Military Academy in Woolwich. In 1842 cadets from the sister institution, the Royal Military College at Sandhurst, were commissioned free too; but Sandhurst in those days was not compulsory, and the numbers were small. The Commander-in-Chief had power to award commissions to, for example, meritorious NCOs in times of shortage, which meant above all during hard-fought campaigns.

Ninety were thus promoted in the Crimea. But the fact remained that about three-quarters of the entire officer corps, and virtually every officer who mattered (because of his rank, office or regiment), entered and rose by purchase; £450 to start as a cornet in the ordinary infantry (over £1000 in the Guards) and a scale going up to £4500 for an ordinary lieutenant-colonelcy.[47] Could officers thus elevated be professionally competent? Could considerations of honour, duty and so on thrive in such a commercial atmosphere? If Gneisenau's comrades had known about it, they would have thought not; but British reputation was protected in this case as in so many others, by the sheer inability of continentals to imagine how different the British could be.

What the critics alleged against such a curious system can be so easily reckoned that we may concentrate more on the case put by its defenders, who formed so much support in parliament that they delayed its final abolition until 1871. First, they argued, character mattered more than cleverness (that was the common argument of defenders of the old order all over Europe) and purchase was not incompatible with professional competence. A gentleman who had invested his capital in a commission could be zealous and diligent in learning the ropes and would not readily fall below the standards of his peer-group; whatever the norm was, the ordinary pressures of officer existence would make individuals conform to it. This of course was true enough, but it did not meet the criticism that the prevailing norm actually was rather low, especially at the 'high society' end of the army: the Guards regiments and the cavalry, where purchase prices were highest, substantial private incomes most necessary, and snobbery and sporting obsessions most rampant. Significantly enough, it was upon these gorgeous but sometimes idiotic characters (one of the worst was the Earl of Cardigan, who after leading 'the charge of the light brigade' with copy-book courage returned at once to his normal existence of neglecting his troops and quarrelling with his colleagues) that examinations of professional competence were last enforced.

More difficult to answer than the argument that purchase kept merit out of the officer corps was the argument that it suppressed such merit as had got in. Zeal and diligence in fact did very little to advance an impecunious career-officer except on service so active as to bring with it a helpfully high death-rate. Some of the best British officers got on well this way in and around India. But so felicitous a conjuncture of helpful circumstances and outstanding merit could not befall every officer more deserving of promotion than comrades who could afford to buy it. The amount of resentment thus caused was only not very apparent, because the prevailing social atmosphere made it unsafe to be more vocal.

Politically the most significant part of the argument in favour of purchase was that it was better for 'freedom'. In British constitutional circumstances there was not much echo of the continental liberal campaign to 'popularize' the army. Only radical leaders of working-class democratic and Irish nationalist movements regretted the availability of armed force to protect the status quo. Middle-class British liberals could accept that, without fearing – after 1832, anyway – that the same armed force would be used to damage their own political interests. When however they pressed for the replacement of purchase by some system likelier to admit more of their own sort to the officer corps, they were told by purchase-defenders that they did not know what was good for them. Would not any other system subject officer appointments to political control? Was it not constitutionally preferable that officers should have the 'independence' of mind and status which purchase gave them? Such men were less likely to serve as unthinking tools of the executive. The system's defenders, when enthusing on this line, almost made the purchase system sound like a bastion of British liberty.

But it was in social terms that the defence ran deepest, and its arguments were most revealing. The purchase system as it actually worked was found to be eminently suitable to British society, by filling its military leadership with the same class as actually led it in most other respects: the aristocracy and gentry. Exception made for the rather new 'urban aristocracy' which was becoming rich and self-confident enough to keep itself apart if it wished to do so, the gentry (as for brevity we will call them) were still the acknowledged social and political élite in the early nineteenth century, relinquishing none of their social and only some of their political power as the century progressed. If purchase (plus colonels' vetoes) kept key parts of the officer corps full of gentry, the country should be grateful. What was good for the gentry was good for Britain. Nor was this socially as restrictive a system as might appear. The army did not want officers who were not gentlemen, but families with enough money could gentrify themselves either by the classic means of buying estates in the country (the required size of estate shrank as the century progressed; address and status mattered more than acreage and income) or by the great device of the so-called public school, whose sociological function was to make young gentlemen out of those who weren't born so, and to protect those who were from non-gentlemanly contamination. Since these schools, which multiplied from the forties, took over the function of élite definition in a society congenitally prone to defer to élites, a nice accommodation was reached between the middle class's desire for access to share in army leadership and the army's preference for officers embodying leaderly quality. The argument often used against promotion from the ranks – that British rankers would not readily obey in the army men they would not naturally defer to outside it – was inverted to justify purchase.

So purchase went on, despite the sudden upsurge of popular criticism in the middle fifties. By the time it ended, it was no longer necessary to keep the officer corps gentlemanly. Gentlemen still ran the army, coming now for the most part through the standardized channels of the 'public schools' and, from the later seventies, Sandhurst. The sociological advantages of purchase could be retained, without its scandals and corruptions. Despite a few famous examples of 'log-cabin to White House' successes, the British officer corps was still no place for the social outsider.

The Royal Navy may be more summarily dealt with, for its officer recruitment was never controversial in the same way. Connections with men of political or professional influence continued to matter a good deal but purchase had never figured in naval history, professional competence had always been indispensable, and there was nothing in naval life to attract the horse-minded. That is not to say that the navy was immune from British class consciousness. It had its standards, and life in the gun room and wardroom were calculated to make sure that aspirant and newly-commissioned officers observed them. Professional examinations in themselves posed little problem, being merely formalizations of what had long been practised; but it was found to matter not a little, who qualified. That same contempt of the supposedly superior fighting officers for the supposedly inferior 'technical' men which for so long kept the specialized branches of

240

the army in social servitude now showed itself in the navy. 'Masters' were the first to press their claim. No ship could be sailed efficiently and manoeuvred precisely without a good master in charge; he was the arch-technician of sail. But by birth and training he was almost certainly 'no gentleman', and although long since admitted to the wardroom, he did not receive the social cachet of a commission until 1843. Close behind him came, inevitably from the 1840s, the arch-technician of the age of steam, the engineer; not normally from the lower deck, but all the same 'no gentleman' either, and no more welcome in the wardroom (he did not get in until 1847). Whether things were comfortable for him when he did, was another matter.

The duties on which these armed forces were almost ceaselessly employed, though for the most part routine, even commonplace, had implications and an aura which gave them peculiar meaning for the British people and the international reputation of the British State. They included a great deal of war or something so like it as to make no difference. The British army in fact was getting more experience of war until the sixties than the Prussian or Austrian armies, and more than the French until their Algerian campaigns became sizeable in the forties. Either wars or annexations normally involving some deployment of military force were going on almost all the time in Africa and India and countries adjacent. (Let it be noted *en passant* that about half the total number of British-recruited troops in India before the great 'Mutiny' of 1857-8 were in the service of the East India Company, with its equivalent to Sandhurst at Addiscombe, and were not directly in the service of the British crown.) Ambitious officers, especially if they were impecunious, used to go to India or the colonies, because only there had they a chance to distinguish themselves in action and find ways cleared to promotion. The British navy too, knew a large amount of professional busy-ness. It was not so often formally 'at war' but it found itself engaged in endless naval operations in its self-appointed role of police force of the high seas, maintaining what became known as the Pax Britannica in one of the several Roman imperial parallels classically-educated Britons loved to draw; the most ringing of them being Palmerston's claim in 1850 that the ubiquity and irresistibility of the navy had updated *Civis romanus sum* for the benefit of the British subject. That British subjects – even rather

241

seedy ones like 'Don Pacifico' – should be prime beneficiaries of the Pax Britannica was not surprising. But in fact the charting of the seas really was a boon to all who went down to them in ships, as was the suppression of piracy, while the very considerable diminution of slave-trading for which also the Royal Navy was responsible was only not a boon to the cruel men who profited from it, besides being an advantage to humanity at large. What with the Crimean and the various China wars, the destruction of the Turkish fleet at Navarino in 1827, and an assortment of bombardments and 'pacific blockades' on top of all the endless semi-belligerent activity against pirates and slavers – and with the proviso made, that none of this was against an efficient modern naval power like the USA or France – it is clear that the navy, like the army serving overseas, was kept in good operational trim.

Our British section must conclude with a glance at the army serving 'at home'. The UK had big problems of internal security like the other great powers, and one of them had unique elements: the maintenance of order among a periodically distressed modern industrial proletariat. This was already a problem before the war ended; we met the Luddites in chapter 10. But it seems to have presented the British army with no task substantially different from that faced by all armies, pending the invention and implementation of an adequate system of police. A city out of control was a nasty problem in its own right, whether it had steam-powered factories in it or not. London in 1848 was only a different military problem from London in 1780 to the extent that it was a good deal bigger. Industrialization soon brought advantages to the army too; troops for example could get from place to place by rail much more quickly than insurgents could on foot, as the Chartists found out to their cost. Most of the industrial sector of society in any case still inhabited towns and villages more 'rural' in character and setting than 'urban', and Ireland, source of the greater part of the problems for the greater part of the time, was almost wholly so. No – it was not industrialization that stretched British military resources so much as dispersion and demand, a challenge which the railway, when at last it came through the thirties, could only partly meet. In autumn 1828, Spiers tells us, 'every available soldier, excluding [only] those of the capital, was placed at the disposal of the Lord Lieutenant of Ireland', who promptly commandeered most of them. How could 'an organized insurrection' in provincial Britain then have been met?[48] The situation became critical in 1831-2, when rioting relative to the Reform Bill required the presence of 19,000 troops in urban England, London especially, just when Irish society was convulsed by 'the tithe war' – peasants with scythes etc. and the odd blunderbuss resisting military-backed tithe collection, and casualties in double figures a common occurrence.

To some extent the British government could, like all others, stretch its domestic military means by the use of pensioners (over 8000 enrolled by the end of the Chartist disturbances) and politically-safe volunteers; typically 'tenant farmers and small landowners' and cocky young bourgeois, 'officered by local gentry and aristocracy'.[49] Of these there were in Britain about 14,000 by 1838, and not many fewer in Ireland. Yeomanry horsemen found this work congenial but British governments of conservative and liberal hue alike disliked having to depend upon them; their expenses had to be paid, their discipline was unpredictable, and their extreme unpopularity among the lower orders (not least because the albatross of 'the Peterloo massacre' hung round their neck) joined with their natural zest in keeping the poor in their place to give their deployment an imprudently naked and aggravating air of class conflict. It was with relief therefore that British government found itself in the fifties at last becoming well enough equipped with 'civil' police forces to be able in all but extraordinary emergencies to dispense with yeomanry and regulars alike. The Irish police, it must be admitted, was less 'civil' than the British: by 1867, when it became the Royal Irish Constabulary, over 10,000 uniformed and armed men were housed in barracks, not unlike Italian *carabinieri* or the Spanish *guardia civil*; but that was the measure of the difference between John Bull's two islands. Only on the easterly one was the use of regulars in domestic affairs henceforth so exceptional as to become a matter of political uproar.

20

THE MILITARY
MULTINATIONAL

The Habsburgs' military problems increased like all other great powers' at the end of the war. In Vienna there existed a clearer conception than anywhere else that prevention of revolution was to be their main business: 'the iron righteousness of law and order', as the State Church put it.[50] Nicholas I soon acquired the *soubriquet* of the gendarme of Europe; Metternich might just as well have been called its chief of police, vigilant for signs of any political activity that might turn in a revolutionary direction. The Habsburgs, moreover, had an exceptionally wide-angled perception of what was revolutionary. Like all absolute monarchs, they were congenitally hostile to constitutional and democratic movements (*a fortiori* when they were republican as well), but they were hypersensitive also to nationalist movements and to liberal movements with nationalism in them, because from nationalism they stood peculiarly to lose. Nationalism, after all, was politically a two-edged sword everywhere else. Mazzini was a nationalist; but so was Louis Napoleon. *On its own*, nationalism was just as well able to fire reactionary politics as liberal. Through the second half of the century, indeed, it normally would do so. In this first half, it was more commonly allied to liberalism, and monarchs were therefore shy of it. But at least the other monarchs could appreciate the theory and the abstract beauty of it, and hope to use it profitably themselves. The Habsburgs absolutely could not do that. The survival or collapse of their empire turned upon their success in providing something other than the principle of nationalism as a prime activator of their people's and especially their army's loyalty, because ordinary nineteenth-century nationalism could only tear their empire apart. The Hungarian part of it had never lacked independent national feeling, with touchy and cantankerous political consequences. They could now only get worse, as new-style nationalism hit it along with the other, older national groups which had hitherto hardly been in a position to think of such things: Czechs, Serbs, Croats and so on.

Those established difficulties were now compounded by the empire's expansions within the period of this book. First, their annexation of Galician Poland in the first and third partitions; then, in 1815, their absorption of Venetia and Lombardy which, added to their dynastic and military influence over Modena, Lucca, Parma and Tuscany, gave them hegemony over the whole of north Italy. In the early twenties, when their armies were restoring monarchical order in Piedmont and Naples with the blessing and connivance of the Papal States, they effectively occupied the whole of Italy, becoming proportionately unpopular with nationally-conscious Italians. Germany was the other 'external' sphere wherein the Habsburgs were expected to wield counter-revolutionary influence, and there they naturally met with more acceptance. Prussia was not yet challenging Austria's leadership within the German national arena. There was in 1815 no constitutional reason why Austria, not Prussia, should not have become the dominant power within the Confederation's army, to which it was committed to contribute 95,000 troops. That army's main task in early Restoration Europe was, needless to say, the intimidation of France. Prussia with Holland was expected to keep watch on the more northerly stretch of the frontier, Austria to support Baden, Hesse-Darmstadt and Bavaria (in charge of 'the palatinate', in the angle between Rhine and Moselle) along the rest, besides bearing a major share in garrisoning the federal fortresses of Mainz, Landau, Luxemburg and Rastatt. On the southern and eastern sides, the empire's preoccupation remained what it had long been – localization of the Balkan border's endemic tribal disturbances, and maintenance of sufficient force on the Ukraine and Black Sea sides to keep Russia mindful of Austria's equal interest in whatever happened to the Ottoman Empire.

The army of which so many and various functions were expected was a mixture of western and eastern European aspects which many historians and military writers rightly or wrongly have found rather engaging. It was still more like the Russian than any other in its social composition and methods of recruitment, and its disciplinary methods were only a bit less brutal and lethal. Its long-established Military Frontier had contributed inspiration for

Alexander I's military colonies and the later, modified colonies in the Caucasus were found to be like enough to the Frontier to challenge comparison. The military problems of the Frontier moreover were not unlike those of the Caucasus and western Siberia. The Habsburg Empire had a regular contact with the Asian world which the other European powers only knew indirectly if they knew it at all. But Vienna, the administrative centre and normal location of the court, was unmistakeably one of Europe's great capitals, which some Europeans would not allow to be said of St Petersburg. The social structure of the Habsburg Empire likewise was more variegated than Russia's. 'Serfdom' continued until 1848 but the crown had through many years been interposing between landlord and peasant, limiting the former's power and guaranteeing basic rights for the latter, while the prospective advantages of free labour on the land had evoked a sizeable *and public* movement in its favour among many landowners. Peasant riots and rebellions continued, especially in Transylvania (scene of the Hora rising of 1784) and Inner Hungary, but agrarian relations within most of the empire had not the Russian grimness and, for whatever reason, serfdom was not identified as a vicious element in the military constitution of the country. Lack of money to keep enough men under good enough arms was the empire's main military vice, not any chronic defect in the nature of its manpower.

Recruitment continued to be by selective conscription for more or less long periods of service (nowhere except in Hungary approaching Russian lengths) varying from province to province until in 1845 a uniform eight years was applied everywhere. Each regimental district was set a quota to meet when the regimental recruiting officer came round. The selection was supposed to be by lot, but was not often done by so humane and civilized a method; bribery and influence kept the sons of all but the lowliest out, and advantage was taken of the system everywhere by packing the quota with 'undesirables' (or, in the aftermath of 1848, 'subversives' like politically-active students). 'Once they had been rounded up, the conscripts would be chained and taken to the *Kreisamt*. There they were neither allowed to take leave of their parents nor even to communicate with them, but were quickly transported to a regimental garrison which might be situated in any part of the empire.'[51] 'Enlisted men,' remarks a high authority,

246

'were still regarded as potential criminals ... or as children whose every action should be watched.' Discipline being tough, and conditions of barrack life spartan (barrack accommodation was growing here as everywhere, though billetting on inhabitants was still the norm outside cities) and service in perhaps uncongenial 'foreign' parts of the empire, as a measure of political prudence, normal (not to mention service in the Confederation), the desertion rate continued to run high, with this result among others, that in some mountainous regions bands of brigandized deserters 'constituted an intermittent threat to the security of the civil population'.[52] Many classes of subjects enjoyed legal exemption, and all of the rest who could afford it could buy themselves off, such practice being positively facilitated in order to produce a core of quasi-professional regulars re-enlisting once or twice before retiring with the capital accumulated from their bounties and the interest it had earned. A *Landwehr* of sorts survived until 1852 but by 1831 had lost whatever small 'liberal' character it ever had to begin with. From three parts of the empire in particular came specially qualified soldiers hardly matched in any other land. The mountain men of the Tirol enjoyed government encouragement to keep up their traditional skill in marksmanship and were under an obligation to provide up to 20,000 *Jäger* on demand. The Military Frontier continued in its by now well-rooted way, supplying about 12-15,000 men to the colours at any one time and with over 100,000 ready for emergencies. Hungary, finally, compensated for its rather low-grade infantry by the excellence of its national light cavalry, the Hussars, who provided a model universally admired and emulated.

In wartime this army was supposed to be capable of fielding something like 600,000. Its nominal peace strength was about 400,000. Not much more than half that number however was actually to be found with the colours. The empire simply could not afford more. Wars had always ravaged its finances. Even with British millions to help, the wars against France had left it nearly bankrupt. Savings were made wherever possible. Francis I celebrated the Restoration and his acquisition of so much of Italy by selling Venice's fleet – quite a respectable one, after Napoleon's naval building programme – to Denmark. Military expenditure remained tightly restricted. From the end-of-war figure of about half the national revenue, it fell by 1848 to only 20 per cent: a meagre proportion by the side, for instance, of Prussia's, which was nearer 50 per cent. One of the devices by which practical economies were made was by sending troops home on long furlough (unpaid!), recalling them only for annual manoeuvres or emergencies. Another was, obviously enough, retention of weapons and equipment after they had become due for replacement, and strict limits upon 'waste' of such costly stuff as practice ammunition.

If comparisons were invited with Russia on the one side, so were they with Prussia on the other. The two armies, after all, shared many German sources and standards, and most of the western half of the empire, from Austria's Alps up to where the Czech-speaking provinces marched with Saxony and Prussian Silesia, was dominantly of German culture. Austrian society had at least as military an air as the non-Prussian parts of Germany. Public ceremonies increasingly centred on soldiers to the sound of military music. Barracks became regular elements of the cityscape; Vienna and Milan rarely had smaller garrisons than 10,000; imperial security required that the army have a visible presence wherever trouble might arise. The aristocracy dominated the officer corps, regaining until after the crisis of 1866 an ascendancy which had earlier been under threat. Fewer aristocrats were officers than in Prussia, but almost all higher-rank officers were aristocrats, and court and high society alike gave them pride of place, all the more emphatic for their never being out of uniform, so far as a rather surprised French observer could see.[53] Purchase of commissions remained the standard way in and up for all socially-qualified men who could afford it, and no one has ever doubted that Austrian officers were generally less well-educated for their jobs than Prussian; the Habsburg army fell a long way behind the model of professional expertise and staff work set by the Prussian reformers; but a sober if narrow professionalism was to be found in it along with that lack of Prussian-style seriousness which attracted more attention. The artillery in particular was very good. The unusually large bureaucracy was less militarized than the Prussian, but lower-grade posts in the public service – in the tax and customs departments, the police, the railways when they started – were normally filled with ex-soldiers, who might embezzle and scrounge but thoroughly understood the importance of obeying orders and making others do so too. By this means, as

248

indeed more or less similarly throughout the continent, military style suffused 'civil society' and the army could by no means be perceived as a body apart.

Yet between the Habsburgs' army and some of their people yawned a unique gap of sympathy, which not all the régime's effort could paper over. We recur to the peculiarity with which we began. This was *par excellence* a multinational empire, and some of the nationalities within it, if not already possessed of a sense of grievance, were fast learning to acquire one (though it must be remembered that peasants generally remained a-political). If there was one thing the emperors could not rely upon to make or keep their army popular with the politically-conscious outside Austria itself, it was nationalism. National sentiment and its imperialist extension had indeed limited uses, as events in 1948-9 were to show. People in Vienna were miraculously cured of dislike of their army when they heard of its thrashing Italians. Hungarians disliked being kept down by German- or Czech-speaking soldiers, but were all for Hungarian soldiers keeping down Rumanians and Galicians. 'Divide and rule' was a workable imperial policy up to a point, but above that point there had to be a common cement holding from one end of the empire to the other, and in this singular case it was fidelity to the emperor in complete separation from any territorial concept. This singularity, indeed, can be exaggerated. Russian soldiers swore their oath to the Tsar alone. Prussian kings battled to keep their soldiers' oath of loyalty from being extended to include 'the constitution' and won. Nevertheless, the Habsburg interest in the matter *was* singular. The Tsar demanded just such an oath because he was an autocrat; the king of Prussia, because he held a peculiarly high idea of his prerogative as head – real, actively managing head – of his army. The Habsburg emperor was not an autocrat, nor did he seek to play 'all-highest warlord'. But his dynasty alone held the empire together. His multinational subjects had to hold a loyalty towards him and his house above whatever they might feel to their particular linguistic group within his empire. The officers of his armed forces, above all, had to hold such loyalty, for nothing but that and them stood between the creaking great empire (creaking all the more, as it took in ever more nationalities) and dissolution.

Loyalty to the emperor – loyalty of a lively, hearty, personal kind

– was therefore a special thing for the officer corps of the Habsburg army, and explained certain of its characteristics which are not unattractive. The moral tone of the officer corps was, understandably, rather old-fashioned and 'chivalrous'. Their concept of honour (every officer corps of course had one, each with its own twist) was less narrowly self-regarding than most, because of this exceptionally strong external magnet. They therefore, for example, took more seriously than most the laws and customs of war observed by civilized States, because such regard was expected of the honourable and chivalrous-minded, and their monarch could expect of them no less. It is difficult not to conclude that defeat with honour weighed more with them than victory without it. They had been aghast at the rapid ruthlessness of French Revolutionary and Bonapartian warfare; while they were patiently hiring transports and skirting neutral territory, the French would march across it and requisition or simply seize whatever they needed. They were slow – perhaps, of all the great powers the last – to wake up to the rude requirements and temptations of the new warfare. Clausewitz was not an Austrian, neither were any of the Germanic military writers and international jurists of the century who rather relished rubbing readers' noses in its 'realities'. The Prussian military tradition and cast of mind were alien to Austria. So of course was that other belligerent phenomenon of the age, people's war. Spaniards readily slipped into it because it came naturally to them. Prussia could cautiously put on a controlled version of it at a time of national crisis because Prussia after all was a nation and to encourage national spirit (along safe lines) was in the dynasty's interest. But the Habsburgs could find no use for it at all and simply perceived it as a horrid thing, a very horrid thing: lawless, atrocious, indiscriminately hurtful; a way of making war which broke down civilization's laboriously built edifice of prohibitions and restraints, and at once robbed war of whatever could still be chivalrous and honourable in it. The prospect of armed conflict against 'their own people' (which unfortunately now included Italians) in a sort of civil war wherein none of the niceties of proper international war could be observed appalled them. Wars should, they held, take place only between *States*. The Frenchman already mentioned remarked in his 1853 book that the Habsburg army 'does its work like a truly civilized power. Enemies wounded or taken prisoner will always find a protector in an Austrian officer.'[54]

250

So far as I dare judge, that was true. Even in difficult circumstances of popular tumult and nationalist insurrection, an Austrian commander could still trust that the better, not the worse, side of man would prevail. When in the early days of '1848' Benedek felt obliged to move his troops from a Pavia which he could no longer safely control, he issued a proclamation including sentiments which, I venture to think, could not at that date have been penned by any but an Austrian general:

I have the consciousness that during my command of this city I have acted, not only as His Majesty's true officer, but also at all times as an honest and good-hearted man, and I carry with me the knowledge that I have protected the citizens of Pavia from very great evils. I have deserved the thanks of the city and I claim from the authorities and the inhabitants so much sense of honour that they will, in all circumstances, not only respect the wives and children of my officers, and my sick officers and men, as also our property, but will further show humanity where there is distress. These are the words of my leave-taking and events will show whether I have been in error in thinking that the officials and inhabitants of Pavia are honourable people. In the meantime I thank from my heart all those who succour the wives, children and sick of the departing garrison in what must be, in any case, a sad circumstance. And so I take leave, wishing to the Pavians nothing but good . . . .[55]

21

THE MILITARY
SOCIETY OF EUROPE,
1815-50

Within each State, each army and navy developed in its own national (not excluding imperial) way, and each bore the stamp of its own national context. The chapters so far in this part of the book have made the most of their national characteristics. But the attentive reader will have noticed that – just as he expected – many characteristics were shared. How should they not have been, when every armed service came out of the same Napoleonic crucible, when every government was cultivating the same political atmosphere, and when intercourse between the different countries of Europe was becoming easier almost year by year? There were many similarities between their employments, their conditions of work, and their respective social relations; and the sixties gave them all a jolt. Let us conclude this part with a summary sketch.

A fundamental economic condition of almost all was their base in societies still mainly agrarian, trembling on the brink of the Promethean gift. Only the UK by 1815 had unmistakeably received it, and, such being the cultural conservatism of the military élite, the armed services took many years to be affected. Belgium, next to slip on to the industrial rollers, was militarily negligible (though from around Liège was exported a far from negligible quantity of weapons). None of the rest was clearly displaying what economic historians recognize as the symptoms of modern industrialization until at earliest the forties. The arms they used, the men they recruited, the riots and rebellions they were set to suppress belonged more to the pre-industrial past than the industrial future. The fundamental political condition for all, however, was that revolutionary movement which every European government *more or less* feared and relied on its army to protect it against, and from which in particular it sought to protect its army. The 'more or less' is crucial to understanding here, for the fear was

252

relative. The Tsar and the Pope would presumably have been terrified and appalled by much of what the bourgeois sailor king William IV and the bourgeois bankers' king Louis Philippe had learned to live with. Liberalism, the word we have to use for the bundle of progressive constitutionalist and economic doctrines accompanying commercial growth and the growing wealth of nations, only seemed revolutionary to régimes and élites which wholly opposed it. In power itself, or threatened with anarchy, it was quick to dissociate itself from the really revolutionary movements (sometimes its erstwhile allies) which pressed from the left or from beneath. Nationalism, too, so far as it can be distinguished from liberalism, was Janus-faced; aggressive or repressive, according to the challenge of circumstances; a force which reaction could harness as well as revolution. The revolutionary movement we have in view as the fundamental political condition of our armies' existence had therefore no uniform appearance or constant tendency, and perceptions of it depended on the point of view. But it turned up everywhere none the less, even in the UK where Chartism and the United Irishmen gave the government uneasy moments. In some countries it gained a foothold within the armed forces, exactly where rulers least wanted and were indeed most surprised to find it. Nicholas I quickly got rid of its short, sharp Russian emanation, the 1825 Decembrists, and purged the officer corps so thoroughly that he was never seriously bothered again; but in Spain everything was upside-down, liberalism acquiring a permanent lodging in the army and combating 'revolution' in the reactionary shape of Carlism. A similar deviation from the continental norm appeared briefly in Naples. The predictably tricky French case and its unpredictably early and smooth resolution we have examined at some length. Elsewhere, monarchs had no more to fear than some reluctance, sometimes, of soldiers to fire upon not very menacing crowds and the well-understood unreliability of certain nationally-raised regiments if deployed against homeland rebels. (That was why Cossacks, etc., were so useful to the Romanovs, and Croats etc., to the Habsburgs – as, imperially, Gurkhas would later be to the Windsors.)

Disloyalty within the armed forces being then neither a big nor an insuperable difficulty, armies remained suited to their main task, maintenance of order and prevention of revolution. To secure them the better from revolutionary influences, increasingly they were lodged in barracks, in or conveniently close to most large cities. They had to get used to something they did not much like: street-fighting, barricade-breaking, and at revolutionary peak-times the siege and bombardment of cities gone out of control. Often they were doing what we would now see as mere police work; always such police as existed (on the continent they were usually para-military anyway) relied on troops to intervene when things got rough. It is difficult to generalize about their 'popularity' between the 1815 lowering of curtains on the spectacular show of glorious heroes and the rebirth of national military pride and passion following 1846. Much depended on how the events of the wars were accommodated by the Restoration régimes, and how successfully the armies presented themselves as continuing embodiments of a worthy wartime legacy: a profoundly interesting question upon which no systematic comparative study has yet been done. For France (because of political divisions) and for Austria (which won hardly any battles and whose Marie-Louise had married Napoleon in 1809) this was clearly a greater problem than it was in Britain and Prussia. Prussia, Russia and Spain probably came out of the war with the most popularly glorious recollections of it. But, besides those recollections taking such different shapes, the army in each case more and more appeared as the prop and instrument of a régime which could not be called 'popular' without stretching credulity. Superficial phenomena like the cheers of city crowds on ceremonial occasions and the well-staged returns home of victorious squadrons and regiments meant nearly nothing. In the jam-packed, casual-labour-filled cities of those years an excited crowd would readily gather for anything with music in it and almost anything without. The authorities had more trouble preventing crowds than collecting them. Guards regiments were the chief providers of metropolitan military shows, and the building up of them with privilege and splendour was a notable feature of the post-Napoleonic epoch everywhere in Europe; but what they signified, to anyone who thought about it, was the surrounding of the crown with the most expensive soldiers that money could buy, and the régime's frank reliance on sabre, bayonet and the glamour of gorgeous uniforms.

Yet, leaving aside the question whether and in what manner the armed forces of the Restoration can be said to have been nationally 'popular' (as some armies certainly had been not long before), we may note that in several ways they became nationally more conspicuous, even simply more 'national'. The barracks into which they were increasingly put emphasized their presence in, and their potential power over, the cities as, indeed, they were partly meant to do. The fortifications so remarkably thrown up around many cities of strategic importance (those of Paris in the years of the July Monarchy being the astounding showpiece) and the great fortresses either now built from scratch or brought up to modern standards (e.g., Langres, Toulon, Soissons, Coblentz, Ingolstadt, Königsberg, Posen, Linz, Antwerp, Portsmouth) had the same psychological effect. Some of their time now became given to works incidentally of public utility which perhaps blunted the point of attacks on their peacetime size: e.g., Britain's navy's nautical chart-making, its army's marvellous mapping of the UK and the French army's mapping of Spain, the roads and clearances made in connection with the Habsburgs' military frontiers and the Romanovs' military colonies, and the great canals cut through the north-west of France, joining Brest to Nantes and the Loire.

The armies themselves literally became more national in that the enlistment of non-nationals largely ceased. I refer not to the Russian and Habsburg armies which of necessity included a mixture of nationalities, some of which were more enthusiastic about that service than others, and which continued to make openings for foreign-born officers. The British army had been wont to use many foreigners (whole regiments of them, or individuals recruited into British line regiments) apart from German rent-a-regiments. It now virtually ceased to do so, the panic attempt to hire mercenaries for the Crimea being to the best of my knowledge the last occasion of that kind. The Prussian army proudly vaunted its purely Prussian composition (which however might not make conscripts from Posen or Westphalia happier within it). The French army likewise acknowledged the call of national self-respect, shedding its last foreign regiments, the Swiss ones, in 1830, but was able to continue to make good use of foreign military talent from 1831 in its Foreign Legion. The Spanish army gradually shed its Swiss regiments. The Swiss federal constitution of 1848 put an end to the ancient practice of cantons' 'capitulations' to supply so many soldiers for stipulated periods; only the Pope's Swiss

255

Guards, otherwise recruited, remained as meagre evidence of what had once bulked so large in military Europe. The Papal States of course were a special case; the force with which they sought to keep the Piedmontese out of Umbria and the Marches in 1860 was 'mostly Austrian, but including many Irishmen and several companies of Frenchmen and Belgians as well as Italians'.[56] Greece was another; half its army – the more reliable half – for long was made up of Bavarians and Swiss.[57] Constitutionalists continued to hanker after National Guards, but their concept was shedding something originally crucial to it – the power of patriotic citizens thus to defend their interest in the nation against a ruler backed by perhaps alien bayonets. Ex-soldiers, idealists, adventurers, footloose toughs and so on, however, did not lack opportunities for the exercise of their aptitudes and passions. There were at least four new openings, whose combined effect upon world military history must have been considerable. The United States army was one, and with it should be linked the prospect of the United States in general, where the frontier set a premium on armed experience. The central and South American wars of independence, followed by wars *tout court*, were another; to which perhaps should be added the civil wars within the Iberian peninsula, in which at times whole 'legions' of Britons and Frenchmen were participating. Then there were the overseas empires, increasingly offering congenial employments to the tough and pushing, and no doubt relieving Europe of the pressure of some such. And last but not least there were the European national liberation movements – Greek, Polish, German, Hungarian, Italian – which although naturally composed chiefly of men of those nationalities, held so many ideals in common that there was easy interchange between them. Their importance in the story of war and European society is such that we shall keep them for a chapter on their own.

22

THE INSURGENT UNDERGROUND

Their internal security duties presented a double problem to the armies of Europe from 1815 until mid-century because to the commonplace riots and rebellions provoked by hunger, pain, oppression and the sense of injustice were now added the plottings and insurgencies of an international revolutionary movement. We turn now to give it the attention it deserves. The reader who has got this far in the book knows well enough what it was. It was the resistance against the Restoration. Liberals, democrats and nationalists all over the continent had grounds for resenting and regretting the Restoration – grounds which in principle were distinct from each other but in practice often coincided. For all of them, the Restoration was damned by its original sin of rebuffing the People. However large or small might be any non-reactionary individual's definition of the People (and there was of course a nearly unbridgeable gulf between moderate constitutionalist liberals and aggressively republican democrats), it was always too large for the Restoration to be comfortable with.

The Restoration's *raison d'être* was to rescue right principles of government and social order (i.e., what it understood to be morally and religiously right) from popular rudeness. To Restoration ideologues and apologists, all the disorders and disasters of the past quarter-century were attributable, under God, to the overvaluing of the alleged rights of the People. The revolutionary principles of popular sovereignty and the rights of man – mainsprings of the American and French Revolutions and difficult not to discern within the British constitution, though conservatives skilfully acquired a blind eye in that direction – were abhorrent to believers in the sovereignty of monarchs by divine right and the more or less sacred sanctions of a hierarchical social order. Equally abhorrent to most of them was that other mainspring of the French

257

Revolution, the identification of the People with *la Patrie*, the Nation. This had not in fact added much to revolutionary confusion in France because the French people already politically composed a Nation-State of their own. History had thoughtfully provided a *Patrie* ready for them to inherit. The Spanish and, so far as they perceived themselves in similar terms, British and Russian peoples likewise had no problem in this respect. But for Germans, Italians, Poles, Hungarians, etc., there were very big problems, frustrations and annoyances. The Restoration notoriously disregarded the principle of nationality. To have taken account of it would have been to loosen the foundations of the legitimate (i.e., pre-Revolutionary) dynasties now restored or reassured. So the Habsburgs compounded their already substantial nationalities problem by incorporating Venetia and Lombardy; Poland became again almost invisible under the blanket of the partitioning powers; Habsburg and Hohenzollern lowered at each other over a yet again rearranged German Confederation; Finland was taken over by Russia, Norway by Sweden, and what some over-optimistic people in the Low Countries had looked forward to calling Belgium found itself instead in Holland. From these territorial arrangements, nationally-conscious Italians, Poles etc. got no joy at all. Order, which at least the Restoration purported to guarantee, was to their minds a poor compensation for the national liberty whose idea glowed ever brighter in their hearts.

So inextinguishable and ardent were the hopes and beliefs of many liberals, democrats and nationalists that their movement easily survived the immediate shocks of 1814-15 and entered upon a new lease of life. We will henceforth refer to them simply as the revolutionary movement for that is what it was so far as the Restoration government were concerned, and its internal differences were contained within that fact. It also became to a great extent an 'underground' movement. Most Restoration régimes either from the start were, or within a few years had become, so toughly counter-revolutionary that only underground could the movement survive; which necessarily put obstacles in the way of its ever becoming a mass one. By this limitation, however, our revolutionaries were not greatly discouraged. They tended indeed to be extraordinarily optimistic. If they were religious believers at all, they did not doubt that God was on their side, not the side of the kings and courtiers. 'God and the People' became one of their dearest slogans. Their confidence in the potential power of the People, once rallied heartily to the revolutionary cause, was enormous; those who felt the magic of the new National idea most keenly believed that the Nation, once properly roused to militancy, could achieve anything.

These beliefs were so perfect that for many they were virtually 'religious' and capable of stimulating to any amount of exertion, of surviving any amount of practical discouragement. Discouragement was in fact to fall thick and fast upon them. By the fifties, appraisal of revolutionary prospects became more sober. The People in arms, even if they were also that even greater thing, a Nation in arms, after all were not so easily able to pull down well-armed established régimes. Until the end of the forties however it was widely believed in revolutionary circles that they could. This belief was not, between 1815 and 1850, as groundless as the sceptical reader might suppose. Our revolutionaries did tend to be ideologues, enthusiasts, romantics, monomaniacs, even paranoiacs, but many of them were soldiers too. Recent events and contemporary circumstances alike gave them grounds for believing that the resumption and international spread of the Revolution was not impractical. The history of 1789-94, after all, undoubtedly showed what could be done by a people roused enough under leaders bold enough. The tidal wave of 'liberty, equality and brotherhood' then unleashed upon the world had not (they were quite right about this) dissipated its energies. It was far too big, its vehicles and channels were far too many and various, for it to disappear. The idea of popular political participation was abroad in all lands, and what did it see in the seats of power? Generally very restricted élites, sometimes unabashed autocrats, whose claims to provide acceptable government surely could not fool enough of the people for enough of the time to keep them in business against God and the People! The very extremism of the Restoration was to our revolutionaries a source of optimism. The worse a régime was, the narrower its social base, the sooner (they believed) might revolution be successfully raised against it.

We thus find ourselves now entering a stretch of European history when revolutionaries for the first time constituted a kind of underground 'International'; a transnational movement of unusual persistence and vitality, dedicated to the raising of armed insurgencies against established governments under the banners of revolution and/or national liberation. The Restoration governments found themselves under revolutionary pressure and menace from the outset. Some of it, to begin with, came from within their own armed forces. This was not as surprising as may at first sight appear. For one thing there were those meritocratic and thus by definition liberal elements in the composition of the French armies and the allied or vassal armies which copied them. The various armies raised on France's behalf in Italy during the wars had been of this kind, and not all such soldiers disappeared from them during the Restoration's initial purges. In other countries, Spain not least, it was patriotic service against France that had brought progressive-minded men into the army. Whether however their wartime experience was of fighting on the side of France or against it, the general wave of revolutionary ideas could hit officers and NCOs just the same, disposing them to like the style and policies of their post-war régimes as little as in their different way did the real Republicans and Bonapartists of the French army like the Bourbons.

In the event it was from Spain (again from Spain!) that in 1820 the grand inflammatory gesture came, and military men were even more prominent there than in Italy. The Spanish army, it will be recalled, had ended the war under the banner of 'the constitution of 1812', and many of its officers and NCOs had remained faithful to the idea of it through the illiberal years of Ferdinand VII's restoration, which incidentally also saw the dismissal and neglect of more of them than was politically prudent. *Pronunciamientos*, officers' revolts under some proclamation of the national will, were already by 1820 becoming part of their way of life. The instrument therefore lay ready to hand for an attempt by the revolutionary underground to surface and recover, if it could, the constitution it had lost in 1814. Surprisingly, the *pronunciamiento* succeeded; not because it was popular with the people (rather indeed the opposite; they were the same people who had expressly *desired* the restoration of Ferdinand and had even clamoured for that of the inquisition too!) but because the greater part of the army was not interested enough to combat it. And even more surprisingly, in view of the liberals' disagreements among themselves and the national tendency to provincial particularism, the constitutional flag was kept flying for three-and-a-half years. This Spanish 'revolution' preceded and outlasted the Italian ones which took their immediate inspiration from it, while 'the techniques of Spanish military liberalism were taken as a model by Decembrists in Russia and liberal officers in Piedmont'.[58] In those two countries such officers tried, in the winter of 1825 and the spring of 1821 respectively, to advance the interests of the nation (which, presaging an enormously important future development, they assumed their corps to represent) in spite of the apathy or helplessness of the masses. They expected no popular support, and received none. The 1820 mid-summer revolutions in the Palermo part of Sicily and in Naples were more popular, but not in ways that were likely to produce an 1808-style popular insurrection. The Sicilian one turned rapidly into civil war, and was suppressed within a few months by the Neapolitans; the Neapolitan one, which early won an (insincere) concession of a Spanish-1812-style constitution from the flummoxed king, showed more lasting power but was suppressed without difficulty by an Austrian army in March 1821.

By the close of 1825, when the singular sombre and remote attempt at a coup by the Decembrists marked its furthest and for the time being its last ripple, the revolutionary international's first phase had come to nothing, except perhaps in Portugal. There, a constitutionalist party, not unaided by British warships up the Tagus, was just surviving a trial of strength with absolutism allied to anti-British chauvinism. But elsewhere everything seemed to be very much as Metternich liked it to be. Ferdinand VII had been back in the Spanish saddle for two years. Reaction had been triumphant in Italy for longer still. Comprehensive purges, persecutions and imprisonments in Naples and the Papal States ensured that such revolutionism as survived (much in fact did) only did so underground. Mass trials of conspirators, many of them by then safely in exile, marked the end of their hopes in Lombardy and in Piedmont, where Habsburg and Savoy troops had combined to crush them. Louis XVIII's decision to go to Ferdinand's rescue had signified France's move in the reactionary direction. Prussia and the other members of the German Confederation had been moving away from liberalism since 1819 and, followed by Switzerland, bent to the prevailing wind by expelling Italian political refugees from their territories. Only the UK, by now taking a decisively different line from the Holy

Alliance, proved to be what it remained through the rest of the century – a safe refuge for nationalists in exile and revolutionaries on the run.

Such an accumulation of reverses might have excused the complete collapse of the movement. Its members however were made of sterner stuff. Success was going to be longer delayed than the more optimistic of them had thought. The Restoration was not about to yield easily. They put to themselves the question which all revolutionary movements have to face in such impasses: what is to be done? It is no business of this book to review the whole range of answers given. We must concern ourselves only with the more military-minded answers: those from people seriously aware of the real military difficulties facing them, and the means by which they might be met; answers containing at least a glimpse of understanding of what was involved in planning for the people to take on the national army.

Of such answers, the next two decades turned out to be quite productive. But before we examine them, we should note how characteristic it was of our revolutionary movement that it did not let the disappointments of the early twenties depress it into impassivity. Nothing but underground work was possible for the time being in most of Restoration Europe, but exciting opportunities offered elsewhere for forceful men moved by visions of national freedom and thence, they doubted not, the progress of mankind. Latin America was their extra-European magnet, the furthest reach through the twenties and thirties of their transnational concern. Mere mercenaries and men who were at least partly so, like the British admiral Cochrane/Dundonald, who served successively Chile, Brazil and Greece, went there too. But it was idealism (and pure enjoyment) which soon after led Giuseppe Garibaldi, the Mazzinian political refugee, to take up arms successively for the stillborn states of Rio Grande do Sul and Santa Caterina and more successfully, with his famous 'Italian Legion', Uruguay. In Europe, more than a thousand Italians (mostly from Naples) went to Spain to support the constitutionalists in 1821-3. Greece was the next attraction, with Ludwig I of Bavaria egging on German volunteers and Lord Byron lending his unmatched glamour to the cause. So it went on throughout these hopeful years. Political exiles and refugees did not merely gossip, write and spout; some of them, when the way to direct action was blocked in their own countries, went to fight in foreign ones for what they all felt to be a common cause. Even in Britain, where the movement had so much more peaceful a face, mild use was made of such continental advice as was available, but, as G.M. Young remarked, the 'physical force' Chartists 'were unlucky in their choice of military advisers. In no age are Count Chopski and Colonel Macerone names to conjure with in English working circles.'[59] In 1848-9 foreigners were to be found wherever barricades went up and people's armies were raised.

Such, very briefly, were the international ambience and theatre within which the irrepressible activists of our movement found fighting work to do through the long years when there seemed nothing much to do at home. Meanwhile there proceeded a lively debate about how the next steps at home should be taken, with a considerable body of literature to mark its main positions on the two crucial questions: the question, whether a people could liberate itself by means of its own resources of will, courage etc., and the military-technical question as to how a revolutionary or liberation war should actually be fought. Let us deal with the former, the more political question first. It divided men roughly into enthusiasts and optimists on the one side, and those who seemed by way of contrast more moderate or realistic. The idea of a people achieving its own freedom by its own efforts was heroic and inspiring. Some nationalist enthusiasts were incapable of looking beyond it. Some who were capable didn't like what they saw: national independence crippled from birth by dependence on foreign support. Geography forbade Polish nationalists to enter-tain much hope of outside help, but not every subject nation was so awkwardly placed. Foreign support did not have to be considered necessarily humiliating or dangerous, and in any case it might be indispensable. Greece, it seemed, had only managed to achieve independence with British and Russian help; certainly it stood little chance of remaining independent unless the balance of Balkan and eastern Mediterranean power allowed it to do so. Belgium a few years later offered another example of honourable dependence. Francophile Belgians had always interpreted 1792-3 as a liberation (from the Habsburgs) for which they could only be grateful to France; now, in 1830-1, France helped them again and sent in enough military force to scare off the Dutch. True, the Belgium which emerged from the subsequent treaty-makings was hedged about with limitations suiting the interests of its great power neighbours, but in the nature of international things what other sort of Belgium could there have been?

Such were the kind of reflections prompted among the political theorists of unfree nations. To achieve freedom wholly on their own was undoubtedly their ideal; to achieve it mainly on their own was the best the more realistic of them hoped for. In either case, there were practical military matters to be considered. We come now to the very interesting body of writings which accumulated during these years about People's War.

23

PEOPLE'S WARS OF NATIONAL LIBERATION

It was about 1830 that there crystallized a most interesting and, for the future, significant development in revolutionary-military thought : the doctrine of popular guerrilla insurgency for national liberation and renovation; precursor of nothing less than Mao Tse-tung's revolutionary warfare doctrine of a century later, not to mention the national liberation warfare of the nineteen-fifties and -sixties. Its originality and pioneering significance has not been much noticed,[60] probably because so little good ever came of it in practice that when changed political and military circumstances in mid-century made its practice even more difficult and Marxism moreover began to magnetize intelligent attentions, practical revolutionaries simply left it behind. It went out with Garibaldi and with Poland's final insurrectionary fling in 1863. But while it flourished, it displayed in strong measure the flavour of its epoch: extravagant, romantic, utopian; and it swayed many revolutionary minds of that generation.

This doctrine of popular guerrilla warfare had three main tributary springs. First, classic regular military teaching about *la petite guerre*, *kleine Krieg*, inadequately translated as 'small war/warfare', and otherwise known in the eighteenth and early nineteenth centuries as 'partisan warfare'. The word 'partisan' has within the past forty years acquired so strong a contemporary significance that it is important to note that this classic use of it was nothing intrinsically to do with 'the people'. This simply concerned small bodies of mobile troops, detached from their own main armies (who conducted, so to speak, 'big war') and operating on the wings or in the rear of the enemy's. More often than not they were regular soldiers, properly uniformed, under normal official discipline, respectful of the laws and customs of war observed, as men liked to think, by all civilized States. The Russian Cossacks and the

265

Croats etc. from the Habsburg frontiers, sometimes used for this sort of work, went in so much for plundering, rape and homicide, that eighteenth-century writers about *la petite guerre* regularly noted how preferable for it were better-behaved troops who could keep quiet when told to do so and whose ruffianism would not at once alienate the local inhabitants. Such operations undoubtedly invited popular participation in certain political circumstances (e.g., the American War of Independence) and when that happened, neatness of definition and control of consequences became more difficult. There was a vast and painful difference between, on the one hand, a regular cavalry detachment probing to interrupt the enemy army's supply trains, and on the other a feud-minded frontiersman taking the opportunity to pay off old scores. The later twentieth-century observer may call the whole span 'guerrilla warfare' but the late eighteenth-century regular captain would have been acutely sensitive to the distinctions. *His* 'partisan war' no more invited 'the people' to join in than did the general's conventional warfare on the battlefield.

The second spring of 1830s' guerrilla enthusiasm was the contemporary wave of that radical nationalism which we have already noted (above, pp.258-9). This new wave may well be named after Giuseppe Mazzini, who was its leading publicist and among the first to ring these particular belligerent changes in it. The core of this nationalism was a colossal optimism about the possibilities of Man as a self-conscious liberated citizen of his own Nation-State, and about what he was capable of in association with others like-minded. Men in yet-to-be-liberated countries – above all Italy, with the promise of whose coming glory-in-unity Mazzini was obsessed – hardly yet understood what being a Man was. For Mazzini and the rest, the only full man was National Man. *He* was capable of previously unimagined heroism, exertion, sacrifice and so on once he was possessed of the grand national vision. Much of this stuff came of course from the later eighteenth century, when recognizably similar ideas fired the French Revolutionaries. But Mazzini's eloquent pen made it more exciting by making it more explicitly religious. Nationalism – especially democratic, republican nationalism – now became a religion as well as a political cause; a war for the nation was a just war, pleasing in the eye of God; and the people, who after all were going to be its prime beneficiaries, could directly undertake it.

266

So much might have remained merely speculative and gassy, had not recent history provided (this was the third mainspring) a string of examples seeming to support the argument that the people could actually fight a war on their own and perhaps, if highly enough motivated, win it. Such examples, the historian must at once remark, proved no such thing; but Mazzini and his like were anything but objective. The string began with the American War of Independence. Selectively admired by democratic enthusiasts, it became stereotyped as a demonstration of how a people possessed by the idea of nationalism and freedom could successfully make it. From revolutionary France came, first, the *réquisition*, the *levée en masse* and the legend of Valmy, and second, the *Vendée* and the Breton *chouannerie*, 'which struck imagination not only by their bloodiness but also by their obstinate persistence and their repeated rebirths'. From the several wartime episodes offering encouragement, Polish nationalists recalled (select bits of) Kosciuszko's eight months' war of resistance against the partition of 1793 and the 1806, 1809 and 1812 risings in anticipation of French succour; Italian nationalists, unless they were too Francophile to do it without embarrassment, could recall their compatriots' sporadic insurgencies against French hegemony. They got the greater encouragement however from the Spanish people's more successful war against the same blight. It was in fact to that Spanish story, closer than the remote American one, that the Mazzinians most clung. Forgetting the Anglo-Portuguese armies' operations and the sea power that made them possible, they exaggerated in that as in every other instance the power of the people on their own, and took the Spanish popular national saga as gospel.

It is appropriate to specify Poles and Italians together because they were, as it happened, the two national groups most involved in this phase. They had much in common. Both were strongly represented in the revolutionary underground. Both contributed more than their proportionate shares to the common stock of political exiles. Both felt their countries were languishing under odious alien imperial rule. Both had lively military histories behind them; the Polish record was the more modernly impressive but Italians had tried hard to show Napoleon that they were by his standards 'worthy of Nationhood' and it was often remarked that Italy's twenty years' experience of soldiers and soldiering had made the people more war-minded than they had been before. Above all, both nations had early spawned ambitious nationalist movements; the Poles instantly on the heels of the partitions, the Italians a bit later, partly from revulsion against French imperialism. Polish and Italian nationalisms, however unlike each other in situation, were much akin in substance, and were from the early years of modern nationalist agitation among the frontrunners.

Their kinship now became the more apparent when, about 1830, Italian and Polish nationalists in exile began to publish a lot about how their peoples might gain or recover independence by their own unaided efforts. Most were of that category of self-helping nationalists who were either so ingenuously solipsistic about their own national situations that they did not seriously think about international relations or so doctrinairely nationalist that they objected on principle to seeking help from other countries; though there was much Anglophilia and Francophilia among them, and from France especially, after Paris became the Polish exiles' capital in 1831 and Polish *émigrés* dug into French society, some sort of support (even if only diplomatic) was intermittently expected. But none of that had much realism in it. None of these books, in fact, had much realism in them. All these authors' geese were swans. They thought and imagined so much about their nations in detachment from their human and material realities that they slid into fantasy, mysticism and ecstasy. Perhaps because their own lives tended to be hard and comfortless, perhaps because they themselves tended to be of neurotic or opinionated character, perhaps simply because rhetoric came easily to them, they expected of *national* mankind more than *natural* mankind could provide. It is not only the origins of modern guerrilla warfare doctrine we are considering here. These men stood also at the head of the line of that continuing breed, the nationalist in exile, who not only cannot forget but cannot remember either.

To the rule that their guerrilla warfare books belonged to the thirties and forties there is one important exception. The first of them all, not much known until the thirties when began its long run of re-publications, had first come out anonymously in Paris in 1800. It was by Thaddeus Kosciuszko, hero of Poland's 1794 bid for freedom. Kosciuszko was an aristocratic military professional who, like so many young men of his kind, had volunteered for service under George Washington in 1776 and who had served there with distinction. Neither in America nor in Poland's wars of 1792 and 1794 did Kosciuszko actually engage in guerrilla operations himself. Professionally, he was an artillery expert. By not even the most comprehensive definition of guerrilla warfare can it be made out to have won the American colonists their independence. Nor did it help much in 1794. The bulk of the operations against the Russian and Prussian armies were undertaken in regular manner by the remnants of Poland's regular army, supported by regularly-officered militia, whose large use of scythes, flails and pitchforks was rather for lack of anything better than from choice, though the romantic and populist cult of the scythe subsequently sought to obscure the fact. There was little popular insurrection (as distinct from popular sympathy) except initially and crucially in Warsaw (about 2000 civilians killed besides 1000 soldiers) and in Posen. In his 1800 book, however, *Can the Poles recover their independence?*, Kosciuszko minimized the more regular aspects of 1794 and harped on the less regular; not least the one occasion when scythemen really had won a small battle, at Raklawiscz on 3 April. He also engaged in a sort of calculation which was to become standard in this genre – e.g., occupying power cannot assemble more than 300,000 men to put down insurrection; adult male population of occupied country about 10 million; say even only one-fifth of them available to fight, that means 2 million against 300,000 ... – somehow or other, it *must* be possible!

Kosciuszko's calculation became a dogma for military-minded nationalists, and his anonymous booklet a gospel. Several more substantial books by the next generation of Polish nationalists, sometimes military men but sometimes not, followed after 1830-1. With them – for the time was ripe – came several similar Italian writings, about the extent of whose initial debts to Kosciuszko Italian and Polish historians continue to argue. Mazzini, author of the most famous of them, *On the sort of insurrectionary war that would suit Italy*, 1832,[62] would seem to have got a lot from the Polish pioneer, but he expressed more of a debt to Carlo Bianco's first essay in this genre, *On a national war of insurrection by guerrilla bands*, which first came out in France in 1830.[63] All of them, Poles and Italians alike, covered the same range of references and ideas; their differences lay simply in where they placed their emphases.

Upon one thing at least they were all agreed. Success in such

269

a conflict must depend upon the mobilization of the people. Some of them opined that from the people would need to be raised and quickly trained bodies of men capable of conducting regular as well as irregular operations. Others that regular operations could be dispensed with, and they did not doubt that men of conventional military experience could be useful. But they concurred in believing that whatever was to be done, was to be done by the people, from scratch. Outside military aid could never be absolutely relied on and might not be much wanted anyway. The only regular troops, guns and equipment the insurrectionary people could expect to start with were those they might seduce or steal away from the established forces of the régime, or capture from it in battle. It went without saying, that the people themselves – not, as in conventional military and juridical teaching, the 'military' proper – were expected to bear the costs and to carry the consequences of the conflict.

Beyond that point began the differences in emphasis which alone lent variety to this spate of guerrilla books. First, about the people. Were they up to their high – in Mazzinian terms, their divine – calling? Some of our writers had doubts. The most optimistic and trusting assumed that national enthusiasm was already there, pulsing beneath the scaly skin of oppression, in such strength and quantity that it would need little beyond encouragement and leadership to let it loose. Once assured that dawn was coming and given such golden hopes to grasp – hopes which would normally of course include the basic liberal freedoms and, for peasants, land – the people would not stint devotion, energies, belongings and lives. The more pessimistic (dare we say, realistic?) writers doubted whether things would go as smoothly as this, and proposed such corrective means as the dictatorship at first of a revolutionary élite hardened in conspiracy or of a charismatic ruthless leader, and/or the unflinching use of terror to keep waverers and faint hearts in line and to silence opponents. None was so lacking in realism as to doubt that some quantity of popular suffering, injury and death was unavoidable, but they betrayed very different senses of how bad it might be, and what effects it might have on zeal for the cause. None was deterred by the fact that war waged like this could not be kept within the conventional 'civilized' limits.

Second, how would the insurrection be started? There were

those whose belief in the people was such that they believed it would start spontaneously and spread like brush-fire. Others felt sure that more would need to be done by way of preparation; already accustomed to conspiracy and the underground as many of them were, they envisaged the necessity for careful and elaborate planning – simultaneous seizures of fortresses and arsenals, prearranged proclamations and publicity, well-timed shipments of foreign arms and so on.

Third, there was the question of how the insurrection should be conducted. The big difference here was between those who argued that it could all be done by guerrilla warfare (everything from disciplined and expert bands to private homicidal enterprise, 'scorched earth', the poisoning of wells etc.) and those who reckoned that although guerrilla warfare would dominate the opening moves, it would have to yield pride of place to more conventional regular operations as time went by, because established régimes' regular forces could in the last resort only be mastered by conventional means: i.e., sooner or later, battles. About the 'city' problem also there were differences of emphasis. We have already noticed how central the city had become to the question of (according to which way you looked at it) revolution or the maintenance of order. These were the years in which the barricade acquired as much mystique among urban-minded revolutionaries as the scythe had among the rest. But not many of our guerrilla writers had the city clearly in view.

This people's guerrilla war literature enjoyed about two decades' vogue before the experiences of 1848-9 and after (see the next chapter) rubbed its essential impracticality into all but the most enthusiastic skins. The Polish insurrection of 1863 was its nineteenth-century swan song; unless one chooses to count as such the Paris Commune, despite its enforced urban limits. Mazzini's country, not surprisingly, proved to be the ground on which its devotees most often tried it out. It never worked. Always something went wrong. The conspirators were discovered or betrayed, their plans went wrong, bravery and sacrifice were found to be not enough, and above all the people never rallied round in the grand manner the doctrine required. Worse: as the forties turned into the fifties, the balance of advantages increased on the side of the forces of order. Improvements in the range and rapidity of fire of the up-to-date muskets and even rifles with which regular

271

troops were armed increased their superiority over whatever weapons insurgent guerrillas might possess. The electric telegraph and the railway, kept in the hands of government, gave it a tremendous advantage in outmanoeuvring insurgents. And military men on the other side began to produce studies of counterinsurgency warfare. The French veteran Roguet for example followed up his classic 1833-6 review of the lessons to be learnt from the *Vendée* (he only had personal experience of the lesser, later rising, but the lessons were the same) with a small 1850 book concealing under the title *Avenir des Armées Européennes, ou, le Soldat Citoyen* a shrewd review of how to handle revolting cities and what we would now call urban guerrillas. 1848 gave the regulars a lot of practice in this line, and their by now flourishing range of professional periodicals more and more reflected their interest and expertise in it. It would not be long before Engels, an excellently informed military analyst, as well as a revolutionary with a bit of insurgent experience, warned his fellow-travellers that the dream of easy insurrectional wins was only a dream, after all.

24

REVOLUTIONS AND INSURRECTIONS, 1848-63

Europe suddenly filled with fighting and prospects of fighting in 1848-9. It began early in 1848 in an atmosphere curiously mingling surprise with resignation. Revolution had been talked about, threatened, attempted and prophesied for years. In one sense both revolutionaries and governments were prepared for it. Most of them expected it to erupt sooner or later, and each successive season after 1845 made sooner seem more likely, as most of Europe slid into a dark trough of economic depression to which industrial and agricultural workers responded with an unprecedented show of protests, demonstrations, riots and even local rebellions, except where they became too starving to do anything more than suffer and die. Galicia flared into a terrible mixture of peasant *jacquerie* and national insurrection early in 1846. Switzerland survived a commendably restrained civil war late in 1847. Yet what actually happened in 1848 nevertheless took everyone by surprise, no matter how much and in what way they were psychologically prepared for it.

The revolutions began where they were least expected – in Palermo in mid-January, crossing quickly to the mainland. Paris was more expected and more significant. Palermo and Naples were hardly examples for the more advanced societies to follow, but Paris was. Paris erupted on 22 February and the Second Republic was proclaimed on the 26th. The news travelled and took effect so fast that conspiracy theorists could hardly help feeling justified, but it was the railway and the electric telegraph which actually did it, though not all that fast by subsequent standards; Vienna, for example, got its first rumour only on the 26th, nothing definite until the *Augsburger Zeitung* arrived on the 29th.[64] Within a few weeks the fever was everywhere. March was the miraculous

273

month, to such an extent in Germany that historians there have ever since simply called the preceding period the *Vormärz*. Absolutism seemed to have surrendered almost without a fight in Berlin besides – usually without a fight at all – in every other kingdom within the Confederation. The Habsburg Empire was no different. Vienna surrendered even before Berlin, and the non-Germanic parts of the empire at once exploited their opportunity; national liberation risings in Milan and Venice, 'home rule' demands in Budapest and Prague. In Piedmont, the Papal States and Poland the same extraordinary spirit was hopefully abroad. The Tsar felt forced on to the defensive, the British government braced itself for renewed trouble from Chartism and the Irish nationalists. By early April it looked as if the age of the Restoration was decisively over and done with, with infinitely less violence than could have been expected.

For the revolutionary underground, this continent-embracing eruption was what they had long been hoping and working for. So far their efforts had been in vain. Their works had done less for them than their faith. It was not particularly their efforts which now brought about the revolutionary epidemic, any more than it was the steady pressure – here bold and clamorous, there subdued and fearful – of liberal men and ideas working in the open. It was the conjuncture of their efforts and their optimistic readiness with that continental economic depression. 1846-8 were terrible years for labouring people. Famine struck Ireland, Silesia and Flanders. Hunger, unemployment and sickness struck almost everywhere. Working-class rebelliousness was crucial both in getting most of the revolutions going and in determining their fate once they had got going. But there was much more to the revolutions than the working-class rage and aspiration which produced some of their most striking and terrible episodes. It constituted in fact only one of three main revolutionary streams interweaving in these years and now coming confusedly to battle together. Ever criss-crossing and colouring one another, their ideological contents were nevertheless distinct in principle and were seen to be so when their reactions under difficult circumstances separated them out. Let them be recapitulated thus: (1) nationalism, capable of allying with *any* political creed though at this juncture much closer to liberalism and democracy than to the conservative heirs of the Restoration; (2) liberal constitutionalism, the creed above all of the growing bourgeois class though welcoming adherents from above and below it, and only 'revolutionary' from the angle of unrepresentative and obscurantist régimes; and (3) the mainly lower-class assortment of men and women who for various reasons seemed revolutionary to almost everyone socially above them, *either* because, being republicans, democrats, socialists and even (for Marx, Engels, etc. were now at work) communists, they were too progressive, *or* because, being traditionalist craftsmen and peasants indignant at the decline in their dignity and standard of living seemingly due to industrial progress and economic liberalization, they were not progressive enough. It was the mutual incompatibilities of these programmes and the worms within the nationalist bud (one nation against another, class against class) that fundamentally tipped the revolutions towards failure. But it was the inability of the revolutionaries to find armed force sufficient to beat the governments' armies that more immediately brought it about.

Superior force, sooner or later, decided everything. Every established régime entered the revolutionary maelstrom with armed forces in being. What it (or perhaps its provisional successor) actually did with them was determined by the interplay of countless factors: where those forces actually were when the trouble started, what was judged to be their political reliability, the whole range of political and moral considerations in the mind of government as it reviewed the prospects and alternatives, response to the unforeseen, and so on. Every revolutionary body (using the widest sense of the term), when it entered the same maelstrom, had to handle arms, whether it liked it or not: take over the existing armed forces or some of them (and disarming the rest, if they'd allow it), raise its own forces and make sure they stayed reliable, decide what to do with them and how much armed assistance to seek or accept from without, and so on. The outcome everywhere turned, in the end, on which side could muster the stronger armed force and at least seem the more convincingly ready to use it to effect.

The revolutions went with such a swing at first, partly because governments and their generals (sometimes having to make vital decisions on their own) had not enough force to meet the challenge so suddenly and, in local detail, unforeseeably presented. So Field-Marshal Radetsky, the Habsburg commander-in-chief in

Lombardy, decided after five days' fighting in Milan that his only sensible military course was to give it up. His reactions to the rising were characteristic of his class and the crisis; in one sense he was *not* surprised, because he had been predicting something of the sort for well over a year, but in another sense he certainly was ('I was in my office when the storm broke loose so that it was necessary for me to flee to the Citadel in order not to be engulfed by a mob')[65] partly because of his failure to understand the people he was policing. Their character, he reported to Vienna, 'has been altered as if by magic, and fanaticism has taken hold of every age group, every class, and both sexes ... the whole country is in revolt and even the peasants are armed....' He found himself for the time being a classic victim of national insurgency, for which 'guerrilla' is an inadequate, possibly a misleading description: 'all communications are interrupted, a number of messengers have been shot or taken prisoner, and my units meet strong resistance in the barricaded streets and villages. Reconnoitering is impossible, since all communications are broken.'[66] The smaller garrisons in the other cities (e.g., Benedek in Pavia: see above, p.251) were in equally impossible situations. There was nothing for it but to pull out of the insurrectionary cities and withdraw to the relative security of the fortresses of 'The Quadrilateral' (Verona, Peschiera, Mantua, Legnano), there to consolidate and purge their forces and wait for orders and reinforcements. Among the counterinsurgency lessons the generals had learnt by now were the dangers of small dispersed garrisons and guard-posts being swamped by numbers and the psychological damage suffered from even militarily insignificant setbacks. Nothing encouraged insurgency more than success. Radetsky and the other commanders who pulled out of 'their' cities until they could return with irresistible force were doing the strategically sensible thing.

The withdrawal of troops from cities in revolution was however not undertaken for that reason alone, nor were generals (so far as their independent wills went) always so ready to withdraw. The Italian case was like those of Hungary and Poland which followed: made peculiarly difficult by the heat of alien nationalism, and delicate for governments in as much as, the people in arms being a Nation-State *in posse*, the balance of power was going to be affected by whatever happened to it. Neighbours' opinions had to be respected. Nothing less than major military operations on the international war scale were likely to produce a firm result. But things were not thus in the capitals and major cities of France, Austria and Prussia. Revolution there was espoused not only by 'the dangerous classes' but also, even in some places chiefly, by respectable bourgeois compatriots with liberal aristocrats prominent among them. Such men were often rather reluctant revolutionaries, worried about the bad company they were keeping, inclined towards moderation and not beyond compromise. Nor did the liberal constitutional programme which such men typically pursued seem absurd or alarming compared with other political nostrums coming on the market. Experience of constitutions (feeble or for the most part short-lived, it must be said) was quite widespread by 1848. They were less alarming to kings and their ministers than they had been fifteen or twenty years earlier; and they had this virtue within the German and Austrian worlds at any rate, that by definition they were not republican. Republicanism (except in France) went with extreme democracy and other practices no less alarming to most liberal constitutionalists than to all monarchs and conservatives. France was different. For obvious reasons republicanism there held a large and in part respectable constituency. Louis Philippe had been one of Europe's three parliamentary monarchs. If he wasn't wanted on those terms, there was no other reason for him to stay. With extraordinary quietness he went, before February was out. Leopold I of Belgium was at risk too, the ties between the two countries being so close that when Paris caught cold, Brussels was sure to sneeze. Belgian revolutionaries, already living under a liberal constitution, had to be extreme if they were to follow the fashion. Leopold offered to go quietly like Louis Philippe if a national plebiscite in due course told him to do so. Meanwhile he moved troops up to the capital in large enough numbers to make sure there would be no mistake when he acted in defence of the constitution. There wasn't, and he survived. Elsewhere however the voice of liberal constitutional revolution was not relatively so disturbing to monarchs. It is understandable that so many of them at first yielded, and although they evoked some contempt and impatience from ideological ultras and grapeshot-minded generals, their motives generally were not contemptible. Some fear there may have been, but fear of precipitating bloodshed and destruction may have a worthy side. Their hopes may have been illusory, but

277

to do something, hoping for the best, may be more admirable than to do nothing from frozen fear of the worst. It seems to have been the case almost universally that they had long been expecting big trouble, so big that they expected it to be too much for them. The celerity with which they yielded had elements of resignation, panic and self-doubt in it, and surprised contemporaries who had expected something stronger from régimes whose care for their military props had long been so conspicuous.

Those military props in fact remained intact, and after a little delay were brought to bear. Armed force, after all, decided the event. By the autumn of 1848 in most countries, by the summer of next year in all, some measure of reaction and restoration had occurred. Nowhere was it complete, nor did most of the rulers concerned seek to copy the 1815 model. It was impossible this time to deny change with such haughty completeness. But change happened in ways which liberals and nationalists remaining faithful to their pre-1848 ideals were to find disconcerting: nationalism shedding its international idealism, liberalism becoming more nationalistic. How that happened, and with what consequences for the continent and the world, is a main theme of European history which we must skirt in pursuit of our inquiry into how control of armed force determined these revolutionary questions and (in the next chapter) was politically transformed by them.

The centrality of armed force to the resolution of the issues between the Restoration monarchs and their peoples had never been doubted. Most of this section of the book has been about it: the armed force maintained by régimes mainly to deter revolutionaries, the plans and dreams of revolutionaries for succeeding by means of it, and their sporadic attempts actually to do so. In the first months of 1848 they did it in many places, so rapidly and unexpectedly that the real weaknesses of their plans and practices were not at once apparent. Experience and reflection since 1776-89, besides producing the plans for nationwide popular guerrilla warfare sketched in the last chapter, had produced plans more specifically for the towns and above all the national capital, the centre of power, going something like this. First and foremost they required the formation of a National or Civic Guard. This was absolutely standard. The original Paris model and the updated Paris and Brussels ones of 1830 retained their magic. Where the people – above all the people of the capital – had no direct military embodiment of their own, such as the French *Garde Nationale* always tried to be and the Prussian *Landwehr* for a while had been, no revolution could expect to succeed which did not at once become armed enough to protect its achievements and to take on opponents. Opposition and sapping were anticipated from two quarters in particular: 'the mob' (as every man of property perceived it) on the one hand, the army on the other. We will deal with the mob shortly, in its proper context of class struggle. The army was the primary prop of the régime under pressure. What would it do? – and how could it be confronted if it did? Revolutionary practice by now was quite straightforward: building of barricades (and posturing upon them), and subjection of such government troops as were present in the streets to hails of bullets, stones, bricks, tiles and chimneypots, not to mention boiling water, chamberpots etc., from windows and roofs above; seizure of whatever weapons could be found in gunsmiths' shops, gendarmerie armouries, government stores and even, if the troops didn't prevent them, barracks; rushing barracks and, within fortresses, citadels; slamming city gates before government troops secured them; and so on. Professional soldiers, as we have already observed, loathed combat in these close and to them unnatural conditions. A big old city, once in revolutionary uproar, could be exceedingly difficult for regulars to fight in and they had learnt that it was better – time and circumstances permitting – not to do so, but to work on the seat of the trouble by other means: blockade, siege, and bombardment. If time and circumstances did not thus permit, then there was nothing for it but street fighting, tough tactics, remorselessness and terror, such as General Changarnier was to use in the Second Republic's suppression of the June insurrection in 1848 and General Magnan in that of the insurrection against Louis Napoleon's December *coup d'état*. At a pinch, and at great cost to lives, it could be done.

But inner-city guerrilla warfare was sure to be so horrid for people and destructive to property (not so much the breaking as the looting) that bourgeois revolutionaries sought to avoid it. Their hopes were not unrealistic. One thing they could rely on (except in Spain) by the forties, was the army's habit of obedience. The generals would do what their king or emperor told them to do. They would follow the course of politics, not supplant it. So in at least the more moderately-aspiring revolutions there was ground to hope that the government would come to an accommodation with the revolutionaries and switch the army, so to speak, from one side to the other; after which it could be used at once for mob-suppression. This is more or less what happened in the smaller German States and, until the October insurrection in Vienna, in Austria. If all that was too much to hope for, then the army might be split or eroded. Some regiments, even the smartest, might be less loyal than others; Guards regiments in principle were supposed to be the most loyal of all but the *Gardes Françaises* had helped storm the Bastille, and Guards officers were prominent among the Decembrists in 1825. Fraternization with the troops, especially with such as already nursed grievances, could work wonders. It did so in Paris in February 1848, when the troops' only bright relief during their long, cold, hungry and seemingly aimless vigil in the winter streets was the people's sympathetic interest and purposeful radicals' friendly words. Generals learnt the importance of preventing it at all costs. More difficult to prevent was the mass desertion of nationally-raised regiments to national liberation provisional governments. Only the Habsburgs were much troubled by this but it troubled them a lot. They were never able – indeed, they never tried – to station all Italian troops outside Italy, Hungarians outside Hungary and so on. Radetsky's army was as much as one-third Italian in composition. Most of the sailors in Austria's Adriatic fleet and most of Radetsky's Italian troops (i.e., about 20,000 officers and men) deserted or became too unreliable to be useful in the spring of 1848.[67] The political situation of the Hungarian troops in Hungary was confused at first by Vienna's inclination to allow 'home rule' there and therefore to order *all* its troops there, Germans, Italians, and whatever, to take orders from Budapest's new defence ministry. But when Hungarian independence became the order of the day in the autumn, most Magyar regiments lined up to fight for it. Revolutionary and liberation movements generally made little headway against professional opposition unless they had some professional stiffening themselves; Garibaldi's Thousand comes closest to suggesting the opposite, but professional experience was there too, beneath the affectation of amateurism, and the Neapolitan army had little of Potsdam or Saint-Cyr about it.

From the enemy without to the enemy within. 'The mob', to

which passing reference has already been made, was only part of the problem, though psychologically a significant one. Just as landlord families in feudal countrysides had nightmares about peasant risings, so better-off people in cities had nightmares about risings by the labouring, unemployed and unemployable people of the tenements, rookeries, riverfronts, courts and backstreets; nightmares which revolution did nothing to banish. In ordinary times it was the main task of police to keep that potential mob down and under. So long as full-time civil police were inadequate to that task, as on the whole they still were in 1848, their defects were made good by regular soldiers and variously equipped bodies of volunteers drawn mainly from the bourgeoisie (a wide range, from fully armed civic guards at one end to London's truncheoned 'specials' at the other). The better-off urban classes could only coexist with the poorer ones on these harsh terms, keeping the latent class war and urban *jacquerie* from becoming, in hard and disturbed times, actual.

Revolution tended to raise the stakes in this already tense urban situation by extracting from the city the government soldiers ordinarily necessary to its tranquillity and by bringing middle and lower classes temporarily into collaboration. Liberty was not followed on to the barricades by bourgeoisie alone. Labouring people had their own ideas of a better world to live in. Some of them coincided with liberalism's ideas but more did not. The lower-class element everywhere sooner or later fell out with the superior one. Its political spokesmen demanded more democracy than most liberals were willing to give; often they were republicans too; and to a small but significant extent now they might also be socialists. In the economic field above all the contrast glared. Labouring men looked to government to spend more money on them while bourgeois liberals believed it ought to spend less; the 'national workshops' in Paris, the guaranteed dole in Vienna, proved immensely divisive. Unemployment, hunger and tactical opportunism caused the political side of the working-class movement to ally more closely with the rough side of 'the mob' than it would ordinarily have done. Inevitable consequences were, first, that bourgeois elements of the National Guard turned repressive and began to yearn for the sight of soldiers again, and second, that erstwhile revolutionaries actually came to blows among themselves, as extremists and hot-heads espoused causes which made moderates shudder.

The 1848 revolutions (leaving aside *pro tem.* the special Italian and Hungarian cases) failed because they failed to arm themselves adequately. In the three principal countries in question it happened, briefly, thus.

In PRUSSIA, in Berlin, the revolution began in mid-March with the people's indignant reactions to the military's crassly provocative endeavours to prevent and break up meetings and demonstrations which multiplied daily as news of revolutionary achievements elsewhere in Germany flooded in. Frederick William IV's first and tardy concessions were met by a demand that troops, by now present in vast numbers, be withdrawn. When on the contrary they carried on clubbing and slashing at the crowds in public places, firing began ('accidentally') and the barricades went up. Berlin was properly in revolt through the night of 18 March. Next day, after further trials of moral strength between government and people and (within government) between the king and the generals, the troops really were withdrawn; the king, who remained in his palace and formed a new semi-liberal government and agreed to summon a national assembly in May, seemed beaten.

Now pressed the military question, in both short- and long-term shapes. In the short-term, the question was one of immediate national and civic security. Foreign relations do not stop because a revolution happens; throughout these very months Prussia was involved in an *imbroglio* with Denmark over Schleswig-Holstein. The peasantry did not patiently wait until Berlin had concluded its business; it was feared that those east of the Elbe would catch fire from the risings all over south Germany, and the Prussian government was as ready as all the south German ones to use the army against them. In the city itself, where public order mattered most to the struggling new régime, a *Bürgerwehr*/citizens' militia was in charge from the 19th; indispensable both because the regular troops had gone and because it corresponded in general terms to revolutionaries' idea of what an army should be. When the representative Assembly met at the end of May, the army question was at the top of its agenda. It was endlessly debated, as liberal deputies deplored the way the *Landwehr* of the War of Liberation had lost its original character and status, the separateness and insolence of Junkerdom, the desirability – nay, the need, if the gains of the revolution were not to be hazarded – of recasting the nation's army into the more popular and politically safe mould of a *Volkswehr*. The *Bürgerwehr*, meanwhile, did not at first prove itself efficient, and especially by failure to prevent a mob assault on the Berlin armoury on 14 June had discredited not only itself but, to the minds of the increasingly worried bourgeoisie, the very idea of *Volksbewaffnung*.

While all that was happening, the Prussian army proper was girding itself for counter-revolution. Its officers had never liked the 'abandonment' of Berlin and they remained distressed by the king's, as they viewed it, misguided feebleness in going along to some extent with the revolution instead of flattening it with bullets. Such hot-house conditions rapidly bred the notion that the army, and its officer corps especially, was the permanent real essence of the Prussian nation. The generals looked forward impatiently to returning to Berlin. Cavaignac's suppression of the Paris workers in June won their applause; *'Gegen Demokraten helfen nur Soldaten'*/'You need soldiers to deal with democrats' summed up their views.[68] Through the later summer, tension mounted between the openly and aggressively reactionary officer corps and the liberal majority in the Assembly, which was induced by the killing of over a dozen civilians by soldiers at Schweidnitz to pass resolutions expressly requesting the king to tell his officers to toe the liberal line or get out. By now there were over 50,000 troops ringing Berlin. Within the city, the *Bürgerwehr* was doing better but the earlier political enthusiasm had waned and the seemingly endless constitutional confrontation between the Assembly and the monarch was wearing to bourgeois nerves. When the king at last authorized General von Wrangel to march in, on 10 November, Berlin and the Assembly submitted to their fates quietly.

In AUSTRIA's capital the course of revolution was much rougher. Conclusive news from Paris, as we saw, reached Vienna on 29 February. The next two weeks witnessed a steady rise in liberals' hopes, conservatives' fears, and general excitement in which students were conspicuous. On 13 March the excitement boiled over. As in Berlin, the point of no return was when a patrol of troops, thwarted in its crowd-controlling, opened fire. At once riot, shooting and scuffling, arson and looting broke out. As in

Berlin, again, there was confusion and indecision among the royal family and their ministers, and much annoyance among the military, notably Field Marshal Windisch-Graetz, who forcibly expressed himself against concessions from the start. Late that evening, the concessionists triumphed. The troops were withdrawn, security was placed in the hands of the *Militärisches Bürgerkorps*/Civic Guard, a National Guard was at once to be set up and an Academic Legion of students formed. Windisch-Graetz's yearning to pronounce a state of siege was thwarted and the emperor proclaimed on the 15th that he would grant a constitution, convene a *Reichstag* and appoint a new ministry. That was the end of it – for a few weeks. While north Italy rebelled and while Hungary and the Czech provinces drove hard for 'home rule', taking their National Guards with them, Vienna remained relatively quiet under the watch of a Civic Guard which proved competent and the Academic Legion which proved officious and noisy.

Leaving aside the kaleidoscope of international, German and imperial events, and focusing simply on events in the capital, we note this big difference from the Prussian situation, that until well into the summer the government was short of troops. By the middle of June, however, Windisch-Graetz, having turned a blind eye to a mediating mission from the government, had brought the short-lived revolution in Prague to an end. He was free to object with increasing force and frequency to what he viewed as the government's weakness and what many besides him viewed as the emperor's crippling excess of good nature. Feeling like his Prussian counterparts that the honour and integrity of his country in the last resort rested solely in its army, he became ready (shades of Taurrogen!) to compel the emperor's abdication in favour of his more military-minded nephew Franz Josef. Moved by like principles was the empire's other most eminent marshal, Radetsky, whom we met in difficulties in north Italy. By the end of July he was triumphantly through them. Piedmont, which had intervened on the Italian national account, was beaten and suing for peace. Radetsky had officers, though not men, available for transfer to wherever in the empire they were needed.

The military balance of power thus swung against a revolution which by now had got into the usual political difficulties besides being harassed by the internal international difficulties peculiar to the empire. After a relatively calm April there had been a new round of disturbances in Vienna in May, when popular pressure with the Academic Legion and National Guard at its sharp end had squeezed further concessions from government, the emperor had been spirited out to the fortified city of Innsbruck, and Vienna itself had come under the control of a 'Committee of the Burghers, National Guard and Students of Vienna for the Maintenance of Peace, Security, Order and the Preservation of the People's Rights'. Worsening unemployment in the city and its hinterland, political disagreements and class struggle now catalysed bourgeois disillusionment, weariness and fear. Government, in such circumstances, was able to claw back some power and authority. Troops reappeared in the city in September, to help the National and Civic Guards disperse mass workers' protests against unemployment and dole-cuts; the University was closed, the Academic Legion downgraded, the 'Committee of Security' dissolved, the National Guard brought back under government control, and (perhaps the smartest measure of all) 30,000 dole-applicants sent out of the city to build railways.

One last cataclysm preceded the end of it all – one final lurch to the left. A soldiers' mutiny on 6 October led to shooting (who started it was, as so often happened, never established) and consequent mayhem, with the mob in full spate and actually managing to break into the armoury. The emperor was got out again, everyone else who was not still revolution-minded and could get out did so, and Windisch-Graetz was given the full powers he had so long longed for. By 20 November his 70,000 men ringed a Vienna which a Central Committee of All Democratic Associations undertook to defend until fraternal help arrived from Hungary. Not much arrived, too late. After about 2000 of the city's defenders had died and Windisch-Graetz begun another bombardment, the city surrendered. Order was restored to Vienna.

The place of naked power in what happened in PARIS may be quickly dealt with. The revolution got going because, and perhaps only because, Marshal Bugeaud and the army were not firmly instructed to stop it. It came to an end (the June days were its end, for our purposes) when the army was allowed to get at it. This was a particularly neat model of what proved to be the general pattern. It was a neat model of the class war aspect too. As de Tocqueville and a few other sharp observers saw from the start, the revolution in February was also an incident in a continuing class war. The forces which in the absence of serious opposition so easily 'won' the revolution would lose their temporary slight cohesion once the chips were down. In the event it was a class issue which pulled it to pieces. Pressures from the left and from below (i.e., principally from the lower-class districts of Paris) caused the opening of an ambitious programme of unemployment relief. Its expense, apart from anything else, became enormous and seemed potentially interminable. Opinion strengthened throughout the provinces and among middle-class Parisians that it had to be stopped, even at predictable cost of great trouble, and by the end of May the government had begun to stop it. The 'national workshops' were to be closed to non-Parisians and younger men were to be conscripted into the army. The insurrection of the eastern parts of the city which soon followed was put down by the army with great relish. ('What brutal and ferocious beasts they are!' observed Bugeaud to Thiers early the following year: 'How can God allow mothers to produce them like that! Ah, *they* are our real enemies, not the Russians and Austrians!')[69] As in Vienna, the social question precipitated the fatal convulsion. As everywhere, however, it was failure to solve the military question that left the way open for that otherwise inescapable final military solution.

The military question had of course long been familiar to the French political public. Since the first Bastille Day, the National Guard had embodied the idea of the kind of armed force that ardent liberals and democrats alone liked. The professional army inherited from the *ancien régime* had not then been as big an obstruction to their designs as might have been expected, largely because it allowed itself to have its strength, like Samson's, taken from it gently. But what if it had solidly resisted the Revolution? Conservatives through the early nineteenth century continued to remind democrats that things might then have gone very differently. Democrats continued to fear that history would not be so obliging as to repeat itself. Conservatives viewed with relief the steady depoliticization of the army from the mid-thirties but democrats set all the more store on rebuilding the status, rights, duties and armed power of the National Guard. In February '48 they knew exactly what they wanted: the army to keep out of Paris until the new régime was secured beyond all doubt, elevation of the National Guard's status so that it alone was empowered to handle civil disorders, and enlargement of it to include *all* citizens, not just those propertied ones; a chicken in every pot, one might say, and a gun in every closet. They could not demand the exclusion of bourgeois men from the Guard but they could – and through Ledru-Rollin did – demand an end to their overweighting of it by, for instance, the formation of special companies with expensive equipment, which only the prosperous could afford. Their vision of the National Guard was not of an a-political body but of one which represented the political principles of the people, and therefore, if truly democratic, one in which democratic principles would dominate. How obedience to orders was to be assured or even how orders were to be evolved at all, were not the kind of questions that occurred to them; they looked at the army question through the lens of national democracy, not the lens of international relations.

Such was the idea of a National Guard which possessed democrats during the five months of opportunities allowed them. They succeeded in getting the law governing the Guard changed to suit them, too, and on paper dominated it (in Paris, anyway) to the tune of 3:1. But it did not become the force they desiderated.

It was not difficult for the moderates to sabotage the new scheme for arming and equipping the Guard at government expense, and proletarian guards were apt to find that they never got arms. Employers too seem to have put difficulties in the way of doubtful employees who wanted to join the Guard. Moreover, many of the more politically conscious working men preferred, despite the opinion of their more intelligent leaders, to rejoin their own clubs or make groups with old comrades of the barricades when the *rappel* was sounded.... In practice the Guard retained to a very large extent its old bias; and at periods of crisis ... after some initial hesitation, it invariably rallied to the support of those parties which stood for moderation.[70]

In the circumstances of 1848, it settled for order and accepted a perhaps somewhat inglorious role as coat-carrier to Cavaignac's and Changarnier's professionals. But in the very different circumstances of 1870-1, it became for a few vivid months the really

287

revolutionary people's army its democratic and proletarian devotees had dreamed of.

The last stretch of our survey of Europe's wars of revolution and independence takes us through the three countries where revolution and nationalism ran together. National sentiment was not insignificant in the other cases but it was not a primary stimulus to the revolutionaries of Berlin, Vienna and Paris as it was to persons with Budapest, Warsaw and Rome on their minds. In these cases there was room also for the expression of popular national feeling against military régimes odious because they were alien as well as repressive. The nature of armed conflict and the compositions of armed forces were therefore likely to be more extensive and various than in the 'straight' revolutionary cases just considered. In fact they turned out to be very different indeed.

HUNGARY, first. Hungarian nationalists were quick off the mark in March 1848. At their head was Lajos Kossuth, a man of some ability who rapidly became one of international nationalism's top heroes. To begin with, Kossuth and his less than harmonious band of brothers sought only some sort of 'home rule' within a suitably reconstituted empire. In fact they did not actually declare for total independence until April 1849. For many months Vienna conducted negotiations with them and encouraged Budapest to hope that a mutually satisfactory arrangement could be made. Vienna was only partly disingenuous in this. It is true that counsels were divided in Vienna – indeed at some stages of the year's developments it was not clear who or what, from the Hungarian perspective, 'Vienna' actually was; there was room for more than the conventional amount of ambiguity and duplicity in its diplomacy with its many revolting children; and there was in Vienna as in Berlin a military-reactionary 'camarilla' at work beside the apparent government, preparing for a counter-attack when the time was ripe. There was also vast natural confusion in the situation while every part of the empire was in rebellion and disorder. In the early months, moreover, Hungary seemed neither the most rebellious nor most disorderly part of it, and there was some desire on both sides that the two great kingdoms, twin keystones of the historic empire, should stay together. One consequence of this (it was a situation rather like that in the USA as the slave-owning states neared secession) was that the

Hungarian government, though as yet only a 'home rule' one, had an army ready made for it; the army regularly raised in Hungary, with many appearances of national distinctiveness, to serve the emperor in his role as also king of Hungary. So full of chaos and changes was the process by which this army became *de facto* the army of Kossuth's quasi-independent government that its officers – confusingly instructed by Vienna now to take orders from Budapest, now not – were saved the usual soul-searchings of their kind about 'breaking their oath'. Some who had doubts, perhaps also had Hungarian national sentiments to help resolve them. Others of course might decide differently. It was not the least of Kossuth's burdens, that other national groups in the eastern half of the empire preferred to back a remoter Vienna rather than a closer Budapest; anti-Magyar Croat sentiment, for example, led a Frontier commander, Jellačić, very early to begin a double game which kept his part of the army – a part Budapest could reasonably have expected to command – in the camarilla's camp.

Not until late summer was it clear that Hungary was going to have to fight for it. By then it was clear too that Hungary would have to fight alone. Kossuth's nationalism included no fastidious prejudice against foreign aid, but nothing more than good wishes and some diplomatic bluster ever came; the foreign freedom fighters who came from Poland, Germany and so on, came of course independently. In its main aspects it was quite a conventional war, fought and ultimately decided by regular-style armies conducting conventional operations. Regular troops and militia, many of them of course only newly recruited, made up the bulk of Hungary's army, with a sprinkling of partly foreign volunteers.

> By the middle of December, 64 infantry battalions, 10 hussar regiments and 32 artillery units had been set up, [i.e.] roughly 100,000 men and 233 cannons. Weapons and munitions production began, and industry was mobilized entirely for war equipment. The expenses were covered by issuing unsecured notes....[71]

Requisitions were made of all valuable and usable materials in the parts of the country under Kossuth's government's control.

It was a tremendous effort, not unreminiscent of the French

effort in 1793-4. It would have been even more so had the government and parliament ever been able to formulate an agrarian policy that would really have attracted and enthused the peasantry. As it was, the peasantry played little active part in the conflict. With government encouragement, some did useful guerrilla work early on, harassing the imperial invaders' supply lines and so on. But most of the fighting they engaged in was among themselves in outer parts of the country – Transylvania and south Hungary especially – where the confused political situation coupled with every kind of local feud and hatred to produce civil strife and anarchy. Romanians fought savagely on both sides. A Romanian national historian proudly claims that the revolution in his, Transylvanian, part of the empire was, of all the revolutions of those years,

> by far the longest (15 months...), the bloodiest (40,000 dead, compared to 15,000 in France) and the most destructive (230 villages destroyed and an inestimable number of libraries and archives burned).[72]

But whomever all that violence and slaughter benefitted, it was not Kossuth. The Hungarian achievement through early '49 exceeded even that of '48. Excellently and aggressively led by the Polish general Bem and the indigenous Görgey, Hungary's soldiers – by June, about 150,000 strong but with only about 500 guns – did so well that the emperor was driven to swallow his pride and accept Nicholas I's offer of intervention. Against the combined Austrian and Russian armies (280,000 men with 12,000 cannon) the Hungarian army had little chance. Görgey surrendered, Kossuth escaped to Britain via Turkey, and reaction's roll of infamy soon had added to it the name of the general commissioned to restore order:Haynau.

ITALY's was the most complicated of all national liberation stories, partly because of the political and cultural divisions of the peninsula (divisions so profound that peninsular unity seemed to many merely visionary until it actually happened), partly because of the peculiar complications represented by the Pope and the Papal States. Neighbours' views had to be respected anyway, but all the more when the neighbours were Roman Catholic. It was international news if the Pope complained or suffered, and after their honeymoon of misconceptions about him, relations between Pius IX (1846-78) and Italian nationalism became very bad indeed. The question of the papacy apart, however, the progress of national unification turned on issues familiar enough elsewhere: the amount of leadership given by the strongest monarch within the national area, the king of Piedmont/Savoy/Sardinia; and the amount of foreign intervention – i.e., French intervention to counteract Austrian presence, and British benevolent neutrality. That monarchical role was revolting to republicans (an unusually large proportion of Italian national activists). Dependence on foreign aid could seem dangerous to monarchists and republicans alike. Dependence on monarchs and foreigners both was a sad comedown for all who followed Mazzini's faith in the power of the people.

In the event (a long-drawn-out event, by no reckoning less than twelve years) the people contributed a good deal to their liberation, but hardly in the way expected by the theorists of people's guerrilla warfare. The issue was in the end decided by the people, the kingdom of Piedmont, and France together; the French did the heaviest fighting (Magenta and Solferino in June 1859), Victor Emmanuel and Cavour did the political management and international diplomacy, and the people, remarkably personified by the unique phenomenon named Garibaldi, provided a more than sufficiently supportive background and chorus. But although such a summary is true enough, it does little justice to the twists and turns of the story, which included episodes when both French and Piedmontese troops were fighting Garibaldi (not at the same time), when Napoleon III signed an armistice with Franz Josef without consulting his Piedmont ally, and when Garibaldi, whose readiness for direct action in the name of liberty knew no bounds, enjoyed the connivance of the British government in landing a big band of (by international law) buccaneers on the coast of a country with which HMG was 'at peace'. It was all extraordinarily complicated – all except Garibaldi.

We will fasten on to the Garibaldi thread through this maze, because it was so unusual, not least as an expression of the people in arms. Giuseppe Garibaldi we have already met as a 'young Italy' enthusiast emigrated to South America and by 1848, when he happened to return to Europe, possessed of considerable reputation as chief of Montevideo's 'Italian Legion'. At once he threw himself and such of his legionaries as were with him into the liberating work he found afoot. The next twenty years saw him intermittently hyperactive in the cause of Italian freedom and unity; sometimes as his own (or Italy's) man, to the annoyance of the politic Piedmontese, sometimes as their man (and Italy's), with general's rank in their army. His nationalism being of the earlier, innocent, internationalist sort espoused by the men of the underground (from whom he indeed got his first political ideas), it was as natural to find Hungarians, Poles, Germans and even eccentric Englishmen in his train as to find him being offered commands in Lincoln's army (declined) and Gambetta's (accepted).

What made Garibaldi so uncommonly magnetic was the quality of his faith and life. His military talents *in themselves* were not very remarkable; but they had hardly any existence in themselves, so that hardly mattered. They were merely physical extensions of the magnetic, inspiring and heroic leadership he brought, with a unique mixture of boldness, confidence, humility and simplicity, to the services of democracy and national liberation. He had more than enough self-taught military skill and *savoir-faire* to make good, sometimes excellent, use of devoted followers in irregular warfare, and he understood conventional military science well enough to be able to fit in with major conventional operations when he chose. He was not infallible, his boldness sometimes overreached itself, his lack of concern about his own safety (his life seemed so charmed that pious admirers attributed it to God) led him, in effect, to throw away rather more of his followers' lives than was, objectively, necessary. But what did 'necessary' mean in such a man? He defied ordinary assessment. Without the astounding magnetism, or in a colder psychological climate, he would have amounted to little. With it, then, he bestrode the world.

The magnetism was exercised in two directions, each indispensable to the grand result. It not only formed for him the loyal and courageous but usually rather small bands of followers who marched with him and did the fighting. It formed also the social atmosphere which enabled, even encouraged, them to do it. Recalling Mao Tse-tung's maxim that the peasantry are the sea in which guerrillas must swim, we could fairly say that the Garibaldi legend (his fame preceding him) and magnetism nicely warmed it up. He hardly ever lacked the people's tacit support and as time went by could rely on it in plentiful measure. This not merely helped his bands move quickly through countrysides and to get the food etc. and especially the drink they of course needed, it swelled to become an active protection, an enveloping climate of admiration and invincibility he could positively rely on; a climate which even his enemies found it prudent (for fear of what popular explosion might be unleashed if he *were* killed) to respect. This essential point may be illustrated by a passage from Christopher Hibbert's good book about him. In September 1860 his march from Sicily to, he hoped, Rome brought him to Naples. The king having left it and the several well-garrisoned forts within it, Garibaldi hired a special train at Vietri and sent a telegram to announce his impending arrival. On the way a frantic naval officer got near enough to Garibaldi to shout a warning that the royal troops had cannon trained on Naples station.

'Ma che cannoni?/What guns?', the General replied calmly from his seat by the window. 'When the people receive us like this there are no cannon.'

The train arrived, and no cannon fired. Garibaldi and his staff mounted an open carriage which the huge crowd took, not along the route planned but along a street leading straight to one of the forts.

Garibaldi stood up in the carriage, folded his arms on his chest and looked steadfastly at the fort in the scorching sunlight. He was wearing a black wide-awake hat, a black neckcloth and the coloured silk handkerchief which, knotted round the neck, fell loosely down the back of his red, purple-stained shirt. The troops, who had been ordered by the King not to open fire, obeyed their instructions and remained inactive.[73]

The Bourbon troops had not come over to his, and the people's, side, but they had done the next best thing. And although the people never rose in unconquerable numbers as they were supposed to in the Bianco-Mazzini nationalist scenario, what they did under Garibaldi's magnetic influence was the next best thing too.

Relatively little happened in POLAND in 1848. The events of

1846 would have discouraged any nationalist activists but Polish ones: the failure of Mieroslawski's attempted coup in Posen/Poznan, the appalling turn of events in Galicia when the peasantry supposed in Mieroslawskian theory to rise against the Austrian authorities had instead reported revolutionaries to them and burnt their landlords' houses (often with the landlords in them), and the ten-day wonder of the 'Republic of Cracow'. But Polish nationalism was not easily depressed. In the springtime of nations, was Poland to be left out? In 1848 Mieroslawski and Czartoryski led many other exiles back to the promised land, encouraged at first by Prussian liberals whose fears of Russian intervention caused them to smile on the prospect of a Poland restored to grateful and allied independence. In Posen and in Galicia, where Bem was the leading light, Polish freedom fighters began to organize and train. But again it all came to nothing. The reactionary camarillas in Berlin and Vienna were not prepared to see springtime liberalism lose their empires for them. The Polish organizations were broken up by force of arms, Cracow and Lwow/Lemberg were given the accolade of bombardment, and the dark cold night of alien oppression returned, offering no choice but submission and collaboration on the one hand, prison, Paris or Siberia on the other.

Nicholas I's death in 1858 had much the same effect on Russia and eastern Europe as Stalin's death in 1953. People's hopes rose, and some frost began to thaw. Change was soon proceeding by giant strides in Russia itself, but little more than fair words came Poland's way. National feeling became increasingly resentful, to a considerable extent guided by the nationalist underground (some of which was in fact overground, since some patriotic minor officials, priests, army officers and intellectuals more or less followed its line) and the Agricultural Society, a nationwide association of landowners which in the absence of a parliament had assumed the role of the moderates' national forum (like the Church of Scotland's General Assembly). In January 1861, collaboration rather suddenly stopped. 'The Poles [simply] ceased to obey', as Stefan Kieniewicz puts it.[74] There seems not to have been a master plan behind it, though the underground, soon evolving a provisional government called the Central National Committee, embraced it as a development after its own heart and was emboldened to foment a swelling series of demonstrations and displays ('provocations', in the view of conservatives) which continued into 1862. At first dumbfounded, the authorities responded with a mixture of concessions and repressions. The concessions were rejected as tardy and insufficient; the repressions, in such an atmosphere as now was Poland's, only stiffened resistance. A particularly tough tightening of the screw in January 1863 precipitated armed insurrection.

There followed through the next twelve to eighteen months the most nearly popular national guerrilla war since 1815, with the original and forward-looking addition of an alternative civil administration such as Sinn Fein fifty years later was to offer Ireland. The whole movement, in the civil and military branches both, possessed a tenacious flexibility which enabled it to bend, even to flatten, before the Russian wind, and then to resurface and continue much as before. Towns and villages obeyed whichever authority was uppermost at the time; this was not heroic (except, probably, in the local government officials) but it was sensible and it helped the insurrection to last. Peasants did not 'go to the forest' to join guerrilla bands in anything like their proper proportion but they lent the combatants the supports essential to them: supplies and, despite authority's menaces, silence. At no time seem there to have been more than about 30,000 combatants, but the total number who fought at one time or another was much higher than that, because most of them did a turn or two and then, if still alive, returned home – probably with some awkward explaining to do. But secrecy was in general extraordinarily well preserved. Polish society – all of it, that is, except a committedly collaborationist upper-class minority – proved to be just as *opaque* to authority's view as was the English working class wrapped round the Luddites.[75] Only in the spring of 1864 did the Russian police run down the last of the Central Committee, about the same time as the insurrection was petering out. Kieniewicz cites its last leader, Traugutt, saying not long before his arrest in April: 'Things which have been going on in our country for the past fourteen months have not happened anywhere else in the world . . . .'[76] So far as this historian can see, he was right.

EPILOGUE:
END AND BEGINNING

The justification for beginning this book in the last years of the *ancien régime* is that war then was trembling on the brink of revolutionary changes both in its own nature and in the nature of its lodging, so to speak, in the ordinary socio-political structures of the countries of Europe. The justification for ending the book in the 1860s is that just such another revolution in its nature and connections was then happening. It is the business of the next volume in this series to follow the consequences of that revolution and to explore its total social significance. This epilogue is merely a finger post pointing ahead.

All the conscious endeavours making and subsequently exploiting that earlier revolution in war and society were to do with the relations between peoples and their armed forces: how the latter could be made acceptable to the people, even become the people's own; what war should be like and what about. But war proved a slippery medium to master. Limited war theorists of the Enlightenment had written (and their kind has continued to write ever since) about war as a neat and dextrous tool of policy. Some eighteenth-century wars indeed had come as close to that as calculating statesmanship and cautious generalship could make them. But the circumstances and mood of the age were singular and transitory. Only such circumstances could veil the true, rough nature of war: 'a pulsation of violence', 'an act of force to compel our enemy to do our will';[1] and with the revolution, circumstances changed. Not only were the wars of the revolution more 'total' in aims and methods than wars had been since, men supposed, the early seventeenth century; they also tended to involve whole populations and to become, for some of them for some of the time, their total obsession. All this and more was new.

In one respect however they were not much different from or

296

more intense than war was already known to be, and that was in their material equipment – which is to say, their use of whatever opportunities science, technology and their own degrees of economic development placed in their way. The relative wealth of nations was vitally important to them – only Britain's wealth enabled it in the end to *win* – but what that wealth was buying was much the same as it bought fifty years before: the same sort of warships, cannon, muskets and continental allies.

The character of warfare is always determined to some extent by the technology available. Improved weaponry etc. constitutes an offer which military planners find it always difficult to refuse, sometimes virtually impossible. What will kill or sufficiently injure more enemy at a longer distance, or in a shorter time, or simply more cheaply, is not rashly to be rejected. But man is not a puppet on technology's strings. 'Improvement' in weaponry has to be put into inverted commas and looked at from all sides. Is the expense worthwhile? How long before the enemy catches up? What will this do to our armed forces? What indeed will it do to war? What will the neighbours think of us? And basic principles of the international law of war remain relevant: means of killing and injuring must be capable of discrimination, and must not cause unnecessary suffering.... Governments and their military chiefs have to go through such questions, even if only on grounds of economy and prudence. Yet when all is said to that effect, the inclination to adopt the best new weaponry that can be afforded is very great. Returning now abruptly to our epilogue theme, the revolution in warfare of the mid-nineteenth century, it is clear that at this epoch Vulcan was changing Mars's life style more – and more rapidly – than he had done since he gave him gunpowder. The most novel elements in the revolutionary compound this time came, not from political theory and practice, but from science and technology – the science and the technology which was central to industrialization.

Within the limits of this book, it can be summed up under the three headings: steam, railways and rifles.[2] Steam obviously did to wind-and-sail warfare what gunpowder had done to weapons impelled by muscle. First by turning paddle-wheels, then by turning screw propellers (better than paddles, because more efficient and much less vulnerable), the marine steam-engine offered to revolutionize naval warfare. The many technical problems were not quickly overcome, even by 'pure' engineers mentally unhampered by service traditions and lethargic bureaucracy. But by the Crimean War, the British Navy was using steam tugs in all its ports; its men of war, though superficially still just like Nelson's, mostly in fact had a small steam engine driving a single screw – invaluable in calms and during nice manoeuvres; and steam was being used in small gunboats and ponderous armour-plated floating batteries. Close behind the iron-clad wooden-hulled steam warship (*La Gloire*, 1859) came, in the form of *HMS Warrior*, 1861, the first iron-hulled warship in European waters. Iron became steel in the seventies, sails disappeared completely as engine technology vastly improved, guns (we shall attend to them soon) became more like those of 1915 than 1805. Big warships had always been expensive. They only became more so as the most refined technology that money could buy thus became indispensable to national defence. But no country that wanted to make any sort of showing on the seas dared lag behind the leader. With the steam-powered warship building competition between Britain and France began about 1849 that tragically distinctive phenomenon of our modern age, the industrialized arms race.

Railways began to discover military usefulness in the later forties but the idea went further back. Showalter shows that certain industrialists and promoters, leaders of German liberal bourgeois opinion, were already sketching blueprints for a militarily valuable railway system as early as the twenties and trying to interest the generals and government in the idea. Their motives were no doubt mixed – what was going to be good for Prussia and its economic satellites would be good for them too – but it is probably indicative of the diffused militarism of German society that the vision came to just such men, just there. The military's initial scepticism slowly yielded in the light of demonstration and experience, and by the forties some officers, among them the young Helmuth von Moltke, were combining professional with business interests by participating in railway promotion themselves. The first time troops were moved by rail in Germany was in 1839. That was the same year when the British government first made significant use of the railway in its military control of Chartism. Not a lot of the rail acquired within the next decade was exactly where the generals would most have wanted it, but where it was so, it was found invaluable for domestic and foreign uses alike: e.g., Prussia rushing troops to Dresden to back the counter-revolution there in May 1848; French troops moving some of the way to Rome to overthrow Garibaldi in the spring of 1849; Austria moving over 70,000 men into Bohemia within two weeks to overawe Prussia at Olmütz in the late autumn of 1850. By now, the strategic value of railway systems was undisputed among intelligent soldiers, and the question was not whether use would be made of them but whether they would be there to be used, and whether that use would be good. The Prussians, with their unique attention to strategic planning and staff work, steadily forged ahead. France had plenty of railways in its eastern provinces by 1870, but the French army had few plans for using them, and was given no time to improvise better. Moltke and his staff on the other hand had carefully studied the matter for years, learnt a lot by trial and error in 1866, and now gave the world its first lesson in the time-tabled rapid mobilization (only fifteen days) of a mass army.

By 'rifles' Showalter means not just the infantry weapons commonly so called but rifled guns in general. Few infantry rifles had been in use during the French wars (and no other rifled guns at all). Everyone knew they were more accurate, but they were a lot more expensive to manufacture and took somewhat longer to load; rifles were necessary for certain light infantry work, but there were many good reasons why the classic smooth-bore musket should remain the basic infantry weapon. The restlessness of inventors however would not leave it alone. Improvements were made, now in this part, now in that, as generals allowed themselves to be persuaded (it was sometimes a slow process) and treasuries found the money. The barrel was rifled to fire not the old looser-fitting ball but a tighter-fitting conical-shaped bullet; the firing charge was enclosed in a waterproof cartridge, and was ignited by percussion cap in place of flint; finally the formidable problems of breech-loading were solved. The war of 1859 was 'the first in which all the infantry on both sides carried rifles';[3] by 1870 there were breech-loaders on both sides too, firing much further and faster and more accurately than had been possible only thirty years before, not to mention from kneeling or lying positions without having to stand up to load. Cannon went through a similarly dramatic evolution through the same years, with results dissimilar only in that a vast increase in the sizes of the weapon and its projectile was possible. Alfred Krupp established his reputation among the military with his cast-steel rifled six-poun- der field-gun, more or less adopted by 1860, but what caught the world's attention were monsters like the 14-inch cannon displayed at his stall at the Paris International Exhibition of 1867.

This is not the place to recount the ways in which this formidable new weaponry and equipment and modern industrial backing constituted a revolution in the *material* of war which compelled the human side to follow.[4] How quickly the human side followed, varied from country to country and from arm to arm. The officer class has usually been culturally conservative, by no means as eager to snap up dazzling new killing devices as their inventors have expected. The wheels of bureaucracy and political decision often turned very slowly. Economy, practicability, tactical value, appropriate training, all had to be carefully considered; and when the innovation was at last accepted, it had to be meshed into the whole military-industrial complex (with Krupps and Armstrongs, it becomes permissible to use the expression) and its manufacture, transportation, distribution, maintenance etc. all assured from production-line to battlefield. Each army had its technical experts and its weapon specialities. The most 'advanced' weapon in the war of 1870 was the French *mitrailleuse*, a primitive heavy machine-gun, capable if well used of doing enormous execution and psychological damage. But it was very badly used where anyone knew how to use it at all. *There* was the difference between the French and Prussian military systems: the French, unintellectual if not positively anti-intellectual, cultivating courage and obedience as supremely valuable qualities in a quasi-professional army detached from society at large, and laughing at the Prussians, many of whom – could anything be more absurd? – wore spectacles!; the Prussians, unashamed of the spectacles brought into the army by its cross-section of Europe's best-educated population, and with its Great General Staff in acknowledged control of all the arrangements. 1870-1 was not just the victory of the nation-in-arms, new industrial style, over first a rather old-style professional army and then a *levée en masse*; it was also the victory of modern scientific brain over traditional instinctive brawn.

The societies supplying the men, the money and the munitions for these first 'modern' style wars were in outline the societies the liberal Revolutionaries of '89 and subsequently had been groping and striving for: commercially and industrially expansive, internally free-trading, urbanizing; societies in which the middle classes necessarily implied in such developments carried increasing political weight; by bourgeois lights progressive and confident, by lower-class lights exploitative and threatening, by everyone's lights increasingly restless and changeful. Historians of every ideological bent join to acknowledge that in some strong sense this was 'liberal Europe', 'bourgeois Europe'. But it was also what it had not been for more than a generation, a warring Europe. With our eye on its military dimension, and recalling the prominent place the question of composition and control of armed forces held in that original liberal tradition, we must now inquire, what had happened to it? Were these renewed international wars of the fifties and sixties its wars? If not, whose were they?

The answer has to be that of course they were, and that they were so because liberalism, not surprisingly, was changing with the times. The simplest way to explain it is in terms of its contradictions. They have repeatedly been noticed in the foregoing pages. They appeared over the questions: who are the people, and what is the Nation? It was in the name of the people that revolutions were always undertaken, but in every revolution from 1789 to 1848, the people had ended up at each other's throats; bourgeois against worker. Neither side (to put it crudely) stayed stationary. The bourgeoisie was growing in bulk, in importance, in confidence, in boldness. The industrial working class (peasants can be left out of this picture) was growing in numbers, in concentration, in boldness and in menace. The forties were a crucial decade for class relations because they clarified the angry existence on the continent of what had existed, rather more passively, for over a generation in Britain: a proletariat, with Marx and Engels among its prophets. 'The mob' was there as ever, but now socialism and communism had come to stay too. The counter-revolutions of 1848 were fuelled in part by the first 'red scare', and the bourgeoisie was as scared as the nobility and the military. Faced with such terrors (to what extent imaginary, is no matter) in its own towns and countrysides, the class in whom liberalism had its firmest lodging, became habituated to the use

301

of armed force against revolution and disturbance from below (if in the last resort the new police could not handle it); if it could not compose and control such armed force itself, it preferred it to rest in conservative hands than not to be there at all. Only in Prussia of the major powers did there persist after 1848 much open endeavour by liberals to keep the army in their hands rather than yield it up to the conservatives and the professionals; and by 1866, that endeavour had failed too – not so much because of the liberal contradiction about the People, as because of its other big contradiction about the Nation.

The working-class problem being at least temporarily overcome by the blood-lettings of 1848-9 and the political repressions and rigorous policing which followed, and the reassuring sense that if the worst came to the worst the army would intervene to save the bourgeois' bacon, liberals were free to indulge their self-destructive weakness for nationalism. Historians of nationalism like to point out the contrast between its earlier and later nineteenth-century phases: the earlier one retaining from the previous century much of its internationalist idealism and pacific inclination, the later one parting with internationalism and becoming variously imperialist/chauvinist/xenophobic. The contrast must not be overdone. Brissot and Arndt would have felt at home with Gambetta and Treitschke; internationalism never ceased to be a force for nationalism to cope with, and a call upon its conscience. But nonetheless the cleft down its middle widened to expose the contradiction: it was shown to be difficult in practice to be a keen national man without becoming involved in fighting other keen national men. To some extent the fighting was forced upon them by external factors like the ordinary balancing mechanisms of the States system and, after the sixties, the avalanche of vulgar Darwinism and the cult of Nietzsche which persuaded men and collectivities to think they must act tough if they were to be true to themselves; but it was also voluntarily embraced from about the forties as the proper attitude for self-respecting Nation-States. Nationalism having needed armed force to bring it to political birth, kept and cherished it as proof of maturity. By no means exclusively military in its sources, it became militarized, and the liberalism with which it had long kept company caught the contagion. The 'nation in arms' remained the great ideal, but what a difference there was between the democratic, free-thinking,

302

citizen-soldiering original of '92-4 – even the British militia man of 1803 or the *Landwehr* man of 1813 – and the mass army conscript later being barked at by regular officers and NCOs on the barrack square! What a sinister contrast, too, between that original and the doctrine evolving among at any rate the Prussian and Austrian officer corps (Spanish anticipations of this seem insignificant) as early as the end of the forties, that in the last resort their armies *were* the fatherland!

This militarization of liberalism and nationalism achieved during our period nothing like the heights and heat it would achieve by the end of the century. By the end of the sixties, however, it had clearly gone quite far. When did it start? Nothing in history ever 'begins', just like that. Every people and nation had its past to call on if it wished. Flattering fragments survived in folklore and patriotic legend; the pioneers of modern nationalism were busily at work by the turn of the nineteenth century, filling in the gaps. We have already considered how much of a boost the experiences of the wars gave to the national and, so far as it was different, military spirit. We have also taken the measure of Napoleon Bonaparte, the latter's chief inspirer, whose cult and vogue began almost directly after he got to St Helena. Nevertheless the Restoration enforced some measure of hiatus on the militarization process. However glorious the feats of the immediate past, the costs had been great to society (even in the UK there was a taxpayers' revolt the moment war ended) and the risks and anxieties enormous to the rulers restored. European society was war-weary, and governments to begin with did not regret it. But bit by bit, each country moving at its own pace and in its own way, the fascinations of war reasserted themselves, and in alliance with liberalism and nationalism promised to be more potent than ever before.

Eighteenth-century continental monarchs never had to worry about being pushed by their people into wars they didn't want. On the contrary, their problem was more to persuade their people to take an interest in their wars – if the people's opinions were thought to matter at all. But already by the 1840s the people's opinions in the more advanced (liberal meaning of the word) countries were felt by monarchs and governments to have a power not easy to ignore, while the said monarchs and governments, although theoretically caring nothing for the views of the governed, were perceiving that this power, 'liberal' though its credentials were, could be engaged to strengthen their own positions. It was a measure of the character of the process in question, that war fever could now as well vent itself in foolish war scares of self-indulgent demands for war against remote, imagined enemies as in the proper liberal form of preparation for immediate national defence.

The year 1840, indeed, may mark the watershed: the year of the 'return of the Ashes' to Paris, of righteous German readiness for war along the Rhine, of Palmerston's and Thiers's competitively aggressive handling of 'the Eastern question', of the forerunner of an embarrassing series of British panics about French invasion, and of an increase in the extraordinary Russophobia which, attaining near-hysteria level, was to push Lord Aberdeen's government into war fourteen years later. The popularization of military spirit had gone far by the end of the decade. Napoleon III was not in a position to be pushed but he welcomed the opportunity of martial popularity. Austrian spirit was stirred by the Italian victories which prompted Strauss's 'Radetsky March'. German spirit is more difficult to pin down since it experienced the unique difficulty of looking 'inwards' (the great unity question) and 'outwards' (what to do about Poles, Danes and Alsatians within the arguably German sphere, about France, Denmark and Russia outside it) at once. National unity and truly liberal politics turned out to be mutually incompatible. National unity won, and their own inability to resist indulging in patriotic national sentiment during the wars of 1864 (German Confederation against Denmark) and 1866 (Prussia against Austria etc.) in the end undid the German liberals. The labour leader Wilhelm Liebknecht's comment on their surrender at the 5 August opening of the *Landtag* by acquiescing in the bill indemnifying the government for having governed unconstitutionally for several years and for fighting (and winning) two wars in that time, seems superbly apt:

The oppressions of yesterday are the saviours of today; right has become wrong and wrong right. Blood appears, indeed, to be a special elixir, for the angel of darkness has become the angel of light, before whom the people lie in the dust and adore. The stigma of violation of the constitution has been washed from his brow, and in its place the halo of glory rings his laurelled head.[5]

Clearly, the supersession of 'war-weariness' by such a climate of opinion as this was more likely to facilitate the recurrence of war than to discourage it. International war in fact recurred, after the long period of relative peacefulness which the Concert of Europe had done its best to engineer or impose. The Concert was coming to pieces by about 1850; the national question was beginning to force the great powers on to opposite sides of it, and the competitive accompaniments of economic development were making them more conscious of the ways their interests differed than of what interests they had in common. But it is very difficult to say exactly what are 'the causes', let alone what is 'the cause', of any particular outbreak of war. The range of likely factors is both wide and deep. Identifying and evaluating proximate and admitted causes is a simpler matter than long-term, less apparent ones; some variables can more or less be quantified, but others cannot; changes in the climate of opinion must matter somehow, no one can doubt it, but exactly how is much disputed.[6] More concrete and indisputable are factors like internal political pressures, admitted foreign policy aims, and shifts in the balance of power. International war recurred in Europe apropos of the national question. Prussia (plus, in theory, the rest of the German Confederation) was briefly at war with Denmark over the future of Schleswig-Holstein in the summer of '48, while Savoy was more vigorously engaged with Austria over the future of north Italy. Next year came two striking reactionary interventions: Nicholas I's against the Hungarians, and that of Louis Napoleon, then President of the Republic, against Garibaldi and the short-lived Republic of Rome. This latter intervention, in its relation to the national question more like Nicholas's than Charles Albert's, was out of character with what was soon to become the policy of Napoleon III, but its *Innenpolitik* sources were those becoming commonplace in the more advanced countries, whether they were liberal-parliamentary or not: the political advantage to be derived from gratifying the demands and indulging the phobias of significant groups of subjects.

Domestic pressures of that kind combined with orthodox foreign policy calculations and an unusual amount of muddle to bring

305

Britain and France (and later Savoy) to the side of the Ottoman Empire in its war with Russia in the mid-fifties. Only a very limited and peripheral war as far as the western participants were concerned, its consequences for Britain and Russia and for the European States-system were enormous. Austria's unexpected severing of its long-established friendly relationship with Russia left Russia isolated and angry, while the humiliation of defeat put steel into the new Tsar's resolve to grapple decisively at last with the gigantic question of Russia's peculiar institution (see above, p.229). But, the quality of its army and some further humiliations of the peace terms apart, Russia's ability to look after itself was not much affected. Quite otherwise was it with Austria, which never got nearer war than threatening to join in. The Habsburgs found themselves on their own when they sought to retain hold of their provinces in Italy and their ascendant presence in the German world. All had gone by 1866, and defeat did for the Austro-Hungarian Empire what it had done for the Russian – it catalysed the ruling élite's readiness to grasp crucial nettles, in this case the very constitution of the empire.

Austria's losses were Savoy's and Prussia's gains. All Europe's wars from 1859 to 1870, when the series ended, were pre-eminently to do with Italian and German unification. Italy was a single kingdom by the end of 1860, barring only Venetia and the more disputable southern slopes of the Tyrolean Alps and Istrian peninsula, and Rome where a small French garrison stayed until 1866, and French officers until 1870. Venetia was incorporated in '66; the other regions remained to haunt Italy from the other side of the Austrian border until 1919. More astonishing and, for the States-system, disturbing, was the appearance by 1871 upon the map of Europe of a German Empire of hitherto unimagined proportions; the result, first, of Prussia's peaceful expansion of its influence and wealth through customs unions; second, its annexations, following successful applications of 'blood and iron', of Hanover, Hesse-Kassel, Nassau, Frankfurt and Schleswig-Holstein (detached by war from Denmark two years earlier) in 1866, of Alsace and half Lorraine in 1871. Herein lay the most momentous political development of the age: France humbled and mutilated, Germany now by far the most powerful single State on the continent, having become so by force of arms on top of prodigious industrial growth. 'Europe has lost a mistress,' observed Thomas Carlyle, 'and gained a master.' Its presence, its methods, and its means were to disturb its neighbours' sleep and to dominate their thinking about war and society for the next sixty years.

But that is another story.

NOTES

Authors of books listed in the Bibliography are in capitals.

PART I

1. CORVISIER (1979) p.113.
2. WOLFF, p.55.
3. BARDIN, under 'Milice, Naples'.
4. HAMPSON, p.209.
5. KITCHEN, p.23.
6. MATTHEW B. RIDGWAY, cited by M. Janowicz in *The Professional Soldier* (1960) p.223.
7. CORVISIER, p.71.
8. FORTESCUE, iii. p.525.
9. MACARTNEY, p.18.
10. ROSE, p.137.
11. FORTESCUE, iv. p.77.
12. BOND and ROY, ii. p.150.
13. KIRALY, pp.106-7.
14. REDLICH
15. SCOTT, pp.34, 42-4.
16. CORVISIER, p.113.
17. CORVISIER, p.134.
18. CORVISIER, p.81. (My translation.)
19. MARCUS, i. pp.347-8.
20. Meyer in BEDARIDA *et al.* p.170.
21. HAMPSON, p.71.
22. LEWIS (1960), p.318.
23. MARCUS, i. p.382.
24. FORTESCUE, iii. pp.41, 524-5.
25. ANDOLENKO, pp.125-6.
26. MACARTNEY, p.18n.
27. PARET (1966), p.13.
28. GODECHOT, p.119.

29. ANDOLENKO, pp.87-9.
30. FORTESCUE, ii. p.578.
31. PARET, (1966) p.21.
32. DEMETER, p.177.
33. My translation of pp.56, 67 of Ménard's edition (1977) of Guibert, *Ecrits Militaires 1772-1790*.
34. REINHARD, i. p.127.

PART II

1. CLAUSEWITZ, Book 8, ch.3.
2. Ibid.
3. SCOTT, p.49.
4. SCOTT, pp.53-4, 58-9.
5. Quotations from speeches by Barère on 9 July and 26 May 1794 respectively.
6. HAMPSON, pp.198-9.
7. BERTAUD, pp.196-7.
8. BERTAUD, p.251. (My translation.)
9. *Moniteur*, 3 January 1793.
10. SCOTT, p.178.
11. My translation.
12. *La Pensée*, no.85, p.40.
13. ROTHENBERG (1977), p.36.
14. PARET (1976), p.130.
15. Cited by BEST, pp.91, 94.
16. GODECHOT, pp.367-9.
17. HAMPSON, pp.239-40. (My translation.)
18. SMEATON, p.69.
19. *Moniteur*, 10 July 1794. (My translation.)
20. Sent to General Blake, 6 January 1812.
21. From a letter of 10 July 1813 in the Bingham Papers in the National Army Museum; typed copies, vol.3, p.50.
22. ARTOLA, p.182.
23. CLAUSEWITZ, pp.332-9, *passim*.
24. *Despatches*, vi. pp.110-1.
25. *Letters*, ed. B. Liddell Hart, 1951, p.117.

26. The Abbé Zahn, in *Carnets de la Sabretache*, no.111, 1902, pp.135-47.
27. His *Journal* (published 1895), pp.245-8.
28. BARDIN, 'Conscription'.
29. MARKHAM, p.177.
30. LA BARRE DE NANTEUIL, p.82.
31. Ibid., p.167.
32. GODECHOT, p.647.
33. LA BARRE DE NANTEUIL, p.163. Godechot confirms this on p.647; Russia's total payments, he says, 'vary according to estimates from 470 to 514 millions'.
34. MARION, iv. p.321.
35. HOBSBAWM, end of ch.4, summarizing the conclusions of Tarlé.
36. GODECHOT, p.611; BRAUDEL et LABROUSSE, ii., part 1, p.186.
37. LEFEBVRE, 1969 edition, p.209.
38. Ibid. The figure offered for 1792-1814 by Gachot in *Revue des Etudes Napoléoniennes*, vol.13 (1918), at p.156, is 617,000, which seems roughly to tally.
39. Senkowska-Gluck in *Occupants, Occupés*, 1969.
40. For Lithuania see Chabanier in *Revue Historique de l'Armée*, 1973, no.2, pp.29-46.
41. RAMM, pp.83-4.
42. CHANDLER, p.756.
43. GIRARDET, p.16.
44. From Waquet in *Bibliothèque de l'école des chartes*, vol.126 (1968), p.191. Similar mourning rituals were reported from Russia – see ROTHENBERG (1977), p.197.
45. Apart from the works of Waquet I have used Meynier in *Revue des Etudes Napoléoniennes*, vol.30 (1931), pp.26-51.
46. Bruchet in *Revue du Nord* (1920), pp.261-3.
47. GODECHOT, p.605.
48. HINSLEY, p.186.
49. From Waquet's article in *Revue Internationale d'Histoire Militaire* (1970), no.30, pp.185-6. (My translation.)
50. Louis J. Thomas in *Revue des Etudes Napoléoniennes*, 1913, pp.346-66.
51. EMSLEY, p.33.
52. HOBSBAWM, as in note 35, above.

53. Greenwood in *Journal of the Royal Statistical Society*, vol.105 (1942), pp.1-16. The method is to correct both wars' figures to allow for deaths estimated to have been sure to happen anyway, war or no war.
54. MARCUS, i. p.347.
55. INGRAM, p.169.
56. EMSLEY, p.12, following Western.
57. HALEVY, 1924, i. p.62.
58. HAYTER, p.21.
59. Cited by HALEVY, p.76n.
60. INGRAM, p.171.
61. Wellington (1812), cited in HALEVY, p.75.
62. A most excellent historical reconstruction of the Humbert episode may be found in Thomas Flanagan's 1979 novel thus entitled.
63. From 'The Soldier's Friend' in *The Anti-Jacobin*, a brilliantly inventive journal published with government contributions during the parliamentary session 1797-8.
64. PATTERSON, pp.14-15.
65. MARCUS, ii. pp.100-1.
66. SHERWIG, p.310.
67. EMSLEY, p.159.
68. Deane in WINTER, p.100.
69. LEYLAND, ii. p.xix. There are several versions of this story, which I have tried to track to its source, so far without success.
70. EMSLEY, pp.32, 107.
71. Ibid., pp.108-9.
72. See R. Glover in KNAFLA *et al.*, pp.127-43, pp.136-7.
73. From R. Kverndal's article about George Charles Smith in *Mariner's Mirror*, vol.62 (1976), pp.47-51. Smith's observations, sharpened by his religious sensibility, are fascinatingly close to Tolstoy's descriptions of Russian soldiers' chat and shouting during Borodino. Both, naturally, leave out the coarser stuff.
74. LEWIS (1960), pp.135-8.
75. GREENWOOD as in note 53, above, using the *actual* figures.
76. HENDERSON, p.41.
77. *The Times*, 4 October 1813, p.3, col.4.
78. FORTESCUE, iv. p.407.

79. EMSLEY, who so describes it on p.37, covers all its phases with exemplary clarity.
80. PARET (1966), p.16n; (1976) p.59.
81. DEMETER, p.8. English readers may catch the allusion if we describe this system as based on respect for Von Buggins's turn.
82. CRAIG, p.34.
83. CRAIG, p.36.
84. RITTER, i. pp.72-3, summarizing Gneisenau.
85. I rely here on Ritter, Paret and Dorpalen.
86. KITCHEN, p.56.
87. CHARETON, p.15.
88. 'Das Schwertlied'; my translation of the last verse.
89. KITCHEN, p.55.
90. CRAIG, p.60.
91. PARET (1966), p.212.
92. PARET (1976), pp.236-7.
93. See e.g. CRAIG, pp.66-8.
94. ARTOLA, c.p.91.
95. LOVETT, ii. pp.707, 718.
96. LOVETT, i. p.192.
97. NAPIER, end of Book 1, ch.5.
98. WELLER, pp.122-3.
99. PARET (1966), p.199, cited by ROTHENBERG, 1977, p.170.
100. KORNILOV, *Modern Russian History*, tr. 1916, p.119n.
101. That the army's strength fell to about 40,000 men seems generally agreed; estimates only vary as to what number it fell from – Clausewitz's 110,000 being the lowest I have seen. The $1\frac{1}{2}$ m. is from S. W. Baron, *The Russian Jew under Tsars and Soviets* (1964), p.70.
102. *War and Peace*, Book 14, ch.1 = vol.iii (pp.287-8).

PART III

1. Vilar in *Occupants, Occupés*, pp.239-40.
2. WOOLF, p.219.
3. BARDIN, 'Maraudage'.
4. BARANY, p.49.

5. *Economic History of Modern Britain*, ii. p.451.
6. For Stein see Obermann in *Occupants, Occupés*, at p.263.
7. I have gone over this ground more fully in my *Humanity in Warfare*, ch.3, part 1.
8. *War and Peace*, Book 5, ch.21 = vol. ii, pp.548-50.
9. From an article by Woensky in *Revue des Etudes Napoléoniennes*, January – June 1913, at p.191.
10. OMAN, p.449.
11. From his *De la guerre*, 1856, pp.35-6. What gives this passage special point for present purposes is where I found it – among the notes of Gustave Moynier, president of the International Committee of the Red Cross 1864-1910.
12. MARMONT, pp.16, 275, 21.
13. See e.g., TULARD and LUCAS-DEBRETON.
14. See again TULARD, and add GEYL.
15. MARKHAM, opening of ch.17.
16. SAMPSON cites this at p.61.
17. CRAIG, pp.70-1.
18. PARET (1976), p.117n.
19. Prince Frederick Charles, cited by DEMETER at p.262.
20. *Putnam's Monthly*, vol.6 (September 1855), p.306.
21. I gratefully borrow these figures from Lüdtke's big article in *Social History*, vol.4 (1979), part 2, at pp.199-202.
22. Cited by F. L. Carsten, and presumably translated by him, in his fine chapter in HOWARD 1957, p.80.
23. Ibid, p.81.
24. From a review of 'The Military Establishments of Germany' in *United Services Journal*, vol.12 (1833), part 2, pp.18ff.
25. A clear view of this complicated matter may be found in Wolfgang Peter's pp.226-301 of the *Handbuch zur deutschen Militärgeschichte*, vol.4, part 2.
26. Translated and cited by PORCH, pp.3-4.
27. SCHNAPPER, pp.108-9.
28. CURTISS (1965), p.177.
29. Engels, as in note 20 above, p.313.
30. *Foreign Quarterly Review*, July 1841, pp.248-51.
31. DUMAS and VEDEL-PETERSEN, citing Moltke.
32. ANDOLENKO, p.255n.
33. Engels, as in note 20, at p.311.
34. This last bit, from CURTISS (1965), p.286.

35. *United Services Journal*, vol.7, part 3 (1831), at p.28.
36. BARTLETT, p.24.
37. SPIERS, p.36.
38. British figures again mainly from Spiers. The relative size of the British army seems to be exaggerated by Kenneth Bourne in his *Foreign Policy of Victorian England* (1970), at p.6.
39. From R. Taylor in *Mariner's Mirror*, vol.44 (1958), at pp.302-3.
40. BARTLETT, p.308.
41. My calculation based on Taylor in note 39.
42. BARTLETT, p.310.
43. Taylor again, at p.312.
44. Digested from SPIERS, pp.62-3.
45. Charles Buller's cry in the Commons, 22 March 1839, in FORTESCUE, xi. p.510.
46. I here follow BAYLEY ch.3, rather than SPIERS, pp.162-3.
47. See generally SPIERS, esp. pp.109, 17.
48. SPIERS, p.82.
49. SPIERS, pp.85, 79.
50. From a Bishops' Conference message to the troops in 1849, cited by SKED, p.32.
51. SKED, p.35.
52. ROTHENBERG (1976), p.14.
53. He further noted that they had therefore sensibly made it comfortable: CARRIÈRE, pp.26-9.
54. CARRIÈRE, p.7.
55. PRESLAND, pp.68-9.
56. HIBBERT (1965), p.293.
57. JELAVICH, p.72.
58. CARR, p.139.
59. YOUNG, p.52. The Italian's own spelling was Macirone. Dr Rosselli has reminded me that English radicals then may not have found these names as funny as Young did, much later.
60. Except by LAQUEUR in his ch.3.
61. KUKIEL.
62. *Della guerra d'insurrezione conveniente all 'Italia.*
63. *Della guerra nazionale d'insurrezione per bande.*
64. MACARTNEY, p.322.
65. Cited by SKED, p.124.

66. Cited by D. MACK SMITH, pp.143-4.
67. SKED, pp.55-6.
68. HOLBORN, p.87.
69. Cited by SCHNERB, p.78.
70. CHORLEY, p.173.
71. PAMLÉNYI, p.271.
72. Florescu in *Austrian History Year Book*, 1976-7.
73. HIBBERT, (1965) pp.278-9.
74. I gladly acknowledge a large debt to his article.
75. The 'opaque' concept is borrowed, of course, from E. P. Thompson.
76. KIENIEWICZ at p.147. I presume this is his translation, and am grateful for it.

EPILOGUE

1. CLAUSEWITZ, Book I, ch.1.
2. *Railroads and Rifles* is in fact the title of by far the deepest book yet written about it, by SHOWALTER. N.B. its subtitle.
3. ROPP, p.168.
4. The best *short* surveys of it known to me are ROPP's ch. 6, and Christopher Harvie's Units 'Technology and Weaponry 1848-70' and 'War and Technology in the 19th century' in the Open University's courses A309 and A301 respectively.
5. Cited from R. Olden by CRAIG, p.177.
6. These sentences are written after an earnest but unsuccessful endeavour to dig something useful out of SINGER AND SMALL; RUSSETT (ed.); and BOUTHOUL and CARRÈRE. The Frenchmen, like WRIGHT at the back of them all, are however very suggestive and full of historical insight.

GLOSSARY

ab novo	from the very beginning
a fortiori	still more, therefore
Afrancesados	literally, 'the Frenchified' – Spanish Francophiles
Annales	French historical journal of notably social-scientific character
bricone	criminal, ruffian
Brumaire	one of the autumn months in the French revolutionary calendar
Bürgergarden/Bürgerwehr	citizen's militia, civic guard
cahiers des doléances	lists of grievances presented to the Estates General in 1789
Canton	local government district
carrière ouverte aux talents	allocation of rank and status according to abilities, instead of birth
chouannerie	peasant rebellion in north-west France
Civis romanus sum	'I am a Roman citizen'
contrôles	musters
Cortes	the Spanish parliament
demi-soldes	soldiers on half-pay
dirigiste	belonging to or expressing the principle of centralized administrative control

317

Drang nach Osten	drive to the east
émeute	rioting mob or crowd
émigrés	Royalists who left France when the Revolution intensified
engagés	volunteers
Freikorps	armed volunteer bands
gardes-côtes	coast-guards
Grenzer	frontiersmen (Austro-Hungarian)
hors concours	out of the running
Innenpolitik	domestic, internal politics
in posse	potentially, as opposed to actually
jacquerie	lower-class rebellion (French original, 1358)
Jäger	literally, huntsmen; in German armies, skirmishers, light infantry
Junker	nobleman in East Prussia
Landrat	Prussian official at head of rural local authority
Landsturm	roughly, 'home guard' in Germany
Landtag	legislative assembly
Landwehr	roughly, militia in Germany
levée en masse	universal call-up in a state of national emergency
milice	roughly, militia
modus vivendi	co-existence, way of living with
mutatis mutandis	changes being made as appropriate

Notwehr	state of necessity occasioned by national emergency
Ordenanza	Portuguese militia
pari passu	at an equal pace
parlement	high court
pro tem.	for the time being
rappel	call to arms
rapprochement	a drawing together again
Reichstag	national assembly, parliament
Sans culottes	French revolutionary extremists
seigneur	*ancien régime* landlord
soi-disant	self-styled
soubriquet	nick-name
sui generis	unique, of its kind
tiers état	the Third Estate, in effect the House of Commons in the French Estates General
tout court	merely, simply
Volksbewaffnung	arming of the people at large
Vormärz	conventional German term for period leading up to 1848 revolutions
Weltanschauung	view of the world

SELECT BIBLIOGRAPHY

Anderson, M.S., *The Ascendancy of Europe. Aspects of European History, 1815-1914* (1972)

Anderson, Olive, *A Liberal State at War. English Politics and Economics during the Crimean War* (1967)

Andolenko, G., *Histoire de l'armée russe* (1967)

Artola Gallego, Miguel, *La España de Fernando VII*, vol. 26 (1968) of Menéndez Pidál, Ramón (ed.) *Historia de España*

Barany, George, *Stephen Széchenyi and the Awakening of Hungarian Nationalism, 1791-1841* (1968)

Bardin, E.A., *Dictionnaire de l'armée de terre . . .* (1841-51)

Bartlett, C.J., *Great Britain and Sea Power, 1815-1853* (1963)

Bayley, C.C., *Mercenaries for the Crimea. The German, Swiss and Italian Legions in British Service, 1854-6* (1977)

Bédarida, F., Crouzet, F., and Johnson, D. (eds.), *De Guillaume le conquérant au Marché Commun. Dix siècles d'histoire franco-britannique* (1979)

Berger, Martin, *Engels, Armies and Revolution. The Revolutionary Tactics of Classical Marxism* (1977)

Bertaud, J.-P., *Valmy. La démocratie en armes* (1970)

Best, G., and Wheatcroft, A. (eds.), *War, Economy and the Military Mind* (1976)

Best, Geoffrey, *Humanity in Warfare. The Modern History of the International Law of Armed Conflicts* (1980)

Blainey, Geoffrey, *The Causes of Wars* (1973)

Bond, Brian, and Roy, Ian (eds.), *War and Society. A Yearbook of Military History*: vol. 1 (1976), vol. 2 (1977)

Bouthoul, G., and Carrère, R., *Le défi de la guerre* (1976)

Braudel, F. and Labrousse, E. (eds.), *Histoire économique et sociale de la France*: 4 vols. (1970-9)

Carr, Raymond, *Spain 1808-1939* (1966)
Carrière, Colonel, *Les forces militaires de l'Autriche*... (1853)
Chandler, David, *The Campaigns of Napoleon* (1966)
Chapperon, Alessio, *L'organica militare fra le due guerre mondiali*... (1920)
Chareton, V., *Les corps francs dans la guerre moderne. Les moyens à leur opposer* (n.d. but *c.* 1900)
Charnay, J.-P., *Société militaire et suffrage politique en France depuis 1789* (1964)
Chorley, K.C., *Armies and the Art of Revolution* (1943)
Christiansen, Eric, *The Origins of Military Power in Spain, 1800-1854* (1967)
Clausewitz, Carl von, *On War*, ed. and tr., Howard, Michael, and Paret, Peter (1976)
Clogg, Richard (ed.), *The Movement for Greek Independence, 1770-1821* (1976)
Connelly, Owen, *Napoleon's Satellite Kingdoms* (1965)
Corvisier, André, *Armies and Societies in Europe, 1494-1789* (1st ed. 1976, tr. 1979)
Craig, Gordon, *The Politics of the Prussian Army* (1st ed. 1955)
Creveld, Martin van, *Supplying War. Logistics from Wallenstein to Patton* (1977)
Curtiss, John S., *The Russian Army under Nicholas I, 1825-1855* (1965)
Curtiss, John S., *Russia's Crimean War* (1979)

Deak, Istvan, *The Lawful Revolution. Louis Kossuth and the Hungarians, 1848-9* (1979)
Demeter, Karl, *The German Officer Corps in Society and State, 1650-1945* (2nd ed. 1962, tr. 1965)
Dorpalen, Andreas, 'The German Struggle against Napoleon: the East German View', in *Journal of Modern History*, vol. 49 (1969), pp.485-516
Duffy, Christopher, *Borodino. Napoleon against Russia* (1972)
Duffy, Christopher, *The Army of Maria Theresa, 1740-1780* (1977)
Duffy, Christopher, *Austerlitz, 1805* (1977)

Dumas, S. and Vedel-Petersen, K., *Losses of Life caused by War* (1923)

Ellis, John, *Armies in Revolution* (1977)
Emsley, Clive, *British Society and the French Wars, 1793-1815* (1979)
Engels, Friedrich, 'The Armies of Europe', in *Putnam's Monthly. A Magazine of Literature, Science and Art*, vol. 6 (1855), pp. 193-206, 307-17, 561-71
Engels, Friedrich, *Engels as Military Critic*, Introduction by Chaloner, W.H. and Henderson, W.O. (1959)

Fantin des Odoards, L.F., *Journal du Général ... Etapes d'un officier de la grande armée, 1800-1830* (1895)
Flanagan, Thomas, *The Year of the French* (1979)
Fortescue, John W., *A History of the British Army*, 13 vols. (1899-1930)
Fugier, A., *Napoléon et l'Italie* (1947)
Fuller, J.F.C., *The Conduct of War, 1789-1961* (1961)

Geyl, Pieter, *Napoleon, for and against* (1947, tr. 1949)
Ginsborg, Paul, *Daniele Manin and the Venetian Revolution of 1848-49* (1979)
Girardet, Raoul, *La société militaire dans la France contemporaine, 1815-1939* (1953)
Glover, Michael, *Wellington's Peninsular Victories* (1963)
Glover, Michael, *Wellington as Military Commander* (1965)
Glover, Richard, *Peninsular Preparation. The Reform of the British Army, 1795-1809* (1963)
Godechot, Jacques, *Les institutions de la France sous la révolution et l'Empire* (1969)
Gooch, John, *Armies in Europe* (1980)

Halevy, Elie, *England in 1815*, vol. 1 of his *History of the English People in the 19th Century* (1st ed. 1913, tr. 1924)
Halicz, E., *Partisan Warfare in 19th-century Poland: the Development of a Concept* (1975)
Hampson, Norman, *La marine de l'an II: mobilisation de la flotte de l'océan, 1793-4* (1959)
Harries-Jenkins, G., *The Army in Victorian Society* (1977)

Hayter, Tony, *The Army and the Crowd in mid-Georgian England* (1978)

Henderson, James, *Frigates: an Account of the lesser Warships from 1793-1815* (1971)

Hibbert, Christopher, *The Destruction of Lord Raglan* (1963)

Hibbert, Christopher, *Garibaldi and his Enemies . . .* (1965)

Hinsley, F.H., *Power and the Pursuit of Peace. Theory and Practice in the History of Relations between States* (1st ed. 1963)

Hobsbawm, E.J., *The Age of Revolution, 1789-1848* (1st ed. 1962)

Holborn, Hajo, *A History of Modern Germany, 1840-1945* (1969)

Howard, Michael (ed.), *Soldiers and Governments. Nine Studies in Civil-Military Relations* (1957)

Howard, Michael, *War in European History* (1976)

Howard, Michael, see also Clausewitz

Howarth, David, *Trafalgar: the Nelson touch* (1969)

Howarth, David, *A Near Run Thing. The Day of Waterloo* (1968)

Ingram, Edward, 'British Strategy and High Command, 1783-1819', in *Militärgeschichtliche Mitteilungen*, vol. 12 (1972), pp. 165-72

Jelavich, C. and B., *The Establishment of the Balkan National States, 1804-1920* (1977)

Keegan, John, *The Face of Battle* (1976)

Kennedy, Paul, *The Rise and Fall of British Naval Mastery* (1976)

Kieniewicz, Stefan, 'Polish Society and the Insurrection of 1863', in *Past and Present* (1967), no. 37, pp. 130-48

Kiraly, Bela K., *Hungary in the late 18th century* (1969)

Kitchen, Martin, *A Military History of Germany* (1975)

Knafla, Louis A., Staum, M.S. and Travers, T.H.E., *Science, Technology and Culture in Historical Perspective* (1976)

Kukiel, Marion, 'Problèmes des guerres d'insurrection au 19e siècle', in *Antemurale*, vol. 2 (1955), pp. 68-79

La Barre de Nanteuil, H. de, *Le Comte Daru, ou, l'administration militaire sous la Révolution et l'Empire* (1966)

Laqueur, Walter, *Guerrilla. A Historical and Critical Study* (1977)

Lefèbvre, Georges, *Napoléon* (1st ed. 1947)

Leonard, Emile, *L'armée et ses problèmes au 18e siècle* (1958)
Lewis, Michael, *A Social History of the Navy, 1793-1815* (1960)
Lewis, Michael, *The Navy in Transition, 1814-1864* (1965)
Leyland, John (ed.), *Despatches and Letters relating to The Blockade of Brest, 1803-1805*, 2 vols. (1899, 1902)
Liddell Hart, Basil (ed.), *The Letters of Private Wheeler* (1951)
Longworth, Philip, *The Cossacks* (1969)
Longworth, Philip, *The Art of Victory. The Life and Achievements of Generalissimo Suvorov, 1729-1800* (1965)
Lovett, G.H., *Napoleon and the Birth of Modern Spain*, 2 vols. (1964)
Lucas-Debreton, J., *Le culte de Napoléon, 1815-1848* (1960)

Macartney, C.A., *The Habsburg Empire, 1790-1918* (1969)
Mack Smith, D., *The Making of Modern Italy, 1796-1870* (1968)
McNeill, W.H., *Europe's Steppe Frontier, 1500-1800* (1964)
Marcus, G.J., *A Naval History of England*, 2 vols. (1961, 1971)
Marion, Marcel, *Histoire financière de la France depuis 1715*, 6 vols. (1914-31)
Markham, Felix, *Napoleon* (1963)
Marmont, A.F.L. Viesse de, *De l'esprit des institutions militaires* (1845)
Mather, F.C., *Public Order in the Age of the Chartists* (1959)
Messerschmidt, Manfred, see Further Reading, under Prussian Germany

Napier, William F.P., *History of the War in the Peninsula and in the South of France...*, 6 vols. (1st ed. 1828-40)
Nef, John V., *War and Human Progress* (1950)
Nickerson, Hoffman, *The Armed Horde* (1940)

Occupants, Occupés, 1792-1815. Colloque de Bruxelles, 29-30 janvier 1968 (1969)
Oman, Carola, *Nelson* (1947)

Pamlényi, Ervin (ed.), *A History of Hungary* (1975)
Paret, Peter, see also Clausewitz
Paret, Peter, *Yorck and the Era of Prussian Reform* (1966)
Paret, Peter, *Clausewitz and the State* (1976)

Patterson, A. Temple, *The Naval Mutiny at Spithead, 1797* (Portsmouth Paper no. 5) (1968)

Pidoll, Charles de, *Quelques mots sur les colonies militaires russes...* (1847)

Pieri, Paolo, *Storia militare del Risorgimento: guerre e insurrezioni* (1962)

Porch, Douglas, *Army and Revolution: France, 1815-1848* (1974)

Post, John D., *The Last Great Subsistence Crisis in the Western World* (1977)

Prebble, John, *Mutiny. Highland Regiments in Revolt, 1743-1804* (1975)

Presland, John, *Vae Victis. The Life of Benedek* (1934)

Ramm, Agatha, *Germany, 1789-1919* (1967)

Redlich, F., 'Military Entrepreneurship in Central Europe, 1650-1900', in *American Philosophical Society Yearbook for 1961* (1962)

Reinhard, Marcel, *Le grand Carnot*, 2 vols. (1950)

Ritter, Gerhard, *The Sword and the Scepter*, vol. 1 *The Prussian Tradition* (1954, tr. 1969)

Ropp, Theodore, *War in the Modern World* (1st ed. 1959)

Rose, J. Holland, *The Indecisiveness of Modern War, and other essays* (1927)

Rosenberg, Hans, *Bureaucracy, Artistocracy and Autocracy: the Prussian Experience, 1660-1815* (1966)

Rothenberg, Gunther, *The Army of Franz Joseph* (1976)

Rothenberg, Gunther, *The Art of Warfare in the Age of Napoleon* (1977)

Russett, Bruce M. (ed.), *Peace, War and Numbers* (1972)

Sampson, R.V., *Tolstoy: the Discovery of Peace* (1973)

Schnapper, Bernard, *Le remplacement militaire en France. Quelques aspects politiques, économiques et sociaux du recrutement au 19e siècle* (1968)

Schnerb, Robert, *Le 19e Siècle. L'apogée de l'expansion européenne, 1815-1914* (2nd ed. 1957)

Scott, S.F., *The Response of the Royal Army to the French Revolution* (1978)

Shanahan, William O., *Prussian Military Reforms, 1786-1813* (1945)

Sherwig, J.M., *Guineas and Gunpowder. British Foreign Aid...*, *1793-1815* (1969)

Showalter, Dennis E., *Railroads and Rifles. Soldiers, Technology and the Unification of Germany* (1975)

Singer, J.D. and Small, M., *The Wages of War, 1816-1965: a Statistical Handbook* (1972)

Sked, Alan, *The Survival of the Habsburg Empire. Radetsky, the Imperial Army, and the Class War, 1848* (1979)

Skelley, Alan R., *The Victorian Army at Home* (1977)

Smeaton, W.A., *Fourcroy. Chemist and Revolutionary* (1962)

Soboul, Albert, 'Problèmes de la guerre révolutionnaire en l'an II' in *La Pensèe*, no. 85, pp. 33-48

Speier, Hans, *Social Order and the Risks of War* (1952)

Spiers, Edward M., *The Army and Society, 1815-1914* (1980)

Tarle, Eugene, *Napoleon's Invasion of Russia, 1812* (1st ed. 1938, tr. 1942)

Thomas, Hugh, *Goya: the Third of May, 1808* (1972)

Tolstoy, Leo, *War and Peace* (1st ed. 1868-9. Oxford World's Classics ed., 3 vols. 1933)

Trevelyan, G.M., *Garibaldi's Defence of the Roman Republic; Garibaldi and the Thousand; Garibaldi and the Making of Italy* (1907, 1909, 1911)

Tulard, Jean (ed.), *L'Anti-Napoléon: la légende noire de l'Empereur* (1965)

Tulard, Jean, *Le mythe de Napoléon* (1971)

Vagts, Alfred, *A History of Militarism, Civilian and Military* (1st ed. 1937)

Van Doorn, Jacques (ed.), *Armed Forces and Society* (1968)

Vigny, Alfred de, *Servitude et grandeur militaires* (1835)

Weller, Jac, *Wellington in the Peninsula* (1967)

Wilson, Stephen, 'For a Socio-Historical Approach to the Study of Western Military Culture' in *Armed Forces and Society*, vol. 6 (1980), pp. 527-52

Winter, J.M. (ed.), *War and Economic Development. Essays in Memory of David Joslin* (1975)

Wohlfeil, Rainer, see Further Reading, under Prussian Germany

Woodward, E.L., *War and Peace in Europe, 1815-1870* (1st ed. 1931)

Wolff, Otto, *Ouvrard, Speculator of Genius, 1770-1846* (1932, tr. 1963)

Woolf, S.J., *History of Italy, 1700-1860* (1979)

Wright, Quincy, *A Study of War* (1st ed. 1942)

Young, G.M., *Portrait of an Age* (annotated ed. by Clark, George Kitson, 1977)

GUIDE TO
FURTHER READING

GENERAL
AND INTRODUCTORY

Some good single-volume general histories lay the best foundations. ROPP carries the heaviest guns, with vast bibliographical support. HOWARD 1976 is very good, with useful book lists, but very slim; chs. 4-6, pp. 54-115, more than cover our period. FULLER has pace, punch and prejudice. GOOCH goes from the mid-18th century through World War II; especially good on civil-military relations, broadly conceived, and with big bibliography. CLAUSEWITZ *On War* (1st, 1832) is largely historical, much of it 'Napoleonic'; Paret and Howard preface their recent translation (1976) with introductory essays of general significance.

There is an enormous number of big illustrated books about war and its history but the scholarly quality of their prose is usually in inverse proportion to the lavishness and goriness of their pictures. A 'war and society' approach is to be found in NEF, a grand pioneer effort; VAGTS, still very worthwhile; NICKERSON; and the Open University's admirable course A 301, 'War and Society', which ran from 1973 to 1979 and whose handbooks or 'units' must be in many British libraries and homes.

On war and society before the French Revolution, CORVISIER is now the obvious starter. (It ignores naval forces.) ROTHENBERG 1977 comes up to 1815; he also neglects war at sea but is otherwise usefully compendious, not least in bibliography. PARET 1966, a masterly study, is worth mentioning here because it includes comparative elements of rare value. The best book on the post-Napoleonic period is WOODWARD, first-class in its classic style, but short; despite the title, it is mostly about other things! Chapter 5, 'Armed Forces and War', of M. S. ANDERSON is very well done; so is Clive Emsley's strong section (covering more than its title suggests) on 'the European Armies and the Revolutions of 1848' in the Open University's course A 321, Unit 16 ('Surveys and Themes'), pp. 16-21. Particular aspects of our theme are dealt with in BLAINEY, VAN CREVELD, BEST, HINSLEY, CHORLEY, ELLIS (who has good chapters on America, France and Prussia) and SHOWALTER. Valuable observations about military history in general and about Napoleonic-era battle experience in particular may be found in KEEGAN, chs. 1 and 3 respectively. HOWARTH's books on Trafalgar and Waterloo offer better 'depth' descriptions of those battles than any others known to me.

PARTICULAR COUNTRIES
(some additional points of entry)

FRANCE

CORVISIER and ROTHENBERG 1977 not unnaturally discuss France more than any other country. LEONARD and GIRARDET immensely reward those who can read them. SCOTT includes good summaries of recent French research. Napoleon is exhaustively surveyed by CHANDLER; part 3, pp. 133-201, admirably analyses his 'art of war'. Best of the smaller, broader-gauged British Napoleon books is MARKHAM's; the basic French one is by LEFEBVRE. For the Restoration period, see first PORCH, which however covers less than it purports.

UNITED KINGDOM

Of great advantage now are EMSLEY, SPIERS, and the opening of SKELLEY. For the Scottish contribution up to 1805, PREBBLE is suggestive. For the naval side, see primarily MARCUS, KENNEDY and BARTLETT. Best short approach to the army during the French wars may be R. GLOVER. For the Peninsular campaigns, start with M. GLOVER and WELLER. HOWARTH's fine books have been mentioned already. For the Crimean War start with HIBBERT 1963, O. ANDERSON and CURTISS 1979.

PRUSSIAN GERMANY

PARET 1966 and CRAIG are the obvious starting-points, KITCHEN is a good recent synthesis for our period. DEMETER is a mine of surprising and valuable things, RITTER a masterpiece. PARET 1976 reinforces his claim to sovereignty over this field. Readers of German will find much information in the relevant volumes of the Handbuch für deutschen Militärgeschichte 1648-1939, generally directed by Gerhard Papke; i.e., Rainer Wohlfeil, *Vom stehenden Heer des Absolutismus zür allgemeinen Wehrpflicht, 1789-1814* (1964, vol.2) and Manfred Messerschmidt *et al.*, *Militärgeschichte im 19 Jahrhundert* (1975, vol. 4, parts 1 and 2).

AUSTRIA-HUNGARY

DUFFY, *Army of Maria-Theresa* is good but rather early for us. His *Austerlitz*, more lightly written, contains good sketches of the Habsburg army in and out of battle. ROTHENBERG 1976 and SKED between them cover our ground well. For the Hungarian side, dig in DEAK.

RUSSIA

By far the most informative book in English is CURTISS 1965, to which he has added a book about the Crimean. Readers with French should consult ANDOLENKO. DUFFY 1972 provides a good sketch of both armies and the battle, TARLE an excitingly detailed view from the other side of the hill.

POLAND

The historiography of Poland, like that of every other eastern and south-eastern European country, has for many decades been peculiarly bedevilled by ideological partisanship. HALICZ says that his book could not be published there. Compare with it what *could* be so published, the Polish Military Institute's *Military Technology, Policy and Strategy in History* (Warsaw, 1976), much of it about our period.

ITALY

Little for us in English except, plentifully, about Garibaldi - e.g., TREVELYAN's still readable classics, and good recent books by HIBBERT 1965 and MACK SMITH. TREVELYAN's book about Manin should now be supplemented by GINSBORG. Italian readers will find PIERI invaluable.

INDEX

INDEX